Hübener vs Hitler

OTHER BOOKS BY THE AUTHOR

Porter Rockwell: A Biography (1986)

Rockwell: U.S. Marshall, A Novel (1987)

The Porter Rockwell Chronicles, Vol. 1 (1999)

The Porter Rockwell Chronicles, Vol. 2 (2000)

The Porter Rockwell Chronicles, Vol. 3 (2001)

The Porter Rockwell Chronicles, Vol. 4 (2002)

VOLUME 1 IN THE *Faith in Conflict* SERIES

Hübener vs Hitler

A biography of Helmuth Hübener, Mormon teenage resistance leader

RICHARD LLOYD DEWEY

ACADEMIC
RESEARCH
FOUNDATION

ISBN: 0-929753-13-5
Hübener vs. Hitler
by Richard Lloyd Dewey

Copyright © 2003 Academic Research Foundation

Academic Research Foundation
a nonprofit corporation
P.O. Box 1371
Provo, Utah 84603-1371

Design and typesetting: Vance Hawkins
Cover photography: Stan MacBean from Photographic Solutions

First printing: December, 2003

This book is printed on acid-free paper.

Printed in the United States of America

To lifelong friend
H U G H   O L I V E R

who appreciates the love for freedom
exemplified by the Helmuth Hübener group
and who, as a high school teen,
engaged in similar activities
of first becoming self-educated
past the accepted political lies of the day,
and then distributing the written word as well,
also as part of a threesome,
with friend Robert Stall and a third friend —
despite opposition;
but who, unlike Helmuth and his group,
did so in a *free* country
and, because of his love for truth
and the persistence to find it,
eventually came to find and embrace
the most *important* truth.

ACKNOWLEDGEMENTS

A labor of love, like childbirth, goes through phases, starting with nausea, ending with nausea, and when finished, feeling even more nausea. And then a sense of accomplishment. It's supposed to be that way writing and finishing a book. But for me, the day after a book is finished, the feeling when asked about it is, "What book?"

By the time this is read, I will be on to another project, not even looking back. But for right now, I have to look back — with extreme gratitude — for those who assisted in this work.

Special thanks go to Alan Keele and Doublas Tobler, the two pioneer researchers of the Hübener story, along with their German predecessor, Ulrich Sander, who was the first researcher to bring the Helmuth Hübener story to light. Keele's and Tobler's interviews in 1974 with various principals in Hübener's story laid the groundwork for my own interviews with essentially the same group of people, plus additional ones who had a part in Helmuth's story.

Alan Keele and I worked on a documentary film project in 1995 about the Hübener group that never was launched (although years later BYU did produce one that was aired several times on KBYU-TV in 2003), but from that association I became increasingly enamored by the Hübener story, and Alan encouraged me in my quest for additional research on Helmuth. So additional appreciation must go to him.

Assisting Alan in the monumental work, *When Truth Was Treason*, was Blair Holmes, who also deserves substantial credit for his footnote research and translation of numerous Nazi documents and records, and other substantive material originally written in German, used for that book, which helped immensely in the research of this volume.

When Truth Was Treason is Karl-Heinz Schnibbe's auto-biographical account of his days with Helmuth in the resistance, and readers are highly encouraged to acquire it, as Karl was an eyewitness participant in Helmuth's story — and was his close friend.

Credit must also be given to Rudi Wobbe for his earlier interviews and lectures used by the author. (Rudi also wrote a book on the subject, *Three Against Hitler*, expertly co-authored by Jerry Borrowman.)

Further credit is due Randall Dixon and the staff at the archives section of the LDS Church Historian's Office for their labors, assistance, and obliging attitude about bringing pile after pile of research materials out to me, again and again. Also of terrific assistance was the staff of the Special Collections Department at the Harold B. Lee Library of Brigham Young University.

The author is grateful for the candid responses from all those interviewed, including Helmuth's two brothers and their wives — Gerhard and Waltraud Kunkel and Hans and Charlotte Kunkel; Helmuth's close childhood friend and his wife — Arthur and Marie Sommerfeld (who have since passed away); Helmuth's associate in the resistance and friend Karl-Heinz Schnibbe; Herta Schmidt Wobbe, the widow of Helmuth's other LDS resistance associate; and Hamburg church friends and associates, who include Werner and Lieselotte Prüss Schhmidt, Hilda Prüss Müller, Peter Prüss, Klaus Guertler, Resa Guertler Frey, Otto Berndt, Jr., and others.

Additionally, the author expresses his sincere gratitude to the following: Richard J. Harding, who sacrificed many sleepless nights for the gargantuan task of extracting and numbering the endnotes; Wallace Johnson for his one-of-a-kind, superb editing; Don Ricks and Heather Dewey for transcribing interviews; Suzanne Doyle for typing endnote sources; Vance Hawkins for his design, typesetting, and translation assistance; Annalyn Beuss for proofreading; Val King and David Bond for numerous hours of production help; and Stan MacBean for his artistry in book cover photography.

And finally, special thanks to Sharon McQueen for playing a Betsy Ross role in sewing the Nazi flag for the cover photo when it seemed no one was willing to sell us one — at least without a background check — only to see her painstaking craftsmanship ripped up and stomped on for the camera!

CHAPTER **1**

A poignant story of World War II, much overlooked by history, is the account of Helmuth Hübener, the youngest German teenager to organize single-handedly a resistance movement against Nazi tyranny.

He lived in Hamburg, Germany, and, despite the danger of his activities, recruited friends and strangers to assist in taking on Hitler's *Reich*.

Hübener possessed a high intellect and great courage, which prepared him for the task.

His mother and grandparents lived in Lithuania before he was born. His grandmother, Wilhelmina Roesuleit, grew up in Taurothenen and his mother, Anna Emma Guddat, who went by Emma, was born in and grew up in Tilsit.[1] Wilhelmina married a Guddat. There, they all converted to the Church of Jesus Christ of Latter-day Saints.

In 1919 Helmuth's grandfather "built houses," recalls his brother Hans, "and was killed by a brick falling on his head in Tilsit, Lithuania."[2]

Their grandmother then moved to the German side of Tilsit, the second-largest city in Lithuania, for employment,[3] and their mother followed. There, Helmuth's mother met and married a teamster named Johann Adelbert Kunkel on 29 June 1920,[4] and from that marriage Helmuth's two brothers were born,[5] with Hans being born one year before Gerhard.[6] Johann then left Emma over religious differences (he was Catholic) and money problems[7] in 1922.[8] Gerhard remembers, "We, brother Hans and I, were not close to our father — so it did not matter to us about the divorce."[9] At that time, actually, they were merely separated, as Gerhard clarifies.[10] Helmuth, not born until later, would never know his brothers' father.[11]

In 1923[12] their grandmother moved to Hamburg[13] (although she may have moved directly to Hamburg in 1920 after her husband died[14]). She met and married Johannes Sudrow, a widower, in 1923. She then wrote and persuaded the boys' mother to move there as well, whereupon Emma took her two sons to Hamburg that same year.[15]

During interviews with the author, Gerhard explains, "We all lived in the same apartment [building] for about nine years, from 1923 to 1932. After two years[16] Mother moved out, into an apartment in wing C[17] and we boys went with her.[18] My brother Hans and I were getting too big and we needed more room."[19] They left the Sudrows in the late spring of 1925.[20]

Gerhard details, "Our apartment building was the shape of a squared horseshoe, with 90 apartments there. It was five stories high, with six apartments per wing. On the east and west wings was a hallway in the middle, but no such hallway on the main south wing, where our apartments were. It had inside stairs."[21] Hans adds it had "a school across from it."[22] From this building Helmuth would later conduct the most eventful activities of his life.

"A shoemaker left his apartment," recalls Hans in a 1996 interview with the author, "and Emma and we boys moved in; that was next to my grandmother's apartment."[23] And this was still before Helmuth was born.

The two boys took to their new grandfather, "a widower, disciplined, honest, sometimes quiet, impatient, yet considerate," says Gerhard. "He liked us boys. He was active LDS. I took to him like a real grandfather . . . and he was the only grandfather I knew. He talked to us like his real grandchildren, with affection and concern. I suppose it was hard on Grandmother when my real grandfather died, but I knew it was hard on my mother."[24]

Emma worked at the state mint,[25] at the minting press that made *Pfennig* and *Mark* coins,[26] and there she met a man named Karl Oswalt Fater."[27] He was a supervisor of personnel over currency stampings "and he was involved in fraud," says Gerhard. ". . . He forced my mother to give him blanks so he could make extra money" for himself, on the side.[28]

It was some time after that, says Gerhard, that "he raped her."[29] Helmuth was conceived out of wedlock as a result,[30] and was born 8 January 1925 in Hamburg.[31] Years later Fater stepped forward with his identity.

Gerhard also maintains Emma had no relationship with Fater socially, had never dated him,[32] and that he was not the type she would date.[33] At some point he was sent to prison for theft at work.[34] However, one time he did show up at their home, and Gerhard noted he was about 5'4" — later to be Helmuth's height[35] (which was also Gerhard's height[36]). It was the only time Gerhard ever saw him.[37] At that time Gerhard recalls Fater was a dockworker,[38] likely no longer with the mint.

Helmuth's two half-brothers were four and six years older than he.[39] There would be no more children born to Emma.

She left the state mint, working as a "nurse"[40] in a nursing home. All during this period she raised her three boys alone.[41] Helmuth was probably three to four months old when they moved out of their grandparents' apartment because the older boys were getting too big and needed more space, says Gerhard.

Emma then met Hugo Hübener, a construction worker, Nazi Party member, and file leader in the local Marine SA, the storm trooper battalion.[42]

Gerhard recalls, "Hugo began staying with my mother, and they were together for several years."[43]

Also, "When Hugo moved in to my mother's apartment, it was too small, so after one year we moved three kilometers away to a much larger apartment in a much larger building, at the street address of Sachsenstrasse 42. It was in the shape of a rectangle, and was six stories high. We lived on the first story."[44]

Meanwhile, four years after Helmuth's birth, Johann Kunkel — Gerhard's and Hans' father — learned of Helmuth's birth, and "had a big squabble" with Emma over it,[45] knowing the child was not his since they had been separated[46] since 1922[47] — three years before Helmuth's birth.

Johann then took her to court for divorce, upset over learning about the four-year-old, yet coincidentally, 13 weeks later, he remarried, which may or may not have been the real reason for finalizing the divorce. The divorce was granted 14 March 1929.[48] Meanwhile, Emma and Hugo went ahead and got married six months after the divorce — on 19 September 1939.[49]

A friend of the family at church was Marie Somerfeld: "In the beginning as we became acquainted she [Emma] was active."[50] But after the marriage Marie did not see her much or at all,[51] and assumed that she was in another branch of the church. Rudi Wobbe, Helmuth's young friend, reports only ever seeing Emma "once or twice."[52] Otto Berndt, their district president at church, states she was "partly active."[53] Gerhard also reports in a 1974 interview that after his mother married Hugo she had become "quite inactive,"[54] although in another interview in 1996 he recalls his mother not going to church again after Helmuth was born, "embarrassed he was born out of wedlock."[55] It seems more likely — because Gerhard's earlier interview corroborates Marie's statement — that Emma became inactive only after her 1939 marriage to Hugo. Gerhard explains why: "I think the reason my mother became inactive was because of the harassments of Hübener towards the Church. See, he was very strongly against it.

Just to keep the peace in the family or the peace with him she dropped out."[56]

When the boys were older, "Mother worked long hours," continues Gerhard. "I worked after school to pay for my education. Helmuth was home alone a lot then, but spent time . . . in church activities. Hans also was home."

With his mother working away so much, and with her lack of consistent activity in the Church, Helmuth's strongest influence came from his grandmother, says Otto Berndt. He says, "She was a stanch Mormon, really, really good and strong." He says it was her positive effect on him that made the difference in his life.[57] His stepgrandfather had become a member shortly after they were married, says Otto, adding that he was active in what he had to do,[58] but apparently was not the fireball his grandmother was.

Gerhard says Helmuth changed his first name at some point in his teens,[59] adding the "h" from "Helmut" to "Helmuth." (Throughout the author's interviews with him, Gerhard spells the name of his brother "Helmut.") As for his last name, he went by his brothers' last name[60] — which was the name under which he grew up,[61] at least at first; then he went by his mother's maiden name,[62] by which members of his branch at church knew him, at least as far back as his early teens and perhaps earlier;[63] and finally he went by his stepfather's name,[64] when Hugo adopted him in 1941.[65]

At Sachenstrasse 42, "Hugo wanted to be in the apartment alone with Emma and didn't want the boys there,"[66] recalls Hans. His anti-Mormon diatribes annoyed Gerhard and Helmuth, and his pro-Nazi lectures disturbed

6

Gerhard so much that he began arguing with Hugo on a daily basis. Helmuth would also argue with Hugo, but only about religion, because during his earliest years, Helmuth was actually a staunch supporter of Adolph Hitler and the Third Reich.[67]

Helmuth's three closest friends were, like his brother, anti-Nazi. But Helmuth was self-willed and determined to follow the *Führer* faithfully — at least until a series of events opened his eyes. Not only Helmuth, but most young Germans were excited about the revolution inspired by the Nazis, more so than the older generation.

Changes to their country began during his adolescent years. Helmuth and his three closest friends, Arthur Somerfeld, Rudi Wobbe, and Karl-Heinz Schnibbe were all active in the Primary program (for ages 3-11) of the Church of Jesus Christ of Latter-day Saints until Primary was banned.[1] And they looked forward to the Boy Scouts (which was and still is heavily promoted by the Church, with each congregation sponsoring its own den). But it too was banned 1 May 1934,[2] when Helmuth was only nine. That apparently did not much bother many German saints at first because of the offsetting positive changes sweeping the nation.

The Nazis took power 30 June 1933 when Helmuth was eight years old — the year of accountability in Latter-day Saint teachings and also the age at which they are baptized.

His friend Karl-Heinz Schnibbe[3] reports:

"We were herded into the auditorium at school and listened to Hitler's acceptance speech on the radio. All night people paraded through the streets with torches, singing the Horst Wessel Song. . . . The sky was illuminated by the torches from the parade.

" . . . We saw the exciting party congresses on the newsreels and we listened to other Nazi orators like Joseph Goebbels on the radio. 'The nation is getting back on its feet,' we heard them say. There was new hope after years of political and economic decline. A kind of intoxication came over the entire population, especially the young."[4]

The Nazis won the support of most citizens by at first greatly improving living conditions. High unemployment dropped from 33%[5] to 0%.[6] The autobahn was built and other impressive projects completed. The Germans finally had more food and fuel to heat their homes. Runaway inflation was brought under control, flashy parades hit the streets, and the once-depressed populace was now excited and polarized. No longer were 25 political parties vying for power and confusing the populace.[7] Germany seemed to have a new destiny. No longer the doormat of Europe, Germany's humiliating loss of WWI and the debilitating Versaille peace treaty were finally behind them.[8]

Karl Schnibbe reports, "Our branch president at that time belonged to the party and was enthused about it, which one could not hold against him. He saw good in it. At first everything was terrific, everything that the Nazis accomplished."[9]

In their branch, a Paul Haase and his sons joined the Stormtroopers. Rudi Wobbe states, "He was a harmless man, actually. He probably joined the Nazis because he liked to march and sing, and his sons, too." Rudi adds that he was bothered that the man naïvely wore the uniform to church and led the singing.[10] Rudi adds, tongue in cheek, "So we more or less tolerated him. [We thought,] 'Well, that's his bag; let him be that way.'"[11]

Adds Karl, "As I recall, they were musicians and belonged to a military band."[12] And the Nazi "Young Folk" that Helmuth, Karl, and Rudi belonged to wasn't half bad. Karl reports, "All the children joined the *Jungvolk*, and at first it was exciting. Young people were interested in the *Jungvolk* and the Hitler Youth because they employed clever tactics. . . . It was all fascinating to us. We could hardly wait from one home evening to another. . . . We liked it; it was fun for us young guys, the night duty, the field exercises, and the uniform. . . . Sometimes there was also a little shooting. Our food was prepared in a field kitchen. For us youngsters it was really something."[13] The *Jungvolk* (for ages 10-14) provided excursions, hikes, and sleeping in tents.[14] The Hitler Youth (for older boys aged 14 to 18) was more like the military, with premilitary training camps, inspections, guard duty, map reading, radio skills, shooting rifles with real bullets, and carrying a dagger.[15]

Regarding the younger children, those under ten, Karl recalls:

"They won over many because they cared well for the children and did other things that were viewed as being positive. For example, during school vacations, we children often went to . . . hostels along the Elbe river. . . . There were large and beautiful white ships that traveled fast. A horde of children traveled on the boats. . . .

"There was a large playground, a sports area . . . and a beautiful beach where we could swim. . . . The children could build sand castles and play handball, volleyball, soccer."[16]

But then the friendly dragon began to show its teeth. The new government established several agencies of brutal power. They hired thugs and criminals to staff the SS and storm troopers.[17] And the citizenry was soon in a position to oppose nothing about the regime. For one thing, it couldn't — it was disarmed. All weapons were collected at police precincts and it was illegal even to own a firearm.[18] For another, the Germany citizenry didn't really show much disposition to oppose the Reich — they had traditionally been a fatalistic society and rarely overthrew rulers.

But a minority did oppose. When people hung other flags than the Nazi emblems, they were arrested by the newly created Gestapo,[19] an agency that boldly proclaimed its full name as *Geheime Staatspolizei*, or secret state police.

For those left behind — the wives of victims — the Red Relief collected money. This was a Communistic charitable group. Although he was not Communistic, Karl's father donated, and when the Gestapo confiscated their receipt books, many more were arrested and sent to a concentration camp. "My father suffered many sleepless nights about this . . . but he was lucky. Perhaps his name was written illegibly."[20]

Karl's father also learned that the SA was locking people in the cellar at city hall and torturing them. "They were completely outside the law."[21]

Teachers were forced to join the Nazi Party — along with all civil servants — or lose their pensions.[22] In the three year period ending in 1935, Hamburg alone saw 637 teachers dismissed.[23]

Society was revolutionized.

A Ministry of Propaganda was established to censor truth in the news media.[24]

History lessons were altered to cover up the true lessons of history. Only years after 1914 could be emphasized.[25]

Books were banned and burned. One hundred fifty authors were outlawed.[26] Religion was discouraged[27] and in some cases eliminated in school,[28] as were prayers.[29]

General Ludendorff declared the Bible to be the product of an overactive fantasy, an action which Helmuth would later attack in a leaflet, claiming, "they are attempting to take the Bible from the German people."[30]

Traditional moral standards were discarded. A double standard existed for persecuting the mentally and physically handicapped and homosexuals — because homosexuals reigned in the governing circles of the dreaded SA,[31] the

"Stormtroopers" who were known for their street fighting and brutality. This special police was largely made up of former and aspiring criminals. Many citizens considered them common "thugs."

Churches, including Helmuth's Mormon group, were persecuted. Rudi Wobbe states that they were threatened, having windows broken when Hitler Youth threw rocks[32] "when we were having our MIA meetings during the week." Also, "There was kind of an incline where our branch meetinghouse was, and they marched up and down singing the Nazi songs to interrupt our meetings."[33] It was blatant "harassment."[34]

Frederich Peters, another youth who knew Helmuth, reports, "The Mormon church is not political. But nevertheless in 1938 the first American missionaries were expelled from the country."[35] He also recalls that in 1936, "many members were arrested, interrogated, mishandled and put in coercive detention."[36]

In addition to the Boy Scouts, the Nazis dissolved most youth groups in 1933. Within a few months of their takeover, 20 youth groups disbanded and joined the Hitler Youth.[37]

The militaristic *Jungvolk* and Hitler Youth grew to 8.7 million children.[38]

Informants were appointed to oversee the workers' loyalty to the *Reich*. Nazi block leaders oversaw neighborhood blocks and spied on all residential activities. These local spies in turn reported to cell block leaders.[39]

If bosses reported employees as "lazy and tardy" too many times, workers would be taken to a concentration camp for "work education." Even an argument with the boss could get one carted off by the Gestapo.[40]

The entire government was overhauled. The Supreme Court was disbanded and replaced by the political People's Court as the nation's high court.

Laws were transmogrified.[41] The number of offenses for which one could be executed rose from three in pre-Nazi Germany to 46 when the Nazis took power. Political crimes were the worst offenses. Ironically, a nonpolitical criminal would be afforded protection under the law, "and did not particularly need to be fearful."[42] And among the worst things of all, the Gestapo was given status *above* the law. On 10 February 1936 it was actually awarded legal status, so the country was now a bona fide police state.

Helmuth's friend at church, Rudi Wobbe, states in a 1987 fireside lecture to Latter-day Saint youth:

"I remember we had torch light marches, twelve abreast, at night. The brown shirts and the SA storm troopers — they watched anybody that didn't salute the swastika flag, and they walked by, and people were beaten with rubber hoses and night sticks. I was just a little tad. I remember my grandmother calling me by name, saying, 'Rudi, do you see the color of that flag?'

"'Isn't it the color of blood?'

"'Yes it is,' she said, 'and blood is what they will spill.'

"I remember that so vividly, as if she were saying it to me today, and how prophetic her words were — and I had to experience them afterwards. . . .[43] This ominous statement always came back into my mind . . . ."[44]

Then, of course, there was the Holocaust. Many Germans turned their backs on the Jews, yet only a comparative few knew the whole story of what was happening.

Gerhard reports, "The BBC never told us of the death of the Jews. Most people in Germany never knew about it either. That only came out after the war. The German soldiers never even knew about it. Only the SS who guarded and killed the Jews in the death camps knew about it."[45] These are the same SS who would mow down hundreds if not thousands of the rank-and-file German soldiers who tried returning to Germany after the war (as Gerhard details later in this volume). Gerhard adds, "The only Jew I knew was our family doctor to whom Mother took us. One day he disappeared."[46]

Nevertheless, while most Germans did not know of the Holocaust, they did tolerate the Jewish persecutions and other disagreements they might have with the Nazi system because they were sick of being Europe's odd man out, so their sudden emergence economically — coupled with soon-to-come swift military victories — gave them a certain, sudden pride. They had power and respect once again among European nations. And they went along for the refreshing, exciting ride.

On 29 March 1937 Adolf Hitler was officially elected.[47]

Then one year later on 13 March 1938 the Nazis marched into Austria. A Latter-day Saint and resident of Germany at the time, Sanford Bingham, recalls, " . . . I remember it was a Saturday morning, March 12, [when] they marched into Austria, the *Anschluß*. I recall very vividly the next morning in priesthood meeting, and you could just feel the tension in the air. And there was one old brother there that knew that he had my confidence. He came up and was chatting with me off to one side, and he said, 'Brother Bingham, this means war. Make no mistake about it. Hitler's leading us to destruction. I'm telling you this in confidence because I know you won't report me.' But he said, 'This is the beginning of the end.'"[48]

Seven months later — on 10 October 1938 — the Nazis took over Czechoslovakia, and less than a year later — on 1 September 1939, they attacked Poland, which officially launched World War II.[49] England and France declared war on Germany. And five weeks later Hitler's army officially captured Poland. They also blitzed through Austria, Norway, Denmark, the Netherlands, and Belgium.[50]

As Karl Schnibbe analyzes, "On the western front nothing was happening. The French played soccer and the Germans watched, but a man such as Hitler could not sit still, and one day he attacked there, too."[51] That was 10 May 1940. Six weeks later they conquered France.[52]

The victories were fast and furious, and most Germans were amazed at their newfound strength.

While no percentages have been estimated, Helmuth's friend Karl Schnibbe felt many German citizens were *against* the marches on neighboring nations.[53]

Arthur Gaeth, the first mission president of the Church of Jesus Christ of Latter-day Saints in Czechoslovakia and a former war correspondent who covered the Nurmberg

Trials, says that many Latter-day Saints were opposed to the war but kept quiet.

"I think they were aware of the fact that they were in a police state, that if they expressed themselves counter to Naziism they could get picked up and they would suffer, and as a result they didn't express themselves in that area at all."[54]

Official data reveals that in the 12 year period of the Nazi regime, from 1933-1945, three million German citizens were placed into a prison or concentration camp for political purposes. Eight hundred thousand were held for active resistance.[55]

Arthur Gaeth, in his research about resistance, found differing numbers — only 200,000 — resisting out of the German population of 65 million.[56]

But in the Latter-day Saint community, the setting was ripe for resistance.

Most German members of the Church of Jesus Christ of Latter-day Saints were influenced greatly by the cultural convictions of young American missionaries who talked of freedom back home and of their own religious doctrine of free agency. While Naziism was the antithesis of free agency — running the country through force, threats, and intimidation — the Saints were pulled another direction — in supporting existing governments as stated in the twelfth Article of Faith: "We believe in being subject to kings, presidents, rulers, and magistrates, in obeying, honoring, and sustaining the law." Rudi comments how he and some other Saints nevertheless viewed the twelfth Article: "a statement of our belief . . . not a commandment." He analyzes, "We can never apply this to a Hitler, a Mussolini, an Idi Amin, all these murderous villains that are the heads of state. They are not ordained from God."[1]

In Hamburg were three Mormon congregations or "branches," which belonged to a "district," with several districts comprising a "mission." Helmuth and his three closest friends belonged to the St. Georg Branch, named after that section of town.[2] Arthur Zander was their branch president. Despite Zander's loyalty to the Nazi Party, Helmuth's three anti-Nazi friends looked up to and liked their leader.

Helmuth was Zander's church secretary, the branch clerk, performing all clerical duties for him.[3] Helmuth's district president also recalls him being the district clerk.[4] Gerhard Kunkel agrees that Helmuth was trusted more than most boys of that age would be for such a responsibility.[5] Also, he could type, "which of course," says Gerhard, "for a boy over in Germany is quite unusual. They don't learn typing in school."[6] Before Helmuth, Gerhard himself had been the branch clerk,[7] in addition to Helmuth's third close friend Arthur Sommerfeld. Arthur confirms, "I was the branch secretary when Zander was branch president. Then I was drafted into the labor service, and Helmuth took over my job."[8] Interestingly, most of the men in the branch eventually were taken into the service,[9] leaving even less male leadership from which to choose.[10]

Arthur Sommerfeld reflects, "As for our branch president, Zander, he was a good organizer, a very good fellow in many ways, and all things considered he was a very good guy. He supported the Nazis, but many people in Germany back then looked upon the Nazi Party as Americans today look upon Republicans and Democrats. To them at the time it was just another political party."[11]

Hilde Prüss Müller echoes his words, adding Zander was such a good man that even her extremely anti-Nazi father befriended him at church.[12] Nevertheless, because of Zander's political views, he made obvious errors, but this is understandable as he did not have the capability of consulting with Church headquarters in Salt Lake City, Hilde points out. Additionally, like many German church members, Zander did not have sufficient church experience compared to local leaders in the U.S. *and* he was only a fairly recent convert of five years when he became branch president.

One mistake he made, for example, occurred in about 1938 when he posted a sign forbidding Jews,[13] which was certainly out of place in a church.[14] This disgusted nearly all branch members.[15] One member of half-Jewish descent, Salomon Schwarz, regularly attended the Barmbeck Branch, the one into which he had been baptized.[16] He wished to attend choir practice and Priesthood Meeting at the St. Georg Branch — but was forbidden by Zander.[17]

Gerhard says that Zander and others "were forced to do it," as were all three branches in Hamburg.[18] Apparently Gerhard had a line on what was happening at all three branches in Hamburg because he had a girlfriend in the Barmbeck Branch — the branch president's daughter. "I was going there quite often," he says.[19] And he had friends in Altona. By contrast, Rudi, in dismay, believes theirs was "the only branch in all of Germany that ever had a sign on the front door."[20]

Herta Schmidt Wobbe, another daughter of the Barmbeck branch president (who would later marry Rudi), and younger sister to the girl Gerhard dated, believed no such directive came from the Church *per se* — above the branch level — and does not remember her branch posting such a sign.[21] Nor does her brother, Werner Schmidt, who is quite certain it was never posted there, as he also states in an interview with the author.[22] In fact, Rudi recalls that their father told off Zander about disallowing Salomon: "Not in my branch, not in my branch."[23] One member, as described below, actually tore down the sign the first week it was posted. (See Appendix A for more about the sign.)

Zander did show too much zeal — he also reprimanded storm trooper member Paul Haase's wife, Emma, for bringing to church an anti-*Reich* flyer dropped from Allied aircraft.[24] In addition, he occasionally locked his flock in the building before a weeknight youth meeting called Mutual would start, in order to have them listen to government leaders on the radio[25] — although he did back down on this brazen behavior when his first counselor reprimanded him, "This is a church of God, not a political meeting."[26] That first counselor was Otto Berndt, who later became Zander's district president.

Karl summarizes about Zander, "He went a little overboard."[27]

Rudi, being so anti-Nazi, felt torn over Zander, as evidenced by his interviews relating to his experience. Zander, ironically, was the man who actually baptized Rudi and his mother,[28] and that tie of love and concern between convert and the one performing the ordinance is almost never broken. Rudi does state, "He was a good man,"[29] and recalls that Zander looked out for him all his days, but at the same time Rudi was so diametrically opposed to Zander's aforementioned political actions that his memories are bittersweet.

Gerhard paints a rather fearful picture for church leadership. "There always was somebody from the Gestapo in our meetings. We never knew them, you see, . . . and they listened to the talks which were given and we had to be real careful."[30]

Rudi says, "We had several Gestapo agents that listened in on all this," and he feels it was assumed by branch members that there probably would be an agent spying on them.[31] He adds they had "almost steady visitors from the Gestapo."[32] Rudi continues, "The brethren were cautioned not to talk about the gathering of Zion and all this," nor could they sing such hymns as "Israel, Israel, God is Calling." He also says, "Anything with Zion or Israel, that was taboo," and everyone was counseled to make certain they did not mention anti-Nazi doctrines in church talks.[33]

Herta Schmidt Wobbe recalls, "The SS came to the Barmbeck Branch meetings — mainly Sacrament Meeting — several times a year."[34]

Therefore, most of the Saints were afraid to voice any opinion against Hitler. Karl explains, "You don't talk about that stuff. . . . That is suicide."[35]

Rudi's reaction was different than others, however. While many simply rolled over and thought, "We better follow the line," he felt "irked" by the visitors,[36] a defining trait in his character that would lead to his later choices.

Karl reports, "I do not wish to leave the impression that any of the Saints, including Arthur Zander and Franz Jacobi (one of his counselors), were evil persons. They were not. Zander was a dedicated branch president, a natural leader of young and old, who took charge of things in the branch and made things happen. . . . He . . . knew how to organize people[37]. . . . We called him Chief. He was good . . . . He was actually not a bad guy."[38]

Karl hyphothesizes that Zander and the few other Nazis in the branch likely opposed the treatment of the Jews on *Krystallnacht* (as discussed later herein). He thinks they would have said, "They didn't have to go that far."[39]

Gerhard says Zander "had some kind of position in official business and so he had to be in the party."[40] He was an office manager for a company named Henckel,[41] a chemical plant.[42] Gerhard discounts Zander's dedication to Naziism, doubting how much he actually believed in National Socialism. In order to get ahead he may have simply gone along with whoever was in charge. "He wanted to get ahead in his profession. And he thought that if he belonged to the party it would be easier for him to get ahead. Which in some ways was true because if you wanted to get into an elevated position, no matter what company it was, the party always was involved."[43] Despite his feeling that he understood Zander's motivation, he is not an apologist for what he feels were Zander's mistakes. "I had quite a few strong run-ins with him myself before I got drafted. . . . I was absolutely not for the regime. I just couldn't stand it, the ideology of the whole regime. It was contrary to my beliefs. . . . I don't like any force.[44] . . . We believe in the free agency of man, and the free agency of man was totally taken away. . . . This was my strongest point which turned me against Hitler."[45]

Marie Sommerfeld was opposed to Zander's party involvement. ". . . We didn't like it. All of us didn't like it."[46] Gerhard feels most of the saints were unpolitical and "just more neutral,"[47] being "working class people."[48] Yet it was that very working class element which the resistance most often targeted, many being open to anti-Nazi sentiment.

When asked if perhaps 10 percent of the German Latter-day Saint population were pro-Nazi, Rudi responds "Ten percent is rather large. . . . I would say about five percent." He adds, "In the St. Georg Branch we had maybe five members at the most that were actually pro-party,"[49] which would be closer to 2½ percent. Rudi also thinks that perhaps 10 percent were opposed and 75 percent were not interested in political affairs.[50] Even with those low numbers of Nazi sympathizers, Rudi felt the St. Georg branch was "the hierarchy of Nazi sympathizing . . . the high point of our district."[51] In a 1988 interview he calls the branch the "high castle of Naziism in all of Germany,"[52] although there were only five members or so who were pro-party. Otto Berndt asserts that with Zander, St. Georg had the only pro-Nazi branch president[53] among eight branches in the district. The district consisted of the three Hamburg branches, and Lübeck, Rostock, Gluksadt, Stade, and Cuxhaven. The only other Nazis, besides the small handful at St. Georg, consisted of one member at Altona and one at Lübeck, he says.[54]

Rudi Wobbe and Herta Schmidt Wobbe place into perspective that the Barmbeck Branch was "absolutely not" a sympathizing branch.[55] Herta says of the Jewish member there, Soloman Schwarz, ". . . We were all sympathizing for him."[56] Her own brother, Ernst Schmidt, an army sergeant, supported Schwarz and risked his own life by attending Schwarz's trial in uniform. Schwarz, just ten years older than Helmuth, was taken directly from court to Auschwitz, where he died.[57]

Marie Sommerfeld feels she speaks for the majority of the St. Georg branch when she says, "We held onto the Church and we were not for Hitler. We were not for National Socialism. Except a few . . . a minority."[58] Rudi agrees the majority of the Saints looked upon the regime with "indifference," while Herta defines "caution" as the general tone of the time.[59] Rudi adds "distrust" as a main factor.

When asked if "maybe 10 percent of the membership" supported the Reich, Marie's reply mirrors her son Rudi's as she responds, "I don't think so. Only a few."[60]

Those few apparently included Zander; second counselor Franz Jacobi[61] (whom Otto Berndt thinks was not a Nazi, only anti-American later in the war[62]); Paul Haase, as mentioned; Herbert Harms, who was SS; Alvin Brey,[63] an early World War II district president who also lived in the St. Georg Branch;[64] and interim mission president Anton Huck,[65] (who resided in Frankfurt[66]) and who, as Gerhard states, was "inclined" toward the party, but may not actually have been a party man.[67]

As for Alvin Brey, Rudi describes him as "a little tainted,"[68] and clarifies that Brey was politically oriented only "up to a point," accepting it "as a necessary evil, probably," and only leaning "a little bit towards it," being a very successful ship's broker,[69] while Herta Schmidt Wobbe adds her opinion that Brey was inclined to support it "a little bit because of his business."[70] In an interview with the author, Resa Guertler Frey (daughter to former second counselor Hans Guertler) thought that Brey was not truly pro-Nazi and that to any extent he did show signs of supporting the *Reich* it was only to protect the Church, agreeing basically with Rudi's assessment. Her father, who was decidedly anti-Nazi, was very close friends with Brey.[71]

Disconcertingly, Huck's two sons were both SS and, like Harms, appeared at church in uniform, as did everyone who was drafted into the service, because of Zander's influence.[72] Marie states, "They said they had to act the way they did so the Church would not be bothered and we wouldn't be persecuted,"[73] and they may indeed have been attempting to ward off concerns by the Gestapo that the Church was perceived as an American religious institution.

Meanwhile, Brey was the district president during Zander's early years as branch president and, although he may have leaned toward the Nazis, he actually overrode Zander on one occasion when Zander opposed the baptism of a Jewish convert, Rudolf Kaufmann.[74] (As analyzed in

Appendix B, Zander either took that stance for political reasons or to protect his branch.)

Other local leaders *opposed* to the Third Reich included Alfred Schmidt, Otto Berndt, Hans Guertler, Paul Prüss, and Richard Prüss.

Otto Berndt rose up the leadership scale quickly, and soon became Zander's first counselor, as stated, then Zander's superior as district president (and later as acting mission president). He was thoroughly anti-Nazi, not hiding his beliefs from the church members by actually preaching against the Reich at the pulpit.[75] "I never kept quiet about it."[76] In defiance to the Reich, he used to walk openly with Salomon Schwarz and his sister, and sit with them in streetcars, despite the Jewish symbol Salomon was forced to wear. "I know people were aggravated against us when we were there. They said, 'What are Jews doing here in the streetcar?' and said they should leave. I told them, 'If they leave, I leave too. They are in my company.'"[77] Otto says he was against the regime since 1933,[78] during its beginnings.

Gerhard got to know Otto Berndt quite well, as Otto was the branch historian when Gerhard was the branch clerk, and they worked together "very closely," says Gerhard.[79] "He was opposing the Nazi Party," but at that time was "very careful" not to speak openly. Nevertheless, he and Otto conversed about it.[80]

Likewise, Paul Prüss, former branch president, was also anti-Nazi, according to his son Peter and his nephew Klaus Guertler in interviews with the author.[81]

Paul Prüss's second counselor was Hans Guertler, who wrote perhaps a dozen anti-Nazi poems that were distributed among family members and friends. These poems were three stanzas and a page each, and copies were made for trusted friends in the other branches of Hamburg as well as nearby towns. His daughter, Resa Guertler Frey, five years younger than Helmuth, reports one "hate-filled" St. Georg Branch member — not Zander or any of the others mentioned herein and whose name she cannot recall — who threatened to report her father, but her father joined the military and "exonerated" himself in the eyes of this pro-Nazi, she says.[82]

Richard Prüss, brother of Paul Prüss and a Sunday School Superintendant, took action to support the Jews. He boldly told Zander he was tearing down the sign forbidding Jews — and did. It only hung "one week," says Prüss's daughter, Lieselotte Prüss Schmidt in an interview with the author.[83] Her sister, Hilde Prüss Müller, also adds in an interview with the author that her father spoke up in meetings that day, saying, "We have no right to put this sign up because we belong to the Church of Jesus Christ. We believe in Jesus Christ. We pray in the name of Jesus Christ. We preach of Christ. And Christ was a Jew!"[84] He then reminded his brethren that the Jews were the Lord's chosen people, and it was wrong to forbid them.[85]

Richard's daughter Lieselotte reports, "He *never* did a '*Heil Hitler.*'"[86] In business meetings, a fanatical Nazi business associate in uniform always greeted his associates with a brisk salute and *"Heil Hitler,"* whereupon Prüss would always respond, "Good morning."[87]

Richard's other daughter Hilde reports they as children were not allowed — ever — by their father to do a *"Heil Hitler."*[88] Her brother — Ziegfreid Prüss — was obviously influenced by his father and stood up to the Nazi machine: He was dragged out of bed in the middle of the night several times by the SS in attempts to recruit him. But he refused to join. Consequently, they hazed him by forcing him to wash toilets, according to his sister Hilde.[89]

Richard also supported the Jews by befriending not only Salomon Schwarz but another Jewish man, a nonmember, who came to their home a number of times even when Richard was threatened by a Nazi neighbor across the street who said he would report Richard and send him to a concentration camp. Furthermore, Richard's family put themselves on the line by helping the French, Dutch, and British prisoners of war who were imprisoned nearby and were given certain freedoms. Richard's wife Rosealie, for example, did the laundry for the Frenchman who would walk past the house each day. Because Richard had been treated well in World War I as a prisoner of war in England, he and his family treated the British POWs particularly well. Later, when their house was bombed, Richard recruited Russian POWs to help rebuild part of their house and he treated them likewise well, feeding them, etc. His children played with the prisoners as a German guard would watch the Russian POWs, whom Hilde pointed out were not true Communists or in the least bit violent.[90]

Hilde finds it significant that the branch did not just "roll over" and sheepishly go along with Zander's mistakes — as exemplified when (a.) her father Richard tore down the sign forbidding Jews; (b.) Otto Berndt defied Zander about playing the radio in church; (c.) the branch members, including the most timid ones, objected to Hitler's picture being displayed — and almost immediately Otto made Zander take it down;[91] (d.) Alvin Brey overruled and ordered Zander to baptize the Jewish convert, Kaufmann; and (e.) the branch members threw out Zander's recommendation that they salute each other with *"Heil Hitler."*[92] ("We never did it!" declares Otto,[93] but "three or four" did. "I never saw a Christian assembly so unified. . . . They all said, 'No, we say, "Good morning." No politics here in church. Everybody can do outside what he wants, but here you say what the Lord says and we say, "Good morning."'"[94]) (See Appendix C for more details about Otto demanding the picture to be taken down.)

In a 1945 *Deseret News* article, Max Zimmer, the next regular mission president in Germany, reports another local leader at odds with the Nazis. In Alsace, branch president Paul Kayser refused the admonitions of the interim mission president "by clinging to the rod of iron . . . and the Brethren let him alone, and he ran his branch after the old order of things."[95]

Helmuth's close friends had fathers who were also anti-Nazi and influenced them significantly.

Rudi Wobbe says, "My father took me aside and said, 'Son, don't ever get mixed up with those people, the Nazis.

They are a bad people.'" He says his dad was a quiet man who usually spoke when there was something profound to say. "His words made a deep impression on me that day. . . . And I believed my father."[96]

Karl Schnibbe similarly reports, "My father had an influence on me. In the privacy of our home he would say of the Nazis, 'They are powerful, they are to be feared, and they are wrong.' He had a great influence on my beliefs — both religious and political."[97] His father, a Social Democrat[98] and "devout Mormon"[99] viewed Naziism as a "competing religious system" that was the opposite of the gospel of Jesus Christ, as it "enticed people to place their absolute faith in a man and in a political system created by men."[100]

(See Appendix D for more information on the topic of Naziism as a competing religious system that actually opposed Christianity — although the preponderance of non-Christian writing seems to claim Naziism is an example of Christians persecuting non-Christians.)

Meanwhile, Karl's mother was nonpolitical. "My mother didn't say one word. I don't know what she was. . . . She was a sweet mother. That's all I know."[101] (See Appendix E for more of how Karl's home life affected his distaste for the Nazis.)

Rudi meanwhile developed an intense distaste for the regime firsthand: His parents one night were talking with neighbors in the apartment courtyard where a Communist flag was being displayed by one of the neighbors when a car pulled up. Out jumped a group of Nazis who began beating up people, including innocent bystanders. Rudi reports,

"They didn't even stop for children. We got our share of whacks, too."[102]

He continues that a month later was a torchlight parade through the streets by Social Democrat and Communist Party members. The Nazis stationed a machine gun on a roof and killed and injured a number of the marchers, who ran atop the building. "Shortly thereafter I saw the machine gun and several bodies flying off the roof."[103]

That same week Rudi and his parents saw a car overturned in the street. Another car zoomed towards it, with gunmen from both cars firing at one another. The oncoming car swerved wildly. Rudi's father half carried him and his mother into an apartment house entrance to escape the hail of bullets.[104]

These two close friends, Rudi and Karl, were thus anti-Nazi from the start, but had little influence on their strong-willed friend Helmuth until his own eyes were eventually opened.

Helmuth possessed qualities that prepared him for his future activities in recruiting others. He made friends quickly and possessed a warmth and magnetism that attracted strangers. His home life likely gave him a mixture of security and insecurity. The latter came from the fact he was illegitimate and was raised without a father. His security came from knowing he was loved, although his mother and grandparents were not demonstrative. Gerhard explains, "My mother and grandmother were strict and quiet, not outgoing and not particularly warm. But we boys felt their love for us."[1]

One display of their love is the fact Helmuth's mother and perhaps his grandparents sacrificed to send him to Brackdamm.[2] Karl also reports the Sudrows "doted on him a lot."[3] Helmuth's mother later wrote that Helmuth "was really my sunshine."[4]

Charlotte Stake grew up with Helmuth and later married his brother, Hans. She reports in an interview with the author, "People were drawn to him. They came to visit him. There were sometimes three or four boys up there [visiting him]. People really loved him. He was really nice. I saw him around the branch a lot. . . . He had a charm about him."[5]

Helmuth's brother Hans also recalls in an interview with the author that Helmuth was a "natural leader" at church,[6] but "did not try to assume leadership — everything came from him naturally."[7]

Karl Schnibbe adds, "I don't think he gave the impression that he wanted to be a leader . . . but when you associated with him as friends it pulls you to him. . . . He didn't say, 'Hey now, I'm the boss. No, no."[8] Karl reveals Helmuth's leadership style: "He was cool and calm."[9]

Rudi Wobbe says it was at Primary that he first met Helmuth, who was "a shy nine-year-old," while Rudi was attending as an "exuberant eight-year-old." He adds, "We found ourselves going to classes together and soon struck up a friendship. It was one of those occasions when you just seem to hit it off with another person."[10]

Rudi at that time attended as a nonmember, due to his grandmother's influence; but he and his mother would be converted and baptized later, when he was nine.

Rudi describes, "I was about half a head taller than Helmuth, but he towered over me in intelligence. . . . He was a straight-A student while I managed only a good average. But in spite of our differences we became fast friends."[11]

Rudi continues, "We liked to do the same things. . . . In the summertime I would visit Helmuth there and together we would to go an outdoor swimming area on the Bille

River. Other times he came all the way to my home in Rothenburgsort go to with me to Kaltehofe, a swimming installation located on the Elbe River. We also enjoyed playing soccer and other games together with other boys our age."

"It was Helmuth that got me interested in reading books on world history. While I was hanging onto the western novels of Zane Grey and others, Helmuth's interest shifted to politics and world affairs. Acting like a patient teacher, he would study a book then pass it on to me with instructions on key parts to concentrate on. After I'd finished, he quizzed me on the important points, and the moral the authors were trying to convey. He had great depth. For one so young he was remarkable in his ability to share his insights with others." [12]

Fellow office worker Werner Kranz concurred Helmuth was gifted artistically, and often made caricatures of foreign statesmen.[13] Gerhard Kunkel explains, "He could draw faces just by looking at them once. . . . His memory was just out of this world."[14] Karl says, "He had tremendous talent. He could take a pencil and whip out caricatures of Churchill and Hitler that were brilliant."[15] Still existing are several such drawings including those of Nazi leadership on a notepad[16] with some of his writings.

His close friend Arthur Sommerfeld recalls that "Helmuth liked popular American songs and sang them. He probably had a preference for American music. He liked jazz music best. He liked classical and opera, too. He liked singing the new songs — hit songs — some American, some German, some British.[17]

He also liked to dance. While the Nazis outlawed American and British "swing dances,"[18] they allowed the traditional dances, as explained by Gerhard. "I attended dances almost every Saturday night from 1937-1939, sponsored by the Hitler Youth for youths 14-18 for our section of town. My girlfriend from the branch and I attended. The dances provided bands of 10-12 musicians playing live music, which were pretty good. All youth were invited. Hundreds came. No uniforms were allowed.

"At church we had dances about three times a year. We had our own branch band of about six musicians, who were all talented. We danced the waltz, foxtrot, and polka. We also had a branch orchestra, of the same musicians plus about six others, including me. I played the violin."[19]

He adds it was a "good orchestra."[20] "We had several good violinists, four of us actually, including Alfred Meier, Arthur Sommerfeld, Karl's brother Bertold Schnibbe, and myself."[21]

Arthur says, "We had about four church dances per year. I was a good dancer, but Helmuth was a bit awkward."[22] Possibly he became better — perhaps considerably better — as later in his teens he became trimmer and more muscular, according to a classmate at school,[23] and likely more athletic.

Helmuth's brother Hans reports other dances they would attend. "In the summer they had dances in a garden outside Hamburg that belonged to people in the city. Helmuth and I would go to dances there. There was a big tent, with tables. We went about once a year over several years. It was just for entertainment."[24]

Arthur reports a fourth venue for dances: "After MIA [short for Mutual Improvement Association, a Wednesday night church youth activity, also referred to as Mutual], Helmuth and I would often go to an amusement street where there was much dancing in the taverns, and we'd go to watch."[25]

Gerhard sheds light on his brother's interest in the arts, along with their friendship. "Helmuth and I went to the operas and operettas together, accompanied by my best friend, Alfred Meier, whom I knew from our branch. He was very tall, and was lead violin in our branch orchestra.

"Helmuth, Alfred, and I went to the operas to see Margot Linde, my girlfriend at that time, a soprano from the Barmbeck Branch, and we also just hung out a lot together. Helmuth and I also talked together. Perhaps because we were closer in age and showed common interests he was closer to me than to his older brother Hans."[26] However, when Gerhard would later leave for the service, Helmuth would become close to his brother, Hans, as well.

Charlotte says, "Helmuth was in plays at church all the time. About two times a year — like Christmastime and summertime. He started when he was about 12."[27]

Arthur's mother, Marie Sommerfeld, reminisces, "I still have a picture of him at home when he was acting in a play at the church."[28] His brother Hans says he was "a good orator and actor."[29] His friend Arthur recalls him in almost the same words: "a *gifted* orator and actor."[30] He details, "We had on the stage some church plays. He was in a couple per year, maybe, going back to age 13 or 14. I was in the plays also — and was a pretty good actor. Rudi was also in the plays. I don't remember if Karl was. I had walk-on rolls with only a few lines, as did Rudi. Helmuth had major roles in the plays."[31]

Arthur also recalls, "The rehearsals allowed us to get together even more often, going to and from them at church." Helmuth was friends with all of Arthur's family. Indeed, he viewed Arthur's mother as a second mom, and Arthur's sisters as his own. Arthur describes Helmuth associating with all of them at their home but spending considerably more time with Arthur[32] — especially walking to and from church activities five times per week, about 45 minutes each way:

He was particularly close friends with Arthur's sister, Mary.[33] Charlotte Kunkel remembers, "She talked to us later about him — that she really liked him as a friend."[34]

Marie Sommerfeld, states, "He was mostly [staying] with his grandparents. . . . But he found he was most of the time with us. We always had nice music evenings and my Eddy would play the piano and we would sing together. We had a lot of fun then.[35] . . . It was a wonderful time."[36] She also said her daughter would accompany him on the piano and he would sing.[37] Arthur's oldest sister Hedi Sommerfeld Radtke adds, "They often played games when they were gathered around the table," and she says he spent "nearly every evening with us."[38] Arthur confirms that Helmuth "would usually come to our home after church meetings and stay for an hour or so, and we would all sing together. We would always sing about a half hour. . . . He would come over Sundays and a couple days during the week, often after Monday night Priesthood and Wednesday MIAs."[39]

The Sommerfeld family was close to all of Helmuth's family. Marie spoke of Helmuth's grandmother Mary Sudrow, saying she and Mary "always cleaned the branch, the meeting facility, together. So Helmuth was always with us."[40] She adds, "We were always together in the ward. We came home together, we lived together, too, lived in the same place [apartment building], and we did a lot of things together."[41]

Gerhard adds that Arthur's mother was also quite friendly with his mother, Emma. "I would say they were friends. . . . And so I've been over there at that place quite a bit. I was going quite frequently with Arthur."[42] Thus not only Helmuth shared a friendship with Arthur, but Gerhard did as well.

Helmuth sang frequently with not just the Sommerfelds, but at church and with his friends when walking together. His brother Gerhard remembers him as "a great singer — a tenor,"[43] but he "did not play a musical instrument."[44]

Charlotte Kunkel recalls, "I think Helmuth did singing and dancing at Mutual."[45]

His acquaintance at church, Frederich Peters, reports Helmuth "had quite a sense of honor . . . and was very active in the church."[46]

Life at church helped define Helmuth's self-concept, focus, personal goals, standards and friendships more than any other aspect of his life.

Helmuth was ordained a deacon 3 May 1937[1] but his membership record never stated he was ordained a teacher. Peters, at church, believes he was a teacher in 1938 or 1939[2] at age "13 or 14."[3] Gerhard believes Helmuth was still a deacon at age 15 when Gerhard left for the Labor Service in 1940,[4] and states that local German leaders were slower to advance young men in the priesthood at that time. Rudi confirms that he himself was never ordained a teacher until much later. "You stayed a deacon a long time. Teacher, longer."[5]

Going to church was an event to which the boys looked forward, not only twice on Sundays but three other days as well for social and religious activities — a total of five trips per week and more, if there were play rehearsals. They met in a factory building[6] next to a school, located at *Besenbinderhof* 13a. To attend church they'd walk down a hill, where the building was located on the left side of the street.[7] "It was renovated into a meeting house," says

Arthur Sommerfeld. "It had a worship room with a stage and separate classrooms."[8]

In their branch, "We were a close-knit group and had fun together," adds Karl Schnibbe. "All our experiences were positive. Even social class differences were largely ignored."[9] When asked about the generation gap that exists in some branches, Rudi denies that existing in their branch.[10]

Irmgard Becker, nine years Helmuth's senior, remembers the boys at church: "In the communion rites of the sacrament, the youths also carried out sacred rites. They also presented — as befitting their age — little addresses and discourses which they had prepared themselves."[11]

Rudi claims Helmuth was an "excellent" speaker,[12] Gerhard says a "good speaker,"[13] having heard him speak in church.[14] He says Helmuth spoke quite good English,[15] which he learned in school,[16] and was better than most students at the subject. "He spoke very clearly."[17]

Marie Sommerfeld recalls, "He was very articulate.[18] . . . I have asked him quite often gospel questions, things I didn't know about. He could always give me answers. He knew exactly."[19]

Karl says Helmuth was "very bright . . . unusually so!"[20]

Charlotte concurs: "He was very bright . . . he had lots of knowledge."[21] Irmgard Becker simply says, "Helmuth had brains."[22] Rudi says he was a "real brain."[23] Lieselotte Prüss Schmidt agrees: "very bright."[24]

As for church classes, Rudi says he and Helmuth both were "good students" and "mostly attended the same classes." Additionally, Helmuth read much Church literature.[25]

Gerhard adds his brother was an avid reader, always reading Church history, and was "quite interested in history."[26] Rudi agrees: Helmuth was an "ardent reader."[27]

Rudi says Helmuth was well liked at church. Otto Berndt says Helmuth was "very likeable."[28] Elenore Bremer, their Sunday School teacher, liked the boys so well that when she bought herself new scriptures she gave her old Bible to Rudi and her *Doctrine and Covenants* to Helmuth. "So we were her favorite students."[29] Elenore Bremer was described by Hilde Prüss Müller as "a really good teacher who could explain things well, very nice, whom I loved very much." Significantly, Hilde's mother was also a Sunday School teacher of the boys. "Sometimes Mother would come home after Church and talk about Helmuth," she says, "And she would say how bright and nice Helmuth was."[30]

Karl says, "Everyone liked him, I believe, because he got along well with people."[31]

Gerhard adds, "He was liked in the branch as he was smaller,"[32] noting that his size, perhaps with its lack of intimidation, along with what others describe as personal warmth, made him appealing and approachable as a person.

He possessed an interesting habit of cocking his head to the side "all the time," and was particularly seen doing that at Sunday School.[33]

Karl says Helmuth was "warm and charming . . . friendly . . . really, really."[34]

Arthur remembers, ". . . Helmuth was warm and friendly. He was a good boy."[35]

Gerhard says, "Helmuth was also cheerful, friendly and outgoing, although in church he was studious. He had an open personality."[36]

Lieselotte Prüss Schmidt recalls him actually greeting the other members of Sunday School class every week and being friendly to them all. He also engaged in intelligent class discussions. She was in his church classes for several years, along with Karl, Rudi, Arthur, and three others — Karla Fricke, Karl-Heinz Fricke, and Gertrude Berndt.[37]

Gerhard notes, "He never gave the impression to me that he was an idealist," nor did he strike him as the kind of person who would fight for a cause "at that time."[38]

Arthur Sommerfeld's mother, Marie, also adds, "He was a good-natured and jovial person."[39]

Rudi describes Helmuth's commitment. "He had a testimony. Of course, the fallacies of youth — we goofed off a little and all this — so that was part of it." But when asked about Helmuth being a committed Latter-day Saint, Rudi replies, "Definitely, definitely."[40] Otto Berndt adds that he believes Helmuth was converted to the Gospel and had a testimony.[41]

In about 1938 Helmuth had a chance to meet the Prophet and President of the Church of Jesus Christ of Latter-day Saints. Rudi reports Heber J. Grant came to the St. Georg Branch for Monday night Priesthood meeting, in which Helmuth was also undoubtedly present. Rudi says, "I still remember that I shook his hands and greeted him as the prophet. Oh, what an experience. It was exhilarating, really. I shook the hand of a living prophet of God. It's like they say, I didn't wash my hand for . . . [laughing]. But no, I was quite impressed. He was a grand man, really. Looking into his eyes you could see the spirituality just radiate from him. . . . Oh, that was a grand feeling, to have a prophet of God come all the way from Salt Lake City to Hamburg, Germany, and shake my hand. That was the highlight of my youth, really."[42] Helmuth's impressions were likely similar. On that visit President Grant spoke through a translator,[43] and "he made it a point . . . to shake everyone's hand in that priesthood meeting."[44] They also later received a visit from Joseph Fielding Smith, at that time an Apostle and later President of the Church.[45]

Conversely, one of the low points of Rudi's youth — and probably Helmuth's as well — was the day they pulled the missionaries out of Germany. "It was terrible," says Rudi. "I was really close to some of those, buddy-buddy with them, you know. They were young people, too, and I was growing up."[46] The first American missionaries came in 1923, so Helmuth had them in his life ever since he was born. Hamburg had 20-plus missionaries.[47]

Helmuth was also close to the missionaries. Charlotte recalls him speaking to them with very good English, even at 14.[48]

Most teenage boys converting to the Church in the "mission field"— the area outside of Utah — can relate to the closeness he felt with the missionaries and the near hero-worship he experienced, finding each one a combination of close friend, big brother, and messenger of "new, revealed truth."

Additionally, it is common Lattter-day Saint belief that missionaries possess a special mantle of their two year calling which fills them with a certain "aura" or "magnetism" that attracts friends and strangers alike, a certain "power" above and beyond that which the young men and women would possess on their own. So when the missionaries left the boys' lives, there was an empty feeling, an "awful feeling" as Rudi describes it.[49] Fortunately, the boys still had each other.

Not only the missionaries' friendship, but also their personal views, affected Helmuth. Rudi says that when the missionaries were over "quite often" for Sunday dinner, "they always talked about freedom of speech, free press, and the freedom they were enjoying in their country and what it meant to be an American, that you could do what you want to do. And somehow it struck a note with me."[50] And no doubt, with Helmuth.

Obviously, though, the lad wasn't perfect and, despite Marie Sommerfeld and teacher Eleanor Bremer's fondness for him, he wasn't admired by *all* the adults in his branch. As Karl points out:

"A few adult members of the branch thought him a bit arrogant, but that was probably because they resented (as any adult German at that time would have done) a young person asking them difficult questions and pointing out flaws in their logic. Helmuth especially enjoyed engaging adults in political discussions, because they were often a bit naïve, and he enjoyed picking them apart if they were wrong. He enjoyed displaying his intellectual and debating abilities. His intention, however, was not to embarrass people but to make them more careful about what they said. . . . In our church classes Helmuth was the one who knew the answers. He had studied the doctrines and knew them very well for a person of his age."[51] Rudi adds that Helmuth would ask "very pertinent questions," and was told "he was too young to ask these questions."[52]

Similarly, Rudi states, "Helmuth enjoyed rattling people's chains just a little, just to wake them up and make sure they were all seeing every side of a question or an argument. It was always done in a spirit of friendly competition, though, without a thought of showing off. If Helmuth really wanted to he could have demonstrated a dazzling display of intellectual fireworks that . . . would have outdistanced even the most educated of the brethren."[53] Additionally, "he spoke his mind," including in the presence of adults."[54]

In an interview with the author, Otto Berndt, Jr., remembers that for those reasons, Helmuth was "not very well liked by older people."[55] Though only 13 when Helmuth was 16, he recalls that Helmuth was "hard to get to know," because, "he was a bright kid and so far ahead [intellectually]." Much of this, he admits, was the age difference, as older teens typically did not fraternize with the younger set. "A few years means a lot of years at that age," clarifies Resa Guertler Frey, who was only 11 herself at that time.[56] Since they didn't associate with the older teens, only a few older teens knew Helmuth very well —

specifically his three friends. The only others were Arthur Sommerfeld's family, his own two brothers, and Otto Berndt, who was in his thirties, being 21 years older than Helmuth, saying he knew him "pretty well."[57] He was also close to his mother and grandparents, but in a different manner, not confiding in them as with his friends.

Gerhard agrees Helmuth was "a little bit" of a smart aleck, and to some extent dwelled on the fact he "knew so much more."[58] Otto agrees Helmuth "was a smart boy, and he let you know that," but that he was not a smart aleck, only "really smart."[59] Rudi agrees: "Not really a smart aleck, no,"[60] saying Helmuth possessed much "self-confidence," yet, "wasn't cocky" and was "not at all" arrogant.[61]

With such combined traits of friendliness, popularity, charm, and brashness, it is no surprise he had a girlfriend.

CHAPTER 6

Giesela Plambeck fell in love with Helmuth and, according to his brother Gerhard, he was likewise deeply infatuated with her. From ages 13 to 16 they dated nearly every day.

"She was not a member of the Church," explains Gerhard. "She was . . . very beautiful. She had brown eyes. She was . . . very intelligent. She went to the same elementary and high school as Helmuth. In advanced school she studied communication. They knew each other for many years and were the same age, but starting at age 12 or 13 they spent nearly every evening together for the next several years. Helmuth had a crush on her and I noticed she had one on him, as well. I recall him telling me his feelings for her several times when we were alone.

"She had only one other sibling: a sister, also beautiful and four years older. They were Lutherans but not active and belonged to the church that we could see from our apartment windows, looking northwest, about 500 yards from us. . . . Helmuth and Giesela may have studied together as both were studious, but likely had no common classes.

"Giesela's personality was outgoing, warm and charming. She giggled and was witty. She was kind."[1]

Because he knew the Gospel so well — and because he observed his own brothers who dated in the faith — he at some point must have foreseen the upshot of dating Giesela if she wasn't interested in converting. Eventually, he would choose "the cause" — the political adventure — over her, but during these formative years he had a strong taste of young love, companionship, and the joys of a two-way, romantic relationship coupled with deep friendship. Morals were generally high among young teens of this era — certainly within the Church — and there is no doubt that Helmuth, coupled with his commitment to the Gospel, kept himself pure.

Gerhard adds the following details about Giesela:

"She lived in the same building as we did, but in a different wing. She was in 137A, the east wing, on the fourth story. Her apartment included the third and fourth windows in from the street, facing the courtyard. She was about five feet tall, dark blonde or auburn hair, blue eyes, and was very well proportioned. She was . . . kind of Italian-looking and full-faced.[2] She started to develop physically quite early.[3]

". . . The Plambecks had pretty flowers in wooden boxes on their balcony, which faced toward the court. The flowers were colorful geraniums. Her mother tended the flowers, and was heavy-set — always on the balcony tending flowers or knitting. "Giesela always had money, as she received a generous allowance every week. She always dressed very nicely, especially compared to the many other girls in the area. Helmuth usually did not have money, so Giesela paid for their baked goods and candies at the bakery next door, just east of their apartment. They went to the bakery a lot. . . .

"She and Helmuth hung out in groups when they were 11 and 12, then paired off after about two years.

". . . Giesela's father leaned toward the Communist Party, but he was not a member. Many laborers in Hamburg also leaned that way. He ran electric streetcars and was paid very well. . . .

"Giesela and Helmuth hung out around the large Norwegian maple tree — the only tree in the courtyard of the apartment building. They would bring chairs outside to the tree to sit there. They also sat and talked a lot on the main floor outside at street level on the east wing, at the north stairs. They also sat on the stairs going up to the entrance of our grandparents' apartment. Additionally they sat outside her apartment and on her balcony. They also took walks down the sidewalk in front of our apartment, Louisenweg, and they walked up and down other streets.

"They often went to the huge park south of the apartment building and waded in the shallow swimming pool. . . . Her parents were not very strict. Since her mother was very heavy, she couldn't do much, but she ate from the bakery next door a lot."[4]

Gerhard has additional, heretofore unknown information about his brother:

"Helmuth also belonged to a street gang of about 12 to 14 boys. Once [while in a street fight] Helmuth fell on the street and got a three inch gash in his forehead and received stitches. It was 2/3 the way up on his forehead, in the center."[5] His gang would find another gang from nearby streets. They engaged in shoving and pushing and wrestling. It was mostly in fun to see who lived on the toughest street; there was no punching or clubbing.

"The boys would spend time together and there was a group of girls who spent time with them; Helmuth would see Giesela then [with the group], as well as spend time alone with her almost every night."[6]

Gerhard delineates life in the neighborhood, much of it revolving around the apartment complex and Giesela with Helmuth: "They would go to the movie, out for a carbonated lemonade, or just visit. . . . I saw her family often, as everyone saw everyone else in the apartment complex all the time, especially in the summers when people spent a lot of time sitting on their steps and visiting. I also often saw her family shopping."[7]

Helmuth had a studious side. His brother Hans reports, "Helmuth grew up in modest circumstances. He could never go on a trip. But by himself he did a lot for his education. . . . Sciences were his hobby. He read very much."[8] Arthur Sommerfeld recalls science as Helmuth's main interest.[9]

Charlotte remembers, "If he had come from a family of money and influence he could have gone to university. . . . He possessed the caliber of intellect that would have allowed him to fit at a Cambridge or Oxford."[10]

Karl admits Helmuth was "absolutely" an Oxford or Cambridge man,[11] adding that a young German needed not only "lots of brains" but also "money" to go to university.[12]

Rudi says, "If Einstein had a 180 on IQ, I would say that Helmuth had 160 — he was brilliant."[13] Charlotte concurs.[14]

Helmuth attended the basic school, Louisenweg[15] from ages 6 - 12, just across the street from their apartment,[16] in the city district of Hamm. Because of his straight-A grades[17] and "above-average capabilities"[18] he was in the upper track[19] beginning in 1938, according to a government report,[20] at a boys' school[21] named Brackdamm.[22] But according to classmates Rolf Attin and Hans-Theo Rob, his final four years went from April 1937 to April 1941,[23] from ages 12 to 16.[24] Gerhard recalls, "He would walk there each day."[25]

Rolf Attin says that Brackdamm was a middle school in Hamburg, "which had the advantage at that time that you could also graduate with your university preparatory degree from the upper track."[26] As with middle schools in the U.S. the students "were joined together from the various primary [elementary] schools," recalls Attin. Brackdamm was later torn down,[27] probably in the 1980s.

At Brackdamm Helmuth excelled. According to his teacher, August Meins, his favorite subjects were geography and history.[28] He liked math the least, according to both Meins[29] and Attin.[30] His mother stated that he also mastered English, typing and stenography.[31] He was allowed two more

years of schooling than most adolescents, and graduated
the month of March[32] or April[33] 1941, at age 16.

Attin recalls life at school with his friend: "In the course
of the four years that we were in school with Helmuth, we
noticed that he could sometimes be a really witty fellow. He
was jovial; he liked to laugh. He was fond of life and open-
minded. He was not a homebody or a loner. Sometimes we
played jokes together. . . . Helmuth was above all really
superb in German and German composition. Mr. Meins once
had him read aloud his essay as a glowing example of how
you should introduce and construct essays. . . . He read
books that were over my head. I thought, 'What the heck
is he reading?' . . . During his spare time he went his own
way. He was a close friend of Franz Prumnitz. We always
saw them together during recess. . . . Helmuth was not
particularly athletic. During our school days Helmuth was
substantially smaller than I; he was a littler chubbier. Only at
the end of our school days was he larger than I was and had
become thinner and more muscular. . . . In the school we did
not know he was a Mormon. Helmuth said nothing about
his private matters. He also said nothing about political
matters. In general we did not talk about political matters
or the Nazi regime. That was not a topic of discussion at
all. And not from the teachers' side either. I only know that
there was a certain pressure for you to join the Young Folk
and later the Hitler Youth. . . . Helmuth was predestined to
take the entrance exam for the university. But he did not.
That was also certainly a matter of the expense."[34]

His teacher, August Meins, reports:

"Helmuth was different from the other students. He was independent and went his own way. But at the same time he did not isolate himself from the others. He was not a braggart. He was a likeable boy, who was very modest — though with a modesty that was clearly like a feeling of inferiority. He never would have admitted this complex himself. There were many reasons for it — his illegitimate birth, his poor circumstances and so forth. Certainly he was never utterly enthused about the Hitler Youth. . . . [Meins obviously saw through Helmuth's cover once Helmuth became anti-Nazi.]

"He never permitted himself to be led or exploited by any groups. He worked a lot by himself and was very diligent. I never had to call him to order. He also particiated in sports by always taking his place. . . . He was a resistance fighter through and through. He sat in the front row, opposite me. I could always observe exactly his reaction in his eyes, when different things in the class were discussed by the class. I knew that in many cases he thought like me. He was a resister, but it was a cautious resistance. Everyone noticed that. [Actually, no one in school knew he was politically resisting, as no one knew his politics.] In truth, many disliked him for that reason. . . . [Actually, he was extremely well-liked.] I knew absolutely nothing about his Christian views. In the upper track there was no religious instruction and our conversation never came around to religion. . . . He was tough, quiet and persistent. Although he often went his own way, you noticed that he could exercise a great influence on people."[35]

In further conjecture Meins adds that Helmuth's views were seen as "Communistic" — supporting labor — yet different than that of fellow classmate Hermann Peters who *was* a Communist. In any case, "He (Helmuth) was the only one in the class with his particular outlook. For that reason he was teased sometimes." [36] [This contradicts Attin's statement that political matters were never discussed.]

Meins continues: "Because of his nature he was teased a lot by the class." [This also contradicts his classmates who indicate he was very much respected.] Meins concludes, "He was never offended and could not be perturbed." [37]

Perhaps the most interesting aspect of his life was his transformation from pro-Nazi to anti-Nazi.

His "second mother," Marie Sommerfeld, recalls:

"Before he talked that way [against Nazism] he became a member of the Hitler Youth [actually German Young Folk, at that time in his life] about which he was very enthused at the beginning. Full of pride he told about 'his' National Socialism, and I needed to warn my children about saying something in his presence which could have been dangerous for them. You need to know that we were opposed to the Nazis and spoke secretly about them." [38]

Further, she says, "In the beginning he was kind of idealistic about the Nazi movement. Yes, he was. Because I really was afraid for Helmuth because I thought he would go the wrong direction, because we were all against the Nazi movement. And that he turned out to be so different I just could not understand. But in the beginning he was very much involved with it and a little bit radical about it, fanatical almost." [39]

Karl indicates Helmuth was absorbed by the public army band concerts. "He stood there and listened. . . . And it was exciting." [40]

In 1938 at age 13, Helmuth joined the German Young Folk [41] which (ages 10-14), he enjoyed "at first," say his brother Gerhard [42] and Marie Sommerfeld, but by November 1938 he would turn against the Nazis and its youth organizations. Later, on 20 April 1939, three months after his 14th birthday, he transferred to the Hitler Youth [43] (ages 14-18) and used it as "cover" to hide his true beliefs. (See Appendix F for government agency mistakes as to when he joined.)

According to classmate Franz Walter Prumnitz, he continued to belong to the Hitler Youth after graduation. [44]

As to Hitler Youth duty, the Senior District Director later included in Helmuth's "Service Certificate" a two-headed report: (1.) that he performed his work to his superiors' "complete satisfaction" and "always distinguished himself through his eager participation . . ." [45] [which was his "cover"], but (2.) that unfortunately he occasionally allowed himself to be influenced "for the worse" by other boys. [46] It also noted he was always friendly towards his comrades. [47] Another report by the Senior District Leader and Hitler Youth Judge states his behavior with others was "disciplined and friendly." [48]

His brother Hans believes Helmuth was at one time a file leader, [49] but the Senior District Leader of the Hitler Youth claims, perhaps in a whitewash to make themselves look better after his defection — that Helmuth never held an office or rank and also never received any decorations or achievements of honor.[50]

Helmuth's "defection" from the precepts of the German Young Folk and the Nazi Party came from a fascinating series of events.

The turning point in Helmuth's loyalty to the *Reich* came the nightmarish evening of 9 November 1938, two and a half years before graduating from school (and five months prior to joining the Hitler Youth). Karl Schnibbe describes walking home late at night and seeing a synogogue in flames and Jewish-owned shops vandalized with window glass broken.[1] Thus the term *Krystallnacht*, the night of broken glass.

In a 2003 newspaper interview with the *Salt Lake Tribune* Karl recalls, "I heard people laughing and yelling. They were parading Jewish women and children through the town in the back of a garbage truck." Afterwards Karl was ordered to vandalize a Jewish home with his Hitler Youth comrades — but he refused.[2]

Detailing this in his autobiography, Karl says, "Once, as I was going home from work, I went along the Grindelallee and came upon a spot where they had herded a group of Jewish people together. The Jews were being spat upon and laughed at on the street by the SS and SA men, who then forced the poor people to climb into their trucks amidst jeering and derision. As I stood and watched, I became terribly upset.[3]

Karl adds this detail in a 1976 *BYU Today* interview: "One day coming home from work I saw the Nazis herding Jews to the camps, spitting on them. I came home and cried."[4]

Karl continues in his autobiography, "Everything that the Nazis seized from the Jews was called 'Aryanized.' Large signs were plastered on the display windows of the Jewish businesses which were 'Aryanized.' Thereafter the party moochers went in . . . ."[5]

In a 1996 interview with the author Karl states that it was this night that "turned me completely off. That was the turning point."[6]

Of all his group, only Helmuth had been sympathetic to the Nazis. But *Krystallnacht* was the deciding event for him.

In the *Tribune* article Karl summarizes, "To me, it was very wrong what [the *Reich* leaders] were doing. I was taught to tell the truth, and to love other people."[7]

Rudi viewed *Krystallnacht* as merely a follow-up to a heart-sickening event he had witnessed five years previously: In February and March 1933 he had seen a shoe store owned by a Jewish family demolished in broad daylight. "They broke all the windows, threw the merchandise out onto the street and dragged the proprietor and his wife and two children out into the street. They started beating and cursing them, all the while calling them dirty names and shouting that they weren't fit to live among the exalted German Aryan people. They used rubber hoses and sticks to beat them. But the greatest indignity of all is that after the family was laying in the gutter in agony, the Nazis urinated on them. . . . I was only seven years of age when this took place but still remember it vividly to this day.[8] . . . It was something awful that bothered me. They were human beings. All that propaganda, to me it had just the reverse effect. I didn't fall for it. It upset me."[9]

He notes that the Nazis had an inscription, "Blood and honor," on their dress daggers. "They used this distorted concept of honor to shed the blood of countless millions in the name of their demented leader, *der Führer*."[10]

Krystallnacht was likely Helmuth's first major disenchantment with Naziism. It is probably from this point that Helmuth began searching for the truth, and it would not take him long to discover it.

Rudi reports that in addition to the Jews disappearing, "Many a loved one would never be seen again. So there was a growing dissatisfaction, or a hatred that grew up in ourselves. We had to do something."[11] He further speculates, "Were we the only ones that could see it? And yet it was going on all around us. We had Jewish doctors and dentists that were hauled away." Rudi reports he and his mother visited their family doctor a week earlier.[12] "We . . . wanted to get in and there was an SS trooper standing in front of the door chastising us. And he said, 'No good German patronizes a Jewish doctor.' My mother just said, 'Well we do,' pushed him aside, and we walked in. She was very resolute."[13] He adds, "Maybe I got it from her."[14]

He summarizes, "So the resentment against the treatment of good, honest, hardworking people that happened to be Jews, good Germans, some of them decorated in the First World War, now all of a sudden second- and third-class citizens or no citizens at all, that's sad."[15]

It was at this point that Helmuth joined Karl and Rudi in a secret project to help the Jews, a project coordinated with other members of the Church.

From the St. Georg Branch in Hamburg, Frederich Peters reports, "I was in a group with Helmuth. Then in about 1939-40 the North German Refinery approached our church because they were very concerned about their Jewish employees. Under the aegis of our system for taking care of our members, we helped the Jews of the North German Refinery by — mostly at night when the streets were empty — loading their things on 'Scottish carts' and then transporting them to the Hanover train station. Helmuth Hübener, Karl Schnibbe and Rudi Wobbe were there. Each time they were underway for two and a half hours,"[16] in an effort to help the jews escape.

But it was not long before Helmuth faced his first opposition. One day he had an altercation with the Hitler Youth. Rudi reports in a 1988 interview with Matthew Heis that after choir practice he, Arthur Sommerfeld and Helmuth were walking home singing American songs, "You are My Sunsine" and "Moonlight and Roses," along with Church songs. "We just bellowed it out." A Hitler Youth patrol stopped and questioned them, and Helmuth "just talked them down to a frazzle . . . left them in the dust."[17]

In his autobiography, *Three Against Hitler*, Rudi adds that on that evening, Karl started out with them but left at Hammerbrookstrasse to head home alone. Rudi and Helmuth [leaving out Arthur in this account] continued their journey. The Hitler Youth patrol stopped them and wanted to see their IDs, demanding to know why they were singing "English songs." Helmuth snapped at them, informing them brazenly they were in fact "American" songs and telling them off for harassing German citizens on the street.

"So intense was Helmuth's tirade that the members of the youth patrol were effectively confounded," reports Rudi. They withdrew, "unable to compete with Helmuth."[18]

Helmuth turned to Rudi and told him that when people are put in a uniform they think they can "bully people around." It is very likely that *Krystallnacht* had not only turned Helmuth against the Nazis but against bullying — period. He now told Rudi their whole country was being run through "threats, intimidations, and even brutal force. And something has to be done about this!"[19]

Rudi believes this personal experience with bullying is what pushed Helmuth to take action. He further noted to Karl, "These Hitler Youth uniforms look just like the military ones. Obviously they are preparing us to be soldiers too."[20]

On his next encounter with the Hitler Youth, Helmuth declared war. He, Karl, and Rudi were together when they were ambushed by a Hitler Youth patrol. This time they *physically* fought back. "Where we were we knew every bush," says Karl, so we disappeared." They ran from the patrol through a park, snuck behind bushes, and *attacked* the Hitler Youth, pelting them with rocks. They left, triumphant.[21]

Helmuth's disrespect for the Hitler Youth was multiplying, as he now referred to them as "these dumb kids,"[22] to his closest friends.

Meanwhile, Rudi and Karl had their own run-ins with the Hitler Youth. The first problem they had stemmed from the fact they had to join. "Oh, we talked about it quite frequently," says Rudi. "It really upset me. Of course, being forced into something, no way."[23] Nevertheless, since he was forced to go, he went.

In 1938 when Rudi attended his first Young Folk meeting, he heard the Jews accused of outrageous crimes. Rudi asked for proof and they turned on *him*.

The next summer at Hitler Youth camp when they had political indoctrination sessions they attacked religious concepts. Rudi defended religion, and they made fun of him. Later one of the Hitler Youth leaders stole Rudi's package from home and handed out all his cookies, then read his mother's letter aloud and made fun of it. Rudi told them off, and they hazed him with shoe polish and toothpaste, saying they were administering "the Holy Ghost."[24]

After that camp was over, "I hurried to the party office to return the uniform. . . . I didn't want anything more to do with those people."[25]

Later Rudi was riding his bike past a Hitler Youth patrol and did not salute the flag. They tried stopping him. He rammed into one boy and knocked him over, then peddled away. They couldn't identify him, so couldn't catch him.

Rudi had another showdown with the Hitler Youth. When he was 16 he started his apprenticeship as a machinist. Since he had his weekends and nights filled with classes in math and engineering,[26] he skipped Hitler Youth meetings. So he was called in to explain why he wasn't attending.[27]

". . . Pretty soon I had to go there and *show* to them why I wasn't at their duty meetings. So I took all my certificates and receipts to show that four nights out of the week I was going to school. So they excused me, especially after I made a spiel that, 'Didn't the *Führer*, Adolf Hitler, say that he wants the German youth the best educated youth in the world? I am doing just that. I'm going to school.' So I got excused.

"Except on the way out, one of those bully Hitler Youth leaders stopped me and said, 'Hey, you have to stay here, we got duty for you tonight.' I said, 'I have an excuse. I don't have to stay.' 'But I am telling you, you stay.' By that he pushed me against the wall. I said, 'Hey man, hands off.'[28]

"'Why, what do you want to do? I'm wearing the uniform.'

"I said, 'Then get out of the uniform, you coward.'

"He pushed me again and I had an awful short temper in those days so I just hauled out and decked him one good. [Rudi also says, "I let him have an uppercut . . . which caught him square on the jaw."[29]] I conked him out cold. He fell to the floor and I just took my bike and ran over him and out I went."[30]

Karl Schnibbe had a similar experience. Once when he went to a Hitler Youth meeting his youth leader wanted to disgrace him for not wearing a uniform. "He wanted to let me have it," says Karl, who adds that the fellow wanted to drill him in the mud. Karl snapped back, "Are you nuts or something?" The leader demanded to know, "Where's your uniform?" Karl says he always told them it was "in the laundry," but this time they caught on.[31] Karl continues, "My tormentor was not any older than I was, so when I had had enough, I went over to him and told him to lay off and asked him if he was completely normal. I said, 'Leave me alone!' . . . One word followed another, and then I gave him a shove. He yelled at me and I told him to shut up. He then yelled even louder, so I punched him in the face. By the finish I had trounced him in front of all the others. I was a little bigger than he and I really had gotten hot under the collar and I finally told him that he could kiss my [rear], and then I went home.[32] . . . Thereafter, when they had duty and drilled, I always went past naturally dressed in civvies. All my friends saw me and I stopped and smirked at them."[33]

Nor did Karl have a great deal of respect for the Swastika. "Whenever I saw the flag come I turned the other way.[34]

A few weeks later, at the end of 1939, Karl received a letter from the area leader and was called in for an honor meeting. He was expelled from the Hitler Youth for the earlier incident of not obeying an order[35] to harass the Jews.

Rudi adds this about the Hitler Youth: "What really upset me was when I was just about ready to join the Boy Scouts. And oh, I was dreaming about it.[36] . . . We had been waiting for several years to be Boy Scouts. When we were finally old enough we were told that this organization had just been disbanded and we were forced to join the Hitler Youth."[37]

Helmuth now had five reasons to oppose Hitler. First and foremost was the treatment of the Jews. Second was the Reich's propensity to bully people using the Hitler Youth. Third, the scheduling of Hitler Youth duty on Sunday which, according to historian H. W. Koch[38] was a deliberate attempt to interfere with German boys attending church. Fourth, the Hitler Youth had broken windows by throwing rocks at the church meetinghouse. And fifth, when Gestapo spies began attending Sacrament Meeting, normally an oasis from the chaos, Helmuth became incensed.

On one particular Sunday the boys arrived to find in their congregation several Hitler Youth attending for the ostensible purpose of disturbing the meeting, but apparently they chickened out, and left quietly after a few minutes.[39]

No doubt Karl, Rudi and Helmuth glared at them, and certainly Karl had a reputation among the Hitler Youth, after beating up its leader, of being one not to be messed with.

"Perhaps they lost their courage or saw one of our leaders in his uniform," muses Karl.[40] This was the sixth and final reason that ignited Helmuth.

They began having private political discussions. And at first, that's all they were, discussions.

Karl reminisces, "I often discussed with my friends Helmuth and Rudi what we thought about such things. We saw each other once, twice or three times a week and talked."[41] Karl says they analyzed current affairs: "Could one really believe [the Nazis]? Joseph Goebbels was a completely calloused and hard-boiled minister of propaganda who could lie without blushing."[42]

Arthur Sommerfeld said that to his credit Helmuth was able to figure out more on his own than most citizens.[43]

Then an event occurred in Helmuth's life that opened his eyes more than he probably ever expected.

CHAPTER **8**

One day in 1940 Helmuth went swimming at the Bismarck swimming pool. He was intrigued with what a group of boys were discussing. They had revealing information about the *Reich*, relating the little-known fact that the Nazis were actually anti-Christian. He soon learned these boys were Communists, were non-Christians, and seemed objective on the issue.

He quickly befriended them and began going to the apartment of one of the boys — and there he was introduced to the BBC.

Arthur Sommerfeld says, "He already knew from his own understanding that the *Reich* told lies. But the BBC awakened him to a bigger realization of how large the lies really were."[1] Hans backs that up: "The BBC just filled him in with a better realization."[2]

According to the mother of one of these youths, Helmuth became strongly influenced by the boys regarding Hitler's anti-Christian activities. Although they were not Christians they regarded Helmuth as a devout Christian who would be interested in this information, and indeed he was.

This woman, Ida Wieczorek, also said Helmuth did not share their Communist ideas, but joined in as they listened to foreign broadcasts. This continued from 1940 into 1941, while Helmuth was still in school.

The boys often swam and talked at the pool with other friends, not part of their group, perhaps non-Communists like Helmuth, but opponents of Hitler nonetheless. At the apartment of one of these boys, the group would "lay there in the dark many nights, listening to foreign stations," says Ida, in whose apartment they met.

Two of the other boys were Paul Liedel and Hans Baier. Another was Joseph Wieczorek, whose mother and father were involved in resistance work. His father, Jupp Wieczorek, had actually been imprisoned for illegal political work. The boys, including Helmuth, assisted them, says Ida.

When "things were hot" they met either in a cellar beside a courtyard behind their apartment or in the country cabin of a Dr. Horn, an attorney for whom Josef's mother worked.

Helmuth was an integral part of this group. However, in February 1941, when young Josef entered the military, Helmuth probably ceased going to the boy's apartment. He would graduate from school the following month of April.[3]

Ida Wieczorek states, "I would just like to mention that Hübener was an upright, clean, fine lad that I immediately took to my heart.[4]

Rudi confirms in his autobiography that Helmuth had "cultivated ties with Communistic youth organizations, like the Wieczorek group, which he met at the Bismarck bathhouse in Altona."[5] (See Appendix G regarding Helmuth's discretion in sharing with his friends his activities.)

After having been exposed to the BBC and his revolutionary friends, Helmuth's curiosity became unquenchable. Soon, he would make *another* important discovery.

With the war stepping up, Allied bombing raids were hitting Hamburg. Bomb shelters were built, and people were running to their designated shelters.[6]

Herta Schmidt Wobbe recalls: "As teenagers we had a different outlook on the war than the adults. After awhile, when the sirens sounded, if we were asleep we wouldn't go down to the bunkers, but would stay in our beds. And if we were at a movie show, we'd walk behind the facades along the sidewalk and make our way home, rather than go into a bunker."[7]

Gerhard says, "Most of the bunkers in the city held about 200 to 300 people. Eighty to ninety percent of them were built underground. Some held a thousand or more. Some held less than 200. Bunkers located in high density areas of the city could hold more than 1,000 persons.[8]

Helmuth also experienced the excitement of bombing raids, which began in early 1940, according to Rudi. The first bombing in Hamburg took place close to the Altona branch of the Church in the St. Pauli district. "I remember we went from St. Georg on foot all the way up to St. Pauli just to look at those bombed out homes. . . . We received some damage in our branch house, too, where we had large windows and they were blown in by the bomb blast and some fragments got thrown in so we had to clean it all up."[9] Hilde Prüss Müller muses that as children they had a hobby of searching the next morning, after bombs had dropped in the night, for "the best shiny bomb pieces," and showing them off to their friends.[10]

Rudi says the bombings did not disrupt their meeting schedule because in the first part of the war the bombings were not too prevalent, but later on they occurred with such frequency that as citizens they had air raid guard duty.[11]

Helmuth pulled at least one stint of "bomb watch:"

On New Years Eve, 1 January 1941, while Helmuth was in his next-to-last year of school, Helmuth, Arthur, and Rudi received, according to Arthur, "an assignment to watch the factory building where we attended church," which, incidently, was a building used to make medicine from herbs.[12] Karl could not join them that night, says Rudi.[13] Also with them was an elderly man from the branch, Heinrich Worbs. On the top floor was a room where the air raid warden sat through the night to watch over the complex, so that if a bomb hit he would call the fire department or try to douse the fire.[14] The government had assigned an air raid warden to every block. The warden was in charge of seeing that every building had a guard, particularly at night in case of fire, to warn the residents. Rudi says their branch always furnished "one or two members" to be night guards.[15]

Regarding that evening Arthur says, "We celebrated together."[16] Rudi adds about Worbs: "First he told us ghost stores and stuff like that, just to entertain us. But then he took to the scriptures and read and expounded the scriptures to us, a very spiritual man. I loved the man. He was a good man. Anyway, his only fallacy was that he spoke how he felt.[17] At one point Worbs prayed aloud and made anti-Nazi statements. The boys warned him to be careful and Worbs responded, "I tell the truth and nothing but the truth and I cannot tell a lie.[18]

Rudi remembers a radio being present that night, from which Helmuth attempted to tune in unauthorized *Reich* stations, but that night he could find only Radio Basel/ Switzerland and Radio Liechenstein.[19]

Worbs, it should be noted, would later play a part in the boys' determination to face the regime head-on.]

Meanwhile, during his last 2½ years of school, according to his young friend at church, Frederich Peters, Helmuth tried to "maintain his cover" about his anti-Nazi sentiments.[20]

Rudi reports Helmuth concealing his real intentions as far back as 1938 — no doubt after his experience with *Krystallnacht.* Rudi had asked Helmuth how he felt about joining the Hitler Youth, to which Helmuth replied, "Rudi, don't you ever believe what people are saying to you, especially in politics. They're always large in words, but small in action. Only time will tell." Rudi adds that Helmuth told him why: "Because they are trying to win the working class over right now by providing employment and temporary economic gains. But only time will tell."

Rudi says he replied, "It sounds like you're not really sure of them," to which Helmuth replied again with a smile on his lips, "Time will tell." Rudi states, "Then I understood that which he was trying to convey to me—that he wasn't the ardent follower of Nazi ideology he pretended to be, but rather was putting up a clever smokescreen so others could not see his real conviction. Pretty clever, I thought, and my respect for him grew even more."[1]

His brother Hans also saw Helmuth using "cover." He declares that although Helmuth was at first enthusiastic about the Nazis, after his conversion to the truth he continued to act enthusiastic, but only "to cover himself."[2]

Karl maintains that Helmuth continued to be active with his Hitler Youth meetings, unlike he and Rudi, "just to camouflage himself."[3]

Hans adds that this was only in order "to get the government job with the social administration. He liked to 'go up,' and definitely wanted that position in the government."[4] Karl concurs that he even wrote a pro-Nazi graduation thesis in early 1941, "to become eligible to go into the office" for the government job.[5] Rudi agrees Helmuth was pretending in order "not to make waves."[6]

With regards to his graduation thesis, a government report states, "He then submitted for his leaving certificate a political essay, 'The War of the Plutocrats.' . . . One would not assume from the style in which it is written that he was only 15 or 16 years old."[7] Rudi says the "Plutocrats" paper even included illustrations[8] — of his own craftsmanship[9] since he was a skilled illustrator. His brother Hans recalls the thesis utilized "many books with political and economics contents."[10] And then he finished school, rated as "extremely good"[11] on his leaving certificate.

So the Nazis were impressed. They analyzed from his thesis that he "possessed a sufficient capacity of political discernment."[12] They also wrote, ". . . a completely positive attitude to the Fuhrer is to be observed,"[13] which, indeed, was more camouflage.

He must have been frustrated that he could not continue his education because of lack of finances; nevertheless, he found himself in that exciting transition between finishing the grind of school work and entering the workforce, allowing him complete freedom each night when the workday ended.

In April 1941, when he was 16, Helmnuth was placed into the upper administrative track of the Hamburg city social welfare department.[14] He was actually "apprenticed" to the clerical civil service[15] — a slot for those who had excelled in school. He worked in the Bieberhaus[16] that was later named after him,[17] which was part of the city hall.

Gerhard explains, "Helmut did not do National Labor Service or army duty, because he got a deferment by nature of his work in administration, and still was below drafting age, which was age 20."[18]

Meanwhile, their brother Hans had finished his four-year apprenticeship as a shipbuilder, "working for the company that built the *Bismarck*," says Hans.[19] In 1939 after the attack on Poland, Hans was drafted for one day, but they sent him back when they learned he could build ships. Two years later they drafted him again — this time for submarine duty — but sent him back when they learned the same fact. He served no National Labor Service for the same reason.[20] Hans's shipbuilding apprenticeship began at age 14 or 15, "while going to school,"[21] and lasted four years.

Neither Gerhard nor Hans was in the Hitler Youth,[22] as they were past the age limit. Nor did Gerhard belong to any Nazi organizations until he was drafted into the Labor

Service and the army. The only organization to which their mother belonged was the government labor union, Deutsche Arbeitsfront.[23] All the boys they hired were already tops in school — and he was a cut above all of them.

At work Helmuth built a solid reputation. His supervisor, Heinrich Mohns, reports him as an "excellent and dependable colleague." Later, the government reported, "He showed an intelligence at central administration far above the average for boys of his age."[24]

Having had his eyes opened by his revolutionary friends — whom he had stopped seeing two months earlier — and by the BBC, and having secured the career he desired, his next step was to learn all the truth he could about the Nazis, since he now had no homework and free time.

His next big step in that direction actually came *at work*. There he had access to storerooms in the basement of the city hall, where *forbidden books* were stored.[25] He would bury his mind in books during numerous trips to the basement, ostensibly for the purpose of filing papers as part of his job. Possibly he would sneak there after hours and read, then check for security guards and sneak out of the building late at night. He read everything possible on European history, foreign policy, domestic strategies, and world economics.

According to his brother Hans, "He read books about the USA, about the Soviet Union and other countries. . . . Consequently he got acquainted with the 'enemy powers' as he studied their strengths. Although the Nazis appeared to be doing well in the war, he proved that in the long run a victory against such an enemy is not possible, just on economic grounds alone."[26]

Rudi adds, "He was reading all those forbidden books down in the basement — the archives — that were forbidden — like Thomas Mann, Heinrich Heine, VonHouever and others. He also read a lot of literature about political science"[27] and the classics in German literature.[28]

Gerhard adds, "Being employed in the civil service he probably knew more about things which were going on in the background than we really know."[29]

Karl recalls, "Helmuth always told [Rudi and I] things that caused us to say, 'My goodness, how does he know that?'[30] . . . Helmuth always said to us, 'I need to make you a little more politically educated.' He presented comparisons and forced us to think. I was always astonished at his knowledge and intelligence. I called him 'the Professor.' . . . He was always hungry for knowledge. I am convinced that Helmuth read many books which ordinary mortals never encountered in Germany at that time. . . . We asked, 'Man, how do you know that?'"[31]

But then he made a discovery that would change his life even more dramatically.

As stated, his stepfather Hugo Hübener was a member of the SA,[32] and a file leader.[33]

This was the infamous *Sturmabteilung*, the Storm Detachment, also known as the storm troopers, whose members had earned membership in it by belonging to the Nazi Party's own, private military group years earlier. Previously, Hugo had been in the Steel Helmet, the

Stahlhelm.[34] But in the SA he had achieved the rank of corporal, being a member since 18 February 1934.[35] He joined the Nazi Party itself on 1 May 1937.[36] By profession, Hugo was in the merchant marine and "loved the military ways," says Gerhard.

Gerhard says it was 1937 when Hugo moved in to live with them and it was 19 September 1939 when Hugo married his mother.[37] "He and I did not get along.[38] Every day he tried to push the Nazi Party on us. At first my two brothers and I would leave the room, then I began arguing with him about it, until we argued daily. Hugo was also opposed to the Church, so I argued with him about that as well. Helmut joined in with me on those arguments about once a week."[39] But it was probably only on religious matters that Helmuth participated, because even though he sided with Hugo on politics until *Krystallnacht* in November 1938, he kept his politics afterwards under wraps.

By contrast, Hans Kunkel remembers, "Hugo was a friend. He was in the Nazi Party, but did not try to force it on the boys."[40] This discrepancy could be understood in light of the young men's differing personalities, as Gerhard and Helmuth were more aggressive and argumentative with Hugo, while Hans was shyer, like their mother, so both Hans and his mother got along well with Hugo.[41] Gerhard also explains that Hans was "not really interested" in anything at that time, such as politics, because he was sick and always depressed from his sickness. He had become ill from spraying synthetic lacquers at work without wearing a mask, and he had gotten some into his lung. It took years to get over it.[42]

The first to move out was Gerhard. "I had to get away from Hugo so [about April 1939] I moved back to my grandparents,"[43] to the same apartment where he and his family had lived.[44] He got a job in Mutzen Fabrik.[45] Earlier he had enrolled at Technicum Hamburg in 1936 in electrical engineering, and had graduated in July 1940, a year after moving away from Hugo and his family.[46]

After Gerhard left for the National Labor Service in August 1940,[47] Helmuth moved in with their grandparents "sometime during the year," taking Gerhard's place.[48] Helmuth moved out to get away from Hugo. Karl confirms that Helmuth did not get along with his stepfather,[49] as does Rudi, who says Helmuth told him personally about it.[50] Rudi says the clash was "personality and political." Gerhard adds it was the religious conflict.[51] Helmuth let Rudi know what he thought of his stepfather, owing to Hugo's anti-Church, pro-Nazi positions: "'Oh yes,' Helmuth said, 'He's one of those idiots.'"[52]

Hans reports that he joined Helmuth[53] either after Helmuth moved or at the same time: "Helmuth and I were at the Sudrows when Gerhard was gone. We ate with them[54] and they took care of us. We did homework up there in their apartment. We slept in a room downstairs[55] where Mother had lived. Two beds were in there."[56] Gerhard adds that his two brothers stayed in the middle room where he had stayed,[57] right below their grandparents' flat.[58] Hans lived there until his own marriage[59] on 9 May 1942.[60]

It was convenient for the boys to move because not only was there conflict in the home, but both parents were away from home working, according to a later government report.[61]

Life improved for everyone because of the move. Helmuth was still able to visit his mother several nights a week.[62] And Hans likely joined him.

As to politics, living at his grandparents' place opened up a whole new world of opportunities to resist the Third Reich.

The Sudrows were older and went to bed early. Also, they were not as quick and observant as Hugo and Emma, so now Helmuth had a veritable field day to explore his anti-Nazi truth-seeking activities. But first a significant event had to take place with his brother Gerhard.

Gerhard recalls, "In the Labor Service from August 1940 to April 1941 I was in France[1] . . . stationed at Craile,[2] 30km north of Paris."[3]

One day in Paris two weeks before coming home,[4] "I went to the little stands on the street where you could buy anything on the black market — fruit, sausage, chicken. And I bought a small Rola superheterodyne radio, about 15 inches wide by 13 inches high by nine inches deep. It weighed about five to six lbs. It was plastic and brand new. I paid 25 marks for it — which was 5,250 francs."[5]

Back at the base, Gerhard noticed, "Nearly all the men had a superheterodyne. Some had models that were big and fancy. They all received short, medium and long wave."[6]

In 1974 he clarifies that his radio had two bands — shortwave and middlewave. "The BBC was in shortwave mostly in the evening, but also middlewave during daylight hours." He adds that it was not easy to receive because of the jamming station" of the Nazis.[7]

Ironically, for all the grief German citizens at home would suffer for listening to the BBC, myriads of German boys — the para-military servicemen in France — were getting their daily news from the BBC! Continues Gerhard, "[I] listened to music on it every night, but on about two occasions, for a half hour each, I listened to the BBC in English, as I knew English. About six or seven other boys would wander in during the newscasts. They didn't know English but, even if they did, I trusted them to not report me and they didn't. I also listened to the BBC in the German language on other fellows' radios for about the same amount of time during the couple of weeks before I bought mine. . . .[8]

"In my room, four of us listened to it often — in fact most men did [in their rooms]. Even the service officers came into our rooms, sat down, and listened with us, as did administrators of the para-military Labor Service."[9]

Nazi records later reported that Gerhard returned from France in March 1941.[10] "I spent a week home before my orders to the army came, which I had to report to immediately. The next day I went to basic training."[11]

As to the radio, Helmuth would have immediately noticed from the bright logo it was a Rola brand[12] shortwave radio,[13] better than the cheap radios to which the citizenry had access and which could not pick up shortwave. The

Propaganda Ministry ordered this cheap machine to be
built in 1933, which received only medium wavelengths —
and which picked up only the stations in the three German
cities of Hamburg, Berlin, and Frankfurt. It was called the
"people's receiver."[14] Gerhard details that this *Volksempfanger*
"was a version of a reflex radio receiver. It was not a
superheterodyne, it was a reflex and limited in distance,"
and was "thought up . . . intentionally" to be very primitive
in order to receive only those local stations.[15]

Gerhard details Helmuth's interest in it. "After I went
home to Hamburg, I told Helmut about my shortwave."[16] "The
Rola radio was kept in a closet in the hall of the Sudrow's
apartment. The closet was about six feet wide, six feet high,
and one-and-a-half feet deep. It had three sections. I had one
section, and the radio was kept there on the middle of three
shelves. I kept my musical instruments on the bottom. They
were a violin, a mandolin, and a mandola."[17] He also had in
the cabinet some paintings and wood carvings, including
quite a few railroad cars he had carved from wood.[18] . . .
Only I had a key."[19]

During this visit home from France in April 1941 Gerhard
reports seeing Helmuth with Giesela "every night," because,
"they were crazy about each other." He also had seen
Helmuth with her every night eight months earlier, the last
time Gerhard was home.[20]

Then Gerhard left for the army. Probably immediately
Helmuth eyed the hallway locker.

Gerhard reminisces, "I don't know how he did it. He
somehow jimmied the lock and opened my locker and

got my shortwave from the locker. I was amazed when I found out."[21]

But the radio needed repairing.

Gerhard Kunkel maintains the Rola was working when he had it,[22] but government records show that Helmuth had it repaired right after he got it. Three possibilities exist: (1.) the radio broke in transit from France, unknown to Gerhard, (2.) Helmuth broke it immediately upon trying to listen to it,[23] or (3.) The radio was not working properly by the time Gerhard brought it home, and Gerhard may have forgotten that detail. To support this possiblity, Rudi believes that Gerhard actually *asked* Helmuth to get the radio repaired.[24]

Karl believes the repair was minor and that Helmuth had "connections" to get it fixed,[25] which is plausible since listening to shortwave was expressly forbidden by the regime and repairmen in general would not have touched it.

By late April,[26] Helmuth received it back.[27] After the Sudrows retired for the night[28] Helmuth had the freedom to dive into the radio. Excitedly he turned the dial, looking for the BBC — then he found it.[29] And he began listening to it each night in his grandparents' apartment,[30] while his grandparents had no idea of his activity.[31]

At 10 o'clock[32] every night came the first four notes of Beethoven's Fifth Symphony,[33] played three times,[34] then the words, "The BBC London sends news in German," or "This is the BBC London, German news broadcast."[35]

Of course with his revolutionary friends he had first heard the BBC, but now he was able to listen at his leisure —

and once again recognize the truth. Opponents of the regime often listened to foreign radio stations for the truth.[36]

Helmuth became addicted. He listened four to five times per week.[37] Since he knew shorthand,[38] he took notes,[39] then typed them. The timing couldn't have been better.

———————————

On 22 June 1941 the German army attacked Russia.[40] Helmuth knew from his forbidden reading material that no European country had ever attacked Russia and succeeded. He also figured that Germany had no natural resources for running a war. He predicted its tanks and airplanes would grind to a halt since the allies could cut off Germany from its oil sources. He saw the Reich coming down like a house of cards and knew Hitler had to be replaced before they were all destroyed.

The BBC's reports confirmed his every fear. It would not cease broadcasting the truth of Germany's indescribable disaster. To make matters worse, he next learned Hitler would not retreat even once that he knew his armies were in a hopeless state; rather, he continued the march into Russia, sacrificing hundreds of thousands of German boys.[41]

Meanwhile German radio spewed its propaganda, claiming one German victory after another. Helmuth discerned who was telling the truth. He knew, not only from the BBC, but from both his forbidden books research and from the increasing obituaries in the newspapers, that his fatherland hadn't a firefly's chance in sunlight. He confided to his friends, Rudi and Karl, about the German news media,

"These aren't the facts. This is not happening." He was also concerned that the German people were now being called upon by a lying government to sacrifice more than ever. Many common foods and household items were no longer available because of the war; a war, they were told, they would win.

Karl says, "Helmuth told us about the attack on Russia. 'It cannot succeed!' He had thought about it a lot and was firmly convinced of it."[42] At this point his friends did not know of the Rola or his forbidden books and documents to which he had access at work. They did not know where he came up with so many facts. But his reasoning had a ring of truth to it.

Yet the blissful majority in Germany knew nothing of the facts. They thought their armies were victoriously marching away, still conquering the world.

In his mind it was time Helmuth did something about it. The regime, with its lies, its political murders, its mistreatment of Russian prisoners, its persecutions of the Jews — he did not know of the exterminations — and its wholesale destruction of its young soldiers, had to be exposed.

So Helmuth, armed with the truth, determined to do his part in toppling the Nazi government!

CHAPTER **11**

After making the decision to take action, his first step was to recruit others.

Nothing is known about his attempts to recruit his girlfriend Giesela. Where he did begin to bring in others, however, was within his Mormon congregation, a naturally fertile field.

Arthur Sommerfeld reports, "Helmuth was my best friend for five years. I lived 30-45 minutes from him. On the way to church I would walk past his apartment and stop there. We'd walk to church together. On the way back from church we would sometimes separate. He would stop at his apartment, or he would continue walking with me to my apartment."[1]

It was not long before Helmuth targeted Arthur to join him in the resistance campaign.

Arthur admits, "I listened to the BBC with Helmuth.[2] . . . We listened many times together to the news on the BBC. We walked together from the church and turned the radio on and listened to the news on the BBC. We listened . . .

not on a regular basis. About once a week. . . . Helmuth and I thought the BBC told the truth because the news the German radio told the German people was not true. . . . They would tell us a British ship sunk, then they would announce it again and again as if they were different ships, to make themselves look more successful than they really were. They wouldn't let the Germans know what was going on.[3] . . .

"Helmuth told me he was distributing flyers. I warned him sometimes to not pass out flyers — on several occasions I warned him — whenever I found out he was distributing the flyers. I was always against it. I told him he shouldn't do it at all . . . He never asked me to distribute flyers. . . . I would [only] listen with him to the radio. I did not warn him to not listen to the radio.[4] . . .

"He never tried to get my sisters to distribute flyers. I don't think he approached my sisters to listen to the BBC."[5]

On the other hand, Karl thought Helmuth did approach Arthur's siblings once. Karl says Helmuth said to them:

"'Tell me, if you had the chance to listen to English broadcasts, would you listen?' He did not say that *he* did it. They said, 'No, that is much too dangerous.' Then he knew exactly how they stood."[6]

Arthur continues, "I didn't tell Mother many things that were going on. It was a secret then. I don't think I told her we listened to the radio."[7]

His mother adds, "He [Helmuth] often asked Arthur to visit him in his apartment late in the evening. But I would not permit it. 'What do you want to do?' I asked. 'Helmuth's grandparents are already asleep and you will only disturb them.'" In hindsight she adds, "But Helmuth surely wanted to initiate Arthur into his secret."[8]

Arthur continues, "The labor service took me at that point."[9]

So, having experienced only limited success with Arthur, and still needing help in distributing flyers, Helmuth turned to his two other close friends — Rudi and Karl — who seemed riper for resistance anyway, what with their run-ins with the Hitler Youth.

Helmuth would later successfully organize others into his resistance movement, but his main work was now launched with just these two, where the camaraderie and trust he experienced among them would never be replaced. All three boys were finished with school and two were still apprentices when their resistance activities began.

Marie Sommerfeld, Arthur's mother, vouches for Helmuth's friends Rudi and Karl, "They were good young men."[10] Otto Berndt, Jr., says all three "were always there in church — and were quite faithful." However, Rudi and Karl were not as *dedicated* until later years, he adds,[11] which Rudi and Karl both freely admit.

Rudi, born 11 February 1926 in Hamburg,[12] was the youngest of the trio, a year younger than Helmuth,[13] and he was an apprentice mechanic.[14] His mother was a war widow and worked as a cleaning woman. He was an only child, born to Gustav Emil Albert Achilles Wobbe and Marie Louisa Meyer,[15] four years after their marriage. Initially baptized a

Lutheran a couple weeks after his birth, his pastor dubbed Rudi a "Boy of Thunder," "because when he sprinkled me with the baptismal water a loud thunder clap was heard from the storm that was raging outside," reports Rudi.[16]

Rudi was nine when his father succumbed to the aftereffects of a World War I battle injury — a grazed kidney[17] — and it emotionally derailed Rudi. "Oh gosh, he was my idol. Big, broad-shouldered man, good craftsman, he could do anything with his hands. And whenever he made a statement, that was gospel for me. I just adored him."[18] . . . I absolutely could not understand why he had to go. I still needed him and wanted to do so many things with him. I was just nine years old then and I felt a terrible loss."[19]

He then became very attached to his mother, who sacrificed to keep them alive. After his father's death, she arose 3 o'clock in the mornings to clean offices,[20] then came home to help get Rudi ready for school, probably worked more, and was home when he got home from school.[21] Nevertheless, she told him that from then on he would be the man of the house and "should look after her."[22] She also took the death of her husband very hard.[23]

On 7 June 1935,[24] three months after his father's death, they both converted from Protestantism to the Church of Jesus Christ of Latter-day Saints through his grandmother, who had readily accepted the missionaries when they found her by door-to-door tracting, whereupon she had told them, "I've been waiting for you all my life. Come on in."[25] She was baptized 9 November 1930 in Hamburg.[26] Similarly, Rudi's mother, before finding the Church, "was quite a religious

person, always looking for something, always searching."[27]
Before she and Rudi were baptized she and Rudi had been
attending MIA with Rudi's grandmother before his father's
death, so they "knew about the Church" already, says Rudi.[28]
His grandmother had also been teaching his mother the
Gospel.[29]

At that point Rudi and his mother were baptized 7 June
1935[30] in an indoor swimming pool at a "bathhouse."[31]

It was therefore at age nine, in 1935, that Rudi came
into the church. "I went to Primary, of course. We held it
during the week, and that's where I met my friend Helmuth
Hubener."[32]

Rudi explains that they had "a wonderful branch
president, Paul Prüss, a very spiritual man,"[33] who was later
replaced by Zander when Prüss's several-year stint ended.
(It was Prüss who had confirmed Helmuth into the Church
and Josef Kraus who had baptized him at age eight; Martin
Bergmann had blessed Helmuth as a baby.[34]) Prüss, says
Rudi, administered a priesthood blessing to Rudi's mother
after the doctors had given her up as terminal, "and had
even moved her away from the other patients to die."[35]
She had been in a coma for several weeks. After the
blessing she awakened to find Rudi beside her, crying. Rudi's
grandmother got the doctors. "My grandmother told them
that by the power of the priesthood of God and the prayer
of faith her daughter had been restored to life." The doctors
did not understand and were skeptical, "but had to admit
that there had been a miracle." She lived until 1961, dying
in Salt Lake City.

Their discipleship is evident in the sacrifices they made for the Kingdom, such as their walks to church five times per week, 45 to 60 minutes each way,[36] a common sacrifice for many European Latter-day Saints. The five trips consisted of Sunday School in the morning, Sacrament Meeting at 7 or 8 o'clock at night, Monday night Priesthood Meeting and Relief Society, Wednesday night MIA, and Friday night choir practice.[37] The troupe consisted of Rudi, his mother, and his uncle, "with a bass fiddle on his back carrying it all the way."[38]

Rudi also was a member of the German Young Folk before joining the Hitler Youth in 1938.[39]

His aspirations for a career were not initially those of a machinist, which he did eventually become, but rather as a sailor. "Born on the waterfront and sea, . . . I was in and out of the freeport aboard ships, so that was my second life." He wanted to go to sea, and thought about joining the Navy for 12 years. But at either school or the recruiting office, they talked him out of it, saying, "You learn a trade first and then you go to sea."[40]

Rudi's one other ambition in life as a youngster was to emigrate to America. "That was my ideal,"[41] to "go to the land where all those smart-looking American missionaries came from."[42]

Rudi was not only close to them, but he and his mother also had them "quite often" for Sunday dinner, where they "always talked about freedom of speech, free press, and the freedom they were enjoying in their country and what it meant to be an American, that you could do what you want to do. And somehow it struck a note with me."[43]

There were several members that emigrated, says Rudi. When a Sister Krause and her daughter went to the United States, "I still remember her leaving, and we gave her a farewell party. . . . I kind of envied her that she could go."[44]

Church was not only a religious event, but a social experience.

The boys enjoyed reading detective novels for fun, and even read in church.[45]

Rudi states that towards the end of 1938 — 2½ years before Helmuth listened at his grandparents' to the BBC — Helmuth approached him "with the idea of forming a detective agency." As younger teens they had been reading the ten cent novels of authors like John Kling and Ralph Torring, and he describes it as a "real treat" to read the twenty-five cent Lord Lister series. He says, "Because of our admiration for this heroic writer, Helmuth made up some identification cards and names for us, 'The Lord Lister Detective Agency.' His badge number was number one and mine was number two. He also wrote up some rules of conduct to govern our behavior as detectives.

"We scoured the newspaper police reports section to find any unsolved crimes that we might look into. Then we tried to get some clues as to where, when, and 'whodunit' questions that intrigued the curious mind.

"We even befriended one of the detectives from the local police station. Helmuth had a way with people to the extent that this detective became very friendly with us. He told us at one time that a streetwalker had been stabbed to death in Rothenburgsort and asked us if we would snoop around to find the killer. For many nights we scurried around the streets in our area looking for anything suspicious. We kept running across a rather shady character by the name of Franz Seemann. He was a street bum who was always looking for a handout and a free drink. As we talked about it we remembered seeing him in the company of the streetwalker in question just a few nights before her murder. We told this to the detective and he pulled Franz Seemann in for questioning. Three days later we learned that he had confessed to the crime and that we had solved the case. Wow, did we feel great. We solved the case and were true detectives. . . . Unfortunately, this was the only success we had. The other cases we tackled were a lot more difficult, so after a while we lost interest and drifted to other interests, except that we still carried our I.D cards."[46]

Days later Rudi tried to show off. He tripped on the edge of the windowsill, fell into the window, and cut his left wrist. His mother wrapped a towel around it and took him to the grocery store and called a cab. At the hospital emergency room he was put under with anesthetic as they sewed his artery back together.[47]

But when he awakened, "there were two Gestapo agents standing by my bed to question me. It seems that as the doctors and nurses had gone through my pockets they had found my Lord Lister I.D. card. That prompted them to report me to the Gestapo as a potential enemy agent. The Gestapo questioned me about the Lord Lister Detective

Agency asking what kind of a subversive organization it was and what foul goals this distinctively English detective agency had. Or they asked was it a cover-up for a secret underground movement. I was still groggy from the anesthetic and could not concentrate very well but they kept pushing, trying to trip me up. I tried my very best to convince them that it was not a subversive or underground movement to overthrow the government, but just a game to be played by two innocent boys."[48] Rudi continues this report in another interview: "The doctor in the St. Georg Hospital called Rudi's mother and made a "big deal" out of it, saying, 'You know what's going on here? He's a member of a secret gang.' She found it so ludicrous that she told him off. 'Oh, baloney,' she said. 'They're just playing. I know both of those boys. . . . They just have a good time, [and] want to have something special for themselves."[49] In his 1988 interview Rudi finalizes his description of the scene: "After an hour they finally left me alone. But the incident wasn't entirely forgotten I learned later."[50]

———————

Rudi sat with Karl and Helmuth during Sacrament meetings. He says that one day during a meeting he noticed Karl reading a book and asked what he was reading. Karl closed it, and Rudi saw that it was a *Book of Mormon*. Inside it were illustrations of "a lot of Indians and trappers." So he went straight to his mother and told her, "Mom, I've got to have that book." He reminisces, "I was real excited by Indian stories and so on." Upon receiving a copy for himself, he recalls, "Oh, was I disappointed. I looked and there were no pictures in it." Karl had not been reading *The Book of Mormon*, but *The Last of the Mochicans*, and had put it inside a *Book of Mormon* cover to fool his father. His dad had "always looked over" to see what he was doing. Karl and Helmuth snickered and laughed at "how they fooled me."[51]

Rudi says they passed the Sacrament and gave talks. Rudi recalls "shaking like a leaf" during his first talk at church.

Among the soon-to-be core resistance group from church, the oldest of the three was Karl Schnibbe. Born 5 January 1924, he was a year older than Helmuth.[52]

Years later Arthur's mother opines, "Helmuth went around a lot with my son and with Wobbe and Schnibbe. Schnibbe was a regular go-getter and 'daredevil,' who always had everything possible on his mind. We would have thought him more likely than Helmuth to be involved in a resistance activity. It could be, also, that Helmuth was influenced by him.[53] Helmuth's brother Hans clarifies this: "In my opinion Schnibbe did not induce Helmuth to resistance; he [Karl] only came to it later."[54] Karl states they may have influenced each other, but Helmuth was clearly the leader, and was "absolutely" smarter than either he or Rudi.[55]

Although a year older than Helmuth, Karl admits further that Helmuth was not only the natural leader of the group[56] but a "natural leader," period.[57]

While Rudi and Helmuth were still in their apprenticeship programs,[58] Karl, who was a year older than Helmuth, had actually finished his three-year apprenticeship[59] and was a journeyman painter.[60]

Although an average student according to his father,[61] Karl excelled in the arts.

Karl reports that during the course of his apprenticeship he continued his close association with his friends, most of whom were from church, because the Church of Jesus Christ of Latter-day Saints kept its youth involved.[62]

Gerhard's wife Waltraud remembers, "Karl Schnibbbe was a joker, and in Sunday School would always try to make the rest of us laugh. One time he pulled false teeth out of his pocket and made them click together. We all laughed. Rudi was also a cut-up, but not nearly as much as Karl, who was that way every week. However, Helmuth was more serious in church."[63]

Karl reveals in his autobiography, "My closest friends, though, were Helmuth Hübener and Rudi Wobe. They were the ones who came often to my house and the ones with whom I went swimming or to the movies. . . ."[64] Karl clarifies to the author, " . . . but not all three together. . . . Helmuth and I met often and we walked, and we talked."[65] But Karl also paired off with Rudi. "We went swimming together and all that stuff."[66] He also went to Rudi's home. "I spent a lot of time at their home on Sundays between meetings.[67] . . . We were good friends."[68] As a threesome, however, they associated mainly at church, although Rudi says they did go to town for "a good time."[69]

Karl further tells the author, "I liked good conversation and I liked to talk about music. I always liked classical music, so Helmuth was right for that," he states.[70] Karl also admits listening to outlawed "swing music" with a group of friends, and states there were swing-dance places in Hamburg,[71] even though it was forbidden. Helmuth also likely attended such places, as he and Arthur Sommerfeld visited numerous dance establishments "for entertainment."[72]

The fertile field of friendships was ripe and ready to harvest for Helmuth's next step of the resistance campaign . . .

CHAPTER 12

One Sunday at church Helmuth made his first move to recruit Karl. He invited him over, then, "When I entered Helmuth's apartment on that fateful evening, he showed me a radio. I didn't have any idea what this radio could do, this attractive, neat, little thing.

"Helmuth said to me, 'It has shortwave.'

"I replied, 'Oh, *short*wave. What can you hear on it? France?'

"'Oh yes, and England, too,' he answered.

"I said, 'Man, are you crazy?'

"'No, not yet,' he responded. 'I want to show you something.'

"Then he showed me a flyer he had written based on the British newscasts. I read it.

"'Man, where did you get this? It can't be possible. It is completely the opposite of our military broadcasts.'

"'That it is,' he said. 'Do you have time?'

"'Sure,' I answered.

"'Then let's hear it.'

"He turned out the light in the room and turned on the radio. The feeble light illuminated the numbers of the shortwave dial. He turned the radio up gently and at exactly 10:00 p.m. we heard the first four notes of Beethoven's Fifth Symphony. Then coming out of the ether in clear German I heard, 'The BBC London sends news in German.' The Nazis often tried to jam such broadcasts, but on that night it was crystal clear.

"My heart was beating like mad, because I knew well that listening to enemy newscasts was strictly forbidden and severely punished.

"The first newscast that I heard dealt with the Russian campaign, code-named Barbarossa.

"The official German military press releases printed in the newspapers and broadcast on German radio stations boasted of great successes in Russia. The number of enemy soldiers killed and captured was phenomenal, but little or no mention was made of German losses.

"'That can't be,' Helmuth whispered to me. 'Somebody's lying.'

"Then I remembered other recent discussions with Helmuth at the church. He said on several occasions that the military press releases were lies.

"'Do you believe them?'

"'Why not?' we said. 'Why shouldn't we believe them?'

"'Because they are lying, that's why,' Helmuth replied. 'Look,' he continued, 'it just doesn't make sense. We march into Russia and kill so many of their soldiers, but they have guns. They are shooting back. Put two and two together and you'll see that we're going to have some casualties on our side, too. And these British reports have a lot more details than ours, and they give their own casualties, not just the enemy's. Our news reports sound like a lot of boasting, a lot of propaganda, and theirs sound more realistic. I'm convinced they are telling the truth and we are lying.'

"From Africa the German news service had informed us that Rommel won over and over again. The British reported to the contrary that Rommel had received many setbacks, but admitted that Rommel had also won some important battles. There was something about the English broadcasts that was, somehow, more realistic and credible. In contrast, the German transmissions were more vague and wanted to color everything and represent it gloriously. Naturally, it was clear that the Germans had lied.

"Listening was fascinating. It was impossible to leave it alone, because you just wanted to know more. . . .

"The German people were being duped."[1]

Most, but not all. Ironically, on the eastern front, Helmuth's brother Gerhard was stationed, coming to the same conclusions as his brother. "I listened to the BBC about a half hour almost every day for years, while both in Russia and in Italy, since I was an observer [forward artillery observer] and radio operator."[2] There, he had a large transmitter, as "I was a relay operator for the German army. And I listened to the same broadcasts. Not only to the English one, I also listened to all the other countries around, even the Russians."[3] . . . They were broadcasting I would say, about 80 percent in German and then they were broadcasting also in English. And then I would monitor the Russian broadcasts."[4]

His side note is Interesting. "I had figured out the Nazis long before I got the radio, but had not discussed it with Helmuth or anyone else."[5] Likewise, Otto Berndt had also figured out the propaganda but did talk about it with others, either.[6]

As with Helmuth, Gerhard discerned the lies of the German stations. He says the German radio, "talked about things that supposedly happened in Russia on the front, at a specific area that I was in, where there was big fighting, that the Germany army was glorious again and so on. In truth, nothing happened whatsoever."[7]

He adds, "So all these things were just dressed up to the German people to raise their hopes."[8] And certainly to keep resistance activities at a minimum, because if the populace knew of the slaughter on the eastern front, where now over a million German soldiers were dying, there might have been more underground activities resisting the *Reich*.

Karl continues, "The newscast ended at 10:30 and I had to see to it that I got home. As I said goodbye, I asked Helmuth if I could listen again the next time he did. 'Of course,' he said. 'Only you know, Kuddl, keep quiet.'

"I listened often with Helmuth to the English newscasts. The anxious feeling that we were committing a crime abated gradually. Nevertheless, it was a certain thrill.

"We began to concern ourselves with it more intensely. We obtained maps and followed the advances precisely."[9]

Karl attended Helmuth's radio sessions once a week. He asked Helmuth to record the other broadcasts that he missed, and Helmuth did so. Since Helmuth was skilled in stenography he recorded them faithfully.

He next began another phase of his resistance movement:

Says Karl, "Helmuth surprised me. One night at his apartment he recruited me to start distributing the flyers. I tried to speak with him about it to see if there was some other way, but he was completely convinced and would not be moved by any arguments. He declared to me again the abomination of the Third Reich and made it clear to me that it was the moral duty of every truth-loving person to combat the regime. I told him I would think about it, because "to speak the truth these days is a fatal luxury." . . . He thought if we were careful it would work. I could not get it through my head that he was so cool and resolute. He said to me, "Think about it again and tell me for certain on Sunday."[10]

Helmuth wanted him to take some flyers that night as a test run and leave them in telephone booths and mailboxes.

"I felt a little fear, but agreed. On my way home I distributed a bunch into phone booths and mailboxes in apartment houses. After I left the flyers off, I was all worked up, especially when I met two policemen on the street where I lived. I greeted them with a *'Heil Hitler!'* and they cheerfully reciprocated. They asked where I was going so late. I replied, 'Home,' and that I was out visiting a friend. They wished me a good night and hoped there would be no air raids. I wished them a goodnight also and clicked my heels together with a salute, and left. At home my parents were in bed when I arrived. I went straight to the toilet, hit with a powerful attack of diarrhea from fear."[11]

Karl recalls his resistance activity beginning April 1941.[12]

"The next morning, my mother confronted me why I was so late. [I told her] time passes dreadfully fast when you're having fun."[13]

Karl says, "The following Sunday in church he saw me coming and he waved at me and I waved back and he yelled through the church, 'They haven't arrested you yet, have they?' I said, 'Will you shut up?' That was Helmuth — joking."[14]

When they got a chance to speak privately, Karl reports Helmuth's first words to him:

'Well, how is it going?' he asked . . . He then said, 'If I know you, you got rid of everything all right.' I told him, 'And a lot more.' He said, 'How come — what do you mean?' Then I laughed and told him that the blasted leaflets had given me the trots. I felt like I had been through a meat grinder."[15]

As both boys laughed, Rudi came up and wanted to know what was funny. Karl told Rudi he was too young for such things, then Karl and Helmuth plotted to meet together the next Saturday night.

So the next Saturday, Karl appeared at Helmuth's apartment. Karl reports that Helmuth opened the door, saying he had a surprise. His grandparents were in the living room, so after Karl greeted them, he and Helmuth went into the kitchen. And lo and behold the surprise was Rudi.[16]

"I was totally astonished to see him there."[17] Karl asked Rudi what he was doing there. Rudi asked Karl the same thing, then added, "You, too?"[18]

Neither Karl nor Rudi knew Helmuth had been sharing his radio broadcasts with the other, and they had a good laugh. Helmuth had for weeks been testing them both.[19]

Now, the boys knew Helmuth's secret — that *all three of them* were involved. And it was here that Helmuth's launched his "group."

CHAPTER 13

Rudi explains the events leading up to this night of grand discovery:

First, before the radio event, he had visited Helmuth's home "several times" as just friends.[1]

Then, Helmuth had told him of the radio when he first got it. He had also learned of it needing to be repaired. "Of course, Helmuth had to try it out,"[2] he adds, tongue-in-cheek.

Finally, Helmuth had told him one Sunday, undoubtedly at church, "Rudi, you have to visit me again. This time I got a treat for you. Come a little later."

Rudi adds, "His grandparents usually went to bed with the chickens, you know, and so I visited. We talked a little. They said, 'Well, don't stay too late, Rudi. Both of you have to go to school (or work) tomorrow.'[3]

"We put our ears together to the speaker to listen to it. They invited us to compare the BBC London news with that of the German newspapers. 'You will find a great discrepancy in that.' We did.[4]

". . . [At] 10 o'clock Helmuth turned on the radio and said, 'Now listen to this, not too loud.' So we glued our ears to the radio receiver there and it does Beethoven's Fifth. And 'This is BBC London with the German news broadcast.' . . . Helmuth in shorthand wrote all those things down. And oh my, it was fascinating. We did that a couple times. . . . And apparently Karl listened to it, too."

So Karl and Rudi next learned they were part of Helmuth's "group." Rudi reports what happened next:

"A couple weeks later Helmuth says, I got something for you. So he handed me a handbill, you know, on red paper. And there was the news we listened to on BBC London with the headline, 'Hitler, the Murderer. He is guilty of executing General Von Schroder, the Balkan commander in chief.' And I said, 'Wow. When did you do that?' 'I've got a typewriter here. I'm the branch clerk and I've got a typewriter at home to write *Feldpostbriefe* [letters mailed to the soldiers from the branch]. So I'm using it in my spare time.'[5]

As time went on, Rudi and Helmuth "listened several times."[6] They would not listen as a threesome, but would pair off — Rudi and Helmuth together, and Karl and Helmuth together.[7] But then all three would *meet* together. Rudi reports, "We talked about it in our meetings when we got together, the three of us. Oh, we went out together and had a good time in the town, went to an ice cream parlor together, stuff like that."[8]

And the reasons Rudi, Karl, and Helmuth listened? "It was adventurous, something new, out of the ordinary," says Rudi.[9] Nevertheless, they knew full well the dangers involved. "We all knew there was a law about listening to foreign broadcasts." He adds that rumors floated around to "watch out," as a neighbor might turn them in, so they were "quite secretive" about it. "But then later on when we got involved, I think it became quite daring. It was more or less a lark for us."[10] Otto Berndt also believed at first it was "just adventure" for them,[11] but later agrees it became a "great conviction, an idealism, a crusade."[12]

In an interview 14 years later, Rudi adds, "At first I thought it was a lark, it was an excitement to do something against the forced-upon-us Hitler ideology. And all this forced-on us stuff by the Hitler Youth . . . and probably in the back of my mind I realized the pen is mightier than the sword. . . .

"So that's the feeling that we had. And Helmuth said, 'We have to do something about this. We cannot just sit idly by and let it happen. We have to do something about it.'"[13]

He explains that they were "getting more absorbed in it," and then, "we realized we were actually doing something against that evil system Hitler had established in Germany."[14]

He says in 1974, "We wanted the other people to know what was really going on,"[15] adding that it was "our duty as human beings," and that it was "humanitarian."[16] He agrees there was a lot of idealism in it, yet states that there was "the excitement of doing something secretive," and says,

"We always had, between Helmuth and myself, we always had a little something going on, he was the captain of this, and I was his lieutenant. A little game we played, a little secret organization. So that was part of the lark.[17] . . . At first it was a job to do [sprinkled with fun by Helmuth] and then later on it became a conviction."[18]

In looking back, Rudi reminisces, "Through all this, I don't know, maybe as a youth you are more daring because you don't have any responsibility, don't have any children or a wife to watch out for. In those days we thought we were doing the right thing."[19]

Helmuth became, from Rudi's standpoint, actually obsessed with political matters.[20] His conviction eventually spread to Rudi's thinking.

It was then that Helmuth labeled them "The Musketeers." Bringing Rudi and Karl aboard was part of phases six and seven of the campaign [as described later] — getting friends to listen to the BBC, then distributing the flyers. On that night the three boys listened to the BBC together, as Karl recalls, then all three went outside and waited till 10 P.M. to hear the news. It was pitch dark, since allied bombers were expected. They joked outside and were nervous, waiting to perform their illegal act, but according to Karl, the only one who was "as calm and cool as a dog's nose" was Helmuth.[21]

They knew the danger if they were caught. Newspapers reported listeners receiving up to three years imprisonment.[22]

When they entered the apartment Helmuth's grandparents were already in bed. Helmuth attempted to tune in London, but the Germans were jamming it too strongly. They went their way, and according to Karl, that was the end of their first night of trying to listen to the BBC as a threesome.

In looking back, Rudi remembers only pairing off with Helmuth when listening to the BBC. But Karl recalls several occasions in which all three boys listened together.

Karl says, "We met together again [as a group] and listened to the newscasts three or four times, and were captivated, fascinated. It was hard to bide one's time before hearing the BBC.

Each night when they were together the boys listened to the BBC with delicious abandon. They clearly saw through the Nazi propaganda machine and realized their countrymen were buying into it. Helmuth and his two friends developed private jokes. They labeled the club-footed minister of propaganda, Joseph Goebbels, "The Billy Goat from Babbelsberg," and called his German radio report, "Doctor Club Foot's Story Hour."[23]

Lieselotte Prüss Schmidt says during this period the three boys would sit in her Sunday School class and engage in unusual "whisperings." She was the only one of the "other" class members who would approach them. She'd say, "What are you whispering about?" "'Oh, it's secret,'" would always be their response. Sometimes they'd say, "'Top secret.'"[24] This, she adds, went on "week after week."[25] Sometimes the three boys sat right beside her, which made it particularly intriguing. Despite their desire for privacy, the boys always sat with the other class members — at times in a circle but usually on "a couple rows."[26] Lieselotte figures they chose

Sunday School class because they did not have a chance to talk together as much in the other meetings.[27] Noteworthy to her is the fact Helmuth had a dual-track mind and could perfectly keep up with the Sunday School class discussion — answering questions and making detailed comments — while simultaneously engaging in the intense whispered conversations with Karl and Rudi.[28]

She also says that during this time Helmuth would begin showing his political colors in Sunday School class by subtly "mixing political philosophy with gospel discussion," feeling safe he could expose *some* of his political beliefs to fellow youth branch members.[29]

Helmuth then announced to Karl and Rudi — perhaps at Sunday School class, perhaps elsewhere — *a full-scale* informational campaign against the Nazis with an even wider distribution of his flyers.

Karl reports his reaction to Helmuth. "I said, 'Man, are you nuts? Are you completely off your rocker? What are you thinking of? Surely you don't suppose that we three can overthrow the government?'

"No. . . . He was not so naïve. 'But,' he said, 'We can inform people, then many persons can start to talk.' Then came a long pause. I could not make up my mind at first. I had to think about it, and Rudi also was hesitant about distributing the flyers."

But Helmuth turned on his full powers of persuasion. "He said we have been taught since children to stand up for the truth. He said simply he was convinced that other people must hear the truth. 'We can warn the people. We can wake them up. We can get them to start asking questions. And when enough people hear the truth . . . then who knows?'"[30]

So Rudi and Karl agreed and, with Helmuth at the helm, began making more detailed plans.

Rudi recalls, regarding him and Helmuth, "We more or less made a pact: We were willing, regardless of circumstances, whatever happened — we want[ed] to let the rest of the German people know what the truth is."[31]

Karl adds about the three of them, "We decided then and there, whoever might be caught should take all of the blame. Helmuth said, 'Good,' and stuck out his hand. 'Shake on it,' he said. For a minute we held our hands firmly together."[32]

Karl then reflects, "Thank heavens there were some good persons who helped the persecuted and put their lives on the line. Now we boys were also part of this effort."[33]

At that point Helmuth left the room and returned with stacks of papers for the boys. He had transcribed all English newscasts for them, plus German newscasts for comparison.

Karl recalls, "I . . . was flabbergasted at his thoroughness. [Helmuth said,] 'This way, when you can't listen, I always have the latest news reserved for you.' I was excited about the idea, because it was not always possible to visit Helmuth every night or every other night. Karl says he then told his friend, 'That's just the ticket, Helmuth.'"[34]

Soon — possibly that same night — Helmuth suggested the boys not just read the newscasts for themselves. Rudi reports that Helmuth said, "Why don't you just take a stack and pass them out, but be careful."[35] Rudi says that on his first time, he took 20 copies and left. Karl recalls all three of them taking flyers this same night that they made a pact, and wishing Rudi good luck.

Rudi says he distributed his first handbills from Louisen-weg through Oldenburg,[36] while Helmuth kept about 10 copies for himself.

Typically Helmuth would take half the flyers for himself and give half to Rudi.[37]

Of this night that they made a pact, Karl says as he and Helmuth stood at the door, he said, "So long, Helmuth . . . stay cool." Helmuth replied, "My regards to your family. Don't fall among thieves." Karl responded, "Cheer up, there's worse to come," and then he departed.[38]

It was the boys' first night of full-scale resistance. They had decided with unalterable resolve to take on the Behemoth.

All three lads became more daring. The more they faced danger, the more exciting it became, and their fear gradually abated.

Rudi explains where he put the flyers: He tossed them in stairwells and mailboxes and attached them to bulletin boards in stairwells.[1] He details, "One of the leaflets we put in mailboxes. You know in an apartment house you run up to the fourth floor, drop it in there and then hurry down and drop it in [again, on the next floor]. Never start on the bottom. By the time you've come back from above, they've caught you."[2]

He also placed them in hallways and attached some papers to residential bulletin boards.[3] . . . His targeted area was a blue-collar worker section named Rothenburgsort.[4]

As for the residential bulletin boards, Rudi says that every apartment building had, in the entrance hall, a bulletin board run by the Nazi Party — with the latest news and proclamations from the party posted on it,[5] all stamped with a swastika.[6] Rudi says they even put handbills on those party bulletin boards too![7]

Karl details, "We stuck our handbills there with a thumb-tack. For the Nazis that must have been very shocking."[8]

Rudi adds, "Of course we disguised them a little bit."[9]

Karl explains how: "Helmuth even procured a stamp with an eagle and a swastika. [All the flyers we posted] looked like official communications. When I think about it today, I still get goose bumps."[10]

Rudi comments, "It was exciting . . . running up and down the stairs there, 'and we escaped them again. . . . They don't know what we're doing.' Then we became braver. More daring." They thought, "Freedom above all."[11]

Rudi says people would be taken by surprise. They would be grouped together reading the bulletin board, and would say, 'Oh, we got another bulletin here. 'Hitler the Murderer.' What's going on?"[12]

At the writing phase of his campaign, Young Helmuth began typing small,[13] four inch by six inch[14] post-card size[15] flyers with only a few words, such as, "Down with Hitler!"[16]

Rudi says the first one was:

HITLER THE MURDERER.
He is guilty of the murder of General Von Schroder.[17]

Rudi lists the titles of several more:

HITLER IS TO BLAME

THE BOMBING RAIDS OVER GERMANY

WHO IS LYING? THE COMPARISON BETWEEN GERMAN AND BBC LONDON NEWS BROADCASTS

THE HITLER YOUTH YOU WERE FORCED TO JOIN[18]

Rudi admits he never did any of the typing because, for one thing, "I didn't know how to type then."[19]

At first Helmuth ground out a new leaflet every one to two weeks.[20] Then as Karl and Rudi grew *more* dedicated and daring, Helmuth wrote and produced a new leaflet *every* week. And then *two* per week.[21] The Nazis later thought the flyers were being written only every eight to 14 days.[22]

Helmuth launched his next phase: At the beginning of autumn 1941,[23] after Helmuth distributed all the small flyers, he immediately began writing something entirely different — no longer small flyers, but *full-page leaflets*[24] with detailed, accurate accounts of military and geopolitical issues. Some of these treatises were derived from BBC broadcasts.

Helmuth's brother Hans describes the leaflets as "the newscasts of the BBC" in which he commented on them from his political and religious viewpoint."[25] Rudi explains, "BBC London was just strictly about the war news, like 'The *Europa* got sunk for the eighth time now,' and stuff like that. That's what he picked out [from the BBC], and he'd just write it in shorthand and say, 'Hey, this is good stuff!'"[26]

Clearly, however, Helmuth authored a certain number of flyers from scratch. Rudi addresses that issue, as well, stating that the one about the *Reichsmarschall* — the "Fat Duke" — was Helmuth's entire creation, as well as the long leaflet where he talks about Schiller.[27]

1 2 1

Helmuth's flyers ranged from sarcastic exposés of the *Reich*'s propaganda regarding the war, to two calls for outright insurrection against the Hitler Youth.

In one leaflet he writes, "Hitler and his accomplices know they must deprive you of your free will at the beginning in order to make submissive, spineless creatures of you. Therefore we are calling out to you: Do not let your free will, the most valuable thing you possess, to be taken away. Do not let yourselves be suppressed and tyrannized by your leaders — highhanded kings in miniature — but rather turn your back on the Hitler Youth, the tool of the Hitler regime, for your destruction."[28]

In a second, Helmuth warns, "You are especially mistreated in the Hitler Youth. 'You are the future of Germany,' they will tell you, but then you are tyrannized and punished for any little offense. The 'Weekend Jail' is an affront that tops everything."[29]

Rudi describes a third leaflet: "Later on Helmuth wrote longer dissertations like *HITLER CALCULATED EVERYTHING, WEEKEND INCARCERATION OF THE YOUTH.* 'If you are caught not going to Hitler Youth duty, and if you are caught going to a movie that is not allowed for you, and if you are picked up by Hitler Youth guards on the way out, you spend the weekend in jail.'"[30]

Rudi describes a fourth, humorous leaflet: "We had a guy by the name of Hammond Goering. He weighed about 300 pounds without bones. But we called him, 'HERMAN THE FAT DUKE.' That was a good leaflet that went over good."[31]

A fifth flyer informs the populace that the supply situation in Germany is in trouble, but the Allies' resources are inexhaustible. A sixth warns of the oil shortage that would guarantee victory for the Allies. And a seventh calls for the German people to end the war by overthrowing Hitler.[32]

An eighth was *THE WAIVE OF OIL* — about the gasoline shortage in Germany. Others were *THE GERMAN-ITALIAN AXIS, THE RUDOLF HESS MYSTERY* — why he took flight to England — , *SPEECHES OF ADOLPH HITLER*, and *DO YOU LOVE THE TRUTH?* which asks, "Do you dream of a land where you can say what you want to say without getting punished for it?"[33]

Helmuth's dedication grew, as reflected in the subject matter of his leaflets. He describes the brotherhood that he feels with his closest friends as he takes an oath from the play, Wilhelm Tell: "We want to be a brotherhood united, to never part, despite danger or want. We want to be free, as our fathers were — and rather have death than to live in slavery. We put our test in the Almighty God and are not afraid of the tyranny of man."[34]

Helmuth launched distribution of these *longer* leaflets August 1941 — in the city districts of Hammerbrook and Rothenburgsort — in hallways, house mailboxes, mailboxes of the German Post Office, and on the street.[35] Helmuth's brother Hans says, "They distributed the leaflets in the worker districts, because from those who had suffered the most from war and National Socialism, the workers, they anticipated understanding and support."[36] He adds, "I knew he put flyers in the mailboxes and telephone boxes."[37]

The Gestapo had only a comparatively few turned in. Those that were came from the city district Hammerbrook from house mailboxes and a public telephone booth.

Later they figured the mysterious resistance group had produced and distributed 20 different subjects of these longer leaflets.[38] Only nine different kinds of small flyers were confiscated.[39] Thus, the Gestapo gathered and saved 29 different tracts. They figured only about 60 total copies made were of the small flyers,[40] But they had no idea of the possibly staggering numbers produced.

From church, Helmuth initially received a portable typewriter for the purpose of writing letters[41] to the inducted military personnel from their branch,[42] and for preparing minutes[43] and performing other clerical work for Zander. Nevertheless, Zander knew nothing of Helmuth's resistance activities.[44] Later, through the church custodian, Dierdrich Meier, Helmuth borrowed a Remington,[45] claiming to Meier that Zander had lent it to him,[46] which was not entirely true.[47]

From church, Helmuth also took paper, again without Zander's knowledge.

Karl states, "He often said, 'Our only real crime is taking this paper from the branch.' We had no idea where he got the rest of the paper."[48]

Zander soon gave Helmuth a key to the branch house, and there Helmuth had the ticket to forge full-steam ahead. He used the Remington to type most of his flyers[49] and the mimeograph machine[50] to copy them in vast numbers, although the copies were a bit dim and blurry,[51] so he preferred using the Remington not only to type but to duplicate as well, using carbon paper.[52]

He performed this same work at his grandparents' apartment, using the Remington which he took home. He'd make seven or eight copies at once and sometimes he typed a flyer twice (with carbon paper behind it) to produce even more copies.[53]

In their investigation, the Gestapo later believed the 20 longer leaflets were duplicated mostly on a Remington.[54] The Nazis determined that the Resistance produced at first two copies of each flyer[55] and later [because of Karl and Rudi's helping to distribute[56]] three to five copies of each flyer, then six to seven copies of each.[57]

On most of the detailed leaflets and the short flyers, Helmuth wrote, "This is a chain letter, so pass it on," in order to boost the widest distribution possible.[58]

But while the boys' dedication grew, so did the Gestapo's.

Soon the Nazi agents had what they thought was a major break-through: They figured out that the paper for the smaller leaflets was used exclusively at the social administration.[59]

But — they could not find the culprit. Helmuth no doubt smiled as he saw them snooping about, leaving each day frustrated. While their suspicions grew that the guilty party was an employee there,[60] Helmuth's courage accelerated.

The boys were having a field day, and Hamburg's 20-plus Gestapo agents were left standing in the wake, scratching their heads.

The Nazis were baffled by the operation. They figured dozens, if not hundreds, of adults were involved — thinking these were operatives of an elaborate British government operation.

The reason behind the Nazis' concern was fear. The fear that the *Reich* had for the truth was far greater than any other fear, as pointed out by German researcher Ulrich Sander: "The Gestapo was more concerned when they found a typewriter that was used to fight with than if they had found a pistol. The typewriter was far more dangerous."[1] Rudi's appreciation of the old maxim was accurate — "The pen is mightier than the sword" — especially when an entire regime was built on a house of cards and even the most dedicated Nazis knew it.

Despite the rage and fear of the Nazis, "Helmuth, Rudi Wobbe, and Karl Schnibbe always raised their sights to higher and higher goals,"[2] reports Hans. (See Appendix E for more information on the leaflets.)

Karl reports their continued efforts:[3]

"At church on Sundays, Helmuth would sometimes say, "Hey, we haven't seen each other for a long time. Why don't you come over and visit me? Let's do something together.

"That was our signal. Then I knew Helmuth had cooked up a new set of leaflets and wanted us to help distribute them."

One night Karl was out with flyers when air raid sirens wailed. When he returned to his apartment, an adult Nazi friend and neighbor named Otto Schultz came into his living room. They spoke while Karl's parents and Otto's relatives went outside to watch the skies.

Karl felt he trusted Otto, and he showed him the flyer. When Otto read it he turned pale.

"He exploded. 'Man, you idiot, where did you get that?' He demanded I burn it, so I burned it with a match in an ashtray. He said, 'Don't do this again. They will smash you like a bug.'"

Karl was shaken by the experience. He told Helmuth about it at church next Sunday, and Helmuth was angry. "Are you crazy? You told a Nazi Party member? You leave recruiting to me!" Karl wanted to quit, but Helmuth came to his senses and, after calming down, sought to reassure Karl and to give him a pep talk. Karl decided to stay with him.

Later, when Karl was out distributing, he thought people saw him, so he burned the fliers. Other times he cut them in pieces and threw them into the wind.

A number of times he shared them at a "gathering place" of friends in a cafe where he visited. He did this in the Landwirt train station on Saturday nights. At first they were flabbergasted. They wanted nothing to do with it. But as time went on he read several flyers to them and sometimes they were curious and would listen for awhile.

"They were interested . . . they wanted to hear . . . to an extent. Sometimes," says Karl in his interview with the author,[4] they met once a week, but whenever he offered them new flyers they'd respond, "Oh, no, no . . . I want to go home right now. I have to go, my friend.[5] They were too afraid. "But not one of them said anything [to the authorities]."[6] Karl admits with laughter there was someone in that group who interested him. "I kind of liked one girl but, like I say, it died a natural death."[7]

Significantly, *no one* reported the boys. They grew even bolder: Karl put flyers in coat pockets at a cloak room. There, he targeted the coats of high party functionaries![8]

Rudi even placed some in the mailbox of the local Nazi Party branch office![9] He says smilingly of this flyer, which reads, *HITLER THE MURDERER*, "I thought they needed to be informed, too, that Hitler was a murderer."[10]

Karl says, "After a while we weren't afraid anymore, though we were really playing Russian roulette."[11]

The number of people who knew of the boys' secret resistance was confined to only five — the three lads themselves plus Arthur Sommerfeld and Hans Kunkel.[12]

The question was, would the Gestapo ever know?

Helmuth was still adept at covering his tracks. Even his closest friends still did not know everything he was doing. For example, neither Rudi nor anyone else knew of Arthur Sommerfeld's involvement — just as Rudi did not know of the Bismarck group — until years later.[13] (Rudi and Karl even perceive each other involved in varying degrees. See Appendix H for a discussion of their perspectives.)

Consistent with Helmuth's propensity for privacy, he at first did not share the fact others were involved with him in the resistance. Neither did he tell of Arthur's listening with him to the BBC. Nor did he initially share his attachment to the Bismarck group.

At church one day came news of a nightmare. One of the members in their branch, a kindly old gentleman named Heinrich Worbs — the same who had spent New Years Eve with the boys on night watch — was arrested by the Gestapo.[14]

Arthur Sommerfeld recalls in 1999, "I knew Brother Worbs well. He wasn't too open in the branch. He didn't talk much. He came to our home. . . . He liked to be in our place. He liked to eat nuts — I remember that. He came several Christmases and would come Christmas Day. He was friendly."[15] Rudi adds that Worbs was "a simple, honest, good man,"[16] a strong member, a convert of several years.[17] And the boys had known him since they were little.[18]

The reason for his arrest? He had muttered *one remark* at the unveiling of a statue[19] when he was standing on a streetcar.[20] "My goodness, now we have one more butcher that we must salute."[21] And/or he may have said, "So they've unveiled another monument to one of those criminals."[22]

Someone overheard and reported it to the nearest policeman and Worbs was imprisoned. He was released after six months (or a year[23]) in a concentration camp[24] (either Neuengammme[25] or Geesthacht[26] near Hamburg, depending on conflicting reports), and forced to sign a statement that he would tell no one about his experience.

But with his insatiable curiosity, when Helmuth saw him back at church in his beaten-down condition, he set out to learn what happened. Worbs would not talk about it at first, but, as Karl reports, "Helmuth didn't give up. . . . he started asking him at church. Finally they went someplace and sat down together and Heinrich Worbs broke down and told him."[27]

Rudi recalls, "He was just a shadow of his old self. He was a broken man. He was just shaking like a leaf."[28]

Worbs also related his experience to his district president, Otto Berndt,[29] who "took him under his wings and comforted him and talked with him," says Rudi.[30] One of Berndt's accounts is the same — but not as detailed — as Rudi's account. Significantly, Otto and Rudi both report hearing it from Worbs firsthand,[31] at church,[32] while Karl does not give a firsthand account. The following experience of Worbs is related to the reader through a combination of Otto's and Rudi's six different accounts:

In 1987 Rudi says that he, Helmuth, and Karl approached Worbs.

"When we asked him what took place and what they did to him, he said, 'I'm forbidden to talk about it.'

"So the three of us took him into the corner and said, 'Heindrich, you can trust us, we're your friends — tell us.'"[33]

In 1988 Rudi states that it was just two of them with whom Worbs spoke — him and Helmuth:

"And since we knew him well, Helmuth and I cornered him also and said, 'Heinrich, what happened to you? You look terrible.'

"He said, 'Oh, I'm not supposed to talk about it.'

"'Heinrich, we're your friends. Don't you remember? You taught us the gospel up in the air raid watch there,' and so on.

"And he finally broke down and told us what they did to him."[34]

In 1974 Rudi adds this detail — that when Worbs first told them that he could not talk about it, he stuck to his guns and did not tell them — until later. Rudi also says that when they finally did have a chance to talk with him, it made the same strong "impression" on Helmuth as it did on Rudi, who adds, "We were quite shaken up over it."[35]

The combined account continues: "And with tears in his eyes he was telling us that he was stripped naked in the middle of January, knee deep in snow. He was shackled to a stalk.[36] . . . With his hands shackled in front of him they poured water over them so it froze to ice just demonstrating how cold it was.[37] . . . Then the guards laughingly came by and broke the ice to warm his hands with a rubber hose[38]

. . . a couple of times."[39] They also taunted him with the words, "This will keep your hands warm."[40] To which Worbs replied, "Don't put me back in the ice house, please don't put me back in the ice house."[41]

Otto adds additional detail: ". . . He was treated as an animal. He said sometimes they took them out at night in wintertime and put them in the block. . . . His hand was stretched out and water was dripped all night on top of it and, because it was freezing, there was ice on his hand. Then every four or five hours somebody came with a rubber hose and was pounding on his hand until the ice was loose and the bones of his fingers were broken. They would sit in that block for 48 hours. He showed me his hands.

"He came back without teeth. His mouth was all swollen so he couldn't hardly speak. He showed me his back. I would say it was totally [thrashed].

"They had to watch when somebody was executed. They'd hang them in that camp. They had to stand around that gallows and then the commandant came and pointed to someone from the prisoners. Then that man he picked had to go up and hang the man on the gallows. If he wouldn't do that, the commandant told that man on the gallows to come down and they'd hang the man who had refused, instead."[42]

Rudi comments, "This could've put him out of his mind with fear,"[43] and adds that while relating his experience to the boys "he was just all the time looking left and right to see if somebody would come for him, just so scared. We said, 'Be at ease, be calm, you are among friends now, don't worry. We love you. You are our brother.'[44] Worbs then said, 'Those are terrible people. They beat you up and starve you to death and all kinds of terrible things they do to you.' And then he broke down and cried every time he talked about it."[45]

Rudi wraps up the account: "It was an ordeal he had to suffer while living in that concentration camp. . . . Two months later he died."[46] A significant fact involves the boys' caring and warmth — all three befriended him while much of the branch was uncertain how to approach him.[47] So these young men were likely his last friends.

Otto says he did not keep the incident quiet — and told the church members, then adds, "They were shocked, like me. But I believe that there were many people who didn't know about the concentration camp."[48] While everyone knew of concentration camps, Otto analyzes that only some members — and other Germans — knew of political prisoners' harsh treatment in the camps. And while they had seen the public treatment of Jews, very few knew of the actual killing of the Jews. Otto's wife, Frieda Berndt, says she did not know much about it,[49] while Otto states that he actually went searching for the truth and for what was happening in concentration camps. He thus admits he was better informed because he "tried to get information."[50] He talked with soldiers on the front who learned of the killing of the Jews,[51] although generally only the SS knew about it. A main problem, Otto feels, is that the German populace was indifferent to learning what was happening.[52]

Karl explains *his* family's reaction:

"After church, on our way home, Father was very upset over the arrest of Heinrich Worbs. 'They have nothing better to do than to chase and badger old people. Why don't those bullies volunteer for the front? They are all overstuffed with food and don't have the strength to go. But the more they arrest, the more indispensable they become.' That is how my father talked to himself in a rage as we walked.

"My mother said, 'Be careful with your blabbering and don't talk so loud. You will cause trouble for us. If someone is standing behind the door in the staircase, he can hear everything. Just think what has happened to Heinrich Worbs. The same thing can happen to you. So please, keep quiet. *You can think what you want, but don't think out loud.*' '[Yes], you are right, Paula, but it is still true,' my father grumbled. . . . "

Karl confesses:

"The story about Brother Worbs so staggered me that I needed to sit down. I recognized more profoundly the danger in which we had placed ourselves. It could as well have been the three of us who were caught. I was convinced that the state police were hunting the persons who were distributing flyers and inflammatory handbills in Hamburg."[53]

But nothing slowed Helmuth.

With renewed vigor and perhaps consumed with anger, Helmuth and the boys set out to blanket the city with their flyers of truth. Certainly Helmuth's daytime job, followed by his burning the midnight oil for the resistance, was taking its toll on him.

Helmuth's old classmate Rolf Attin reports, ". . . Helmuth once crossed my path here in Hamm; he looked considerably older. More mature somehow. I noticed that immediately. I thought to myself, 'His must be a difficult life.' It must have been in the fall of 1941."

At work Helmuth often discussed current events with the other apprentices and admitted later to wanting to know more than they.[2] He also assumed they suspected he listened to the BBC because he was generally known as "the man with connections,"[3] a term in which he no doubt took great pride.

At work he befriended a certain fellow apprentice named Gerhard Düwer, and in early January 1942 Helmuth asked him if he wanted to join "a secret club."[4]

The next day Düwer asked him "what the deal was with his club." Helmuth told him it involved a spy ring to overthrow the regime[5] and that he was receiving orders to make flyers. He urged Düwer to join the ring[6] and told him the name of the club was "S.P.I."

Later, Helmuth admitted he had lied[7] as he was in no way involved in such a ring[8] but it had accomplished what he wanted: He had found Düwer not only responsive to the flyers but willing to become extremely active in his resistance movement. Perhaps that had been part of his motive for concocting the story.[9]

Düwer, born 1 November 192[10] was two months older than Helmut[11] and had been in the Hitler Youth since 1939.[12] He had also attended middle school 1935-1941 and, like Helmuth, was an administrative apprentice at the social administration, although he had been hired about four months before Helmuth, in December 1941.[13]

Thus far Helmuth's steps in the resistance movement had included a dozen phases:

(1.) Turning against the *Reich* from the November 1938 *Krystallnacht*, turning against the Hitler Youth and actually fighting them; befriending boys at the Bismarck pool and learning from them about Hitler being anti-Christian; also, engaging in conflict with his anti-Mormon/pro-Nazi stepfather;

(2.) Listening to the BBC with his revolutionary friends;

(3.) Reading forbidden books from work;

(4.) Sharing information from his books with Karl and Rudi;

(5.) Repairing and listening to Gerhard's shortwave, thus gaining more information from the BBC;

(6.)   Inviting Arthur, Karl and Rudi to listen to the BBC
with him;

(7.)   Writing and duplicating nine different small flyers;

(8.)   Writing and duplicating 20 different large, detailed
leaflets;

(9.)   Distributing flyers himself;

(10.) Persuading Karl and Rudi to distribute flyers;

(11.) Bringing Gerhard Düwer into the BBC's listenership;
and now, in a major step forward . . .

(12.) Launching a larger resistance section the authorities
never discovered.

In this new resistance section, Düwer and his friends
often met with Helmuth to listen to foreign stations and
distribute flyers. The group grew, according to Düwer, first
"in a narrow . . . [then] an outer circle of acquaintances."
He continues, "When we had become more accustomed to
it, we began to distribute the flyers in greater numbers. . . .
The circle got bigger and bigger and we found more and
more people to work with us."[14]

They posted flyers in three primary city districts, on
not only the usual Nazi bulletin boards, poster columns,
and mailboxes, but now in the coat pockets of guests at
festivities, shows, and dances![15]

Soon, in the 13th phase of Helmuths's resistance campaign, they enlarged their operation to include a printing
press at Kiel, which agreed to produce the flyers in even
greater numbers, with secretive printing work taking place
during the graveyard shift by two employees. The numbers
of flyers they could now print would dwarf the number that

Helmuth initially produced in typewriters and the church mimeograph machine. However, it's not certain that this operation ever got fully underway.[16]

Rudi confirms this larger printing operation: "He did mention that there was a contact — he found a contact — . . . it rings a bell that he was going out of town to get the leaflets printed."[17]

Next, in phase 14, they started sending flyers in letters to the front.

A government report later states Helmuth discovered a way to distribute his flyers to dissident German soldiers, and that somehow he obtained "a card file of the military addresses of soldiers who were not entirely reliable and patriotic."[18]

One leaflet reads, "Comrades in the South, North, East, and West." Later Helmuth convinced the Nazis that it was so titled in order to impress his small circle of colleagues.[19] But it was likely targeted to soldiers on the front. His brother Hans substantiates this work with the military: "They soon duplicated flyers. Then they sent them to the front, and that was subversion of the military forces!"[20] Hans was amazed at Helmuth's bravado.

Karl says he had no idea about Helmuth's new recruit at work, Gerhard Düwer. "Helmuth had never mentioned Düwer, because Helmuth was very cautious."[21]

Nor did Rudi know of this other branch of Helmuth's resistance group.[22]

The 15th phase of the resistance movement was to expand recruitment — including old acquaintances and current office workers. Despite his growing power and success, not everything Helmuth touched turned to gold. He approached one old classmate friend, Franz Walter Prumnitz, over Christmas vacation 1941 when Prumnitz came to visit him, but Prumnitz wanted no part of the group.

Franz and Helmuth had attended the upper-track school at Brackdamm together, and Franz had visited Helmuth at his grandparents two or three times, where they had done school work together. After graduation, they had only visited while on duty with the Hitler Youth. Then Helmuth wrote him a letter during Christmas vacation of December 1941.[23] Franz subsequently visited him at his apartment. As Franz was about to leave, Helmuth showed him a flyer.

Franz told him he wasn't interested, and did not see him again. Days later, Helmuth sent him a handwritten letter about Rudolph Hess. Franz wrote back but didn't mention the touchy subject.

In the next month Helmuth sent him mail two or three more times, which consisted only of envelopes containing a flyer. Franz read the first, then claimed to have torn up the others unread, and thrown them in the garbage.[24]

Helmuth also found no glitter with Horst Willy van Treck, a close childhood friend.

He had known Horst since they were young children, playing together. When they were older and going to school, they continued to associate by going to the movies together. Towards the end of school they quarreled temporarily but reconciled about graduation time — March or April 1941. After that, Horst visited Helmuth at his grandparents' apartment five or six times where they talked shop and listened to music, visiting one to one-and-a-half hours each time, so that Horst was home by 9:30 or 10:00.

In July or August 1941 Helmuth gave him 10 or 15 flyers. Horst claimed he tore the handbills into pieces in Helmuth's presence and stuck them in a storm-sewer grate in front of the house. He said Helmuth tried to take the handbills away from him.

Helmuth, who had nothing to lose in his report of the matter later, likely presented the more truthful version when he agreed with most of Horst's report but maintained Horst did not rip the handbills in his presence nor did he stick them in a storm sewer grate in front of him. He claims he presented Horst a certain number of copies but Horst searched for those that were written most clearly, which consisted of five or six copies of different flyers. A week later Horst gave him "at least ten copies" more.

They did once argue over the flyers in front of Horst's house, where Horst told him that what he was doing was not right. Horst further said that some day he could get in big trouble over it. He also told Helmuth that in the future he would not accept any such handbills from Helmuth.

Helmuth states, "I did not offer him any again, and it was never discussed again." He claims during the argument that Horst wanted to give back the handbills, but that he would not take them back. He says they separated after that, rather agitated with each other. He summarized that he figured Horst possibly destroyed the handbills following the argument, but in any case did not believe Horst distributed them — since, from the beginning, he was opposed to the distribution.

On 29 August 1941 Horst was inducted into the National Labor Service. After that they visited several times but never spoke of the flyers. While Horst was away, Helmuth sent him four or five letters. In his next-to-last letter Helmuth included information from a BBC newscast.

Horst wrote back, telling him to discontinue sending such material in the future. Helmuth sent mail once more, consisting of an envelope containing only a flyer. Horst read it and destroyed it immediately.[25]

Helmuth later added a few details to this account, but the results were the same — Horst refused to get involved. Noteworthy is Helmuth's "persistence." So confident was he in his persuasive abilities, his charm, and the truth of his message that he figured most of his friends would join him, given enough effort. Soon, however, he found that his abilities had limitations. Namely his inability to persuade everyone. This really pushed his buttons.

Others held Helmuth in high esteem and joined him wholeheartedly.

Seeing success among friends Helmuth became more brazen and soon launched step 16 of his resistance campaign — the final and most reckless step of all.

CHAPTER **17**

On New Year's Eve, 31 December 1941, on the way to a church dance, Helmuth's brother Hans sensed trouble. "We went dancing together, and on the way home we talked about everything." *Everything* included Helmuth's newest plan — to reach and incite hundreds of thousands of French POWs held near Hamburg, and eventually all two million in Germany.[1] Possibly Helmuth was becoming a victim of his own success. "They . . . wanted to produce the flyers in French. . . . That was dangerous; I warned Helmuth about it. But he had become somewhat careless because of his successes. Nevertheless," continues Hans, "they raised their sights higher."[2]

Hans figures Helmuth was feeling successful because both he and Helmuth were hearing people "whispering about the leaflets."[3] But Hans suggests that they were coming into contact with "too many people."[4]

Meanwhile Karl had seen Helmuth only a couple times during the 1941 Christmas holiday. Karl had gone to his aunt's farm in Ludelsen for a week in order to bring food home, since food was getting more and more scarce from the war. Then, a few days into the New Year, Karl returned to Hamburg and saw Helmuth at church. Helmuth told him to come visit at his apartment.

"When I did, he had new flyers again. They were very vehement things. This was in the middle of January."

The next time they would see each other would be under surprising circumstances.

Meanwhile, Helmuth continued planning his French POW project, for which he sought assistance. Until then, Gerhard Düwer was the designated go-between to recruit others at work.

Among those Düwer contacted was another apprentice, possibly named Neuss,[5] to whom Düwer showed a flyer. Additionally, Düwer read flyers at a private party at his own home when his parents were absent, as well as sticking some in mailboxes.

The Nazis later learned of Düwer receiving only 15 flyers from Helmuth. Twice Düwer told Helmuth that Düwer had held parties — one was at his home and another was at a friend's,[6] ostensibly for the purpose of recruiting. Helmuth reported later that Düwer did not tell him what went on at those parties, except that they played records "and that it was completely terrific."[7] Helmuth added that he bought about 20 records of dance music for Düwer (certainly an unusually generous move for someone with limited income unless Helmuth's resistance activities could benefit —

which they likely did if the dances were used as recruiting venues.

Düwer said that Helmuth's ring spread wider and wider, and that it was he who helped Helmuth find the printing press at Kiel. Also, Düwer may have been instrumental in expanding the ring as wide as it went — if indeed he is accurate.

Helmuth was now ready to launch his French POW project.

Like the Romans, the Nazis had rounded up slave laborers from conquered countries. Two million Frenchmen had been taken by the Reich.[8]

Helmuth was determined to get his flyers to the French prisoners of war[9] who labored in the Altona district of Hamburg,[10] but he needed someone who could translate his flyers into French.

At his office, he found an acquaintance who could do the job. Werner Kranz happened to share a dance class with Helmuth every Thursday night for four weeks at the Holzdamm.[11] Otherwise, the two boys did not socialize.[12]

On 17 January 1942, while they shared a class in the administrative school, Helmuth, who sat adjacent to Werner, discovered him taking notes in a tablet for French vocabulary. Possibly during a class break, Helmuth asked if he knew French. Werner said he did. Helmuth asked if he would do him a favor. Werner replied, "It depends." Helmuth told him he needed something translated into French. Werner told him he needed to first know what there was to translate and what its contents were, because he was not perfect in French. Helmuth answered that he could not tell him any more about it.

Three days later Helmuth tried again. This time he took Gerhard Düwer along. Together, they approached Werner at work.[13]

"Hubener shared with me quietly that 'they' were producing inflammatory brochures, which they wanted to give to the prisoners," Werner later reports. "I told him that such a thing was out of the question for me and urgently advised him to cease his activity. He repeated, however, that he wanted to bring 'something' to me on Monday. With that the conversation ended. On Monday, January 19, 1942 we had not talked about the matter and Hübener had also not given me any papers. On the following day, the 20th of the month, he tried secretly to press some folded papers into my hand. I did not accept the writings and declared to him that I, under no condition, would accept or read them. The administrative apprentice Düwer, who had entered the room with Hubener, was present at this conversation. They left the room together again after I refused."[14]

Helmuth had impressed so many with his wildly witty writing style and superb sarcasm of Nazi leaders, that he now felt confident he could convert most anyone to his cause.

But Werner Kranz wouldn't bite. In fact, this was the deciding incident in Helmuth's downfall, because the moment Kranz refused the folded paper in his hands, *their boss happened to look up and see the curious transaction . . .*[15]

Helmuth's boss was Heinrich Mohns.[1] He was the *Betriebsobmann*, the "overseer" of loyalty, "with political and social control" in their office.[2] He also saw Gerhard Düwer *helping* Helmuth in approaching Kranz. Mohns claims later he said to them, "I hope you fellows are not involved in any forbidden business; watch out, that you don't end up in a concentration camp!" At that, says Mohns, "Helmuth and Düwer left the room laughing. As soon as both of them had left the room, I requested an explanation from Kranz."[3]

To Mohns, Werner Kranz spit out everything. He told Mohns he was supposed to translate an inflammatory leaflet into French, because Helmuth claimed to have connections with French prisoners — but Werner told Mohns he turned Helmuth down.[4]

Werner had been able to determine — even from the quick glance of the folded paper that Helmuth tried giving him — that the material was anti-Nazi, and now he reported it to Mohns.

Mohns persuaded Werner to bait a trap: Werner agreed to tell Helmuth he had a change of heart and wished to obtain Helmuth's flyers in order to translate them. But the next time they spoke, Helmuth's sixth sense kicked in and he told Werner to forget it.

The next day, 21 January 1942, Mohns summoned Düwer, and the bubble burst. Mohns demanded that Düwer obtain more copies from Helmuth as hard evidence.[5] Düwer, obviously torn over what to do, tread water for several days. He stalled and lied, saying he had no flyers.[6] A later investigation, contrary to Mohn's own report, claims Mohns then pressured him on *numerous* occasions.[7] For 13 days Düwer struggled, tormented, not knowing what to do.

At last, on 4 February, he handed Mohns two copies of Helmuth's flyers,[8] admitting he had still more at home. Mohns told him to bring them the next day.

But the next day Düwer came to work, saying he forgot them. Mohns, out of patience, reported everything to his superior, Mr. Graf, who took further action.[9]

In hindsight Düwer shouldn't have given his boss any flyers. Equally important, he should have protected Helmuth and others by not *telling* Mohns anything. Third, he should have told Helmuth about Mohns. Helmuth no doubt would have hidden or destroyed all evidence. He could have returned the typewriter to the church and given Düwer a harmless, concocted flyer that would have protected all involved. A cool head prevails, and Helmuth was the coolest of the bunch. Düwer, in retrospect, made the biggest mistake of his life (and ultimately of Helmuth's, Rudi's, and Karl's) by not simply conferring with Helmuth about the pressure Mohns was exerting.

Werner Kranz was also conflicted. He says he did not sleep the night before he was caught by Mohns, so torn was he over helping Helmuth versus turning him down. Obviously Helmuth's charm and engaging personality were difficult to resist, but Werner was also fearful of the Gestapo — and no evidence suggests he even believed in Helmuth's cause.

Life then came crashing down on Helmuth.

CHAPTER 19

His hopes and dreams were dashed the second he looked up and saw the agents entering his office. At 5 P.M. that day, 5 February 1942, the Gestapo arrested Helmuth,[1] along with Gerhard Düwer.[2]

Rudi reports that at some point Helmuth "stood up on the top of the table in the social services department at the government and said, 'There's something rotten in the state of Germany. You better remember this.'"[3]

Watching Helmuth and Düwer cufffed and escorted away, the other apprentices — and especially Werner — were no doubt horrified.

The first thing the Gestapo did was to take Helmuth home and search for incriminating evidence.

Helmuth's brother Hans details what happened next: "I saw Helmuth when the Gestapo came to the apartment. When I went to visit my grandmother, a knock came on the door. Two men from the Gestapo came in to look through the house. That was the first time we knew something was going on."[4] [This was *not* the first time Hans knew something was going on, because Helmuth had told him of the French project and the letters to the front, which he recalled in an earlier interview; but his detail of the two agents bringing Helmuth home in this interview is for the most part apparently accurate — and terrifying.]

"The two agents had leather coats and leather hats. Both were tall, over 6'3", in their early 20s. They were heavy and harsh when they talked.

"They wanted to search the house. . . . They came in with Helmuth. They said, 'We want to look for propaganda material.' They didn't talk further. Helmuth was pale; he was white, scared." However, Hans recalls, "He had not been beaten."[5]

As for being beaten, Marie Sommerfeld recalls in 1974 that Helmuth's grandmother told her the Friday following the arrest that when the Gestapo brought Helmuth to the apartment, "He was terribly beaten up, and his grandmother cried out in terror when she saw him."[6]

Hans continues, "He stood by the door while the two agents looked around. Grandfather, Grandmother and I sat on a sofa."[7] The agents found the Remington with seven carbon copies still in the roller. It was his last flyer, and was entitled, "Who Is Exciting Whom?"[8] They confiscated the leaflets and the typewriter[9] that belonged to the church.

Marie Sommerfeld reports that the two Gestapo agents also found the radio, a pile of assorted leaflets, some notebooks, and manuscripts of handbills, along with shorthand notes. As Helmuth was leaving, his grandmother wanted to ask him, "Why were you arrested, what has happened?" Helmuth wanted to speak to her, "but the officers tore him away. They were not permitted to exchange a word."[10]

They escorted him outside and sped him away in their Mercedes.

The same day three more handbills were turned in by a Frau Bertha Flogel, a Herr Schwedlick, and a Herr Frehse to cell leader Herr Weltien. Two had been found in mailboxes and one in a phone booth — all less than a block from Hübener's grandparents' house were he lived[11] — such was Helmuth's increasing recklessness.

Marie Sommerfeld details what happened next:[12]

"I was well acquainted with his grandmother; every Friday we cleaned the church together. One day when I came to work, I noticed his grandmother. She was kneeling in front of the podium and had raised her hands and prayed and pleaded[13] ["and she shouted," she says in a second report[14]] aloud to God[15] [Marie adds in the second report], and I waited there until she finished."[16]

Continuing her first report:

"I walked up behind her and she did not notice me. Then I tried to calm her: 'What is the matter?'

"'Something terrible has happened,' the words gushed out of her.

"I asked if perhaps something had happened to Gerhard, who was stationed at the front; if he had been killed.

"'No, but I wish that Helmuth had been killed, that he were dead.' [Fearing the Gestapo as did all Germans,

Helmuth's grandmother wished he did not have to face the ordeal before him.]

"'But why Helmuth?" asked Marie. 'Nothing could have happened to him.'

"Then she told me everything exactly."[17]

In the second report Marie adds, "Oh, and when I think about it, you cannot imagine how I felt."[18]

At Gestapo headquarters Helmuth and Düwer were formally placed under arrest.[19] Three days later, Karl and Rudi learned about it at church:

Karl reports, "On a Sunday [8 February 1942], we were asked by the branch president to remain a little while after the meeting. He had a very regrettable announcement to make, he said, and he told us to be there. There was nothing unusual about that and I was not concerned."[20] Then, after the church meeting was over, Zander dropped the bomb.

He said, "A member of our branch, Helmuth Hübener, has been arrested by the Gestapo. I cannot give you any details, because my information is very sketchy, but I know that it is political. That is all.[21]

Karl continues:

"My heart fell into the seat of my pants and I wanted to die at that moment. I have never been so scared, and I was literally sick. I looked over at Rudi and he looked at me. He was pale [and "stunned," says Rudi[22]] but we could not speak. 'What?' some other members of the branch around me were saying. 'Helmuth? That is impossible!' I did not wait for Rudi to leave; I just wanted to go home. . . .

"I did not want my parents to think anything was wrong. I could not tell them anything. All they said was, 'I wonder what he did.'[23]

Rudi adds, "We waited for Helmuth — Karl and I. We waited for Helmuth, he didn't show, so we just went in and had kind of a foreboding feeling, you know. Then Zander got up and announced that Helmuth . . . was arrested. He didn't know the details, but he knew it was political."[24]

Helmuth's mother had made a rare appearance in church that day. With her were her parents, the Sudrows, who were active members. Rudi reports that one of the members, Frederich Jacobi, said aloud, "If I would have had a gun I would have shot him myself.[25] According to Otto, Jacobi was not pro-Nazi, but obviously was fearful and, after the war, he went inactive with the Church.[26] (See Appendix I for more information on the announcement of Helmuth's arrest.)

After both Rudi and Karl learned the news about Helmuth, Rudi says they got together to decide what to do. "'Wow, looks like the roof is coming in on us,' one said to the other. We talked about it. . . . 'Should we take off for Switzerland or something?' . . . But we couldn't do it because our parents would be heartbroken. And I talked with Karl's sister, Karla, and her girlfriend, Lucy."[27]

After church, Rudi's mother questioned him.

"She said, 'Rudi, what do you know about it?'

"'Nothing, Mama, nothing.' I didn't want her to worry about it. [In his interview 14 years earlier Rudi says he had told his mother what he was doing and her response was always, "'to be careful,' and that's it."[28]]

"And then she said, 'We have to talk.' So, oh my, a lot of tears and a lot of questions, and 'Why did you do this, Rudi?'

"I said, 'Well, Mom, don't you remember what they did to Heinrich Worbs?' I said, 'I cannot stand by and do nothing. I don't want to become part of it. I don't want to be guilty of omission. I want to do something about it.'

"She said, 'Oh gosh, what a price you have to pay.'

"And, of course, I start worrying what I should do — should I escape, try over Switzerland or over Holland or over Sweden? I contacted several people on the sly. . . . It was ten days I had to worry about it."[29]

Rudi's confusion played a part. "I didn't know where to go, and so I stayed."[30]

Rudi claims that a 16-year-old boy could have made it. "There would have been a way. So I was almost close to going to Sweden because one of the workers had a Swedish uncle, and he was always talking about Sweden. And we got interrupted by the Nazi [overseer] who said, 'What are you talking about — Sweden? You should talk about Germany.' And then the master, Trübe was his name, came in. 'What is this, a political orientation meeting? Shut up and go to work.'"[31]

Each day Rudi was on pins and needles. "Every time I walked past a policeman, I thought, 'Is he going to grab me?' I went to work and it just wasn't the same. Finally I said, 'No, I better not [flee the country]. I better face the music. Otherwise, if I escape they will grab my mother and my relatives and put them in concentration camps.' I said, 'No.' So I stayed."[32]

In jail, Helmuth stayed true to their prearranged story, which was . . . that the first one caught would take full blame for writing and distributing the flyers. It was well known the Gestapo could learn anything from a victim in 24 hours maximum.[33]

It took them 48 hours to learn anything from Helmuth — and even then it was only a tip of the informational iceberg. Yet they never would know it was so little.

When Helmuth finally did break under the torture of beatings, he *mentioned* Karl and Rudi, but only as curious acquaintances, not as conspirators. He also stated his friends were with him only once when he tried to listen to the BBC — and that it was jammed. Rudi adds, "He told me that after many, many days that he finally had to tell [about him, Rudi]." Alan Keele provides trenchant analysis in his response to Rudi: "You can see that he was telling you the truth, too. He didn't break right away. In fact, he only mentioned your name in passing. He was talking about something else and it just sort of dropped out. You can notice as you read this [the Gestapo documents]."[34]

Then the inevitable happened to Rudi and Karl.

"Tuesday morning, February 10, I went to work as usual," says Karl Schnibbe. "I was working with a colleague in an empty apartment, when right at noon someone rapped on the door.

"Sensing impending calamity, I went to the door myself. . . .[1] I opened the door and there stood two guys — about 6'4", 6'3" tall, with that long, dark leather coat — and he lifted up his lapel from the coat and there was the badge — Gestapo,"[2] . . . and I immediately knew the game was up.[3] . . . He said, 'Are you Karl Schnibbe?' I said, 'Yes I am.' He said, 'You know why we're here?' I said, 'Yes I do.'"[4]

They escorted him away, drove him off and stopped at his home. They tried tricking him into a confession, claiming Helmuth had talked more than he actually had. But Karl did not fall for it. The agents searched his house for an hour while no one else was home. Since the Otto Schultz incident, Karl had learned to bring home no flyers.

"Then we got back into the car. The suspense was terrible. What should I say, what should I not say? They told me if I lied, they would beat me to a pulp."[5]

They took Karl to the city hall, the headquarters of the Gestapo. They entered through the rear and went into a special elevator.

Rudi details the news he received of Karl's arrest: "On February 10, 1942,[6] I was waiting for Karl outside the branch house on that incline there. Then I saw his sister, Karla, and her girlfriend, Lucy Erickson, come down, and Karla just walked up to me and said, 'Karl has been arrested by the Gestapo. [In 1974 Rudi reports she asked the question: "Did you hear Karl-Heinz has been arrested?"[7]] You will be next. What are you going to do?' 'I don't know.' [In 1974 he says he said to his mother and sister at a "meeting around that time," which is perhaps this same conversation, "'I guess I will be next now. . . . Well, I expected so much. I'm surprised I wasn't pulled up yet.' So we talked about what to do. I said, 'Well, I guess we have to face the music, whatever happens.'"[8]] By then it was time to go in. As a zombie I marched in and sat down, and then the announcement came that Karl was arrested, the second of the perpetrators . . . was caught. . . . Oh, I just sat there, you know. And I heard the people whisper, 'I wonder who else is there? What made them do this? Are they crazy? Oh, those poor boys, they were always so nice.' And somebody says, 'I bet he is one of them.' That's when I got up and ran out."[9]

As an apprentice, Rudi worked five days and went to vocational school one full day on Wednesdays. The next Wednesday was 18 February 1942.[10]

Rudi reports, "While I was sitting in a class of the vocational school . . . on February 18, 1942, I was called out of the class . . . ."[11]

Specifically, the principal came up to his class and said, "Wobbe, there are two gentlemen outside that want to talk to you."[12]

So Rudi went downstairs to the principal's office and saw the lapel of one of the men with the Gestapo sign on it.[13] The men had leather coats and black hats.[14]

They asked, "Are you Wobbe?"

Rudi answered, "Yes."

The agents replied, "You're under arrest."

All Rudi said was, "I have to get my books."

They responded, "Never mind your books. You won't need them anymore."[15]

Rudi says they went down to the car, and the men drove him to his home. They had been there before and had told his mother of the charges against him.[16] Differing from his 1974 and 1988 reports, Rudi states in 1961, "She couldn't believe it, for I had never told her anything of this activity. But now I had to admit to her that it was so and left her heartbroken."[17] (The other reports say he had indeed earlier told her of his activities.[18]) In any case, the news was especially hard for her due to the fact she had assigned Rudi to look after her when her husband had died.

"When my mother opened the door I could see tears in her eyes,"[19] says Rudi. "I was sweating blood at that time."[21]

Unlike Karl, Rudi kept his leaflets in his room. But he kept them hidden. He describes his room as a "little half room" where he slept on a chaise lounge.[21] The Gestapo searched every square inch, ripping all the books from shelves and tearing apart everything, looking for evidence. Rudi stood there racked with fear, waiting for them to discover his "secret hiding place."[22] Rudi says that as they searched his room, that's "when I prayed the hardest."[23] He says he prayed, "Oh, strike them with blindness, Lord."[24]

Finally the two agents noticed the tapestry hanging on the wall. It was of a bellowing elk, and the agents laughed at it, but never looked behind it, and continued searching elsewhere. In one sense Rudi had the *last* laugh — because behind the tapestry was "the secret hiding place." There, the wallpaper had come loose, "creating a small pocket in which I had hidden several of the large leaflets."[25]

When Agent Wangemann had reached for the tapestry, Rudi said to himself, "Oh, now he gets it. He finds it." But Wangemann merely flipped the tapestry and made a comment about it. "He just flopped it down and grabbed me and said, 'Out.' Oh, if they would have found that, they would have arrested my mother on the spot."[26] More than anything, Rudi feared for his mother's safety.[27] The agents then left, taking Rudi with them.

His youthfulness added to his fear. "I turned 16 on the 11th, and on the 18th I was arrested."[28]

In summary, Gerhard Düwer was arrested the same day as Helmuth on 5 February 1942,[29] Karl Schnibbe five days later[30] and, eight days after that, Rudi Wobbe.[31] But only at Helmuth's apartment were flyers discovered.

The first thing the Gestapo wanted to know was, "Who are the adults that put these kids up to this?"

Hans Kunkel analyzes, "The Gestapo could not imagine that a 16-year-old alone, by himself, carried out this scheme and composed these clever flyers without adult help. They believed he was a member of a large adult resistance organization."[32] Rudi says of his interrogators: "They thought there was a conspiracy behind us, [involving] grown-ups. . . . We were just the leaflet carriers . . . the distributors. But behind us [they thought] there was an organization of adults that were instigating the whole thing, the whole resistance group.[33]

Then, out of the blue, one man stepped forward, ready to rat on the Mormons.

Helmuth's stepdad, Hugo Hübener, who never had liked the Saints,[34] told the police he suspected "that liberal" Otto Berndt had influenced Helmuth.[35]

Otto was then hauled in by the Gestapo for questioning.[36] He recalls, "I guess it was a whole week later that they arrested me, and I didn't even know why they arrested me. They had never told me. They told me this later on. . . ."[37]

While being taken to Gestapo headquarters, Otto, as district president, knew the future and fate of all the Mormons in the Hamburg area — if not nationwide — lay in his hands.

Rudi says that Otto later told him, "The fact that the office equipment of the Hamburg District, of which I was the President, had been used in typing and mimeographing this dangerous information caused much concern."[38]

Otto reports in a 1974 interview, "As I was sitting there in front of that room before they called me in I was scared to death, so scared that I had to hold my knees because they were shaking. And I prayed to my Father in Heaven."

He tells Rudi, "I prayed like I had never prayed before [Rudi adds, "that the Lord would let him say the right words."[39]]." Otto states in 1974: "I knew I had the feeling that my life was at stake as I was sitting there. And I asked my Father in Heaven to bless me that I could go through this, what was ahead of me. And as they called my name and I went in that room all the fear was gone. It was so quiet in myself that I could hardly believe it. . . . I was sitting down, and this is as true as I sit here, I felt as if my spirit left my body and another spirit came and took possession of the body, and this spirit answered the questions."[40] He told Rudi that he felt that other spirit "took over my thinking."[41]

"For three days I was thoroughly questioned by the Gestapo." (In 1974 he says "four" days.[42])

To Rudi he adds, "I was asked hundreds of questions in rapid succession and I, or I should say the spirit or the higher power that had possession of my body, was able to answer them all without any hesitation. I was very sure of myself. [In 1987 Rudi adds, "He told us later that he didn't even know what he was saying."[43]] After three days of questioning the officers felt that I or the church I represented had nothing

to do with the crime committed by these three young men."
He later told Karl, "After three days they told me, 'You can
go home.'"[44] In a third interview, Otto reports, "In the course
of the questioning I was able to show that our church was
not an American church and that we had nothing to do with
the U.S. government. All our records had been confiscated
by the Gestapo. They were checked and later returned. . . .
When I was questioned by the Gestapo I was told to see
that the accused Helmuth Guddat was to be cut off by the
LDS Church. I flatly refused to do this and explained to
them that . . . the Church had no right to excommunicate
him.[45] In 1974 he reports he also told the Gestapo, "He
will get his punishment from you, and we think that it's
enough punishment for him. Why should we excommunicate
him?"[46]

Karl also relates that Otto told him that, "In the interview,
they said that they didn't believe that Helmuth, Rudi and I
[Karl], that we did this sophisticated job . . . they wanted
names."[47]

Karl adds, "You see, this was our dilemma. They didn't
believe us. How can a 17-year-old boy and his friends
produce leaflets so sophisticated . . . so ironic . . . so nasty
. . . so that we made fun of them . . . they couldn't believe
it. They said we need the names. . . any price . . . . Kill them
if you need. But there were no names. My gosh, there were
no names!"[48]

Otto hypothesizes that Helmuth's mother, "had probably
told him [her husband] of my battles with Zander and my

whole attitude against the Nazis. So that's why they arrested me too."[49]

When Otto was released, a Gestapo officer walked with him from his cell to the exit. "I recall one sentence as they released me from the Gestapo. They treated me well. There was nothing to complain of. I told them what they wanted to know and they had me sign a copy of it.

"The man in charge asked me, 'Were you afraid?'

"I said, 'Yes. You know that the Gestapo does not have a good reputation in Germany and he who falls in the hands of the Gestapo has cause to fear.'

"He said, 'But we have done nothing to you.'

I said, 'No, you didn't, and I'm grateful for that.'"

Then occurred one of the most eye-opening moments in Otto's life, as the Gestapo officer said to him, "When this war is over and our troops come home in triumph, there will be no room for your church and your members here in Germany." Otto adds, "And he said it in a tone that I believed. They would have put us in the gas chambers just as they did with the Jews. I know that."[50]

Elsewhere Otto reports the officer as saying, "Make no mistake about it, Berndt. When we have this war behind us, when we have the time to devote to it and after we have eliminated the Jews, you Mormons are next!"[51]

Otto continues, "I didn't feel it as a threat. For him it was a fact. He stated a fact, that's all."[52]

He concludes, "There was a feeling in my heart to say to him, 'That never will happen. It won't take long and you will be wiped away, from Germany and from the whole earth.' But I had had enough after these four days, so I kept quiet."[53]

The Gestapo in fact did categorize the Mormons as a sect "dangerous to the state,"[54] but did not place them on the "active" extermination list.

Afterwards when Latter-day Saints expressed hope for victory in the war, Otto confronted them: "You be grateful to God that we will not win it."[55]

Other Latter-day Saints prayed for the regime to die early and for their people to lose the war. (On record are four such Saints — Rosa Bohringer, Johannes Kindt, Walter Krause, and President Willy Deters of Bremen.[56])

As for Otto's dealings with the Gestapo, he wasn't finished with them. On another day he wrote them in order to get the church's typewriter back.[57] Not succeeding, he went down to their office and retrieved it.[58] Additionally, he had other encounters with them. "The Gestapo always came to me. . . . They were watching me and calling me in for another interrogation."[59]

After the arrest, branch president Arthur Zander advised Marie Sommerfeld and the rest of his congregation that writing Helmuth would do no good since letters would never reach him.[60] Knowing this, it is highly unlikely that Zander ever visited Helmuth in jail, nor did he ever even know of his actions before the arrest, according to Karl Schnibbe in an interview with the author.[61] Therefore, it is extremely unlikely Zander ever had any discussions with Helmuth about his resistance activities — before or after the arrest.

The only conjecture among primary or secondary sources that Arthur Zander *might* have known about Helmuth's activities comes from Arthur's mother, Marie. "Whether he didn't like him [Helmuth] I don't know. But he mentioned very often to him that he should be careful."[62] When asked in her 1974 interview if Zander knew Helmuth had "some kind of ideas against the government," Marie responded, "I think he felt it. I think because he warned him."[63] This hypothesis is likely inaccurate because Zander would have quickly confiscated his typewriter, taken back the office keys, and probably released Helmuth from his calling as branch clerk had he possessed even a particle of suspicion that Helmuth was involved in the resistance, just as he did Otto Berndt from his Mutual position as counselor when Otto merely showed anti-Hitler sentiments.[64] (Ironically, the very next year Otto became Zander's "superior" on the district level — although in Latter-day Saint beliefs, higher authorities are mainly in place to serve those "below" them, rather than to oversee or "pull rank," even though some overseeing is inherent with the office.) Thus, Helmuth indeed would have been careful around Zander, given Helmuth's dedication to the principle of "cover." Helmuth knew how important it was to camouflage himself, to hide his activities, to fake his true beliefs.

Meanwhile, a certain consternation consumed the members in Hamburg, especially Helmuth's St. Georg Branch, where President Zander feared repercussions.

With now four arrests under their belt from the St. George Branch in recent months — counting not only the boys but Brother Worbs — the Gestapo placed an even more watchful eye on the Saints. Many feared for their lives, as well as the Church's very existence in Germany.

———————

In consideration of these factors Zander wrote "excommunicated" on Helmuth's membership record on 15 February 1942, ten days after his arrest, apparently with the consent of interim mission president Anton Huck. However, there is no evidence of Zander holding a church court or even notifying church headquarters in Salt Lake City.[65] District President Berndt says no court was held[66]] and that Zander and Huck did it behind his back. "I didn't know about it at all. I was the one that should have decided that, as district president, but I wasn't informed. I got a letter from the mission office saying that he should be excommunicated, and I wrote them back and said, 'Nothing doing.'"[67]

The excommunication efficacy is questionable, but in any case it was overturned after the war.[68] (See Helmuth's membership record in Appendix J.)

Although he opposed it, Otto reported later that the excommunication of Helmut[69] was a matter of show and paperwork formalities to appease the Nazis, in order to protect the other Saints. So he understood Zander's fear of the Gestapo when the three lads were nabbed.

Nevertheless, some church members were vehemently opposed to the action, as expressed by Helmuth's acquaintance Friedrich Peters: "I was very enraged about it, after I heard it."[70]

Zander's protection motive was certainly viable, although Alfred Schmidt, president of the Barmbeck Branch in Hamburg, also disagreed with it. He felt the action unnecessary.[71] (However, President Schmidt had not had four branch members recently arrested.)

Backing up his defiance to the Nazis, Otto still refused to sign the excommunication. Even when the Nazis persisted later.

Just a year after the war, Otto had Helmuth's excommunication reversed[72] On 11 November 1946, he and new mission president Max Zimmer wrote on Helmuth's membership record, "excommunication done by mistake." The next mission president, Jean Wunderlich, took the matter to Church headquarters in Salt Lake City for complete clarification, and on 24 January 1948 the First Presidency of the Church ordered a similar notation placed on Helmuth's membership record.

Helmuth was actually posthumously ordained an elder, says Gerhard, and "was rebaptized to make sure on 7 January 1948 and endowed on 8 June 1948." Gerhard reported he has that information on temple sheets that were returned to him, which state, "All the temple work was done for him."[73] In a dramatic turn of irony, when Karl Schnibbe soon learned of the excommunication he figured he *also* was excommunicated, and assumed that for the next six years.[74] But he and Rudi never were.[75]

CHAPTER **21**

Rudi says that after being carted away by the Gestapo: "I was now taken to the police headquarters and questioned and threatened for a whole week. The investigating officers tried to get me to admit that my mother was also mixed up in this affair. This I couldn't do, which made the officers angry to the point that they roughed me up but good."[1]

His main concern continued to be his mother. "My fear was that . . . the Gestapo was trying . . . to implicate my mother, that she had part in it. . . . So I tried everything that said, 'Oh no, she had no knowledge of it whatsoever,' and she actually had. . . . She knew."[2]

Rudi says that on his first day they stopped beating him for some reason, possibly because it was late. At 5 o'clock the van left for Kolafu, where they would be imprisoned each night. Rudi was led to the prison bus and then driven to the prison, near the airport where there was a prison, a penitentiary, and a concentration camp, all in one — a large complex. There he was put in a cell with a former SS accountant[3] who had been set up by his boss to be arrested. This much older man had attempted to borrow money for his wife's birthday from his boss. His boss had told him to get it from the office "till," and leave an IOU. This he proceeded to do. However, his boss had removed the IOU and "set him up" to be arrested the next Monday morning. The SS guards beat him mercilessly, and nobody believed his story. So as Rudi's cell mate he warned Rudi to clean everything in his cell, as high in the room as he could reach. But the SS guards were tall. So during Rudi's first night, the guards performed a white glove inspection, reaching as high as they could, which was higher than the two prisoners could reach. They found some dust. One of the guards took a key ring of large keys and slapped the old prisoner across the face, tearing his cheek open.[4]

The next morning Rudi was taken back for more interrogating. "I was scared, I was scared, oh my."[5]

The bus came for him and took him to Gestapo headquarters.

Rudi details his second morning of capture: "The SS guards were just waiting at the gate for us, to meet us for the daily beating and kicking, [to take us] into the Gestapo prison, where we had to stand that close to a wall — the point of our nose was touching it. If you dipped you got beat over the head. For hours on end — standing there. With all the other prisoners.[6]

Karl continues, "At the Gestapo headquarters we had to go into the Hall of Mirrors. It was on the floor where the Gestapo offices were. There were large lights in the room.

The first time it was terrifically hot and there was a terrible, dazzling light."[7]

Rudi describes this "Hall of Mirrors," which was a waiting room in which the prisoners had to agonizingly wait for their interrogations in smaller, private rooms. "There wasn't a single mirror in it. . . . And why they call it the 'hall of mirrors' I don't know; maybe it's time to contemplate, a time to look into yourself; but that's what everybody called it."[8] Also, the walls were painted white, so the lights reflected brightly, perhaps giving it a mirror-like effect.

The room held about 20 prisoners.[9]

Karl adds:

"We had to stand at attention again facing the wall, with our noses approximately one inch from the wall. You wanted to do it right, so that you did not attract attention, because of fear of the horrible kicks. You did not know when they would come, when suddenly you would be kicked and your face smashed into the wall and made to bleed.[10]

"Then you had a real problem, because you made a mess on the wall.

"If you concentrated too hard, you could not hold out for long, because you became dizzy and fell down."[11]

Sometimes they took the prisoners to the Hall of Mirrors where they stayed for the whole day waiting to be interrogated. "So you stay in that Hall of Mirrors the whole day. . . . It was awful!" says Karl.[12]

Elsewhere he reported he was not only kicked but beaten — and his nose was broken. He was also tortured by being forced to hold a huge rock in his arms while standing in the squatting position for long periods of time.[13]

Rudi reports, "After an hour and a half I got called by the guard sitting there and escorted up. And then my second interrogation. This time there were two agents, Wangemann and Müssener. Wangeman, he was the brutal one. Müssener was kind of nice, or maybe that's just a role he played. So he [Wangemann] had a rubber truncheon in his hand and where he was beating his hand it left a blood stain. So I noticed hanging in the corner was a towel, a bloodstained towel. He just wiped his hands and the truncheon off on it. And so somebody else was there ahead of me. And I noticed there were drops of blood on the floor, too. Nice way to step into it. So I had to stand there and they were shooting questions at me left and right, you know. I was telling the truth more or less except when it came to my mother; then I lied, because I didn't want her to get involved. I was trying to shield her."[14]

What astounded Rudi was an increasing awareness of the Gestapo spy network. When interrogating him during his third interrogation[15] they actually dug up a strangely detailed incident from his childhood — they had kept a dossier on him — and no doubt on the entire population who had performed anything remotely "questionable." When Rudi had been a small child, living in a "working man's neighborhood" that was strong in Social Democratic and Communistic political influence, he and the other neighborhood kids were handed little Red flags to run around with, as part of child's play. Now, "believe it or not," says Rudi, "the Gestapo knew about it. . . . And even back when you were a child you were being spied on by the Gestapo. . . . They knew about it, that was the crazy thing. And they asked me about it. . . . They asked me if I still had affiliations with those people."[16]

Rudi says they asked, "How about Heinrich Koch and Gustav Binder who gave you those red flags when you were a little boy? Are you still in contact with them?"

He adds, "That's when that came up again. So their spy system and their informants, that reached way before Hitler took over power of Germany."[17]

". . . I said, 'For goodness sakes . . . .'[18] After recovering a moment from that absurd question and explaining the episode away, he revealed that he only passed out the leaflets.[19]

Then they brought up his file on the Lord Lister Detective Agency I.D., when he was 13![20]

The Gestapo continued their questioning — of where he distributed the leaflets. So Rudi named the streets, wherever he dropped them off, including where he put them on the bulletin boards. Rudi reports his dialogue with the Gestapo agents:

"'Why there?'

"'So the people could read better.'

"'Don't get smart with me.'

"I got on my knees one time. He was beating up on me so bad, beating on my arms, and shoulder, and head. I was just like this, you know, to protect my head. Got it right here.

"And then he changed his tune. And Wangemann sat down and Müssener came. Kind of lifted me, a kind of a fatherly type, and said, 'Now you know what he will do to you. Why don't you tell us? Is there anybody else? How about your Uncle Alfred? Did you tell him about it? You know, on the sly?'

"Oh, I was wide awake. I knew exactly what they were driving at. So I said, 'No, no, no, they didn't know anything about it. As a matter of fact, my mother doesn't even know anything about it. She was quite surprised that I was involved.' So that's where you have to lie just to shield people, and it was hard. My mother drummed it home to me that whatever you do, tell the truth. But I couldn't. I couldn't involve other people. I knew what they would do, and we all knew what was happening around us.

". . . The Gestapo asked, 'Anybody in the Church take part in this? How about Zander?'

"I said, 'Zander, he's a Nazi.'

"'How about Berndt?'

"I said, 'He doesn't know anything about it. No, nobody in our branch knew anything about it.' Arthur Sommerfeld knew but he never actively participated. He knew about it, he knew about us but he was too good a friend to squeal [against]."[21]

By 1988 Rudi changed his theory: He says Karl, not Helmuth, had mentioned his name during interrogations. "I found out it was Schnibbe that gave my name, not Helmuth. He said, 'Yes, I showed Wobbe some of those leaflets.' So the cat was out of the bag, that's how they got me."[22] This took place, says Rudi, at Gestapo headquarters at Stadthausebruke, at a holding cell, as well as upstairs in their interrogation room.[23]

Karl says he was beaten and interrogated throughout the day. One can only speculate, but Helmuth probably received the same treatment until he "confessed." He was likely confined with metal hand and feet bands to the sides and feet of his bed at Kolafu during the night — actually beginning 5 P.M., after interrogations — until the next morning. According to one researcher, unyielding prisoners were sometimes so subjected.[24]

Rudi says he tried to live up to his promise not to involve anybody else. His interrogators demanded to know if anybody else knew. Rudi told them, "Nobody else."[25] When they tried to trip him up and say that Helmuth had said something contradicting him, Rudi told them, "No, that is not so. Hübener couldn't say that because that's not true."[26]

The boys generally stuck to their plan and their story not to implicate others.

Rudi reports, "I saw the other conspirators, Hübener, Schnibbe, and Düwer, once a day during exercise time in the courtyard of the prison. However, we were not permitted to speak to each other and we never did."[27]

By contrast, Karl recalls seeing only one of his colleagues — Helmuth — one time, "about two days after his arrest,[28] coming out of the Hall of Mirrors.[29] "The [Gestapo] slipped. . . . It never should have happened. . . . I saw Helmuth standing up there and I walked by him and he saw me coming and he grinned—you know, smiled—and then I knew that he kept his mouth shut and he only gave names as friends. That was our promise to each other. . . . I saw his face and I thought, 'Oh my gosh what have they put you through?' . . . He looked like he had been in a meat grinder.[30]

Karl states further that he went into interrogation "every day for three weeks."

During interrogations Karl admitted that he tried listening to the BBC, but claimed it was jammed. He also admitted that Helmuth earlier wrote broadcast notes for him at his request. He further stated Helmuth showed him a flyer once, but nothing more.

Because of Helmuth sticking to their story, Karl says he now had a ray of hope.

"Had I not known that he had promised to take the blame upon himself, perhaps I might have contradicted him in some way in my testimony. [But] I stuck by my statement; it made no difference how they twisted and turned things, or how the questions came.

"I did not tell them that we listened night after night. I told them that we tried once.

"The interrogators were the same people who had arrested me: Müssener and Wangemann. A blonde female stenographer was there; She saw a lot of tears and sorrow. She must have been a totally hardened sow, because a normal person could not endure such a thing."[31]

After seeing Helmuth emerge from the Hall of Mirrors it was evident to Karl that the Gestapo had treated him with particular harshness, certain they could get from him the names of the adults behind the ring. Agent Müssener's cryptic report is easily deciphered by writer Uli Sander: ". . . Only after lengthy remonstrances [beatings] and emphatic admonishments [torture] was Hübener moved [forced] to make a confession about the extent of his destructive activity."[32]

Rudi says he was interrogated three times, with severe beatings each time. "The last time I had to sign my confession. They had it typed up."[33]

Gerhard Düwer admitted to his interrogators that he had taken flyers. But he stated it in a way to cover himself: He said he did so in preparation to turn Helmuth in. They didn't buy it. Long after being interrogated, Düwer owned up to the fact he had said that so his sentence would go lighter.

To Düwer's credit, despite his catastrophic mistake of not conferring with Helmuth after Mohns confronted him, he did show a heroic side: Gestapo agent Mussener said that, during interrogating, Düwer was hesitant with his comments, and gave the impression of being "stubborn."[34]

Each night they were kept where Rudi spent his first night — in cells at Concentration Camp Fuhlsbutte,[35] abbreviated "Kolafu." There, brutal captors beat and harassed them, letting them sleep very little. This prison had a reputation of torturing its inmates in the prison church so their screams would be drowned by music from the church organ.

Rudi and Karl were never taken to the prison church, but Helmuth's fate while at Kolafu is a mystery.[36]

Helmuth never told the Gestapo of the other branches of his resistance group — the Bismarck boys or the larger circle he and Düwer had apparently established — nor did he ever spill the beans on the Kiel printing press.

In summary, the month of February 1941 was a nightmarish one for all three. Helmuth was held from 5 to 26 February, while Karl and Rudi spent part of that time anticipating their arrests and the other part actually being held in custody and interrogated. Karl was arrested 10 February and Rudi on 18 February. Their treatment, though possibly not as bad as Helmuth's, had some similarities — they spent their evenings at Kolafu, then were driven in a van to Gestapo headquarters on the fourth floor of Stradthaus, the City Hall, and there they faced the Hall of Mirrors and interrogation rooms each time.

As for the Gestapo, the Hamburg office alone was staffed with over 20 agents.[37]

In his 1974 interview, when asked what the nature of the torture was — whether fisticuffs or kicking or what — Rudi responded with only two words: "Rubber hose."[38] He adds two revealing comments in 1988: "No, they don't use fists. They don't dirty their fists," and, "If you say something they didn't like, you got it."[39]

Müssener and Wangemann, Helmuth's interrogators, were high-ranking Gestapo officers ["not the highest, but they were pretty high," says Karl[40]]. Rudi reveals that the agents were on opposite poles. It was Wangemann as "the tough and brutal one" vs. "the kind, fatherly Müssener."[41] They were, according to Karl, alternately "threatening . . .

sweet talk . . . and beating up in between."[42] The two agents "were intelligent persons," whom Karl describes as the type who attended the opera.[43]

On 27 February 1942 the four boys were finally finished with their interrogations.

What awaited next was a different kind of stress on their minds and souls . . .

CHAPTER **22**

The boys were told to get ready to go. Their new home would be the Investigatory Prison at Hamburg.[1]

Karl reports to the author that the Gestapo shoved him into a van and took off. "Then they slowed down and they drove to a gateway and I said, 'Where are we?'"

The new prison was six stories high. They locked him in the basement. "The first thing I noticed was how quiet it was." Every night the previous three weeks "was like this — screaming, yelling, crying . . . unbelievable . . . and there it was so quiet. I didn't hear a word. That was the first night I slept."[2]

The boys had no idea how long they would stay there — or just be shipped off somewhere, or what. Waiting to learn their fate was agonizing.

Karl reports, "We were told by some in the UG [Investigatory Prison] they thought we would appear before a juvenile court, a court for delinquents. Others thought we would go to a court of lay assessors. Still others thought the special court in Hamburg would handle us."[3]

Not knowing their future was torturous.

There, Rudi did not see Helmuth or Karl because "they made sure that we were on different floors."[4]

Karl reports, "I had a solitary cell. . . . I sat at a little, scrawny table. There was a stool, but that was all. There was nothing to read! We received toilet paper afterward, newspaper actually, cut in small squares, which I tried to read. There was absolutely nothing to do. Now and then you heard a rustling at the door, and you knew that the guard was peeking through the spyhole to see what you were doing. . . . You were not permitted to lie down."[5]

Karl adds:

"I do not know when my parents learned about my arrest. In any case, they did not know at first where I was. I vanished without a trace. I did not come home. 'Where is the boy?' 'I don't know.'

"They contacted my boss.

"My mother went to Police Precinct 24 on the Lübecker Straße, and they said, 'Leave the name here. We will inquire.'

"Mother told me later, she did not know for a few days where I was.

"My parents inquired of the Gestapo, and then they knew that I was involved with Helmuth. . . . They told my mother she could bring laundry to me each week, as well as a hand towel and soap, toothpaste with a toothbrush, and socks and so on."[6]

Irmgard Becker, seeing his parents at church, recalls: "The parents of Schnibbe were downright sick after the arrest."[7]

Karl describes this second prison. "There were a few more interrogations, but they were civil. They asked everything again."[8]

Rudi reports of their six-month stay in this second prison. "There was no violence and the food was fair."[9] Later he says, "The food there was a lot better than it was at the concentration camp, believe me," although "meager."[10]

Karl explains what "meager" meant: "We received some soup so thin that it went right through to your bladder. We called it 'radio soup,' because on the radio they always said, 'We'll be right back.'"

He says his mother could visit only once a month for ten minutes. "She also wanted to smuggle in a little chocolate or marzipan by sticking it in the laundry, but it did not work. The package was opened in the cell by an SS man, and he emptied everything piece by piece. When the candy fell out, he said, 'Ah, what do we have here? Chocolate? Do you really think we would allow you swine to eat chocolate?' Then he ate it before our eyes or stuck it in his pocket, perhaps for his girlfriend."[11]

He also says he could now receive visits from his mother, "who was permitted to visit me every other week."[12] (Later, he says "once a week.[13] and that only his mother came to visit.)

Karl's mother was allowed to visit once a month for ten minutes, recalls Karl.[14]

Possibly because they had different guards on different floors Rudi's report varies somewhat from Karl's regarding refreshments, as well, as he states his mother "probably" brought him a piece of cake when she brought him fresh underclothes each week and that he was able to eat it. "There wasn't SS there. It was just a regular Justice Department guard."[15]

Rudi wrote his mother every week. "Of course, you always have to be aware of it, everything you wrote down, everything you talked was overheard, censored, read. So you always had to make sure that what you were writing was that you were sorry for it and stuff like that, you know."[16]

In addition to his mother's mail, Rudi notes sarcastically, "I received a letter from the Hitler Youth. I received a dishonorable discharge from the Hitler Youth, saying my charge was preparation to high treason. And it broke my heart."[17]

Rudi explains the boredom they had to face, as "one could only sit there." He asked for books but did not receive them. "Once a day for 20 minutes you could walk around the courtyard in the goose fashion, one after another. And that was the only exercise."[18]

It was here that Rudi received a "spy" as a cell mate, a Gestapo plant to ask him questions — a common practice for the Gestapo.[19]

In the cells were three bunks for three prisoners. "And one day this guy, this Bernhard Rubinke came in."[20] Rudi later learned this fellow had never finished his schooling, and had come there from reform schools.

Karl says, "The Gestapo had told Rubinke something like: 'Listen, sniff Rudi out a bit and tell us everything that he says, then we will make it a bit easier on you.' They called it 'reduction of punishment.'"[21]

He asked Rudi, "What are you in for?"[22]

Rudi reports, "So I told him more and more. . . . I was too naïve. . . . I was always outspoken, too much. . . . I was just blabbering. I felt bad about the Nazi regime and I voiced my opinion always. . . . [i]f there was something I didn't like, I'd talk about it. So anyway he pumped me and pumped me, and then I got my indictment papers and I was asked if I wanted a solitary cell. I said, no. I didn't want to be by myself, and then of course they said, 'What's it all about?' So I just kept telling them what we did, what was on the leaflets."[23]

"So of course, Rubinke made a beeline for the Gestapo. Then I was down. Oh gosh, he accused me of being part of a robbery because I was telling them about some ration stamps, some meat stamps I got for just two *Marks* from a guy at the vocational school. And at the time I got them I didn't think about it, but probably got them through a robbery or something. All that was told to the Gestapo. I was part of a robbery and I got those ration stamps and everything. I had a hard time getting it all straightened out what was really true. So Rubinke was a spy."

Rubinke later certified five were probable lies.[24] In his defense Rudi countered Rubinke's accusations.[25] Nevertheless, Rudi had trusted and confided in the wrong man. He probably *did* tell Rubinke the three primary points that got him in trouble: Rubinke claimed that Rudi said, (1.) the German troops in Russia were always retreating, (2.) those volunteering in the SS were committing suicide, and (3.) Adolf Hitler was the greatest mass murderer.[26]

Meanwhile, being warned of stool pigeons, Karl had not talked to the other prisoners. "In the beginning at Kolafu someone had told me: 'Trust no one! Trust no man! Pay attention, my boy, you are alone here, completely alone. Keep your mouth shut and trust nobody. They are all bums; they are all stool pigeons. They all want to earn brownie points and to have their sentences reduced.'

"Knowing this kind of thing happened, I did not say anything, especially to the other prisoners they put into my cell. When they said, 'What did you do?' I replied, 'I smoked in the movie theater. What did you do?'"[27]

Despite Rubinke's lack of credibility as a witness, they took him to Berlin for the trial; however, the day of the trial he disappeared. By error he was shipped back to Hamburg. Rudi comments, "I was glad. . . . He could have hurt me. They actually contemplated the death penalty for me also. I have it all in black and white in that file [his personal file he donated to the LDS church]."[28] Thus, a major miracle occurred for Rudi when Rubinke was carted back to Hamburg.

Karl continues:

". . . We were told to pack our things, and we were moved into cells down on the first floor, which was exactly above the place of execution.

"I figured, from glimpses and sounds, that five to eight people were executed every morning at the Hamburg UG."

It is unknown about Helmuth's imprisonment, although it is known they allowed him to write at least one letter to his mother.[29] In it he states, "It is not easy for me to sit day after day from morning until evening between these four walls."[30] In a poignant, optimistic summary he closes, "The day will come when I will be free again and then I will also be present when you celebrate your birthdays or feast upon your Christmas cake with obvious relish."[31]

In the same letter Helmuth writes, admitting, "Now when I read daily of the bravery and endurance of our soldiers on the eastern front and think about Gerhard [his brother], who is one of them, when I catch sight daily of new reports of the heroic battles of our submarines and air force, I can't imagine that I once could have been so stupid and stubborn to read the newspaper with so much prejudice, and place more faith in the inflammatory and biased reports of those in London who cook up abominations, that is, those of the London radio. For this stupidity, I now have to sit here behind bars, and I believe it is for the best."

According to Alan Keele, their interviewer, Rudi and Karl felt that this portion of the letter was "an ungenuine extortion under duress, and served as the only means of communicating with his family."[32]

Marie Sommerfeld reports, "At first I had a terrible fear that they would seize my son Arthur, too. He had always been with Helmuth, and perhaps he also belonged to the resistance group. Arthur had just been drafted into the Labor Service. At that time he was lying sick in a Berlin hospital."[33]

Arthur clarifies, "I was in the hospital because of an injury I received while in the National Labor Service. We were building a road in Lochow, Poland, leveling the ground to store ammunition, when a root broke on a tree. The tree fell on me and split my skull. I was unconscious for six days, then taken for two weeks to a hospital in Warsaw, then spent nine months in a Berlin hospital."[34]

Marie continues, "I told my sister [actually it was her daughter[35] — or it was her daughter *and* sister], 'Let's go to Berlin. We have to go there. We have to find out from Arthur whether he knows anything about it.' . . . We wanted to know whether he was involved too."[36] Once they were there, Arthur told her, "'I was twice or three times up there [at Helmuth's apartment] and listened to it, to the bands, to the radio. But then I was drafted, and [it] was lucky for me. . . .'"[37]

She adds, "Otherwise he would have been in prison too."[38] (Of course she knew it was illegal to even listen to the BBC, so her son was not out of hot water yet.) . . . "I fasted and prayed that he would not be implicated, involved."[39]

The visit itself is substantiated by Arthur's sister, Hedi Sommerfeld Radtke: "After the arrests we traveled to visit my brother [Arthur] to find out if he knew about it and had taken part. Helmuth listened to the English stations himself and printed flyers in the church office, my brother told us."[40]

Hedi further reports that their mother was grateful that Arthur had been shipped off to the Labor Service; and she recalls her mother saying, "It is lucky that Arthur was

not here, perhaps he would have been involved also."[41]
Their mother likely sensed some sort of activity with which
Helmuth was involved: "Even when he went to school he
was always politically interested. [Earlier, she says in *favor*
of the Nazis.] . . . I said, 'Well, don't get involved in those
kinds of things,' I told him. But then I didn't hear anything,
and then my son didn't say anything."[42]

Arthur was never investigated.

Rudi wrote in one letter to his mother, "I read your letter
many times a day and am very unhappy that I now must sit
in prison. I regret it so much, I can not cry any more."[43]

Karl reports, "During the entire time of the visit I looked
out the window. I was hungry for freedom, to look outside.
My mother always held my hand and said, "This won't be
so bad, will it?" That was a terrible time.

"Once they put someone in my cell with me. He was
a repeat offender, a professional criminal. He had been
imprisoned six or seven or eight times.

"It was strange that he, as a professional criminal, had
still been running around, and Helmuth, who did something
once, had been thrown into prison, never to return to life.
That's how the Third Reich was. They seemed to have
more fear of Helmuth than of all . . . the professional
criminals."[44]

After languishing a month at the Investigatory Prison,
on 25 March 1942 there was finally movement in their case.
They learned that the Attorney General of the Higher Court
of the State of Hamburg had given all his information on the
four boys to the Attorney General of the Reich in Berlin!

The highest court in the land would be reviewing their case.

And two months later — on 28 May 1942 — the boys finally heard what would happen next, because at last their indictments came.

Karl says, "I picked up the indictment, and as I looked at it I thought I was done for. The entire indictment was stamped, 'Secret.'"[45]

The charges against Helmuth and Rudi were "conspiracy to commit high treason" and listening to and distributing foreign radio newscasts. The charges against Karl and Gerhard Düwer were similar but less incriminating: listening to and/or distributing foreign newscasts.[46]

Karl continues, "I read the trial would be . . . at the People's Court in Berlin. I already knew about the People's Court. It was talked about. It was feared. It was a great surprise that I was to be shipped to Berlin. I was shaken."[47]

The trial would be in another ten weeks — on Tuesday, 11 August, at 9 A.M. — so the boys had even more time to worry over their fate, and being with the highest court in the land, the wait was now even more excruciating.

The *Volksgerichthof*, or People's Court, was created 24 April 24 1934 and replaced the Supreme Court.[1] Anything that came from the court was deemed of the highest importance.

Karl states:

"After the indictment [came], at least five or six officials came to my cell to see the man who had to go to Berlin.

"[They said,] 'A juvenile delinquent is going to the People's Court? Schnibbe, you have to go before the People's Court? My goodness, what did you do?'

"[To them it] was like the seventh wonder of the world. The People's Court was infamous as being the worst there was. I had the feeling that the officials respected us.

"They said, 'I'll be . . . ! Man, you guys are really something!" They thought perhaps we had been functioning as spies for England. They thought they had gotten a pair of real hot dogs.

However, because he was in solitary confinement, he had to "brood" over his indictment.[2]

Karl's father wrote a heartrending letter to the Attorney General of the People's Court, requesting the trial to begin soon, "in order that we be freed from this disquieting uncertainty of what will become of our boy."[3]

Equally heartfelt is a letter from Rudi's mother: "I hereby request an acceleration of the above-mentioned case, because my son, who is 16 years old, is suffering greatly emotionally in confinement. It is also for me, as a widow, very hard to be required to watch my only child go to pieces emotionally from the results of his confinement. I am a war widow employed as a custodian. . . . My nerves are all frayed because of my son's grief. I request, therefore, once again an acceleration of the case of Hübener, *et al.*"[4]

On 30 June 1942 Karl's father wrote the court again, requesting to attend the trial and to learn the address of the defense attorney in order to contact him. In his letter is a final reminder: "We would like to ask the Attorney General not to judge his offense too harshly."[5]

Meanwhile, Helmuth's brother Gerhard reflects, "In April 1942 when I was home again on medical leave, I noticed my closet door slightly ajar. I figured Helmuth had somehow jimmied the lock. I did not even check inside the closet to see if anything was missing."[6]

When he returned to the Army at Warsaw, Poland, for Officer Training School, he was yanked from his training and pulled in for interrogation. Government officials told him of Helmuth's resistance activities. It was his first time to hear about them.[7]

"Later I learned Helmuth listened to English and German BBC broadcasts." That did not surprise him since "he and I both had four years of English in school."[8] Also, he had "learned quite a bit from the missionaries."[9]

Three months later, with Helmuth still awaiting his trial, Gerhard had another encounter with Helmuth's girlfriend:

"In June 1942 I caught malaria in the swamps of Russia. I was sent to the Hanover hospital where they treated tropical diseases. I went home on a four-week medical furlough in July.

"At that time I saw Giesela. I ran into her as she was in a hurry going somewhere. It was July 1942. We spoke only a few minutes. She said she was going to be drafted into office work and would probably leave the city of Hamburg, probably to work at a camp outside the city, as most young women drafted went to camps there. She was cheerful, friendly, and outgoing then. I [later] saw her a second time."[10]

To the author Karl recounts that the next step for the boys was being taken to Berlin for trial.[11] In his autobiography he adds the detail that it was in the green Minna prison van that he saw Helmuth, Rudi, and, for the first time, Düwer.[12] He recalls, "I didn't know who he was."[13]

Rudi similarly states, "All four of us were put together and I said, 'Who is he?'"[14]

Karl continues, "We were driven . . . to the Altona train station where there was a compartment reserved for us on the express train to Berlin."[15] In the van they were each handcuffed to a police guard.[16]

But on the train they were not cuffed.[17] However, each of the four prisoners had a guard sit across from him. "They minded their own business and we talked our business."[18] Rudi does remember the comment of one guard: "'I don't think they would do much to you. If I would be the judge, I would give you a good spanking, a good licking, put you in uniform and put you to the front.'"[19] Rudi says that on the train they could talk — and that it was the first time since their arrest to do so — but not about the case. ". . . But we slipped in a couple of words: 'How come?' I said [to Helmuth]. 'I had to or they would have killed me,' he said."[20] Rudi adds that "they were quite lenient," and were just prison escorts,[21] obviously not SS.

"When we could converse a little [on the train], we could whisper a bit among ourselves. Helmuth referred to the interrogations. He said, 'I am sorry. I could not do otherwise.' But he had protected us fairly well.[22]

If there was any question as to whether or not Düwer felt innocent and should not have been included as part of the group, Rudi says that on the train, "He was acting the part of all of us,"[23] so it was evident he felt he was one of them, despite telling his interrogators he should be excluded.

Next they arrived by train to Berlin to face "the highest Court[24] of the land, the *Volksgerichtshof.*

And there Karl, Rudi, and Gerhard Düwer saw courage displayed by Helmuth that they had never before seen.

In northwest Berlin the boys were first taken to the city's oldest prison, Moabit,[25] which held 620 men,[26] to await trial.

Karl says, "We were separated again and isolated in louse-ridden cells. It was a filthy hole. There was an overpowering stench!

Rudi adds, ". . . In Berlin, the minute we got there, the guards, they called us Communists, traitors, scum, just the lowest form of it. They opened the little window where they shoved the food through. 'Here you Communist swine, have your swill.' And the food was just about that." He says they were held in solitary confinement.[27]

Karl has the same memory. "We had to listen to all manner of profane language. They called us swine, curs, scoundrels, criminals, traitors to our country and so on. It was obvious that we were already guilty."[28]

The boys were forced to work, preparing mothballs. The strong chemicals were almost unbearable.

Rudi states, "But there in Alt-Moabit, which is the oldest prison, it goes back to medieval times, that was the oldest one there, it was terrible. And then, of course, one day came the call I should meet my defense attorney, court appointed."[29]

Karl says, "[My attorney] was already too friendly, too chipper. Then he said, 'Tell me, what did you guys do?' I did not trust him in the least! The system of course was completely corrupt, a system of cogs, one turning the other."[30]

Rudi analyzes, "In the first place, all the lawyers belonged to the national socialistic law club. So that was the pool the court would draw them from. They were all Nazis. And he treated me like he was a Gestapo agent and just kept interrogating me. So I didn't trust him. I asked him, 'What is Bernhardt Rubinke doing here?' He said, 'Oh well, he's just being called as a witness, not to worry about it.' I said, 'Why don't you find out about it?' One interview with the attorney, that's all. . . . Just a sham."[31] Rudi does feel that his attorney was going to try to lighten the sentence.[32] Nevertheless, the Gestapo only approved of certain lawyers.[33]

After a week in the filthy Moabit prison, the boys were told to get dressed at 8 A.M. on 11 August 1942.

Karl recalls, "When I put my suit on, someone said, 'That can't be your suit.' It hung so loosely on me that I looked like a scarecrow!"[34]

Rudi reports, "Since my arrest in February to this time in August, I had lost fifty pounds due to the meager food supply, bad treatment, and mostly worry."[35]

The boys were handcuffed and taken in the green Minna to the justice building. There, they were locked in a cell to await trial. They had their handcuffs released — all except Helmuth — whose hands remained bound in heavy chains behind his back.[36] After only a 20-minute wait, their attorneys arrived and led them upstairs to the courtroom of the highest court in the land . . .

CHAPTER **24**

Karl says that on the way to trial, ". . . We suffered more verbal abuse from the [Nazi] functionaries running around. It was an exciting thing for them. In their eyes we were important criminals. We were symbols, resistance fighters.

"I particularly recall one of them, a short, fat fellow running around. He really gave us a hard time.

"He said, 'Now we'll see what kind of mess you've gotten yourselves into! Now you're gonna pay the piper, my friends!'

"People were still snarling at us, even here at the trial."[1]

The boys entered a packed courtroom.[2] The crowd stared with astonishment as four mere adolescents entered. It was a large room,[3] like a university-style classroom with high ceilings and wood panels.[4] Adorning the walls were Nazi flags.[5] Behind the judges was a huge picture of Adolph Hitler.[6]

Rudi says, "I had a feeling the minute I entered the courtroom that we were already sentenced. It was just a show they were putting on, just a big show."[7]

The four prisoners sat on an elevated stand with the lawyers in front of them. In front of *them* was an empty area, and then across the room [about 20 feet,[8]] the judges sat on an even more elevated platform.[9]

When the judges entered, everyone had to stand.

According to original court documents, the judges and their staff consisted of seven people.[10] Rudi says, "We were over to the side with the four lawyers in front of us, and then the regalia of clowns as our judges.

But a bigger shock I got when I saw their blood-red robes with a big . . . vulture on their chest . . . the 'vulture of defeat and ruin.'"[11] Elsewhere it has been described as a "large golden eagle" and a swastika.[12] The three primary judges wore the blood-red robes.[13]

This was the infamous "blood tribunal."[14] Rudi elucidates: "That's what they called 'the blood trial.' Besides, they probably did from the sentences they handed down."[15]

A newsreel had shown a German military general literally quaking in his boots before this court. Now before them were four boys. Three of them were decidedly nervous, but Helmuth sat calm and confident. He knew his fate and was prepared to *confront* his captors.

The three wearing red robes were:[16]

(1.) Vice President of the People's Court, Karl Engert, who presided;

(2.) Chief Justice Fikeis (who Rudi says was the "chief judge" and "spokesman");[17] and

(3.) Motorized SA Brigade leader Heinsius.

Others of the staff who sat on the high bench were Senior District Leader Bodinus and Senior District Judicial President Hartmann.[18] Then, as representatives of the Prosecuting Attorney, there were First District Attorney Dr. Drullmann and Judicial Minister Wohlke.[19]

Attending were the following whom Helmuth knew: Gestapo officer Müssener, who had interrogated him; Heinrich Mohns, who was Helmuth's supervisor at work; Werner Kranz, from work; and Karl Schnibbe's father, who was the only parent, friend, or supporter given permission to attend.

Rudi reports only a few spectators were present while "the press turned out *en masse.*"[20] In contrast, Karl recalls *many* spectators there and only two or three reporters.[21] In any case it was a "big crowd."[22]

Only one witness was there whom Helmuth did not personally know: a witness to whom Gerhard Düwer had given flyers.

According to Rudi the trial began at 9 A.M.,[23] 11 August 1942, although Karl remembers it at 10 A.M.[24] in his auto-biography and 9 A.M.[25] in his interview with the author. In his 1988 interview Rudi is also an hour off: "Shortly before eight we got there," he says.[26] Despite minor contradictions, Karl's and Rudi's accounts of Helmuth's story, including this trial, are remarkably consistent.

The trial began with opening statements and formalities. Each person stood when his name was read, and acknowledged if it was correct. Each stated his birthdate, residence, profession, etc.

Then the judges went down the row of attorneys who represented each of the accused and asked if they had anything to say. Each said, "No."

The next phase of the court consisted of a small intelligence test, wherein a few general knowledge questions were asked. Rudi says they had to stand in front of the judges' bench,[27] and he describes what happened next: "They gave us an IQ test first — if we knew the Party program and if we knew when Hitler's birthday was and all this,[28] including how many points were in the party program [25]."[29]

Rudi adds, "Then we were tested in our knowledge of the Party and its political aims. Helmuth Hübener was asked what he thought about the Party according to his beliefs. He answered that he didn't like the Party and held the Church of Jesus Christ of Latter-day Saints in high esteem."[30]

Since Helmuth startled them with such honesty, Rudi says they began to concentrate on him, "that he should be judged as an adult."[31]

Then, as Rudi says, "For eight hours they hammered away at us."[32]

The judges began interrogating about the prisoners' crimes.

Karl attests, "Helmuth was sharp as usual. He answered with flying colors. The rest of us were completely speechless, the result, in the first place, of lack of sleep, and then of our nervousness and state of agitation. In spite of that Helmuth answered immediately. He did not seem to be bothered by all this in the slightest."[33]

Karl adds that he and Gerhard Düwer spoke very little and that Rudi stuttered.[34]

Rudi says he was questioned about being "antisocial by buying these ration stamps . . . on the black market," which he had mentioned to Rubinke the spy. Rudi says the judges looked at the ration stamps purchase as "a bad sign;' and then, "they asked if I ever participated in a robbery. I said, 'No way.'"

Rudi adds that the prosecutor said, "What about this and that?" — things Rubinke had said.

"I said, 'That's a lie.'

"'Okay, we've got bigger stuff to talk about with you anyway.'"[35]

Rudi believes these questions came to him, Karl, and Düwer *during* the course of interrogating Helmuth about the flyers.[36] However, Karl reports that the judges asked them *before* they interrogated Helmuth.[37]

Karl also reports seeing his father during court. "I waved to him and he waved back as if to say, 'Chin up, boy, it's not as bad as all that.' But after he heard how the proceedings were going, he sat there despondently, hunched over the whole time."[38]

Karl's father also no doubt became increasingly sickened by the battered appearance of Helmuth: "You could tell," says Johannes Schnibbe, "from his face the agony of his detention."[39]

After that, witnesses were called. After giving their information they left.[40] Werner Kranz, from Helmuth's office, was reprimanded for not turning Helmuth in sooner, nor on his own, but was not punished.

Gerhard Düwer's contact was next called. His name was Horst Zumsande. In late January 1942 Düwer had handed two leaflets to him and his brother Kurt. The two brothers lived together[41] and were the same age as Düwer.[42]

Düwer had presented two leaflets to the Zumsande brothers, of which Horst now claimed in court to have read only the first few sentences. When he realized the flyers were subversive, he returned them, he said. Thereupon, Düwer stubbornly read the leaflets to the two brothers.[43]

Horst Zumsande testified of Düwer telling him and his brother about the African theater of the war on an earlier occasion.[44]

The Gestapo had learned of only one other of Düwer's contacts: Karl Horst Pipo,[45] who was also present at court.

The witnesses claimed that when Düwer had read flyers to the Zumsande brothers, Karl was present.[46] This had taken place in late January, just days before the arrest.[47] (See Appendix K for more information on the leaflets.)

Mohns was then called as the main witness. He boasted that he "tried to keep his office free from impure political thinking."

Finally, Gestapo agent Müssener was called. After his testimony, the judges called a recess, in which they had lunch. The four prisoners were taken handcuffed to the cellar and given nothing to eat.

After lunch the trial resumed. First, the judges had the spectators removed. The reason, the judges gave, was for state security issues since the leaflets were to be read aloud.

The judges then read and discussed every flyer.

Rudi states, "Helmuth claimed a total of 60 handbills were done."[1]

Most of Helmuth's writings angered them. In some flyers Helmuth attacked Hitler and his speeches.

Rudi details, "They went through all the material and then finally we were asked questions and Helmuth always answered. 'Oh yes, I remember this. That's the report from the BBC London about the infantry division that lost so many people in Russia.' And the clothes and goods, *Wolle und Wintersachen Spende*, where the public was required to give all their furs and warm clothing for the freezing soldiers in Russia, and so on and so on."

Rudi reports the judge as then saying, "You mean you wrote all this?"

Helmuth answered boldly, "Yes."[2]

One of the more unintentionally amusing reactions to his leaflets comes in the official written summary by high court judges Engert and Fickeis when they denounced one of Helmuth's leaflets about the Asian theater of the war: "The leaflet 'Who's Inciting Whom' contains inflammatory statements about the entry of Japan into the war [by attacking Pearl Harbor], which in a venomous manner is given for the outbreak of the war with America."[3] (Venomous indeed. Attacking Pearl Harbor meant nothing to the judges, but criticizing Japan was seen as venomous, and they *blamed* Helmuth for criticising Japan.) Almost equally absurd was the prosecutor's report at the People's Court — from the Superior Attorney General of the *Reich*: "In the leaflet, 'Victorious Advance into the Shining Battles of Annihilation,' the Japanese successes are labeled as meaningless and the outlook for Japan's victory is placed in doubt."[4] This blatantly obvious fact struck the judges as incredulous. It happened to be the last leaflet Helmuth ever wrote.[5]

Another flyer, "The Nazi Reichmarshall," referred to "good old fat Hermann:"

"Oh yes, he has something on the ball, this little rogue with the saucer eyes."

Speaking sarcastically and in highly inflammatory terms the flyer declares he has "a dazzling career, a pretty actress, and a very ample salary that is not to be sneezed at, but no brains. No, really not, as big as his head is."[6] This particular flyer, surprisingly, caught the judges' sense of humor, and the somber occasion was broken by chuckles from the bench. Despite their political bent, the judges appreciated Helmuth's clever wit.[7]

Rudi explains this moment in detail, "They even handed those handbills out on the bench. Some of them, they even snickered and laughed about it, those SS people there. Especially the one that says, 'Herman Göring, they call him, "Herman the Fat Duke."' So they snickered. The chief judges had to say, 'Order, please, order.' He called them to order."[8]

Karl reports the judges laughed heartily at that flyer: He said he was speechless as "they sat there and snickered."

He continues, "I was astonished how cool, clear, and clever Helmuth was. The court went over every detail in the leaflets and he recalled everything. He knew precisely when, how, and where he had conceived an idea and what he meant by it. . . . Throughout the entire trial Helmuth stood like an oak."[9]

The judges asked, "Why did you do that?"

Helmuth said, "Because I wanted the people to know the truth."

The judges: "Does that mean that the British atrocity stories are correct?"

Helmuth: "Exactly!" Sometimes Helmuth was sarcastic towards Chief Justice Fickeis.[10]

Fickeis at one point asked, "Would you have us believe that the British are telling us the truth? Do you really believe that?"

Helmuth responded, "Yes, surely, don't you?"

The judges asked, "You don't doubt Germany's ultimate victory, do you?"

Helmuth replied, "Do you actually believe that Germany *can* win the war?"[11]

Karl says at that point all Hades broke loose.

Helmuth's attorney, Dr. Hans Georg Knie, "turned around and scowled, as if to say, 'Are you out of your mind?'"[12]

Karl and Rudi report that when Helmuth was asked again why he did what he did, he replied, "I wanted others to know the truth."

The prosecution then asked, "Are you suggesting we are lying?"

Helmuth replied in a manner showing some contempt by using the familiar form of "you": "*Jawohl, Ihr lügt.*"[13]

Rudi reports, "And then they asked, 'Helmuth, why? You did this especially in earnest.'[14]

"'Hamburg stays reactionary[15] . . . the working class is still reactionary[16] . . . they will never join the Party,' he said."[17]

Rudi adds, "He was also asked why he had passed handbills among the working classes.[18]

"He answered: 'Hamburg will always stay in opposition to the Party,[19] . . . especially in the labor sections of Hamburg where the laborer, the common worker, cannot be fooled like the rich people.' It was his statement.[20]

". . . The judge screamed out, 'You snot-nosed kid, what do you know about it?' Really abusive, verbal abuse. They called us scum, and traitors, and ungrateful boys."[21]

When Helmuth snapped back with an answer, the judge, amazed, responded, "Quiet, you impertinent boy."[22]

Helmuth was then beaten by the guard and pushed down.[23]

Karl analyzes, "It was completely clear to me that deep in his heart Helmuth knew prior to appearing before the People's Court that he would be sentenced to death. I believe he had made up his mind to conduct himself with courage and dignity."[24]

Karl's father later said Helmuth gave a courageous "account of himself."[25]

Rudi summarizes: "A lot of courage. He stood there like a man ten feet tall, steady. He was not intimidated whatsoever, and he stood his ground. And always he tried to focus the attention on himself,[26] . . . trying to take away the limelight from us, not to be important, but to shield us, to protect us. I noticed it, and so did Karl. We noticed it right away that Helmuth was trying to take the blame. 'I am the one. I'm the one that wrote the handbills and the dissertations. I'm the one that started it. I'm the leader, I am the one to blame. Leave these alone,' in so many words. And this went on for quite a while.[27] . . . Then came the court-appointed attorneys, who had their say. They didn't say very much. We had a feeling that they were just part of the parrot arrangement there — they just had to say a few words.[28] . . . They had about one minute each, which was ridiculous, it was a sham.[29] . . . And then the prosecutor came forward [with his recommendations to the bench]. He said, 'Death penalty for Helmuth Hübener. He has to be tried as an adult. Wobbe, he was too much involved, seven years imprisonment. And for Schnibbe and Düwer, a minimum of two years.' And then they deliberated."[30]

According to Rudi, the judges said, "Bring the public and the press back in."[31] [Karl says the spectators and the press had been ordered out of the courtroom only for the discussion of the leaflets, but Rudi says they were also out for the discussion of Rudi's robbery accusation, the testimony of the witnesses, and the prosecutor's recommendations.[32]] Karl says the door was opened and all the spectators poured in again.[33] The Nazis, of course, were nothing if not dramatic.

Karl states that the judges then withdrew to decide the verdict, while Rudi recalls the judges not leaving the room to deliberate.[34]

"Then the judge and his assistants and the party officials in uniform stuck their heads together," says Rudi,[35] ". . . for a few moments on the bench, and then announced that they were ready for sentencing."[36]

This method was attested to by victims of other trials. Worse, judges commonly met with the prosecuting attorneys before a trial to fix the outcome.[37]

Karl reports the climax of the court scene. "Fickeis berated us terrifically. He called us traitors to the fatherland, scum, asocial elements. 'Vermin like you,' he said, 'must be exterminated.'"

CHAPTER **26**

In their written summary, judges Engert and Fickeis later added, as part of their indictment against Schnibbe, a prophetic definition of chillingly frightening possibilities when one is expected to abide by *politically correct* thinking: "It goes without saying that the good, healthy common sense of all politically right thinking persons dictates that this deed deserves to be punished."[1] Such expectations of *political correctness* were typical from the Nazis.

The judges then told the court of Helmuth's mental abilities. They considered him far advanced for his years. His school thesis, they claimed, written by a boy "in his 15th and 16th years," as well as his leaflets, his general knowledge, his political knowledge, and his appearance and behavior before the court, "show without exception the picture of a precocious young man, intellectually long since having outgrown his youth."[2]

Ironically, so anxious were the Nazis to indict him, that they established his credibility, intelligence, maturity, political knowledge, writing brilliance, persuasive personality, and "ability to make judgments." He was the very type of creature they were most afraid of — and they had to build him up in order to destroy him, which is one of the greatest of all ironies in his story.

Rudi elaborates on this moment during court, reporting the judges' comment on his thesis as, "so well written that it could have been the work of a thirty-year-old assessor"[3] — an assessor of law[4] — which would have received "all honors,"[5] or which could have been written by a 30-year-old "university professor."[6]

Despite his earlier conversations with Helmuth, Rudi now realized, "That's when actually it hit me, 'Goodness sakes, he really went out on a limb there and really studied this in depth.'"[7]

Then came Helmuth's sentence.

"My knees were knocking," says Karl. "I had no hope."

At that moment they read Helmuth's verdict.

According to Rudi the judges "announced" the sentence: "'For Helmuth Hubener, charged preparation of high treason, aiding and abetting the enemy, we sentence him to death. And the forfeiture of his human civil rights for his lifetime," which apparently means they could mistreat him all they wished until his death.

The official court sentence document states, "The defendant was aware of the danger of his propaganda and of the reasons for it. Therefore the death penalty, which is compellingly prescribed, must be imposed on him. . . ."[8]

Karl recalls, "When this sentence was pronounced, the room grew deathly silent. . . . The people were shocked. Then I heard people whisper, 'The death penalty for the lad? Oh, no!'"[9]

The other three then waited for their sentences, no doubt standing there in horror.

Rudi reports the judge's pronouncement:

"'Wobbe, the maximum of ten years imprisonment, preparation of high treason, aiding and abetting the enemy,' . . . 'Schnibbe, for distributing broadcast news, five years imprisonment.' Not preparation of high treason. 'Düwer, for distributing minor information, four years imprisonment.'"[10] (See Appendix L for Karl's and Rudi's discussions on why Rudi's sentence was higher, and other disagreements they had on some facts.)

Gerhard Düwer was sentenced to less than the others because it could not be proved he ever listened to the radio.[11]

Ironically, the judges possibly prescribed steeper penalties to all four boys because they had not been deprived of Hitler Youth training![12]

Rudi says, "We were asked if we had anything to say. We were choked up. We couldn't believe it."[13]

Says Karl:

"They began with Gerhard Düwer, who said, 'No, I have nothing to say.'

"'Schnibbe, do you have anything to say?'

"'No.'

"'Wobbe?'

"'No.'

"'Hübener?'

"'Yes.' Helmuth stood up and faced the judges fearlessly. He said, 'Now I must die, even though I have committed no crime. So now it's my turn, but *your turn will come*.'"[14]

Rudi reports, "Then Helmuth — he turned into a man and stood up and said, 'You have sentenced me to die — me, a son of Germany. My time is now. Your time will come!'"[15]

Rudi details the scene a bit further beginning with the judge:

"'Do you have anything to say?'

"Helmuth [replied], 'Yes,' and he stood up. 'You have sentenced me to die, me a son of Germany, for just telling the truth. My time is now, but your time will come.'

"'Quiet, push him down.'

"The guard just pounced on him and pushed him back on the seat. Sixteen years old, seventeen at that time."[16]

Karl reports elsewhere, "And Helmuth stood there and said, 'I have to die now for no crime at all.' He said, 'But your turn is next.'"[17]

Rudi similarly reports elsewhere, "We were then asked if we had anything to say. Hübener was the only one who responded by saying: 'Wait, your turn will come also.'"[18]

Karl's father later told Marie Sommerfeld, "When Helmuth heard the sentence, he [momentarily] collapsed. His friends wanted to help him, but . . . Karl and Rudolf were held back."[19]

Rudi adds, "I am sure Helmuth did not expect to be executed at that time,"[20] although Karl analyzes, "It was completely clear to me that deep in his heart Helmuth knew prior to appearing before the People's Court that he would be sentenced to death. I believe he had made up his mind to conduct himself with courage and dignity."[21]

Helmuth was the first underage defendant to be given the death penalty as punishment for disobeying the radio law of September 1, 1939.[22]

Legally, this was made possible by the decree of 4 October 1939, which took youths 16 and over out of the juvenile system to the stricter adult system, if they possessed adult mental abilities,[23] which the court deemed Helmuth to have.

Just seven years earlier, a group accused of similar offenses to that of Helmuth received sentences of only one to three years in prison.[24]

The trial had lasted only one day and it was now 5 P.M.[25]

After the trial, Karl's father asked Kunz, Karl's attorney, to obtain permission to visit his son. Kunz went quickly to the judges before they left. They deliberated a long while, then gave Karl's father just five minutes to see his son.

Rudi says, "We were marched out of the court room.[26] The hallway was lined with people left and right . . . As we were paraded through them, everyone of them took off their hats, their head gear, and bowed their heads. In silent support, respect ."[27]

Karl adds, "For me it was clear: this act was in solidarity with us. They could not say anything or they would have been in deep trouble themselves."[28]

Rudi adds, "One whispered to me, 'Have courage. *Halte deinen Kopf hoch* [Hold your head high] . . . '"[29]

The boys were then placed in a large holding cell.[30]

Karl says he, Rudi, and Düwer were all present in the cell with Helmuth, but Rudi remembers only he and a Swiss spy there with him. Rudi says they were all together in a cell later, but without Helmuth.[31] (See Appendix M for Rudi's version of this scene.)

Rudi reports, "I spoke with Helmuth for a short time ["for about an hour," he says in 1974[32] and 1961[33]]," while Karl says the visit lasted 45 minutes.[34]

Rudi adds, "I don't know why they put us all together in one room, but it was the last chance I had to talk with him."[35]

In 1961 Rudi adds, "We were both in a state of shock and were not able to say much. At this time we could not fully comprehend the extent of this judgment. We had heard of fake trials and didn't really know what to expect and if we should take this sentence serious. We recalled what the guards had told us on the train to Berlin and didn't know what to think."[36]

Karl reports:

"We were fed bread, and the handcuffs were removed from three of us, but Helmuth's hands remained cuffed behind his back. . . .[37] Rudi and I fed Helmuth."[38]

"I broke up the bread and put pieces in his mouth. I was still shaking like an aspen tree. Rudi and I talked with Helmuth. 'Helmuth,' I said, 'I do not believe they will do it. They will reduce or cancel the verdict. They only want to establish an example so others do not start anything. They will not kill you. You are too young; that will be how it is.'

"'No,' he said quietly. 'They will kill me. Look at the walls.' The walls and iron gate were completely covered with writing. There were small names and verses: 'I must die,' and 'I do not want to die,' 'Farewell, beloved,' 'Goodbye, Mother,' and such.

"Every square inch was covered with references to people's death sentences. There were things written there in foreign languages — French, Polish, Czech."[39]

Rudi says, "We heard the rattle of keys in the door.[40] Karl continues, ". . . Then all of a sudden the gate opened — the big iron gate."[41]

Rudi says the guard stated, "Wobbe, you shouldn't be here."[42]

Karl states that the guard said, "'Pack your things, you're going back to Hamburg. . . . Wobbe, Schnibbe, Düwer, get ready to go!' So we had to leave."[43]

"Now I had to say goodbye to my friend, Helmuth.[44] Saying goodbye still haunts me today," says Karl.[45]

Rudi states, "Then Helmuth said simply, 'Goodbye. And I only could say, 'Helmuth'[46] . . . The last embrace. We wept. It helped me to see my friend."[47]

Karl reports, "We each embraced Helmuth. [I said,] 'Farewell!' Helmuth had large eyes and now they were full of tears. He said, 'Goodbye, my friend.'"[48]

Karl elsewhere reports, "Helmuth had blue eyes. I mean really big, dark blue eyes. And I never saw Helmuth emotional. He never showed his emotions when something happened. And when I put my arms around him and I told him, 'I'll see you pretty soon,' his eyes filled with tears, and he said to me, 'I hope you have a better life in a better Germany.' And then he cried."[49]

Rudi adds, "Then I was taken out. That was the last time I saw him."[50]

Helmuth felt he had done the right thing. Rudi feels that as a result of the trial, Helmuth had become even more convinced that the regime was corrupt,[1] and did not feel at all sorry for what he had done. Rudi states, "He held his posture right to the very last."[2]

Karl says he was led from their cell, upstairs to a room behind the courtroom where he saw his father for the agreed-upon five-minute visit. Johannes Schnibbe had come to comfort Karl, but Karl ended up comforting his father. "When he entered the room," says Karl, "he completely collapsed. I said, 'Now it is not so bad. Do not be concerned. I am still alive.'"[3]

Karl reports he, Rudi, and Düwer were taken to the cellar, and the guards took them back to Moabit prison.[4] Meanwhile they took Helmuth to Plotzensee prison.[5]

Rudi states, "Oh, the daily verbal harrassment from those guards there, especially that one, he just said, 'Oh, they changed that [your sentence], you're going to hang. They're going to get you for sure, you Communist.'"[6]

At Moabit Rudi sunk into a heavy depression: "In thinking ahead I could not comprehend how I could be locked up like this. It was solitary confinement at that time for the next ten years. I felt very discouraged and my morale was very low."[7]

In 1988 Rudi states, "I was so, what do you call it, discouraged and I even contemplated ending my life. I was so down.[8] . . . If you're humiliated every day and every time you turn around, you were reminded how worthless you were, that you were lower than dirt, and a couple other choice words the guards had for me. . . ."[9]

This sorrow, especially in light of Rudi's mother assigning him, after his father's death, to protect her, prompted Rudi to record:

"In this state of mind I wrote to my mother and told her that I wouldn't blame her if she would denounce me as her son and if she didn't want to see me anymore after what I had done to her.[10] ["Forgive me that I caused you so much pain," he wrote. "I don't know what I'm going to do."[11]] Then I asked her to write me and answer if she still loved me and wanted me to come back to her, after what I had done.

"Death seemed sweet to me, a liberator from the awful treatment I received in this lonely cell at Moabit. I didn't write it this way to my mother, but she must have read it between the lines.[12]

". . . It's weird. That was the fastest reply I ever got — was in two days I received a letter back from my mother.

She said, 'There's nothing to forgive, son. You always will be my son, regardless what other people say. . . . Pray, try to find Him. And stay close to Heavenly Father. He will be the proper judge.'[13]

". . . She told me . . . to . . . ask Him for guidance and strength and for a strong testimony of the truthfulness of the Gospel, so that I would be able to endure all things. I wept reading that wonderful letter from my mother and received the strength I needed to overcome despair and dejection, and I felt a lot better afterward.[14]

". . . Somehow I wish I had that letter. That sure buoyed me up and I started to pray then. At first I thought after hearing how bad I was and all that, I didn't even think to pray anymore, I felt so guilty. So I asked the one guard who gave me the hee-haw about it, I wanted to see the pastor, the chaplain. And he said, 'Oh wow, you want to repent? It's too late. You're going to hang anyway.' I said, 'Never mind, I just want to talk to him.'

"So he came and I asked him for a Bible. He said, 'No, no, we as Protestants only go by the New Testament.' I said, 'I'm not that kind of a Protestant. I'm a Mormon and we believe in the complete Bible. I'd like to have one if you can spare one.' He did. Argued a little bit with me but couldn't convince me. I started with Isaiah, the hardest one. And I found solace and comfort. The one that I'll never forget is in chapter 55: 8-9, I think, where he speaks that the heaven is so much higher than the earth. 'My thoughts are higher than your thoughts.' It doesn't mean anything to anybody else, but to me it meant comfort. That the Lord knows what's going on. And the seventh verse, 'Seek the Lord, ask for forgiveness.' So that turned me around. [Later he says of this scripture, "Isaiah 55 especially gave me comfort that the Lord knows what's best."[15]] That was the verse that stuck with me. I read it over and over again. . . . [S]o I started to pray really, on my knees and wrestling with the Lord. And I received comfort and strength.[16]

". . . That's the message I received out of the scripture. That even heaven is higher than the earth so His thoughts higher than mine. So I may not understand it now but He does and there's a reason in being punished, being brought down. So I could grow and gain a testimony.[17]

". . . In reading the Holy Scripture I began to understand the Gospel of Jesus Christ. I had gone to the Church of Jesus Christ of Latter-day Saints in Hamburg because of my mother's influence. I didn't have a testimony in those carefree days in Hamburg with my friends, who were now in the same prison with me, but now I prayed and I read the scriptures and understood, and felt a great joy in my heart. Was this the reason why the Lord had permitted that I'd be taken to this place of hopelessness?"[18]

Later he comments on a prayer: "'Let me overcome this and be able to go home one of these days, years,' whatever, and that I'd be able to survive with His help. And I received comfort."[19]

He also expounds: "When the chips are down, so to speak, and you really are put through a test, that's when you realize what you actually have. And the realization came to me when just about the roof caved in on us. . . ."[20]

He further talks about his faith: "Those were hard times, but if I learned anything it is that the Lord sometimes sends us trials to test our strength. Oh sure, at times, we wavered and weren't quite as strong, but I learned to pray. Oh yes, I learned how to pray. And to keep in close touch with my Heavenly Father. I believe I received a testimony there, like in *The Book of Mormon* — the Zoramites who were humbled by being kicked out of the synagogues because they weren't appreciated and accepted. Sometimes you have to be humbled to seek the Lord. And a lot of people lost their faith because of the atrocities and the grievous pains they had to endure."[21]

Rudi remembers their stay in Berlin as 20 days,[22] while Karl recalls it "about a week before the trial"[23] and "two or three days" after the trial.[24]

After that, Rudi says he and Gerhard Düwer went from Berlin in a prison van to the old Huettenstrasse Prison for a day, then to the Glasmoor prison at Hamburg for one week — September 2-9. They were separated from Karl during that week, and bedbugs feasted on them.[25] However, Karl recounts that the other two boys went *with* him from Berlin straight to Glasmoor prison, north of Hamburg.

Rudi recalls he and Gerhard Düwer joined Karl at Glasmoor on 9 September 1942.[26] There, they dug peat for prison fuel, "a dirty, hot job that left the prisoners exhausted."[27]

The three boys were fortunate to be assigned to the prison tailor shop, sewing prison pants. There, the shop director took a liking to them. Karl remembers him as Staff

Sergeant Eggers,[28] while Rudi recalls him as Master Taylor Franken.[29]

Meanwhile, in Helmuth's last prison cell on death row, he had only a small stool, a little table, and a bed of planks. Heating pipes were torn out so no one could hang himself. For his clothes, he was given only a smock and nothing more, so he couldn't strangle himself on regular clothes.

No fixed date was set for his execution. Part of his punishment consisted of not knowing when it was to occur.

Marie Sommerfeld reports, "After the death sentence, I tried to comfort his grandparents. They were completely in despair."[30]

Three days after his trial, his mother wrote a poignant note to the Attorney General at the People's Court, desiring three things: (1.) for her and her mother to visit Helmuth, (2.) for clemency, and (3.) for an opportunity for him to make up for his actions. She summarized, "Please heed the pleas of a sorely tested mother. Helmuth was really my sunshine and was such a good boy. . . ."[31]

Marie also says, "We wrote to him. We tried to help him and comfort him in his difficult imprisonment. . . . I wrote a consolatory letter. . . . He never received the letters. However, his relatives who visited him informed him that we had written. He was very thankful for that."[32]

Week after week he waited. Apparently six appeals for clemency were submitted,[33] including: one from his fellow employees;[34] one from the Hitler Youth unit;[35] one from the public authorities in Hamburg;[36] one from his attorney,

Dr. Knie;[37] one from the Berlin office of the Gestapo(!)[38] [although it could have been officer Müssener who had this letter sent from Berlin, as the signature of the one signing the letter is illegible]; and one from his stepfather, Hugo Hübener,[39] who may have officially adopted Helmuth during his detention time and given him his name.[40] This, Marie Sommerfeld believes, occurred in order to help Helmuth, since Hugo was a loyal Nazi and on good terms with the Party.[41] Helmuth's mother may have prevailed on her husband to do this, although one source states Hugo adopted Helmuth five months before his arrest: September 4, 1941.[42] His brother Gerhard, who says the adoption came through "just shortly" before the arrest, confirms this.[43]

Portraying a different motive for Hugo adopting Helmuth, Gerhard believes that Hugo *wanted* Helmuth as his son, as Hugo had only one son and one daughter from his former marriage[44] and that he wanted another son. "And so it just came in right handy that way. . . . And Helmuth at that time was not of age. He had no say in it."[45]

One letter that went against the grain, that actually *requested* Helmuth's death sentence, came from the Berlin office of the Hitler Youth, written by the Senior District Leader and Hitler Youth Judge, named Nille,[46] who obviously felt burned when Helmuth turned against the *Reich.*

Karl writes, "His last months must have been miserable there on death row."[47]

He was given no blankets. For the rest of August he may have been comfortable, but during those colder months, he likely shivered and waited for his death.

Meanwhile, Gestapo agent Müssener, who had caught and interrogated the boy, did an unexpected thing. Inspired by an apparent change of heart [perhaps from Helmuth's remarkably bold defense and confrontation of the judges, not backing down and even *warning* those judges that they would be judged someday by a Higher Judge] he went before the High Court and begged for the boy's life![48]

But Müssener's request for clemency joined the others in being deep-sixed by the National Minister of Justice on 15 October 1942. The decree of execution was signed. Dr. Crohne from the National Minister of Justice office wrote his signature on Helmuth's death warrant. His official cover letter states, in its direction to the Attorney General at the People's Court in Berlin dated 19 October 1942, that a certified copy of "the decree of 15 Oct 1942" is attached with "the request that you arrange with the greatest haste for all necessary subsequent actions."[49]

On 27 October 1942 six men showed up at Helmuth's cell — two officials from the Attorney General of the People's Court, Ranke and Renk, along with a Mr. Rohde (a representative of the prison director) and a Dr. Schmitt (the prison doctor) accompanied by two prison guard officers. They appeared to Helmuth at 1:05 P.M. and "read slowly and clearly" to him the judgment of the People's Court of 11 August (as if Helmuth needed to be reminded). They also read the decree of the National Minister of Justice of 15 October, which stated that he — the Minister — would not make use of his right of clemency, "but to let justice run its course." He then told Helmuth the execution would take place that night after 8:00 P.M., and recommended that he prepare himself for his final hour, and said he could make his final requests, if there were any, to prison officials. During all this Helmuth "remained completely quiet and calm." The officials then left the cell.[50]

CHAPTER **28**

At 6 P.M.[1] Helmuth was permitted to write four letters —
to his mother;[2] to his brother Gerhard;[3] to his grandparents;[4]
and to Arthur Sommerfeld's mother,[5] Marie, who loved him
like a second mother, according to several people.[6] In fact,
Marie says, "He always called me Mother Sommerfeld.[7] She
later wrote from memory some of the contents of his letter
to her.[8]

The letters to his mother and grandmother were
destroyed during the 28-29 July 1943 bombing raid of
Hamburg.

But the letter to Marie Sommerfeld met a different fate:
According to Arthur's *wife* Marie, "Arthur's mother Marie
lost the letter going from Czechoslovakia to Hamburg, on
the handcart expedition."[9] This was a pioneer-like handcart
journey from Czechoslovakia to Hamburg at the end of the
war, in May 1945, when the Russian troops were advancing
on Czechoslovakia, causing the Sommerfelds to flee over
treacherous mountain roads to safety.[10] However in another

account, the older Marie Sommerfeld recalls the letter as "lost in the bombing attack."[11] In a third account Arthur's sister Hedi speculates, "We could no longer find the letter after the death of my mother and assume that she had placed it at the disposal of a journalist and these people had kept it. Unfortunately we cannot prove anything, so this piece of history is lost. We would not have given it away and treasured the value of the letter."[12]

Marie also adds: "I no longer remember verbatim what he wrote. But the letter was very long. I still know some passages."[13]

Arthur's brother Werner Sommerfeld reports, "When we first read it, we opened it and we saw at the end you could see the ink it was blotted out because he must have shed some tears because he knew that it was the end of his life on this earth."[14]

Marie reports from memory two versions of Helmuth's letter.[15]

The first reads:

"When you receive this letter I will be dead. But before my execution I have been granted one wish, to write three letters to my loved ones [actually four].

"I want to thank you for the letter you sent to me, dear Sister Sommerfeld, which they withheld from me.

"I also want to thank you for the many happy hours I was able to spend in the circle of your family.

"Please remember me kindly.

"I am very thankful to my Heavenly Father that this agonizing life is coming to an end this evening. I could not stand it any longer anyway. My Father in Heaven knows that I have done nothing wrong. I am very sorry that in my last hour I have to break the Word of Wisdom [as explained in the letter to his grandparents, below].

"I know that God lives and He will be the proper judge of this matter.

"Until our happy reunion in that better world I remain,

"Your friend and brother in the Gospel,

"Helmuth."[16]

The second reads:

"Dear Mother Sommerfeld,

"When you receive this letter I will already be dead. I was permitted to wish for something before my death. I wished to be permitted to write some letters. I thank you for your consoling letters, which I unfortunately did not receive. But I am happy that you have not completely forgotten me. Unfortunately I have broken the Word of Wisdom in the last hours of my life. Soon everything will be over. Keep me in good remembrance. I have not done anything wrong. I thank God that I will soon be released from this agony."

Keele analyzes the Sommerfelds' letter: "It's very pure, very straightforward, very moving, and simple. But the theological argument is very strong — because he realizes he's within a few hours of meeting his Maker. But it's amazing how calm he is. And how quiet in his conscience he appears to be."[17]

He also wrote his brother, Gerhard Kunkel, who was serving in Russia as an artillery observer at the time[18] for two years as a noncommissioned officer.[19] "When I received it I burned it, feeling impressed that it could get me into trouble, but memorized it and recorded it in my journal the next day. This is the letter as I recall it. The translation is as follows:[20]

"'I am very grateful to my Father in Heaven that this agonizing life will shortly come to end this evening. I could not stand it any longer. My father in Heaven knows that I have done nothing wrong. I know that God lives, and that He will be the judge in this matter. Until our happy reunion in a better world, I remain your brother in the Gospel. Helmuth.'"[21]

Gerhard's short letter is very similar to the fifth paragraph of Marie Sommerfeld's letter. Meanwhile, the letter to his *mother*, according to church district president Otto Berndt who stayed close to the situation, contained at least one moving sentence: "I have only two hours left, then I have to appear before my God,"[22] which leads one to logically conclude that the first letter he wrote was to his mother, since he began writing at 6 P.M.

Hans read his mother's letter and recalls, "Helmuth wrote her a letter of farewell. The letter was heartrending."[23]

As for the fourth letter, to his grandparents, Charlotte Kunkel reports, "Only once did Grandpa Sudrow talk about the letter.[24] . . . When Grandma Sudrow received Helmuth's letter she came out to us. We lived with my parents. She came lots of times to visit us because she was worried about Helmuth. So when she got the letter she came to us at my parents' in Bellstedt. She would take the streetcar and it would take a half hour to get to us. She normally visited us once a week there, but as soon as she got the letter she came [directly] to see us."[25]

She continues, "It said he had to drink cognac, when taken to his death. It said, 'When you get this letter, I will be dead.'"[26]

She summarizes, "We never like to talk about it. It hurts to talk about it. It brings back lots of stuff. It was a painful time in our lives. Helmuth had spent a lot of time with Hans."[27]

Acts of courage give birth to emotional pain — for the heroes who sacrifice and for those left behind. Helmuth himself knew his life was significant. Listen to Arthur Somerfeld's mother:[28]

"I still recall today how Helmuth often said, 'You will yet hear something really great about me. I will be known everywhere.'[29] She adds, "When I read the letter I had to think about his words."

In 1974 Marie further details, "Very often when he would come home he would tell me, 'Sister Sommerfeld, *I will become something great* [author's emphasis].' When I asked him, 'How do you mean that?' he said, 'Well, you'll just have to wait.'"[30]

She concludes in a statement published later in Hamburg: "At that time he was already involved in his resistance work, about which we, however, knew nothing. He did not say it because he was a braggart. It was more of a promise to those around him that he would someday really apply his intelligence, which he possessed, to something meaningful. But we did not know what to make of it."[31]

With Helmuth not yet in the execution chamber, the predictably precise Nazi record keepers detailed their cold, careful manner with which they carried out his execution. These were his last moments, as reported detail by detail from the Attorney General's office:

The executioner, Rottger, reported to two government officers, including the Executive of the Secretariat — Renk — and the Director of Execution — Ranke — that he and his assistants were ready.

In the front of the room was a table covered by a black cloth. On it were a crucifix and two burning candles. The back of the room was partitioned off by a black curtain. The above two officers stayed behind the table, while in front of the closed curtain stood the executioner, his three assistants, and a government administrator named Rohde.

One of the two government officers, Ranke, who stood behind the table, ordered Helmuth to be brought into the room.

At 8:13 P.M. Helmuth appeared with his hands shackled behind him. He was escorted by two prison guards into the room, where the door was locked behind them.

The other government official, Ranke, then identified Helmuth, and told the executioner to proceed. Ten seconds passed from the time Helmuth entered the room until he was turned over to his executioner.

Helmuth was calm as the curtain was withdrawn, revealing a guillotine. His shirt was removed and he was placed upon the apparatus, showing no resistance. Almost immediately . . . the blade fell.

Only eight seconds — a remarkably swift eight seconds — had passed from the moment he was handed over to the executioner, was placed upon the guillotine, and was executed, *including* the brief time it took for the executioner to make his report that the sentence had been carried out!

Thus, Helmuth had been in the room less than 18 seconds before he was killed.[32]

The National Minister of Justice recommended that his body be delivered to the Anatomical Institute of the University of Berlin.[33] By law it had to be given to some institute.[34] His family was given no information of his execution or of his grave.[35]

Hans records, "We never received a letter that informed us where he was buried."[36]

Hans says his mother learned of Helmuth's death in a most unusual manner . . .

CHAPTER 29

The Nazis made a nationwide "example" of Helmuth, announcing his death with thousands of blood-red posters all over Germany.[1] His mother happened to see the placard on a cement wall[2] on 28 October, her birthday,[3] according to Hans, while he himself first learned about it from his grandmother after she received Helmuth's letter.[4]

The local newspaper in which it was announced was the 28 October 1942 issue of the *Hamburger Anzeiger und Nachrichten*, consisting of one long paragraph, a quarter page long.[5]

Adding absurd aggravations to the whole affair, the Gestapo came again to Otto Berndt, wanting Helmuth excommunicated.(!) Otto's response was, "'He's dead. Why should we excommunicate a dead man?'" [6]

Hans continues, "My mother suffered a great shock at that time."[7]

Marie Sommerfeld adds, "After the death sentence, I tried to comfort his grandparents. They were completely in despair."[8]

Helmuth's acquaintance at church, Frederich Peters, states, "I first learned about the execution in 1942 by the red placards and the newspapers when I was on leave in Hamburg. In the branch no one knew anything about it.[9] [Obviously it must have just taken place.]

Marie Sommerfeld further reports, "One evening [28 October 1942], some weeks after the judgment, I was sitting with my daughter. She was reading in the newspaper. Suddenly she read aloud: 'The death sentence of Helmuth Hübener was carried out yesterday.' I was very shaken and cried: 'Now they've executed him after all.' My daughter asked: 'How come, do you know a Helmuth Hübener?' 'But of course, that is Helmuth Guddat!' You must know that we knew Helmuth only by the name of Guddat."

Meanwhile at prison, on 28 October, Rudi recalls Master Tailor Franken[10] calling Karl Schnibbe, Gerhard Düwer, and himself into his room and showing them an article in a local newspaper, announcing Helmuth was executed the day before.[11]

Rudi relates his feelings at that time: "We'd heard nothing of our friend until this awful moment. All our hopes and yearnings were smashed. Everyone started crying as Master Franken showed us the newspaper. He told us how sorry he was to be the bearer of sad news and gave us a little time to collect ourselves.

"I was numb the rest of the day, overwhelmed by shock and grief. That night I couldn't sleep but tossed and turned on my bed, thinking about Helmuth. Just what did they mean by 'Deprivation of Civil Rights and Honors?' Did that mean they denied him even the basic comforts and necessities of human life before he died? Did they treat him even lower than an animal? I kept seeing his face as we departed, realizing the torture he must have faced as they walked him to his execution. It was early the next morning before I finally wept myself to sleep."[12]

Rudi adds:

"Many a night after that [newspaper] statement . . . I lay awake praying, crying, hoping that change would come. I didn't receive an answer to my prayers. It was my grandma that did. She was the one that brought us all into the church. She had a personal relationship with our Heavenly Father. She wrote me that she wrestled with Heavenly Father for an answer to her prayers. That I would return. She said, 'I heard a voice, saying, "I heard your prayer. He will return. Not just yet."'

"Somehow this letter from her got through the Nazi censorship. Don't you think it was a life saver for me? He knew that my faith was wavering. . . . Especially when these nice guards come and tell you, 'Where your buddy got executed, you're going to be next!'

"It happened, but it took three and a half years in these camps before we were finally liberated by the British army."[13]

Helmuth inspired numerous others with his courage. Some have even acted on his example. The White Rose and other resistance groups would later rise up in Nazi Germany. The White Rose was similar to Helmuth's in that it consisted of German young people — but somewhat older, as they were enrolled in university. Like Helmuth, they would write and distribute leaflets. (See Appendix N for the philosophical position of the White Rose group.)

Apparently there may have been one other LDS male imprisoned for resistance, although his name is not known. This apocryphal account states that his politics leaned to the left, he rode a motorcycle, and he refused an invitation from the SA to join them, so he was imprisoned.[14]

Helmuth's life served as an inspiration to those determined to resist evil.

German researcher and writer Uli Sander states, "Of course I wish for Helmuth's sake, that he had lived. But I am also thankful to him that he took all this onto himself, like so many others. If they hadn't how could we live with ourselves?"[15]

Douglas Tobler places into perspective those who fought for the resistance: "These people provided then the moral soil for the rebirth of Germany."[16]

CHAPTER **30**

Fascinating adventures were soon experienced by Helmuth's family and closest friends.

First is the amazing chronicle of his brother Gerhard Kunkel.

Gerhard was still at Warsaw, Poland, attending artillery officers' training school when Helmuth was caught.[1] He was there because of his knowledge in electronics technology.[2]

Helmuth's other brother Hans believed at one point that Gerhard had accepted "subversive" documents from Helmuth[3] while he was in the army, but Gerhard maintains he never received any.[4] Gerhard explains his fate:

"When Helmuth was caught I was bumped down from lieutenant to corporal. . . . About one week after graduating, I was called in for a court martial.[5] I was stripped of my just-commissioned officer rank.[6] . . . The reason? They claimed I was involved with Helmuth, but they could not prove it."[7] In a 1974 interview with Douglas Tobler and Alan Keele, he adds that his commandant "thought I may have received some

of the handbills Helmuth supposedly had sent to the front
to someone he knew. I was interrogated for two days. . . ."[8]
In interviews with the author in 1996 and 2003 Gerhard
continues, ". . . They confiscated all my gear — my personal
effects — to search it, then gave it all back. If they had found
a leaflet on me I would have been shot on the spot. . . ."[9]
"I was considered 'politically not trustworthy' and was sent
to the front lines of the Russian campaign in a 'rehabilitation
division' where I was a forward artillery observer, as I had
been before, except now I was on the front lines and was
watched by a supervisory officer for 'reliability.'[10] for what
was to be a period of one year.[11]

"But an incident occurred that allowed me to win back my
respect and remove any doubts about my trustworthiness
as a German soldier."[12]

To better understand his chronicle, Gerhard left for basic
training in April 1941 when he locked away the shortwave
radio that Helmuth discovered, then he received additional
training in the signal corps as a radio operator. He graduated
from that in October 1941 and went to Bad Orb to find his
father, whom he saw for the first and last time since early
childhood. Then he was sent to Russia.[13]

In December 1942, Gerhard was wounded in Russia
during an artillery barrage. Shrapnel from a shell cut open
both his knees.[14] He was treated in the Rhesev, Russia, field
hospital,[15] then left the hospital for Hamburg.[16]

Back on the front lines, still considered "untrustworthy"
as a soldier, Gerhard was surprised by the following:

"In July 1943 I was the forward observer inside the observation bunker when I discovered Russian soldiers. They were in a silent attack entering the bunker from the other side. The light was behind them. They could not see me in the darkened portion of the bunker. I fired at the door — wounding or killing some, perhaps, I do not know.

"I grabbed the small emergency transmitter and escaped out through the emergency exit. Outside, I was confronted by a Russian soldier. We both were out of ammunition and he did not have time to fix the bayonet to his rifle. I had only a pistol and a bayonet. So, with bayonets in our hands we began hand-to-hand combat. I got the better of him and stabbed him in the right shoulder and left thigh, and incapacitated him. Those were terrible times. I still have nightmares about them, although they are less frequent now than in the 1960s and '70s. My wife still wakes me up from such dreams and sometimes I wake up screaming.

"During that Russian silent surprise attack, I used the transmitter to call in "Code blank — fire on all coordinates," which prevented the thousand-plus Russian soldiers from probably killing two divisions of our troops (about 12,000 men), who were hemmed in a valley, unaware they were about to be destroyed.[17]

"Because of my actions, I received the highest honors of battle — the Iron Cross [a medal of distinction which few soldiers received][18] and Medal of Valor [the rarest medal[19]], as well as the Russian Battle Medal — and was given back my former rank, plus I was released from the 'rehabilitation division.' I was politically and morally opposed to the Nazi regime when we fought the Russians; nevertheless, it was an insult to me to have to be supervised and watched over as a soldier."[20] (See Appendix O for an explanation of medals and emblems, including those which Gerhard received.)

All his combat was in Russia and Italy.[21] In Italy he received a "silver purple heart,"[22] one of three purple hearts.

Noteworthy is the fact that after the war, "My oldest boy played with my medals. I was afraid to bring them to the U.S. so I buried them in the back yard, along with my military pistols I still had, but not in a container. I just wanted to get rid of them. They're probably all dissolved in the earth by now."[23]

His wife Waltraud details, "I remember six of the medals. It did not matter to Gerhard to take care of them — I saw the oldest boy playing with them. Gerhard did not even allow the boys to have toy guns."[24]

Immediately after the silent attack in Russia, Gerhard was sent home on honor furlough in July 1943.[25] He visited his grandparents and was introducing them to his fiancée,[26] when the following happened:

Right during their visit, American and British forces began their famous 28 July 1943 bombing attack on Hamburg.

Gerhard says:

". . . My girlfriend and I had been out to a movie and were still visiting in my grandparents' apartment when, on July 28 at 12:15 A.M., the allied bombing raid began. 1,500 planes flew over. My grandparents, my girlfriend, and I all ran outside toward a canal a half mile away for protection.

The canal was about 20 feet below street level. As we ran I remember looking back and seeing an apartment building collapse on my grandmother, killing her. I guess well over 200 others were killed on the street by that one building, plus those inside. Other apartment buildings — in fact all buildings around us — were collapsing. Bombs were exploding across the street as we ran. One could not run in the street itself because of the hurricane-force winds [exceeding 150 mph from the explosions] shooting down the street, creating a strong vacuum that blew people all over the place. So we, as well as a crowd of perhaps thousands, ran on sidewalks as close to the buildings as possible.

"As we approached the canal, about a hundred feet further ahead, I saw my grandfather badly burned, almost beyond recognition. I was pretty certain by his features that it was him, [also] his unusual leather briefcase he still had in his hand was a giveaway. He had become separated from Grandmother somehow and perhaps had been blown across the street to the spot where he now lay, quite dead.

"I had napalm on both my legs. It was burning. I had to stop the pain and burns by jumping into the canal. But the way was hedged up by a crowd of people all crowded to a standstill in front of and on the steps leading down to the canal and riverboat landing.

"My girlfriend and I somehow got through the wedge of people on the steps and made it to the landing, which was about halfway down to the canal from street level. We got separated. I jumped into the water. The cool water immediately stopped my legs from burning. Then another man and I helped catch my girlfriend as she jumped into the canal also. I helped about seven other people in the canal to safety. I don't remember the rest of the night. Perhaps I passed out or slept. The next morning was total devastation. By one look at our apartment building nearby one could see there was nothing worth going back to. The grief of seeing my grandparents killed then sunk in.

"We walked about three hours across the town, now in ruins, to my girlfriends' parents' house, to safety. Although Hamburg was almost utterly destroyed from the previous evening, we were attacked the next night and another night."[27]

Fifty-five thousand civilians were killed and 40,000 injured from a five-day blitz of Hamburg. Also, two-thirds of the housing was badly damaged or destroyed.[1]

The Allied forces threw everything they had at Hamburg those nights — every flyable plane and every pilot.[2]

Meanwhile, at their prison in Glasmoor, Rudi recalls the prisoners seeing the "heavy haze of smoke"[3] blocking out the sun over Hamburg and smelling "burning flesh and homes,"[4] from 30 kilometers away at their prison.

Karl reports the city as "one big, red glow." He adds, "On the following morning the sun shone radiantly, but over Hamburg one could see only a huge, dark cloud. Then the cloud spread out and covered Glasmoor as well, and for three days we could not see the sun."[5]

Charlotte adds, "Then there were two days of no sun. Ashes a quarter inch thick gathered on the vegetables in our garden."[6]

Karl recounts how even the rain was black.[7] Rudi says of the sky then, "The sun never shone. It was black. The smoke was all over that valley."[8]

Meanwhile nearly a million citizens fled Hamburg.[9]

Gerhard analyzes, "The working section of Hamburg was the part most destroyed, which ironically was the section least sympathetic to the Nazis."[10]

According to Helmuth's friend, Arthur Sommerfeld. "On the night of July 28, 1943 . . . I left the shelter to look for something in my apartment that I'd forgotten. Because there were so many false alarms, I figured it was safe. The big bombing attack hit while I was there. I got chemical burns on my neck and hand. I screamed and ran to the bomb shelter where my family was, and got first aid."[11]

For his burns he was treated in hospitals for the next several months while his family fled to Czechoslovakia. There, five months later, he rejoined them.[12]

Helmuth's oldest brother, Hans Kunkel, reports, "When the bombing raid of July 28-29, 1943 came, I was working in the harbor. I was working late when the bombs dropped, then walked home. . . . On the way home from work, I saw many dead people and buildings collapsed."[13]

Helmuth's classmate, Lieselotte Prüss Schmidt, had an altogether different experience: She and her family generally went to a regular bunker, located 5 to 10 minutes away by bicycle, but the night of 28 July when the allied bombers attacked, they were caught in their house so they went to the basement. It was reinforced to protect them like a bomb shelter.

Lieselotte's sister, Hilde Prüss Müller, reports, "Through one-inch slits in the concrete we could see "Christmas trees," which were markers that looked liked Christmas trees being dropped from planes to mark where the bombers would drop their loads. Then we would know which neighborhoods would get carpet bombed."[14]

After their own house was hit, they ran outside and watched the house burn. Since their father was mostly crippled from arthritis, someone helped them carry out some of their furniture, including a piano, which they placed in the street for safety. Her father, Richard Prüss, then stated, "So what if we lose the house — save my genealogy." Someone ran back into the house and saved it all. Then her father went back in to check out the damage, when the house collapsed. The second floor fell down burning, straight into the first floor. Hilde recalls seeing her father inside when the second floor crashed down where he was. She did not know for a few moments that in actuality he had jumped back, out of the house, to safety, "But that initial horror stayed with me — I had nightmares for 20 years," she reports.

As her parents and siblings stood side-by-side and stared at the burning house, her mother explained, "So the house burns — we still have the Gospel and our children."

The next morning, Hilde was amazed to find her sister out in the street playing their rescued piano for neighbors and passing strangers. Hilde describes, "That was my little sister, Lieselotte, playing the piano and enjoying life." She played, in fact, *"Freut Euch des Lebens,"* which means, "Enjoy Life!"[15]

As a postscript, Liesellote's son later returned to Hamburg on a Church mission and tracted in their old neighborhood. The people remembered one thing only about his family: "Oh, your mother was the little girl! She played that song in front of her burned-out house."[16]

Meanwhile, Rudi's parents, grandparents, aunts and uncles all lived close together in the city and were all bombed out. Rudi's family fled to his uncle's designated "garden area" in the country. After they arrived, his uncle built a cottage of bricks for them to live in. After the war, Rudi's family moved back into town.

Meanwhile, Rudi's future wife, Herta Schmidt, and her family were not bombed, but just two minutes away one of her brothers had his home bombed. However, at her brother Werner's apartment building, "A bomb landed next to our apartment house," says Werner, "but it didn't go off."[17]

Three brothers were in the Army. Werner was drafted in January 1945 to Western Germany and was taken prisoner by the British.[18]

Back on the home front, meanwhile, Herta's family fretted. There was no news about two of her brothers — her family figured they were MIAs or KIAs — until they returned home at the end of the war for a surprising, joyful reunion. One of these was Werner,[19] who was interviewed for this volume. The other returning prisoner was Gerhard Schmidt. But her third brother, Ernst, was killed in Russia.[20] This was the lad who had accompanied, in uniform, Salomon Schwarz, the Jewish member, to his trial in Berlin as a show of support.

CHAPTER **32**

Days later, Helmuth's stepfather, Hugo Hübener, found Gerhard at his fiancée Waltraud's parents' place and recruited him to help dig through the rubble. While Hugo and Gerhard were digging through the debris, Hugo announced a fact that Gerhard had not known — his mother, Emma, had died.

During the raid, two people had caught fire and, in a state of panic, had dashed into the crowded bomb shelter where his mother was, catching everyone in the shelter ablaze. All were killed.[1]

Two eyewitnesses had seen and reported the incident to Hugo.

Gerhard recalls, "I felt even greater grief now, knowing she was gone also."[2]

Hugo's future is described by Gerhard: "After Mother was killed . . . Hugo married a third time, but had no children from her."[3]

Soon Gerhard had an unexpected encounter.

"A couple more days passed. My girlfriend's father and I rode bicycles back to the apartment where I used to live, to dig through the rubble ["to find some of my things,"[4] he later adds].

"But to no avail. There, Giesela, Helmut's girlfriend, recognized and called for me. We talked for several minutes. We did not talk of the obvious subject — of Helmut — as we both knew he had been executed the previous October 1942. She told me she had finished school at the Army School in communications and was now working for the German Army Intelligence Office. We parted. That was the last time I ever saw her."[5]

Hans' wife, Charlotte Kunkel, summarizes her and Hans' experience after the bombing raid: "My parents' house stayed intact. Hans had built a concrete bomb shelter under the cherry trees. My parents and I were there when the bombing attack came."[6]

She reports that when it was over the first night, "Hans and my dad went to help other people. . . ."[7]

Two days later Hans went to look for his brother, Gerhard.[8] Charlotte remembers, "All he found was the rubble of rocks and bricks."[9]

Meanwhile, Gerhard looked for Hans and Charlotte in order to tell them about Hans' mother and grandparents, but Hans and Charlotte had taken their baby on a train south to Oberfranken for safety, where they stayed with another family. (The government actually sent families with babies south for safety.[10]) Gerhard found only Charlotte's brother and told *him* the news. Her brother then relayed the message to Charlotte's parents. Two months later when Hans and Charlotte returned to Hamburg, her parents told *them*.[11] Obviously those were emotionally draining times for Gerhard, Hans, and their families.

––––––––––

Meanwhile, Arthur Sommerfeld reports what happened to him and his family, Helmuth's "second" family:

After Arthur had been caught out of the air raid shelter and burned, and after joining his family later in Czechoslovakia, he met his future wife in a small Czeckoslovakian village. (See Appendix P for more details of his journey.)

"I would sing as Marie [who lived in the same apartment building] would play the piano in her living room. We were just friends through this period.[12] I worked for the mayor in the village for two years."[13]

His wife Marie continues: "In May 1945 he and his family left, like pioneer settlers. They loaded everything on a little handcart. They went over mountains."[14]

Arthur reports, "I went with my mother and three sisters. We went north with one handcart, for six weeks, to Hamburg."[15] Marie adds, "They lived in vacant houses on the journey."[16] Arthur says, "It was spring, so it wasn't too cold or hot."[17]

Marie remembers, "Arthur's sister Helena got lost on the journey and made her way back to Hamburg alone. She was lucky not to be taken by the Russian soldiers, who tried luring or even taking girls onto their trucks. It took her about nine weeks — she arrived unharmed about three weeks after the rest of the family had arrived."[18] One can only imagine the turmoil Arthur's parents felt as their daughter was lost on the exodus to Hamburg with the Russian army close behind.

Helmuth's Sunday School classmate, Lieselotte Prüss and her sister Hilde meanwhile left their house in ruins and went with their family out of the area, to Posen, in northeast Germany, for about nine months. They lived in a school gymnasium with ten other families, sleeping on straw sacks and taking turns eating with a single spoon for the entire family.

When they returned to Hamburg, they faced a devastated house and no materials or help to rebuild it. Their father was still crippled from arthritis, and their 18-year-old brother, Richard, worked a job during the day. But miracles began to unfold. Thirty Russian POWs came into their neighborhood and began removing the eight feet of rubble, enabling Richard to clear out the basement and first floor. Next, Richard's boss jumped in with a marvelous gesture of generosity — he gave Richard lumber that he secured from the black market. And finally, through grit, they began rebuilding their home. After work on his job each day, Richard labored on the home until extremely late each night, while Hilde and her mother took turns holding a candle so he could rebuild the basement and first floor — but not the second and third floors, which were too damaged. Since Richard would leave soon for the army, he worked feverishly to finish the house. His mother insisted, "Richard, you have to sleep!" But Richard responded, "I will not stop until I can leave with a roof over your head." The whole family meanwhile lived and slept in one unbombed room in the basement — a washroom with a cement floor — until Richard finished the house.

Hilde adds that she never tasted chocolate in her life until someone gave her two tiny pieces during this period. She went out into a field to savor it. On another occasion, she hauled the family typewriter, used for genealogy, to another town to trade it for a sack of potatoes so they could eat. "Because of our experiences," she says, "we learned *gratitude.*"

Before leaving for the army, her brother Richard told his family he would not kill anyone, and also asked the Lord to take him rather than allow him to kill anyone — especially fellow Latter-day Saints. Two months after D-Day, his prayer was granted as he himself was killed in an ambush on the first day of fighting — at the same spot where his father had been taken prisoner during WWI.[19]

In reflecting on the war years, Otto states that they had enough to eat.[20] In fact they didn't even think, during the years of bombing, that they were in danger. "I think we didn't have even time to think about it."[21]

Otto had been an air raid warden and, one night after a raid, "I wanted to go to bed and kneel down by my bed and pray to my Father in Heaven and thank him that I was still safe. But I was so exhausted and tired that I didn't get up from my knees. I fell asleep and slept for hours kneeling by my bed. We were sometimes scared, yes. But as far as worrying that I should die, no."[22]

At one point a bomb exploded in front of his home. "A big oak door fell on top of me and the walls crumbled." Under the rubble, he could not hear because his ears were clogged with dirt, so he thought at first he was dead. "Oh, dying isn't too hard," he mused. "But my thoughts went back to my family," he continues. He wondered if he would be discovered under the rubble. Finally, he clawed his way out.[23]

Otto kept close tabs on his district. He remembers that the brethren stayed in Hamburg for the most part, while the sisters, children, and older people were evacuated to safer parts of Germany and elsewhere.[24] Otto's three children were sent out of the city — two to the border of Czechoslovakia and one to the Beyreuth School.[25] Then they reunited with their family after the war.[26]

Meanwhile, Rudi, Karl, and Düwer were in the prison camp near Hamburg, having a harrowing experience all the way to the 1945 allied victory.

Karl states that he, Rudi, and Gerhard Düwer were transported from their prison outside Hamburg to Poland.

As the Russian army advanced, they were taken back to Germany, but, on the way, ran out of food, so the prisoners had to forage for their own in deserted villages and in the countryside, as the citizenry was fleeing from the oncoming Russian army. With an acumen for survival, and with his friends sick, Karl provided Rudi and Düwer with food — finding farm animals and anything edible along the journey — and in the process almost got shot.[27]

They returned to their prison at Hamburg for a few weeks, then were back on the road again. Suddenly Karl was told, "You're drafted into the army!"

"'Who me?' Then I started laughing," says Karl.

The officer responded, "What's so funny?"

"I said, 'I'm a political prisoner. Can't you see? My back, there's a triangle on there.'

"He said, 'That was yesterday. Today is different.'

"I said, 'Oh no, it isn't. All these years, I was not worthy to fight in the Germany Army. Now, all of a sudden? . . . No way.'

"He said, 'Either you go or we hang you on this tree.' He got mad."

In his interview with the author Karl concludes, "Guess what I did? I went. Three weeks before the war was over!"[28]

Now a bona fide soldier, but not having to report for duty for several hours, Karl went to visit his mother — the first time in years — before his train was to take off for the eastern front. Since his home was bombed out, he found her at a new address. When she saw him standing there, "My mom almost had a heart attack." She asked what happened, he told her, and she exclaimed, "You are not going. The war is over and you are not going."

"I said, 'Mom, I know the war is lost. . . . I cannot take that chance. With any bad luck they come and look for me, if I don't report to the barracks. And if they catch me they hang you next to me,' I said. 'I cannot take that chance.'" [29]

So Karl took the troop train back to the eastern front. Not many days later in Czeckoslovakia, he was captured by the Russians and spirited off to Siberia to a slave labor camp for four years. [30]

Rudi reports his own adventure. "It's kind of a humorous event if you permit me: Three French prisoners broke out [from their prison]. And Hamburg (had) already capitulated in 1945. . . . As luck would have it, they ran into a French attachment of the British army. They [the British army] . . . raced down, opened the gate, opened all our cells and doors, and we stormed the kitchen and it saved us. A big Olaf, a Norwegian kid, said, 'That guard threw a knife at me when I was picking up some potato peelings out of the garbage can.' He took one of those five gallon cans, dipped it into hot pea soup and hit the guard over the head. [It presumably killed him as] he never ate pea soup again." [31]

Rudi adds, "I can still see that English major there firing his pistol in the air saying, 'No riot here. We'll free you if it takes us all night.' He kept his word. . . . But he didn't open the gates or say 'everybody go home.'. . ." [32]

In 1987 he says:

"It took a week [in 1988 he says "a couple of weeks [33]] till they finally sorted everything out, then [came] the permission of officers of the French army, attorneys, juries and judges assigned to the British army — they reviewed every case. . . .[34]

"My turn was next and he said, 'Rudolph, tell me, why did you do it?'

"I said, 'I wanted the rest of the German people to know the real truth.'

"'Jolly good boy,' he said. 'You can go home now.'

"Whew! It was a long trek home. Everything was in disarray. I marched [past] the city and county building, and the center of Hamburg. All the way they bombed out streets. . . . Everything was bombed out about 80%. . . ."[35]

In 1988 he adds, "And so I just kept on marching and I saw the ruins left and right of me, burned-out apartment houses and I thought to myself, 'Gosh, this used to be this street and this used to be that street.' Hard to recognize when everything is in ruins, shambles. All just a pile of bricks. So I kept on marching, and marching, and marching and finally saw the old water tower."[36]

He arrived at a little sports pavilion. "They remodeled [it] into some apartments where my parents said we were staying. I marched across that football field there — a soccer field. All of a sudden a German shepherd dog came towards me, a police-trained dog. He saw me. In his life, I never saw the dog before, yet he didn't know that. That dog recognized me as part of the family — he danced around me and barked and my mother came running."[37] He adds in 1988, "And I heard my mother across the soccer field 'There's Rudi.' And she came running across. It was quite a reunion."[38]

CHAPTER **33**

In 1987 Rudi continues: "You probably wondered how I survived. That's what this warden asked us one time: 'What is it that makes you tick? It has to be something special. Others escaped, committed suicide — tried all kinds of uncanny things. You guys — you got something special.'

"I told him, 'Well, I believe in a living God. And he will bring me home again. I know this for a fact. My grandmother — she told me she asked Heavenly Father, and he told her I will be coming back home.'

"He said, 'I wish I had your faith.'"[1]

Rudi refers to this conversation in 1988 with more details. "I told him that I had a belief in God. He said, 'Well, I was wondering. There had to be something. Anybody else, they would have been broken. Their spirit would have been broken and they would have been just babbling fools.' Insanity is quite often connected with long prison terms and all that. But he said, 'There was something that just kept you going. Now I understand. You believe in God and you have such a strong belief that it carried you through.' Of course, I used the opportunity and taught him the gospel."[2]

He continues his account in 1987: "Later on I was able to testify for this good man — as they [the de-Nazification officials] were taking his job away being a warden in a prison, and I testified that this was a humane man. Three times I found the Gestapo coming into the camp to get us two out and send us to Auschwitz. Three times he found and stopped them and jeopardized his own job. Why shouldn't I stand up now and testify in behalf of this man to save his job, and his life, to get his job back?"[3]

In 1988 Rudi details this incident: "In '45 I met one of the old guards, *Hauptwachmeister* Eckert, a strict man, but a fair man, good man. And he said, 'Wobbe, are you aware of it, that *Oberregierungsrat* Dr. Kruger is on trial? De-Nazification trials.' And I said, 'No.' He said, 'Do you feel like testifying for him?' I said, 'By all means. He was a fair man, he was a good man, by all means.' So I went to the court hearing. I don't think I received a subpoena, I just went there. And I identified myself and I said, 'I was an inmate in the prison and concentration camps where he was the warden and to my knowledge he defended our presence against some Nazi guards,' and I was told later by him that he actually stood his ground against the Gestapo who were trying to put us in the concentration camp, the extermination camp. And so I said, 'In everything he was a fair man. He favored us political prisoners. He never thought that we were criminals and always treated us fair. Even my request to work in the airplane factory which normally would be taboo because of the length of my prison term, because the opportunity to escape was so great there, but I just gave him my word of honor that I wouldn't escape and I was transferred to the airplane factory. So he actually trusted us and treated us like human beings. So I only can say what you're trying to pin on him is unjust, unfair.' . . . The judge said, 'Well, I don't think we have to listen to any more testimonies. That should do it. Case dismissed. This man should be reinstated.' So he was reinstated in the Justice Department. What do you call it here when you study? Criminology. So I think that was his field, as a psychologist. And so, yes, he was able to go back to work."[4]

Rudi did have that opportunity to escape from prison: "We worked with Poles in the airplane factory. While we were at the fortress, I met a man. He had his master's or doctor's degree, working as a common laborer there. Tadenz Dombrowsky was his name. I'll never forget it. And he said he was working for the Polish underground and he could make arrangements for me to escape. I said, 'I don't know. The minute they find out, they will arrest my family in Hamburg. And furthermore, where would I go? Sure, fighting in the Polish underground against the Nazis, fine, but somehow I want to go home, to see my family again.' He said, 'Well, whenever you feel like it let me know.' Then he asked me if I would in my inspection area sabotage those planes. I said, 'No, that I cannot do. It's against my professional integrity. What I do, I do well. What I build is flawless, and furthermore, that might be my uncle that I am killing or one of my relatives that's been drafted into the army or air force.' No. I did everything possible there and I opposed the system, but sabotaging, no, that's against my grain. So he dropped it as such, but said, 'Nevertheless, whenever you want to leave, let me know. I got it all ready for you.'"[5]

Rudi continues with his 1987 account: "I prayed a lot — I learned to pray. I wrestled with Heavenly Father. And promised him, 'Heavenly Father, if you will get me out of this . . . ,' I promised I'd serve him the rest of my life.

"It is the evil one who tells us not to pray. Wasn't it the Twelve Apostles in England, despondent, bare-footed, their heads bowed . . . and prayed? . . . Above them, the Savior was standing, reaching out to come to Him. 'If you will listen to me, and not listen to him telling you not to pray' — because they were so despondent and discouraged, nothing would go right. Let this be a lesson to us always. Always pray. Communicate with your Heavenly Father. Counsel with the Lord in all thy doings. He will guide you. He will direct you. He will bring you out of prisons, he will bring you out of temptation, out of evil places. The only thing is we have to pray to Him."[6]

Rudi's experience, despite being horrific, took him from carefree youthful days to being a dedicated young man in his faith, as he says in his 1987 lecture about his experiences:

"I'd like to bear you my testimony. That I know without a shadow of a doubt that our Heavenly Father is living. He is a loving Father, and his Son, Jesus Christ, the Redeemer of the World — my Redeemer, your Redeemer, your personal Intercessor by the Father in our behalf — speaks for us because He loves us. I know that this church, the Church of Jesus Christ of Latter-day Saints is true, that the Gospel of Jesus Christ is the true gospel that brings us all the happiness in the world if you are only willing to live it. I know that our Heavenly Father answers our prayers. I know this, I experienced it. I'm a living testimony to that. I bear this testimony to you in the name of Jesus Christ, amen."[7]

As for Karl, eventually he was released and came home July 1949.[8] After his return from Russia, Karl admits being in a confused state. He could not work and subsisted on food stamps available to returning prisoners of war. "I asked the questions a lot of times, 'What is harder, to be a prisoner or a free man?' And I had to realize it was harder to be a free man, and after all of these years, I didn't know what to do. . . . I was lost."[9]

He did make one attempt to visit his former employer, but he was dead. And his wife had given the business to his nephew. In any case, Karl was not ready to work again.[10]

"I was restless. I walked, I talked . . . to 2 o'clock in the morning in Hamburg. Mom was crying and she was upset with me. I said, 'I'm sorry.' It took me a long time to snap out of it. . . . Six months, seven months."[11]

He details his transformation. "One Saturday my mom said, 'Tomorrow we go to the organ concert.' And there they played . . . Mendelssohn — beautiful. All the Jewish composers, they were forbidden in Hitler Germany. And then it happened. Right during the concert I broke down. I started crying and then I cried and I cried. After that the healing started very fast. It was a long, long, hard road but I made it.[12]

Karl adds, "Then I started working."[13]

CHAPTER **34**

Meanwhile, Gerhard, after digging through the rubble to find his things, and seeing and talking with Helmuth's girlfriend, wraps up his war chronicle:

"Within a couple more days I had to report to the local army headquarters in Hamburg in civilian clothing, since my uniform was burned. They said I did not have to return to the Russian front, and they gave me a furlough extension of one more month.

"I spent the next month furlough with my girlfriend and her parents."

He then reported for duty at Frankfurt, and several weeks later was given a one-week furlough to get married.

"We got married on the 25th of September 1943. We took a train to Frankfurt so I could report back to duty. On the way, we had a stopover in Berlin for several hours and went to the Tiergarten Strasse zoo, walked around town, and waited awhile at the station for our connecting train to Frankfurt, where we knew we had only a few days together until who knows when? Those were exciting but emotionally tough times.

"There at Frankfurt we rented a small room for three or four days. I had to report for duty during the day, but at nights I would come home to her. That was our honeymoon. Then we went back on the train to Hamburg.

"Two months later, just before Christmas after a short Christmas leave, I was transferred to Italy, and did not see her again until Easter 1946 [2¼ years later].

"In Italy I operated a large transmitter as a communications link with the army headquarters in Belgrade, Yugoslavia and, like in Russia, listened daily to the BBC to learn what was really going on, since the German war propaganda did not tell the people the truth.

"The war finally ended April 5, 1945, in Italy and two days later in Germany. I heard reports of German soldiers trying to return home across the border getting shot down by the hundreds by the German SS. I decided to give myself up to the Allies, as we were supposed to. I stripped off my emblems and rank and went to them in a basic, olive green/gray uniform. They gave us American army uniforms and took us to an internment camp to work, etc., and held us 13 months. I was one of the first discharged and allowed to return home since I had a wife and now a son at that time. Jens was born in July 1944.

"I waited for hours, then took a train with hundreds of others also married, and arrived at the main train station in Hamburg. I took two different buses and arrived at my wife's and in-laws' house. My wife was surprised to see me since I was declared missing in action. She didn't know I was returning and at first did not recognize me, standing there wearing a mustache and a U.S. army uniform with a "POW" stencilled on the back! I was excited to see my son I had never seen: now almost two and a half and running around the house! What a joyous day that was."[1]

Helmuth's family and friends had unique adventures waiting for them after the war — getting back on their feet, fighting through poverty, and excelling both spiritually and occupationally.

———————————

Rudi reports of life right after the war: "I remember the first meeting I went to. It was at Brother Berndt's garden cabin. That's where he actually lived, and that's where we had our meetings, kind of cottage meeting type. I remember when I was able to partake of the sacrament the first time. I just broke down and cried. After three and a half years I was able to partake of the sacrament. And the way I was received, of course Brother Berndt himself and the people that were left there, they weren't the Nazis, they were the solid-core-type Latter-day Saints and it was great. That feeling was just out of this world."[2]

He describes his social life: "And so the young people always traveled, they want to meet other young people. That's how we [Rudi and his wife] met. And oh gosh, we had some good times together. Whatever we could do. I remember we had a little party and social where we brought whatever we had and had a few goodies to eat and danced in the true MIA fashion, you know, good, clean fun, and we were so glad. There were returned soldiers along with those out of the concentration camp. And that's where I met my wife."[3]

Before the war when they were single, Herta and Rudi had seen each other only at district activities, "[We] were not interested in or know each other" at that time, says Herta.

"When Rudi came back from concentration camp, he came to our branch," and, being older and ready for marriage, they got to know each other better.[4]

While in prison Rudi had promised the Lord he would serve a mission if he endured his experience. He kept his word and, when the war was over and the prisoners were released, he served a two-year church mission from 1946-1948.[5] It began as a stake mission, then Max Zimmer converted it to a full-time mission.[6] Rudi had interesting experiences in both proselyting and church welfare, transferring food from the American saints to German saints. His financial support came from his parents, as well as a 200-*Marks*-per-month stipend[7] for his prisoner of war experiences, and 50 *Marks* "or some ration stamps," to buy bread, from his fiancée, Herta Schmidt,[8] to whom he became engaged three weeks before he left. During his mission he was a branch president and, as he reports laughingly, "for lack of qualified members or members *per se*, I was the district president of the Relief Society." (the church's women's organization). He says Otto Berndt had a "chuckle in his voice" when he gave him the calling.[9]

"It sounds like an old cliché, but it truly was the greatest time of my life, especially after that concentration camp."[10]

Rudi's missionary companion was Werner Schmidt — when they had companions — as sometimes they had to work alone, says Werner. Their missions covered the same two-year period. Rudi, Werner, and two others were *Germany's first missionaries* after the war, he adds. Werner's sister was Herta, Rudi's fiancée.[11]

Since he also worked with church welfare, he saw firsthand help from the American saints. "Talk about a wonderful feeling. You could actually feel it. Some of the clothing had little notes in the pockets which said, 'With all our love, your brothers and sisters in Salt Lake City.' It was a special touch, really. You could actually feel the extended hand from across the sea towards the Saints in Germany. Of course, we were enemies in those days at the time of the war. But the forgiving hand or the hand of love and friendship which said, 'We are your brothers and sisters and want to help you. We know you've suffered. You as Saints especially.' And of course, the government took so much for their own relief efforts, so the Saints and the Church had to ship a little bit extra always. So some of it was turned over to the Catholic Caritas and other relief organizations, which was just fine. Our famous dinner was always cracked wheat with a can of peaches and condensed milk over it. That was our feast."[12]

After Rudi's mission, he would return to Hamburg and marry Herta Schmidt 21 January 1949.[13]

Rudi held various church callings before and after his mission, mostly teaching and leadership, including branch president in a town just outside of Hamburg — Luneburg — in which he took an early-morning train or motorcycle 60 kilometers each way on Sundays, plus trips there on other days each week to fulfill his calling. He also worked 48 hours per week and was newly married.[14] He traveled there from 1949 to 1951, where "I had to quite often give the Sunday School lesson, give the talk in sacrament meeting, bless the sacrament."[15]

For Rudi's career in mechanics, he had to first serve a five-year apprenticeship. Some of that was accomplished before his imprisonment; 18 months were actually earned *during* his prison term as a prisoner of war working in an airplane factory. Finally, he completed his apprenticeship making electric forklifts after the war. Then he completed his journeyman's test, and was finally fully paid in the workforce. Meanwhile he and Herta lived in a tiny attic space of her parents' house until they got their own apartment.[16]

CHAPTER **35**

Otto Berndt experienced challenges and miracles while serving his district after the war.

He says "about 60 or 70 percent" of the members had lost their homes in Hamburg, so what he tried to do was to get the people who had been evacuated from Hamburg back into the city. "But first we had to see that we had living spaces for those in Hamburg." He searched for places for them to live. "We tried to get members to crowd a little to see who could take another family in, or if we could find a basement that could be built out and you could place a family in there."

He corresponded with all the members in his district. "I visited them and every month they got a letter from me so that we always were in contact with each of the families. So I knew where every one was in Germany — even in the whole of Germany," meaning, he knew where all the members of his district were, scattered throughout Germany.[1]

Then in 1946 Ezra Taft Benson of the Council of the Twelve came and called him on a mission.[2] While being headquartered in Frankfurt, Otto became close to his mission president, Max Zimmer, who was from Switzerland. Then, Otto got the ball rolling to overturn Helmuth's "excommunication."

In getting to know Zimmer, Otto reflects that Zimmer's attitude influenced his own after the war. Zimmer felt the Saints should have more aggressively opposed Hitler, yet at the time, Otto and other German leaders felt that to oppose the regime would have meant certain extinction; nevertheless in hindsight, Otto admits feeling guilty he did not pursue that path of opposition. (See Appendix Q for more of Otto's hindsight perspective.)

Otto agrees Zimmer was fearless. For example, he explains he "wasn't afraid to go to the headquarters of the British in Hamburg there." (See Appendix R for an amusing experience reflecting Zimmer's fearlessness.)

Otto details the difficulties they faced with food, and the miracles they experienced.

The years after the war is when they hungered.[3] He elucidates, "The British occupation army confiscated every piece of food that we had, and clothing was almost impossible to obtain." His family often went hungry. They found it was harder after the war than during the war to obtain food and clothing.[4] Fuel was especially scarce the winter following the war,[5] which means they went cold.

Conditions were alleviated somewhat when church welfare began arriving in 1947.[6]

When his first mission president, Max Zimmer, was released, Otto was left in charge of the mission for eight or nine months[7] until Jean Wunderlich arrived.

Otto talks about surviving those times. He says the government rationed food, cigarettes, and liquor to people, and he traded his cigarettes and liquor for bread.

He also sold them to sustain himself the first year of his mission.[8]

The first shipment of welfare supplies came from the U.S. while he was still in charge. His wife sent him a telegram, saying they were over-run with clothes. Back in Hamburg they received 52 boxes of clothes.[9] He rushed home and distributed them to all the people of his district, but in the meantime their house was so full that they had to sleep on top of the clothes. "We couldn't find our beds," he remarks, but "it was beautiful."[10]

He says most of the clothes they received were for women, and that they could supply every sister in the district with about ten dresses![11] Otto meanwhile had only one shirt, which had to be washed every night.[12]

Food finally came — cracked wheat, peaches, canned pears, canned honey, lard, some bacon, and condensed milk.[13] "It was marvelous. I remember the first shipment we got in Hamburg. Every person got 50 cans."[14] The process for distribution was simple: The branch president supplied a list of members of his ward, who came to Otto's house to get their food.[15] Later they got it at Altona.[16]

The food and clothing shipments continued until the next year, 1948, when currency reform stabilized the economy.[17]

Until then, very few items were available, and members relied not only on the black market, but their own variation of it — swap meets.[18]

Otto's wife, Frieda, explains that they had this program in not only their branch, but other branches as well: If somebody had something to sell, they would list it on a blackboard, and also list what they wanted.[19] Otto says the system worked for him personally as well — he traded some cotton for light bulbs.[20]

As for the free food being taken advantage of by people, Otto believes as many as 200 locals in Hamburg joined the Church during that short period in order to receive free supplies,[21] but when the economy improved in 1948 they all left — all but one — a Brother Sommer, he says, who remained active in the Church. Thus, the Church's generosity paid off, not only in helping to feed many hungry people — but spiritually, eternally, for that one soul — although during that period Otto opposed the policy of giving supplies so liberally. However, his mission president, Jean Wunderlich, wisely overrode him.[22]

Otto talks of the difficult choice he had to make in accepting a mission call from Ezra Taft Benson. "I hesitated. I told him right away, 'President Benson, I can't go. Take a look at my house. The house isn't finished and my family with seven children are there and some are very young. . . . You see this dirt floor, and the roof isn't finished. I can't go.' And he said, 'Brother Berndt, we need you. We need you desperately in Frankfurt.' And he said, "I promise you in the name of the Lord, if you accept this mission and when you come back from your mission your house will be finished with everything you planned to do on that house, and it will be a comfort for your family.' And my wife, she sided with President Benson. She said, 'If the Lord told you to go you have to go.' So I decided to go and went on my mission. . . .

"There came this Brother [Jack] Hutchinson in. He was an officer on one of the liberty ships, and he came from New York with a load of corn to Bremerhaven for the American army there. . . . In the middle of the ocean they got a cablegram that they should change their course and go to Hamburg with that corn. So they came to Hamburg. The captain didn't know why, but they obeyed orders and brought the shipment to Hamburg. The first thing that Hutchinson did was [he] went to the headquarters of the occupation army and asked if there are Mormons. And they had my name and my address as district president of the district. So he came. And he came about a couple of days before I was ready to go to Frankfurt. . . . We weren't home, but the children were home. They told us there was an officer in his white uniform. It was amazing for the children. They couldn't believe that. And I didn't believe it either. But he came, then with an interpreter, and introduced himself and I invited him for Sunday to the meeting place. We talked a little bit about it.

"At the meeting place I had my farewell . . . but he didn't know that it was my farewell. And we had one chicken left and we invited him, and I thought, 'How foolish to invite this American for our chicken dinner.' One chicken with nine persons, he was the tenth. But he came. And then he asked,

'What's the occasion?' And with my little bit of English I told him that I had to go on a mission and to be honest I don't know how to get there. And even I don't know where to live. I don't have any money or anything. So he said he would come back after a couple of hours.

"He came back and had a big trunk."

As Otto tells his story, Frieda clarifies it was a "suitcase," but Otto states, "No, that was no suitcase. That was so big and full of food. All what they had in the pantry there [at the navy kitchen]. He brought that and the children had something to eat. Then he emptied his pocket, and I guess it was . . . 700 *Marks*. I said, 'Where did you get that?' He said, 'I got it at the quartermaster and asked him for some cigarettes.' He took the cigarettes in his uniform and sold them on the black market to give me that money. And then he told me the story about it, that the shipment was for the United States Army in Bremen, but they got that call to bring it to Hamburg. And he said, 'Brother Berndt, I know that that was inspired by the Lord.'

"And then he said, 'And I promise you, Sister Berndt, that I write to my wife. I have not much, and we have three boys, and we have not too much. We are not rich. She will tell that in Relief Society and the Relief Society sisters will help you, and they will send you every month a package. I tell them that they should put one carton of cigarettes and a pound of coffee in it. Then they send you some food to make a package. Thus you can sell or trade it in for what you are in need of.'"[23]

Frieda continues their account. She says the family sent the package "every month." She adds, "And one month . . . I was so down. The house wasn't finished and then all this work to do and with seven children at home. And I had to rest that time. I had a nervous breakdown, and the doctor ordered that I had to rest every afternoon at least a half hour. I said, 'I have not the time to rest a half hour.' She said, 'You can do more after you have rested.' I had a woman doctor. And I did. I laid down, and this day I laid down, the same lady who was telling me that they would break in our house years before, she was in my house and did the washing that day for me."[24]

The dirt floor and unrepaired roof were evidently fixed, as Otto says that Ezra Taft Benson's promise was fulfilled.[25]

Otto says the Jack Hutchinson family followed through on Jack's promise for two years.[26] Frieda adds that her daughter, who spoke English, wrote the Hutchinson family every month, thanking them for their help. "Then as my husband came back from his mission he wrote a letter over and told them that his mission is finished and thanked them for all the things, and that we need not the help, he is home now."[27]

Otto then served a second mission shortly afterwards, until 1951, as Jean Wunderlich was released. Otto states, smiling, "And I begged him, I said that he should never mention my name to that new mission president because I'd like to stay home now for awhile."[28]

After his second mission, he was determined to stay in Germany, but could not find work anywhere. He was told he was too old — by now he was 48. Just when he thought he finally got a job, he was told it went to a younger man. So he decided to follow the advice of his now-departing mission president, Jean Wunderlich — to emigrate[29]

But he needed another miracle. He had to sell their house for ship passage money. He was frantic two weeks before they were supposed to leave to the U.S. — as they still could not sell their house. "It was impossible because people didn't have money. We needed the cash for that house and it was impossible to find somebody." Then at the last moment, it sold — two weeks before their departure.

But he needed a second miracle. And he helped to fulfill this one himself. The days ticked away and they still had not been paid for the house, but a week before they were to leave, they were paid. They hurried down to the ship's office to secure passage on the boat — but it was now sold out. The only place to stay was in a hotel because the family who bought their house had already moved in.

Since the next ship would not leave for another four weeks, all their money would be consumed by hotel bills and there would be none left for tickets on the next ship. They checked into a hotel and stewed over their predicament. It was six days before their boat was supposed to leave . . . then five . . . then four. Finally, with three days left before the boat was to launch, Otto got an idea. He marched down to the ship's ticket office once again.

"And that was the first time I did bribe a person. . . . I put 50 *Marks* in the envelope and I told him my condition. I said, 'Sir, we have to have a place on that boat.' And I gave him that letter. He wanted to open that, and I said, 'Don't do it, there is something in it and you go in a closet or somewhere to look in the letter.' And he came back and he said, 'Mr. Berndt, I will do my best.'"

They heard nothing the rest of the day. Or the next. It was now one day before they were to leave, and they were now even 50 *Marks* poorer . . . when suddenly they got a telegram from the employee at the ticket office.

They rushed down there. Otto says, "He found a place for the whole family."[30] An American family had decided to delay its trip for another month, due to illness, so Otto's family got a first class cabin.[31]

CHAPTER **36**

Of Helmuth's family of believers — those friends closest to him, the St. Georg branch of the Church of Jesus Christ of Latter-day Saints — approximately 120 of its 180 members were killed in the bombing raids, primarily the first night.[1]

Despite the onslaught of war, the Saints kept up their dedication to the Church. Otto reflects that attendance during the early part of the war had been excellent — "about 200" — but it dwindled some when the bombers came the last part of the war.[2] Nevertheless, they stayed "on the program" with their meetings.[3]

"I never saw so much unity at any time as during the war," he states.[4]

Otto adds, "People shared more," and gives this example: "In 1942 there was a branch in Essen. They had the first air raid there and most of the people lost their belongings. I asked the families in our branch to look in their closets and find clothes. But I told them right away, 'We want good ones. They lost everything. What they need is what they can use right away.' We had brethren who had two overcoats and they gave the best one away and kept the old one."[5]

After the war, as they reconstructed their lives, the St. Georg Branch members found spiritual strength and continued unity in their fellowship with each other as they attended a new branch.

Herta Schmidt Wobbe says, "The Altona Branch was the only one left standing after the bombing. There were two branches in Hamburg right after the war — the Altona Branch and the Barmbeck Branch."

The Barmbeck Branch actually met in Herta's apartment — before she was married to Rudi — as her father was still branch president.

And after the war, just as before, life pretty much centered around the Church with the same meeting schedule[6] — Marie Sommerfeld states, "Mondays had Relief Society and Priesthood, Wednesdays had Mutual, Friday was Choir, and Sunday had morning Sunday School and evening Sacrament Meeting."[7]

No doubt Anton Huck saw the error of his political leanings. Arthur Zander likely did as well, as he would later write Rudi about it, as mentioned below. As for Huck, Rudi says, "I must hand it to that man, he was devoted to his call. He rode the coal trains, open wagons, railroad cars, dirty coal trains by standing up all the way from Frankfurt to Hamburg just to preside over a conference, district conference."[8]

Then later it was changed. Max Zimmer from the Swiss Mission was made mission president and he said, "We better get organized."[9]

A small handful of Saints likely never saw the error of their ways. Otto reports that after the war, apparently before Jacobi became inactive, "I got my satisfaction out of this Brother Jacobi, who [had] said he would report me to the Gestapo after the war. I was in the Altona Branch, in our meeting place there, and he came and asked me, 'Do you still belong to this church?' I said, 'Yes, I do.' He told me, 'How could you? The missionaries in their airplanes came over Germany and destroyed our cities and everything.' I said, 'Your mind is closed about this. Can't you remember who brought this war upon us? It was your friend Hitler. He was the one. If you lost your home and everything you had, you should complain about him, not about the missionaries who came over here. I'm glad we lost the war. I am so glad for that. You can believe me about that. The lecture I got from the Gestapo in their interrogation with me showed me the future of this church in Germany. I know what they would have done with it.'

"There are people who have closed their minds against all that was true and who will believe only what they believed then, and all the others were wrong. They are the ones who would follow another Adolph Hitler again, even if they saw everything in black and white before them."[10]

Nevertheless, Otto adds, "I couldn't point out anybody right now who still lives in the Nazi past."[11] He indicates that the only ones to have complained about the American bombings were Jacobi, who he felt, as stated, was not Nazi, along with a small number of non-Nazis, and the "few Nazis" themselves.[12]

Otto summarizes, "Even after the war they looked suspiciously upon me. I told them in many of my speeches, 'You should be grateful that we lost that war. That is one of the greatest blessings Father in Heaven has bestowed upon us.'"[13]

But it was met "with a grain of salt," as some or most of the Saints were thinking, "How did he know that?"[14]

———————————

Gerhard gives his postwar report:

"From 1946-1948 we were in the Altona branch of the church, where most of the surviving St. Georg members were living. . . .

"In my first branch after the war were the Sommerfelds, Rudi Wobbe, Arthur Zander, Frederich Peters, and our new branch president, Otto Berndt, among about 60 of the St. Georg Branch members who survived.

"At the Spring Conference in 1948, the mission president, Jean Wunderlich, assigned Arthur Zander and myself to organize and head up a new branch, the Wilhelmsburg Branch, with about 50 members at first, but which doubled by the time we emigrated to the U.S. four years later. At this time I was set apart as the second counselor and Zander as the branch president. The subject of my brother was taboo: We never discussed it.

"Karl Schnibbe returned from his labor camp in Russia to that branch. Rudi also joined us in that branch, as well as the above-mentioned people, all of whom had been at the St. Georg branch before the war.

"The St. Georg branch of the church had been like a family to Helmut and to me. We were all very close and loved each other greatly."[15]

Much can be said for Karl's character, reuniting and accepting the handful of church members from before the war who were Nazis — especially after he had suffered years of imprisonment at the hands of the Nazis. Karl attained a high degree of acceptance, charity, and peace of mind over his trials. In a side note, he is quite certain that Arthur Zander never reported them. "No, he did not. He had no idea himself and whatever he did [in supporting the Nazis] I forgave him a long time ago." Karl adds, "When I came home I saw him quite often in church."[16]

After the war, in a strong statement of support for Karl's resistance, Otto Berndt approached Karl one day and commented, "Karl-Heinz, if I would have known what you guys were doing I would have joined."[17]

As for their old friendships, Karl saw Rudi at church "every Sunday" and at church get-togethers, church dances, and trips, but Rudi was now married with small children and busy with his new, young family.[18] Despite their new directions in life, the Church was the glue that held the fabric of their previous associations together. "The Mormon

Church in the mission field is like a big family," says Karl. "It is much closer. I enjoyed it tremendously. . . . If I could turn the clock back, that is what I miss . . . the associations."[19]

Being single, Karl found a great deal in common with Gerhard Düwer just after the war, despite the fact he was imprisoned due to Düwer's panicking and not consulting with Helmuth. "Gerhard is a nice guy. I forgave him too, you know. It was a dangerous time. *No*, I forgave him. It was no problem."[20]

Interestingly, Düwer "was always a little reluctant to talk about it . . . I mean the details. He helped Mohns get a leaflet . . . it bothered him . . . that's why he never participated in any get-togethers in Hamburg when the government invited him. He always declined . . . so I never put him on the spot or made him feel bad."[21]

He continues, "When I came home from Russia, we became good friends." Their former resistance activities with Helmuth (although separate from each other), coupled with their prison experiences and survival treks to avoid the Russian army, united them in a unique way. Karl adds that he saw him at least four times per week until Karl came to the U.S. two and a half years later. "We went out to eat, we went to the movies, we went dancing." They were single and "had a good time." He adds that Düwer was not interested in the Church, however.

One church member, John Albert Dahl, reports talking to both Rudi and Karl at church in Germany after the war and knowing them both as active members."[22]

Likewise, Otto Berndt, Jr., finally got to know Karl and Rudi after the war. He saw them at church regularly, and found them faithful and active.[23] Before Karl and Rudi's imprisonments, Otto, Jr., was in his early teens and thus was in a different group. But after the war, "I got along with them well."[24]

Arthur and Marie Sommerfeld report of their married life in Hamburg, living near Rudi and Herta. Marie remembers, "We lived in the same apartment complex. Herta would come see me. Our babies were about the same age. We'd visit each other at each other's apartment about once a week and run into each other at the store."[25]

Arthur adds, "Back in Hamburg — the war was now over — I worked for an expedition firm at the harbor docks, checking loads that came from trains and ships."[26]

He would continue this work after the war, from 1945-1947,[27] then he married Marie in 1948.[28] They remained in Hamburg as he worked for an insurance company, and finally they emigrated in 1953[29] to the U.S. with all his family — except one sister,[30] who remained in Germany.

Gerhard Kunkel summarizes his years after the war. "I worked as a subcontractor rebuilding electrical control panels in various manufacturing plants, etc., at about six places for the next six years."[31]

But life was difficult for them all.

CHAPTER **37**

Rudi details, "In the '50s Germany was dead. . . . We hardly could survive. We did hard work and all this. I wanted Germany to revive, yes, in the true democratic sense. Oh yes, I attended political rallies and all that. I wanted to do my part, but somehow I had loftier thoughts and desires. I wanted to chance it over here. . . . We had about 20 members that emigrated at the same time."[1]

They were all from Hamburg, heading to Salt Lake City. The journey was an adventure by itself. Rudi and his wife, as all Hamburg emigrants, bid friends and family *adieu* at church and on the dock. Then as the ship steamed across the Atlantic, Rudi was their branch president on the open seas. He told them, "Do not think that we are going to a true Zion. Maybe we have to find Zion here [in the U.S.], it's in the midst of Babylon."[2]

"On the first of July, we arrived in New York harbor five o'clock in the morning, through the fog — the air was coming out of the water. And I was afraid that we might miss the date with this grand old lady that stands there on Liberty Island. I pressed my eyes to the porthole there, and I couldn't see a thing. All of a sudden the sun broke through and a ray of sunlight illuminated the Statue of Liberty, and I couldn't help thinking about this first: '. . . your tired, your poor, your huddled masses yearning to be free, the wretched refuse of your teeming shore. Send these, your homeless, tempest-tossed, to me. I lit my lamp beside the golden door.' We were quite overcome with emotions, and the four of us — that is, my sweet wife and two oldest girls, Angelika and Evelyn — we knelt down in our cabin and praised our Heavenly Father in thanks, that He brought us into this free county, which is choice above all other nations."[3]

Rudi, his wife, and two daughters took a bus from New York to Salt Lake City and, thoroughly exhausted from a bus schedule mix-up and lack of sleep, they finally arrived at the bus station just west of the temple.[4]

Rudi states with a smile, "For us, the Fourth of July, 1953 was the arrival here in Salt Lake City. And the people of Salt Lake, they liked us so well they gave us a fireworks display, and they've been celebrating ever since." Despite their exhaustion, they wanted to see how America celebrated, and went to their first July Fourth fireworks display that same night.

They lived at his brother-in-law Gerhardt Schmidt's place for a month and got a job at McGee and Hogan as a machinist, riding a bicycle to work.[5] But he worked nights, till 2 A.M.,[6] which caused him to miss out on life. "My family went every night and visited somebody and I couldn't go because I had to work. That bothered me quite a bit."[7] So he found work where he could have his nights free with his family.[8] Then they lived in their own apartment, sharing a house with Herta's other brother, Werner Schmidt, on Almond Street near the capitol[9] where "many more" of the St. Georg Branch immigrants lived[10] until they became more affluent and moved to larger homes in other sections of town. In September of 1956 they bought a home in Rose Park . (See Appendix S for Rudi's trials and triumphs once in the U.S.)

Meanwhile, Herta's brother Werner also married in 1949 and immigrated to the U.S. in 1951.[11] Herta and Rudi lived with Werner and his family awhile.[12]

A fellow employee at Rudi's first place of work was German, and translated for him,[13] but he was desirous to learn the language quickly, so he mostly stayed away from the German branch and attended the English-speaking ward in his neighborhood and integrated himself mainly with Americans. He did attend missionary reunions for decades and the Hamburg Club for awhile,[14] and also belonged to a German thespian group, *Das Deutsche Theatre*, but had to stop when he began shift work at Galighers.[15] After six years he became a citizen.[16]

His father-in-law, Herta's father, the former branch president of Barmbeck Branch during the war, came to the U.S. in about 1957 and was in the German branch.[17]

Rudi's trade in the U.S. was as a machinist at Galigher's in Salt Lake City for over 30 years, and later as a supervisor of the maintenance department. He had also worked one to two years elsewhere as a machinist.[18]

"Rudi had nightmares for decades over his experiences," says Herta. She often would awaken him, but the nightmares became less frequent as the years went by.[19]

Rudi details these dreams: "Oh, it lasted for quite a while. And at night, I couldn't sleep with an open door. I had to be locked in, you know, phobia. And still I'm walking down the streets, especially when I was released and walking towards Rothenburgsort from the center of town from the *Rathaus* [city hall] which they named Adolph Hitler Platz in those days. Anyway, I always looked back, I was afraid of a guard . . . running after me to put me back in there. So I had those nightmares that I woke up in a cold sweat, that I was in the concentration camp again and it's the Tall Paul in his black SS uniform who was beating upon me, or I remember the trial, the shock we received and the blood-red robes, the judges. Then the flashback of Helmuth and how we cried in each others' arms, the last embrace and all those things that haunted me for a long time."[20]

In dealing with those dreams, emotions, and memories, he adds, "Sometimes when I give a fireside talk it kind of wells up and I choke and break down, but otherwise my mission really helped me in that respect."[21]

Facing minimal conflict after the war, one time in the early 1970s, after he had a piece written about him by a columnist named Steve Hale in *The Deseret News*, Rudi received a phone call from a man with a German accent who simply said, "Traitor!" and hung up.[22] Certainly a far cry from life in the Gestapo interrogation rooms, but unneeded distress nevertheless. Otherwise, he never noticed anyone in the German community in the U.S. or Germany who disassociated themselves from him.[23]

He gives one account of dealing with misunderstanding once in the U.S. "I was working with a fellow who was kind of deranged, a jack-Mormon [not practicing]. He turned the light out and followed astrology. If the stars didn't say that it was a safe day for him to ride an automobile to work, he walked. Loony, in other words. Anyway, all of a sudden he handed me a bunch of pamphlets, anti-Semitic, anti-Black, and I said, 'Wait a minute, I'm not going to distribute those. That's just what I got away from over there in Germany. Absolutely not.' He said, 'You must be a Communist.' I said, 'If that's what it takes to be a Communist, I guess I'm a Communist then.' That guy turned me in to the FBI. . . . It was in the '50s. . . . Of course, I was reinvestigated. You know, you get investigated over there before you apply for your visa anyway, to emigrate. So oh, they asked Karl Schnibbe and the fellows I worked with and this one and that one, what kind of a guy I was, was I a Communist. . . . They couldn't find anything that I was a Communist; then I probably was a Nazi. They came to Karl Schnibbe and he said, 'Are you crazy? He spent three and a half years in a concentration camp by the Nazis.' So I finally was cleared. We studied the Constitution and everything, and applied for citizenship and got it."[24]

He says the day he was "sworn in" as a U.S. citizen was "the greatest day of my life." He further details, "I told my boss about it and he called me in and called me 'Mr. America.'"[25]

After living a full, productive and faithful life, Rudi Wobbe died of cancer ten days short of age 66 — on 31 January 1992.[26]

Marie Sommerfeld, Arthur's wife, reminisces, "After emigrating to the U.S. we'd see the old St. Georg Branch friends mainly at the German church meetings the first two years in the U.S. Other than that, we'd see them usually only at weddings and funerals. And we still do."[27]

As for the U.S. meetings, Marie states, "We lived where Deseret Gym is now [since replaced by the LDS Conference Center]. We'd walk to Temple Square. After about two years, when we had too many kids to enable us to go, we quit going to the German meetings and just went to our local ward. We saw Arthur's mother and sisters several times per year on special occasions."[28]

Regarding family life in the U.S., Marie recalls that they lived on Almond Street a short while. "We would visit at each other's houses once in a while. . . . We saw Arthur Zander at the usual gatherings as well."[29]

Charlotte Kunkel adds that once in the U.S. the old St. Georg Branch people would have "a couple parties" and "a costume ball."[30]

Gerhard summarizes, "In 1952 we came to the U.S. and for the next nine years we saw many of our old German friends every month at the Assembly Hall on Temple Square where a service was conducted in the German language. About 1,200 German members came at first but over the years it dwindled to several hundred. When we moved to Idaho in 1961 we quit going. When we did attend [until we moved] we saw the Zanders, Rudi, Karl, the Sommerfelds, and others who had known Helmut growing up. We had one St. Georg branch reunion in the 1980s, where about 40 attended. Friedrich Peters, who remained in Germany, came for the occasion from Germany. We have never been involved socially with our old friends except those once-a-month meetings on Temple Square and the one reunion."[31]

The Hans Guertler family also emigrated in late 1950. But their two children — Klaus and Resa — had to come to the U.S. a half year later due to the fact they had been members of the German Young Folk — even though they'd been conscripted (against their will) in their early teens![32]

The Richard Prüss family also emigrated — in 1951. Hilde, seven years younger than Lieselotte, was single when she came to the U.S. and even dated a man whose father had bombed Hamburg! She also met three other men over the years who admitted they had bombed her city: Two were employees in retail stores who, upon hearing her accent, asked where she was from, then admitted regretfully they had bombed her city. The fourth was her Sunday School teacher in her 17th Ward in Salt Lake City. He took her aside, learned where she lived in Hamburg when her house was bombed, realized *he had bombed her house* on 28 July 1943, and then, with heartfelt sincerity, he asked for her forgiveness, which she granted.[33]

Her sister, Lieselotte, met only one man who had bombed Hamburg. He belonged to her ward in Salt Lake City — and also apologized.[34]

Once in Utah, Otto Berndt was quickly employed — in direct contrast to his heart-breaking attempts and near-misses after his two missions in Germany, just before he emigrated with his family. He worked eight years at the Utah Pickle Company and another 14 for the Church Historian's Office. "And in 22 years I was not one day out of work, not one day. One of the greatest blessings I got here."

Otto and his wife went on two missions back to Germany — to Kassel and Bremen.[35]

Karl reports that he emigrated to the U.S. in January 1952, first staying a couple weeks with his aunt on Long Island. He did not like New York at all. He wondered why he had left Hamburg. But "the minute I came to Salt Lake I fell in love with the city. And with my skill I had a job just like that."[36]

He was an artisan on the fine touches to elaborately constructed buildings, including the state capitol, the Celestial Room of the Los Angeles temple, the Salt Lake Symphony Hall, and his latest job — the Jordan River Temple in Salt Lake Valley. At first he worked for a German company, but has through the years always maintained the status of an independent contractor.[37]

Once in the U.S. he and Rudi got together only occasionally because Rudi had a big family by this time, and both men were busy with their careers; but later on, when they were both retired, they got together regularly, at least once a week, for lunch.[38] He describes their relationship. "Good friends . . . very close."[39] When he had his knee surgery and his wife had to go to school, "Rudi came every morning to me and sat with me there."[40]

Still living in Salt Lake City are Rudi's widow, Herta Wobbe, her brother Werner Schmidt, Richard Prüss's daughters — Lieselotte Prüss Schmidt and Hilde Prüss Müller, Karl Schnibbe, Gerhard and Waltraud Kunkel, Hans and Charlotte Kunkel, Otto Berndt, Jr., Klaus Guertler and his sister Resa Guertler Frey, and others Helmuth knew and loved. Helmuth's third close friend, Arthur Sommerfeld, and his wife Marie passed away since their interviews with the author and before this volume was published. Otto Berndt, Sr., died in 1995.

CHAPTER **38**

Helmuth's story lay in relative obscurity for 20 years after his death — until 1962 — when the group was rediscovered. A German researcher named Ulrich Sander wanted to become a journalist, so he interviewed Helmuth's schoolteacher and classmates, as well as some of his friends from the St. Georg Branch. Sander states, "I was continually writing articles about this group. And from then on, this story wouldn't let go of me."[1]

One of his articles was discovered by noted German novelist Gunter Grass, who became a Nobel laurete in 1999. In the 1960's he wrote a novel, *Örtlich Betäubt* [*Local Anaesthetic*], that was clearly based on Helmuth and his group. Grass states that Helmuth's contribution to the resistance is "what was important to me."[2] Sander states that Grass's novel deals with getting the Nazi problem and resistance efforts, such as Helmuth's story, out to the younger generation, despite the older generation's not wanting to talk about it, and it deals with the resulting tension between the generations.[3]

After the war, Helmuths' legacy received some attention in Germany, while in the U.S. little has been reported of him — certainly nothing in the dramatic film media [as yet] has been portrayed. In 1979 the play *Hübener* was written by Thomas Rogers and produced by Brigham Young University, which was restaged at BYU in 1992 and by Rogers in Bountiful, Utah in 2003, while another play about the Hübener group was written and produced by attorney David Anderson in Salt Lake City[4] in the early '80s.

Rudi says the BYU play was basically Karl's version, as he was the "correspondent" to the playwright on it, and that the project was unknown to Rudi at the time until it was produced. He says it was a "very touching drama with some literary license," which to some patrons pits Hübener in a large manner against his branch president — even though Zander knew nothing of Helmuth's resistance activities.

Rudi says nonetheless the play *Hübener* was "very well received." He states that he and Karl received numerous invitations after that from BYU student groups and that they spoke at firesides and seminars. He adds in 1988 that, after many years, he and Karl are still speaking at firesides.

As for the first play, the one produced first at BYU, Rudi expounds, "We were asked to stand, especially on the 27th of October when it played, the execution date of Helmuth. We were asked to stand there in a silent tribute to Helmuth. Karl and I were standing there [at the end of the play], and they used a spotlight on an empty spot on the floor. It was supposed to be Helmuth and so on. It was done very well, very dramatic." (The author was in attendance on that night as well, learning about Helmuth for the first time.)

The play grew by word of mouth and sold out every performance. By popular demand, the play was extended additional weeks, where every performance continued to sell out. However, after the final performance, BYU's president, Dallin H. Oaks, called a halt to the play, and this caused some consternation among many cast members who had plans for touring with it to LDS areas throughout the U.S., just as the very successful LDS play, *Saturday's Warrior* had done.

Some were confused as to why, and Rudi would someday learn. In the meantime, the script was filed away, and no one could receive permission to restage it, including attorney David Anderson in Salt Lake City, who attempted to obtain the script from BYU [in 1983 or 1984, says Rudi[5]] for the purpose of restaging in Salt Lake City. Consequently he wrote his own script, which was staged by Walk-ons theatrical company in an old chapel on First South and Ninth West.

Rudi says Anderson's production played for quite awhile there, then he and Karl had radio interviews on KALL and another talk station. "We had *Take Two* on Channel 2 television, and I think Carol Mikita came to my home and interviewed me. So there were several public exposures. And then somehow the AP got ahold of it and wrote something. That, of course, went worldwide, and they got ahold of it over in Germany. Then we received a request from the VVN [television network] if they could get a script. They were planning on the 60-year memorial service and so I sent them the script, and somehow it was too churchy for them. They didn't use it. But in the meantime we had an interview with this reporter from the *Sunday Times* of London. . . . He interviewed David Anderson, the playwright, Professor Tobler from the BYU, and myself. And we told them the true story. . . . The article that appeared in the *Times*, it was atrocious. We were very upset.

"All three of us contacted the reporter and raked him over the coals, for what he actually had written wasn't what we told him. He said, 'Well, my editor kind of sensationalizes.' I said, 'Editor, my foot. What kind of a backbone do you have? It's just lies and distortions.' And then somehow there came an article out in the *Deseret News* or the *Tribune*, I'm not quite sure. Somebody [apparently a local newspaper writer] was trying to get ahold of the Public Relations Department of the Church and got through to President Monson [at that time of the Quorum of the Twelve]. And he was absolutely misquoted, which I found out later. But what I read in the paper really got my dander up."

Rudi's bishop wanted Rudi to straighten out the matter directly with President Monson so there would be no ill feelings towards Church authorities. Rudi says his complaint was that President Monson was quoted as saying, 'We don't want to dig up old skeletons,' and 'Who can sort it out now, we don't want to be bothered with it,' and, 'Who knows what is true?'" Rudi adds, "And that really got me upset."

So Rudi's stake executive secretary, who knew President Monson, told Rudi, "Yes, you can talk to him. He's a fellow you can talk to. He's not high and mighty."

Rudi met with him. "I came out of that meeting feeling entirely different. Of course, I accused him of being a Nazi sympathizer. He said, 'Wow, Brother, you go right for the throat, don't you?'' I said, 'Well, I say what I feel.' And I said, 'I'm quite disturbed about it, that the Church is actually trying to downgrade us. Everybody else is impressed and accepts us as heroes. I'm not looking for praise or anything else. We did what we did, what we believed in. But nevertheless, we could use a pat on the shoulder from the Church.' He said, Brother Wobbe, I don't know of any Nazis. I don't want to know of any. I know a lot of good German people. I was a bishop,' and he named several names. I said, 'Oh, I know all of them.' So he said, 'Absolutely not. What makes you think so.' We talked about it. He said, 'Let me tell you something. . . .'"

Rudi says in 1988 that enough years had passed that the sensitive nature of his conversation was over (since the collapse of the Berlin Wall, leaving East Germany no longer an issue). Thus, he could obviously divulge the problem that some felt towards Helmuth's, Rudi's, and Karl's stories. President Monson told him about the temple in Friberg that was to be built, and asked him to keep it quiet. He told him it was important for the Saints to have a temple there and to be able to do the work for their kindred dead. "'For that reason,'" Rudi says he was told, "'we are trying to put a damper on your story. We admire your courage and all this, but just picture a firebrand like you in East Germany, it would ruin everything that we've worked for all these years. That is why. What would you have done?'"

Rudi continues, "I said, 'Exactly what you are doing.' He said, 'When the prophet of the Church calls me in as he did you, there's only one thing: "Yes, sir."'" Then the nicest thing, the personal touch was, he said, 'Well, since you had to wait so long to get ahold of me' — I realized he was a very busy man — he said, 'Maybe I'll give you a copy of *Be Thine Own Self*,' or one of his books. He signed it and gave it to me, and we shook hands. And he said, 'Oh, that's not good enough,' and he gave me a bear hug, both of us having tears in our eyes as we parted. I must say he's a great man."[6]

Other books and plays have been written about Helmuth. In Germany, Alan Keele notes that Helmuth plays important roles in not only Grass' novel, but his play *Davor (Up Tight)*, which has been seen on West German, Swiss, and Austrian television; and Paul Schalluck's radio play, *Helmuth Hübener*, which was heard throughout Germany. "Hübener-types" [fictional figures clearly based on him[7]] also occur in works by [Nobel-laureate Heinrich] Boll, Rolf Hochhuth, and others [who were among the "engaged writers of the German Group of 47."][8] At Berlin's Plotzensee prison, visitors are given a booklet that portrays a photo and short write-up about Helmuth's life.[9] Rudi's autobiographical account was published as *Before the Blood Tribunal* in 1992, shortly after Rudi died. It was co-authored by Rudi Wobbe and Jerry Borrowman and published by Covenant Communications. the 172-page book was retitled *Three Against Hitler* in 1995.

The first U.S. book about Karl's involvement with the group was published in 1984. Titled *The Price*, it was co-authored by Alan Keele, Douglas Tobler, and Karl Schnibbe. At 136 pages, it was abridged and edited down considerably from Karl's original interviews, and is out of print.

A similar volume by the authors was printed in Germany.

Still in print is a much more expanded and enhanced version of Karl's account that was published in 1995 as *When Truth Was Treason*. This 456-page book uses the more complete interviews with Karl and has hundreds of fascinating notes, including translations of all the original Nazi documents involved. The work is compiled, translated, and edited by Blair R. Holmes and Alan F. Keele, with a foreword by Klaus J. Hansen. Originally published by the University of Illinois Press, it was acquired in November 2003 by the Academic Research Foundation, which will republish the book under a different title and redesign it sometime in 2004 or 2005. (Until then, copies of the original *When Truth Was Treason* are available only by mail order, as noted in the back of this volume.)

In December 2002 Brigham Young University finished a one-hour documentary, *Truth & Conviction*, produced by Rick McFarland and Matt Whitaker, and written and directed by Matt Whitaker, about the Hübener group, mainly from Karl's perspective. By design, it consisted almost solely of interviews, and aired on KBYU-TV several times in 2003.

More media productions will likely focus on Helmuth Hübener and his group.

CHAPTER **39**

As for Helmuth's extended "family," his fellow St. Georg Branch members, life in the U.S. continued to show their closeness.

Herta Wobbe says she and Rudi went to Germany only twice. The first time was to pick up their daughter who was returning from a Church mission in 1978, and the second time was in January 1985 — for the occasion of the city of Hamburg's dedication of the youth center in Helmuth's name, which Karl also attended.[1]

It was on this trip that Karl first learned of Helmuth having a girlfriend. In an interview with the author Karl states, "He had his eye on someone that we found out later. But he never talked about girls. . . . When we had the get-together in Hamburg [at Helmuth's 50-year commemoration sponsored by the city in 1992] there came a lot of stories . . . they said he liked one girl."[2]

Rudi states he did not want to return to Hamburg, but his daughter talked him into it. His reason for not wanting to return: "I'm satisfied here and I don't want to tie into old memories again." But she prevailed, wanting to meet her relatives and see Hamburg.[3]

As for his second trip, Rudi remembers, "We visited these places of our incarceration. I still remember this place. But I saw it, and it's what you call a flashback. I see this SS guard jumping on top of me, beating and kicking me. Then this one prisoner was about 16 years of age — right out of childhood — and he pulled me aside and shoved me behind his back and just disappeared, and became a part of the wall. . . . That moment that I had this flashback, I remembered this day his face. He said, 'Rudi, whatever you say, whatever you do, memorize it, word for word. Do not deviate. Otherwise, they'll kick you to death.' I got that lesson. I stuck to my story. Then after about a month or month and a half, there in that concentration camp, I felt every bone in my body. . . . Everything was hurting."[4]

Rudi wrote in October 1988, when editing his 1974 interview, that he "blocked out all tortures they inflicted upon me and suppressed them from my consciousness. It was only in 1985 when I had the opportunity to visit Hamburg again and stood in front of the gate at Kolafu when the flashback occurred, making me remember all the things and persons. For instance, [I remember] my guardian angel 'Hans' who saved my life by intervening for me in front of the *'langen* [tall] Paul.' For 40 years I could not remember his name, except when I stood in front of that gate."[5] [Paul was, according to Karl, a large, sadistic guard who mercilessly beat the prisoners and who, after the war's end, was reportedly spotted on a city street corner by former prisoners. They rushed upon him and beat him to death.[6]]

Karl Schnibbe has returned to both Kolaful and Moabit prisons and has seen the cells where he was incarcerated. He says that the interrogation room at Gestapo headquarters was bombed out, as was the courtroom at Berlin.[7]

Others in Helmuth's story returned for visits to Germany, including his brother Hans and Charlotte, who return every two years. "The first time we went to the [Plotzensee] prison," recalls Charlotte, "was when the wall [Berlin Wall] went down."[8] Hans states, "In Berlin at the Plotzensee prison we saw a plaque on it with his name.[9] Charlotte adds this interesting aside: "In the prison it is cold in the execution room. In there were zinging sounds."[10]

As Rudi and Herta returned twice to Germany, so have Gerhard and Waltraud returned just twice.

Gerhard describes one trip to Hamburg. "When my wife and I visited Hamburg [4-24 June 1994[11]] . . . we found the office where the 50-year observance committee had left their literature.[12] They had somehow obtained Gerhard's name and had begun writing him, whereupon they had corresponded for two years.[13]

"When I went to their office, they had a gallery that included materials about Helmuth. They had the red booklet [a 66-page compilation about Helmuth] in a glass case. They said that was the last one, and they took it out of the case and gave it to me."[14]

Gerhard makes this painful point: "In 1994 we went to Hamburg to see my brother's memorial building, the

Helmuth Hübener House, which in 1985 had been renamed from 'Bieberhaus,' the administrative building for the Hamburg government. But the plaque was now gone and the building has been renamed back to 'Bieberhaus.'

"A street which had borne Helmut's name had also been renamed to something else, and the old street sign bearing Helmut's name had been removed. I suppose the new generation does not know and appreciate their heritage."[15]

CHAPTER **40**

To this day, few photographs of the boys exist, and are owned mostly by Karl.

Herta says Rudi owned the only photo of the three boys together,[1] although Karl (and the author) now have copies. In 1974 Marie Sommerfeld had one photo left of Helmuth[2] which has since disappeared. It was probably one of him acting in a play at church.[3]

As for Helmuth's enemies, the blood tribunal judges got off scot-free. Helmuth's boss Heinrich Mohns, who turned him in to the Gestapo, had this report published about him in 1950 in the *Hamburger Abendblatt* newspaper. "The Court of Assizes particularly took amiss that the defendant [Mohns] still does not see the injustice of his deed at that time."[4] Specifically, Mohns was sentenced on 20 May 1950 to two years for "crimes against humanity." Three years later, on 25 June 1953, upon appeal, the Fifth Criminal Panel of the

Federal Court for Justice overturned the decision, turning the matter over to the Jury Court of Hamburg, where the appeal was upheld. Thus, Mohns never served his prison sentence for turning in Helmuth.[5] It is possible that Mohns did sweat through a few hundred sleepless nights wondering about his impending sentencing and prison term. This may have served as some degree of punishment in and of itself. Still, he got off.

In the final analysis, whenever one takes a stand against evil, they will court controversy. In Helmuth's case, he heroically took on the Third Reich, and in fact felt of his actions, "I have done nothing wrong." Although it is not documented, a few old Germans likely thought he should have toed the line, kept his nose clean, and kept him — and them — from trouble with the Gestapo. Some even today could criticize his actions as foolish, in a pragmatic light, leaving those of his family and fellow church members open to tighter scrutiny — and even arrest and execution — as happened to other resistors' families later in the war.

Yet, ironically, one of the non-Latter-day Saints in his group, Gerhard Düwer, believed he was motivated by religious ideals.[6]

Of deeper irony, after his arrest, Helmuth was told he was bright enough that he could have worked in Berlin in the Propaganda ministry. It is particularly interesting that that is where they needed him most, points out Karl.[7]

All in all, his life portrays lessons of not only amazing perception, but courage. About the time Helmuth's life began to be noticed in Germany, fellow St. George Branch member Frederich Hermann Peters urged members of the Church of Jesus Christ of Latter-day Saints to take Helmuth's life seriously.[8]

One insightful analysis of Helmuth's experience comes from John Albert Dahl:

"We know Hübner was concerned, smart, and educated. Was he also misguided, adventurous, overanxious, or naïve? Some remember him as being a bit arrogant. For his age he shows qualifications of extreme leadership. He certainly was acquainted with Frederick Von Schiller, 1759-1805 [since he quotes six lines from the end of Act II, Scene Two of *Wilhelm Tell*, which is the oath by the Swiss Confederates at Rütli], and is drawn by Wilhelm Tell [as indicated in a flyer of Helmuth's]. He may have felt to be predestined to fight tyranny just as the legendary Wilhelm Tell. In one of his leaflets he quotes the Rütli Oath of that drama. The first and last lines of that oath read, 'We want to be united now as brothers and fear no kind of wicked human power.'

"Schiller, the idealistic and naïve, great German dramatist, poet, and philosopher, was widely known all over Europe in fighting for *Liberte*, *Egalite*, and *Freternite*. He had been persecuted and arrested himself for several weeks.

"The leaders of the French Revolution of 1789 made him an honorary citizen of France. . . .

"Schiller was a defender of the idea of freedom and human rights before these concepts found their place in human rights documents of our generation after WWII.

"Without any doubt Schiller influenced Helmuth deeply in his fight for freedom," says Dahl, to the extent in fact, that he sacrificed his life.[9]

Ironically, while being such a proponent of democracy, Helmuth never experienced democracy himself, points out Alan Keele,[10] but he did have the model of American missionaries "whom he knew well and admired greatly and who had, until two years previously, done the same things, right down to the detail of handing out pamphlets."[11]

Keele further analyzes, "What may very well have started with some measure of adventure gradually acquired political, religious, and philosophical content and depth."[12]

Keele also observes, "As they tortured him he got more and more proud of what he did. This is not what you'd expect someone to do. He didn't break down and begin sniveling and say, 'I'm sorry I did it. It was stupid and so forth.' He said, 'I started listening to the BBC and I had to listen. And then when I found out what was going on I had to tell people about it.'"[13]

Keele also writes in an unpublished essay, "The *Führer's* New Clothes," (a shorter version of which was later published by *Sunstone*), "Far from making him willing to recant, his experiences in prison merely confirmed his worst fears and effectively solidifed his resolve to oppose the stystem to the very end, and it explains why in the interrogatons — not unlike the young Luther — he boldly said that he 'had no choice:' He 'had to listen to the broadcasts,' and when he had learned the truth, he 'had to disseminate it.'" [14]

In the final analysis, Keele observes:

". . .if a perfectly indoctrinated school child of 16 is able — by virtue only of his intelligence and a brief exposure to a few BBC broadcasts — to see through and illuminate for even a few others the fabrications of the entire Ministry of Propaganda under the brilliant Dr. Goebbels, then that young man is a threat to a regime built upon lies greater than any secret weapon or saboteur and upon this one outspoken lad all of the official German fears, conscious or subconscious, about the credibility of the *Führer*'s new clothes, [are] likely to become sharply and fatally focused. Perhaps the pen *is* mightier than the sword.

"[His] enlightened response to an unjustified regime was not enthusiasm, apathy or violent opposition, but a sincere if naïve attempt to change things by educating his fellow man. . . .

"Had the Nazi regime 'held sacred the freedom of conscience' and 'protected men in their inherent and inalienable rights,' by its laws, not 'depriving its citizens of the privilege of free exercise of their religious belief or proscribing them in their opinions,' Helmuth would almost certainly never had become a lawbreaker. His mentality was anything but, and his character was such that he certainly would still have been politically enlightened, he would still have sought out the truth, he would still have studied the issues, he would still have scrutinized the candidates, not allowing himself to be duped by the rhetoric and toadyism of more recent morally unfit candidates any more than he was by Hitler or Goebbels, and . . . with his dedication to the principles of peace and non-violence, he would have undoubtedly been an almost model member of any free society.

". . . Mormons might face situations from time to time in various countries around the globe where the survival of individuals or the very survival of the Church as an institution would seem to dictate a policy of close-mouthed neutrality.

". . . Unless specifically counseled by the prophet to do otherwise, to ride out the storm in situations where evil has already clearly, if temporarily, triumphed, it seems that members of the Church would do better to err in the direction of being more concerned, rather than less, about the survival of those principles of freedom they hold dear.

". . . If his life and his death have taught the world anything, if his legacy is to have any meaning, it perhaps ought to be that more responsible people should follow Helmuth's lead, doing exactly the kinds of things Helmuth had the courage to do then, but doing them here and now, in this and other free countries around the world, before and lest the wicked rule. . . ."[15]

In a shorter statement of Helmuth's and his friends' mission, Karl Schnibbe analyzes in a 1976 *BYU Today* article, "It's a beautiful thing that someone is recognizing that there were LDS boys who fought the Nazis."[16]

The Saints in Germany at the time may have viewed their plight pragmatically, as Herta Schmidt Wobbe explains their situation in answer to a question in 1974 in light of the 12th Article of Faith of the church that states, "We believe in being subject to kings, president, rulers, and magistrates, in obeying, honoring, and sustaining the law." Her response is, "I think this came into the picture that we should just stay to ourselves and not make too much opposition to the government, not that we should go along with it like we couldn't just let Salomon Schwarz down. . . ." Rudi adds in that same response, "The feeling more or less among the members was that they would more or less tolerate it and try to stay out of trouble, don't make waves. . . ." Herta explains the simple, bottom-line reason that cuts through many philosophical arguments: "Otherwise we wouldn't be able to meet at all."[17]

Rudi finishes their explanation: "We were cautioned don't make waves, don't get too important. We might get noticed, and then we're going to get tramped on. That was the general feeling."[18]

But, of course, he and his two best friends, in declaring war on evil, did just the opposite.

Otto Berndt recalls that Zander preached to his flock that it was their duty to support the regime in the spirit of that Article.[19] Otto himself tried to keep the "loudmouthed" members in check to protect them all, but not with that Article in mind.

Rudi analyzes his actions in light of the Article, expanding his comment used earlier in this volume: "There are still some that think we . . . offended the 12th Article of Faith, which I'd like to state here is not a commandment. It is a statement of our belief. And it is a truly American concept. We can never apply this to a Hitler, a Mussolini, an Idi Amin, all these murderous villains that are the heads of state. They are not ordained of God. I believe in the great gearwork of the great clock in the universe. They have a place. They're put on earth at a certain time to be a scourge, to be a temptation, and to bring the Lord's plan to fulfillment in a negative way. Because the Lord knows in his great wisdom and his foreknowledge how certain individuals and spirits were to react put upon this earth. Wasn't it Herod that killed all the children? Nero persecuted the early Christians, and all these evil men. I wouldn't say they're foreordained, but they fit in the great plan of salvation. Our Heavenly Father knows how they'll react under certain circumstances and that's my belief. I got challenged in a priesthood quorum once when I made that statement. I responded, 'Oh, no, no, no. I didn't say they're foreordained. It's somewhat planned, arranged to make this great plan of our Heavenly Father come to a point."[20]

While interviewing Rudi in 1974, Alan Keele refers to Ulrich Sander, who "could not understand why you three young boys arrived at a democratic point of view." He says Sander points out that the three boys did not experience the previous government as they were too young, and that they grew up under totalitarianism. Sander was puzzled why the boys could arrive at a democratic point of view.

As for the boys' democratic point of view — Rudi chalked it up to the gospel, the Church, and the missionaries.[21]

Herta says they felt "differently" than other Germans about democracy because of their membership in the church. "You're something different. And we were there something different entirely."[22]

Rudi adds, "But maybe it's the youth that has to lead out. They're not tied down with families and children, responsibilities. Sure we have parents and loved ones that would grieve, but truth must go on and we should tell the truth regardless if it hurts us. . . . [W]hen it comes to voicing your opinion, I think we have to stand on our hind feet and say, 'Yes, that's what I believe in.'"[23]

Nobel-laureate author Gunter Grass summarizes in the BYU documentary, "This is what it comes down to — a story that has continually torn at me. Why didn't I know these things? Why did he know? This was just the fabric that Helmuth Hübener was made of.[24]

In 1988 Rudi was asked if he would do it all the same again.

His reply: "Yes."[25]

In conclusion, the inescapable topic to ponder is, "Should the churches always resist perceived tyranny in practice, and not just in theory?"

For churches who wish to maintain their existence in dictatorial nations, their leaders have to and do face the dilemma of surviving — for both the church's individuals and the church as an institution. (See Appendix T for more analysis on the Church's survival in a totalitarian state.)

While it is obvious to perceive Helmuth Hübener as a hero, the argument has been made, even by other stalwart anti-Nazi German Latter-day Saints and friends of Helmuth, that in retrospect there is a certain value in religious individuals merely obeying the laws of the land and allowing a government to run its course in order that a higher mission — the activities of a church and its work on a spiritual plane — may take precedence over the more obvious, popular, perceived need for revolution — such as the overthrow of an immoral government.

Thus, a mission of The Church of Jesus Christ of Latter-day Saints and perhaps other Christian (and non-Christian) religions has been to exhort its members to support and obey governments to whichever its citizens belong. If those governments be immoral, then the work of opposing and changing them legally — such as through elections — by individuals who belong to the Church — may be in order. However, in the case of the Nazis and Soviets where, once a government is in power and cannot be removed, the issue becomes more complex.

Even in that case the argument could be made that history should run its course and churches should not get involved in opposing certain governments because, in the spiritual long-term, those who conduct immoral acts within governments — such as Nazi and Soviet leaders — will eventually be held accountable before God, while the mission of churches in each country is to quietly carry on spiritual work and to operate in such a manner that churches do not threaten to topple governments in order that governments will not retaliate by destroying churches.

Adding further complexity is the question, "At what point should one resist the government?" In the Mormon Germans' case, would they have been justified to fight the government if they had known of the Jews' extermination, or known of their own pending extermination?

Another debate centers on the issue of individual conscientious objection. One side may argue that *individuals* should conscientiously oppose and fight evil governments, while the opposing side may argue that if enough *individuals from a certain religious community* fight or oppose a government, they may threaten the overall religious society to which they belong by causing that religious society to be perceived by the government as their enemy.

One theory has it that it is our responsibility to resist evil categorically, and thus sacrifice one's organized religion on the altar of principle. Another is to simply allow the governing body within a religion to determine such policies, since they are in perhaps the best position to determine when and when not to resist, as their particular organization is at stake. Latter-day Saints believe a prophet, who is at the head of their church, makes policy for the overall membership, so that the Lord will protect His church and its members through that prophet.

In any case, Helmuth's work as a religious activist has been seen by certain idealists as productive, and yet again by certain pragmatists as counterproductive. But no one can doubt his sincerity, purity of heart, and magnificent heroism.

PHOTOGRAPHS

Helmuth Hübener's family.

Left to right: Wilhelmina Sudrow (grandmother), Helmuth,

Johannes Sudrow (grandfather), Gerhard Kunkel (brother),

Hans Kunkel (brother), Emma Kunkel (mother).

Rudi Wobbe, Helmuth Hübener, Karl-heinz Schnibbe,
circa 1940

COURTESY OF HERTA WOBBE

Members of St. Georg Branch
of the Church of Jesus Christ of Latter-day Saints
(Helmuth's branch).

COURTESY OF HERTA WOBBE

Helmuth Hübener

COURTESY OF GERHARD KUNKEL
FROM HAMBURG-HAMM COMMEMORATIVE BOOKLET

Helmuth Hübener

COURTESY OF GERHARD KUNKEL
FROM HAMBURG-HAMM COMMEMORATIVE BOOKLET

Gestapo photos of Helmuth Hübener

COURTESY OF GERHARD KUNKEL
FROM HAMBURG-HAMM COMMEMORATIVE BOOKLET

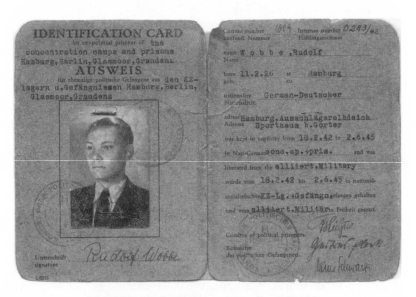

Identification card issued to Rudi Wobbe
by Allied occupation forces after the war

COURTESY OF HERTA WOBBE

APPENDICES

More on the sign

Shortly after the war, Hamburg's third branch — the Altona Branch — had a history written by Johannes Kindt, mentioning that the same kind of exclusion of Jews had to be officially posted.[1] One possible scenario is that a directive may have been given from the district to post such a statement, perhaps even with a discreet side order to branch presidents to use their discretion in heeding it or not, as long as they at least made a statement of "show" to the Gestapo.

While Gerhard Kunkel thought all three branches were forced to post the sign, President Alfred Schmidt of the Barmbeck Branch opposed it. It's possible, however, that he could have put it up temporarily to appease the Gestapo. Schmidt's son, Werner, denies even that as a possibility. "My father simply would not have allowed it."[2] It is possible that Herta and Rudi are correct in their recollections that only Zander ever posted such a sign. Rudi maintains that Kindt's Altona branch report is mistaken,[3] but does qualify his comment with this assessment: "They could have mentioned it over the pulpit . . ."[4], which would have appeased the Gestapo.

More about Arthur Zander

Latter-day Saints believe their church is inspired, even restored from heaven in the latter days, and that its leaders make inspired decisions for its members.

In Hamburg's three branches, among the presidents, only Zander had pro-Nazi leanings. In the St. Georg Branch before Zander, the branch president was Paul Prüss. "He was more Saint than political, a very spiritual man, very devout," and anti-Nazi, says Rudi.

In Helmuth's case, Arthur Zander was described by Karl and Arthur as a "good" shepherd[5] whom the branch followed and liked, but by Rudi and Otto Berndt as someone they "didn't like" because of his political views.[6] Although Otto says he did not dislike him personally,[7] he was someone obviously duped into parroting the party line.

Zander had joined the Church in 1933[8] and served as branch president from 1938 to 1946, according to Rudi.[9] However, his release date was likely earlier than 1946, since he was detained as a prisoner of war in the United States.[10] Furthermore, at the end of the war, his branch no longer existed as the St. George Branch — as only a third of his members survived Allied bombing — so it merged with the other two branches.[11] After the war, a new third branch was started, and Zander was chosen branch president.

Otto thinks Zander was placed in his position at St. Georg as branch president by mission leaders in order to deter government oppression.[12] Yet Otto admits Zander was more liked than himself,[13] leaving one to believe Zander may have had, despite his politics, an easygoing style. Additionally, he was a foreman at work, so was used to leadership.[14]

Apparently even decent people like Zander were deceived by Nazi propaganda, especially when the Nazis did produce some positive results, such as rescuing the country from an inflation-ravaged economy, destructively high unemployment, and the national humiliation of Versailles. It seems that fairly new converts, such as Zander, were easily seduced by the new national optimism, overlooking too many flaws that others were quick to perceive. Rudi could not understand why everybody — especially everyone at church, more especially the "learned elders in the church" who "knew the gospel"[15] – did not share his insights. "Why was it just us young people?"[16] Of course it was more than just the young people, as certain adult leaders were also decidedly anti-Nazi.

Helmuth, like Rudi, no doubt at one time wondered the same thing. But Helmuth initially had been one of those deceived by the *Führer*'s lies, so maybe he understood . . . . Helmuth had discovered the *Reich*'s lies "line upon line," similar to the way the gospel is learned by new converts and indeed everyone.

In regards to Zander's Nazi views, Karl summarizes, "He went a little overboard a bit."[17] Yet, amazingly, many of his decisions worked to protect his flock temporally.

A bishop or branch president's calling, as leader of the Aaronic Priesthood, is to look after the *temporal welfare* of his stewardship — which he did. Simultaneously, the stake or district president is focused on the *spiritual welfare* of that ward or branch — as well as for the whole stake — and Otto Berndt certainly excelled in his calling in that arena.

Rudi feels Zander is "regretful" that he got "that much involved" in Naziism. It's noteworthy that Arthur Zander is the one who baptized Rudi and his mother and, as is generally the case for those who aid in the conversion or baptism of new converts, Zander "always looked out for me," but, "there was something I just didn't understand." Rudi even confronted Zander on at least one occasion long after the war, saying, "I never agreed with what you stood for.[18] Rudi says Zander claimed he was "just following party lines,"[19] and "Well, everybody has to live his own life."[20]

Rudi summarizes their relationship, "We're cordial. I don't have any feeling of animosity or hatred towards him. . . . I don't want to judge him too harshly. He probably repented in the meantime, but he doesn't want to admit it."[21] He says that Zander wrote him a heartfelt letter years later once they were in Salt Lake City. "He said, 'Yes, I slaved to do penance,' and so in kind of an ironic way he wrote me a long letter."[22]

When asked if he thinks Zander still feels awkward about it all, Rudi reflects, "He feels a little funny about it," and agrees that Zander "definitely" looks down at the floor when he sees him.[23]

Otto says, but does not distinguish between right after the war in Germany when authorities were hunting Nazis, or later in the U.S., "People told me that I should report to the government what he did and what Brother Huck did, and soon. I said, 'No. It's against my belief. He's still my brother, and if he erred in that time, there wasn't too much harm done . . . . Why should I?'"[24]

In Church history there have been examples, particularly in foreign countries where inexperienced new converts make up much of the leadership, that a local leader's actions have been a trial for some members. (It's hard enough for veteran, U.S. leaders to not make mistakes, even with both the "power of the Priesthood" and "the Holy Ghost" assisting leaders, as Latter-day Saints believe.) Nevertheless, an entire congregation can grow and its faith and patience can mature in what Latter-day Saints also believe are the rare instances that local leadership mistakes are made.

Even higher authorities err, but when the Church's president "acts as a prophet," Latter-day Saints believe they cannot and will not be led astray by the head of the Church, a promise given to them of the Lord, they believe, in numerous LDS General Conferences.

Zander has since passed away in Salt Lake City, active in the faith, having raised a family also active, even stalwart, in the faith.

Otto Berndt's opposition to displaying Hitler's picture in church

At the warehouse where they met for church, one Wednesday night Otto Berndt walked onto the second story, into a classroom, "to see how the young folks were preparing their Christmas celebration."[25] There, he discovered that the pictures of Joseph Smith and the Savior had been removed and, in their place, a picture of Hitler had been hung. He told one of the leaders to take it down — and to replace the pictures — which was done. Otto was at that time a counselor in the young people's Mutual.

The branch leaders did not like his action, so they released him. He was then drafted, one of the first in the branch.[26] When he came back a year later in 1941, he rose quickly in district leadership, "above" Zander and the branch leaders.

Despite his political actions at church, he never spoke to his children about his politics during the years of the *Reich*.[27]

Otto Berndt was drafted into the army, according to his own account,[28] although his son thought he volunteered for the air force in 1940.[29] He served a year. His stint included only construction work as one of the ground personnel near the Baltic Sea in Germany. He did not go to the front. Soon his spine was injured and he returned home.[30] (His son, Otto, Jr., was about three years younger than Helmuth and was drafted in January 1945, but was never inducted, as the war ended soon afterwards.[31])

Naziism vs. Christianity

As for the myth that the Nazis were Christians who persecuted Jews, the record is set straight by scholar Alan Keele in a 1980 article of *Sunstone* magazine:

"National Socialism was not a simple political, economic, or social phenomenon.

"It was an entirely new world-view based on an eclectic conglomeration of astrological, gnostic, millennialist, Christian, and Teutonic cults and myths. The Nazi inner circles were steeped in this collage of mystical lore. Albert Speer, for example, writes in *Inside the Third Reich* that Hitler and a few colleagues were celebrating his greatest diplomatic coup — the signing of the non-aggression pact with Russia — on the scenic mountain peak of the Obersalzberg, when they looked across to the Untersberg, a place associated with many Germanic legends. There, say the legends, the Emperor Charlemagne sleeps in a cave until he shall be called forth to usher in the millennial *Reich.* As Hitler and his party watched, the Untersberg was bathed in a brilliant red light, which Speer later decided was a rare and remarkably vivid southern display of the Aurora Borealis. The light shone on the assembled faces like a divine show of approval for the historic event of that day. Speer reports that Hitler was deeply moved. Watching the light, he said, 'It looks like this time much blood will be shed.'"[32]

As such, Naziism was a jealous and competing "religion."

He and Douglas Tobler continue in an unpublished essay: ". . . the majority of the Germans . . . had been lulled into believing that Hitler was a committed Christian because of his Catholic background, Point 24 of the Nazi Party Platform promising Nazi support for 'positive Christianity,' and by his effulgent protestations of attachment to German Christian traditions and his 'calling' by heaven . . .

"But the true intent of the party was captured by Hitler's personal secretary, Martin Bormann, in a secret communique in the fall of 1941 on 'The Relationship of National Socialism and Christianity.' Here, he makes clear that the two 'world views' are incompatible, that when children are no longer indoctrinated into Christianity, it will die out. . . . The influence of the churches upon the people must be 'completely and finally broken.'[33]

"Himmler dreamed of the day when he would hang the Pope in full regalia in St. Peter's Square in Rome; that would be a great symbolic act, the end of the Judeo-Christian era.[34]

"Himler's views were, in fact, implemented into the new policy between Church and State in the so-called Warthe region recently taken from Poland. This 13-point program, in a communique from Hitler to Guatleiter Greiser, reads as follows:

"'1) There are to be no more churches in the civil sense, only religious church societies in the sense of clubs; . . .

"'5) Only adults can become members, and that only by written declaration of intent to join. Members cannot be 'born into' this club, but must wait until they are 21 years old to declare their intention to join. . . .

"'6) All confessional [Church] auxiliaries as well as organizations [youth groups] are abolished and forbidden. . . .

"'8) No more religious instruction is allowed in the schools.

"'9) Aside from the club's dues, no financial contributions are to be made.

"'10) The clubs are not allowed to own property, such as buildings, houses, fields, cemetaries, etc., except for their meeting place.

"'11) Furthermore, they are not allowed to participate in welfare any more.

"'12) All charitable foundations and monasteries are to be dissolved, since they do not correspond to German morality and German ethnic policies.' (Hitler to Gauleiter [Governor] Greiser, Warthegau, in *Kirchliches Jahrbuch fur die Evangelische Kirche in Deutschland* 1933-44, [Gutersloh: C. Berthelsmann Verlag, 1948], 453)

"Hitler had earlier expressed his innermost feelings on the subject to Hermann Rauschning, The Mayor of Danzig:

"'As far as the Churches go, they're all the same. They have no future. Not among the Germans, at any rate.

Italian fascism can go ahead and make its peace with the church. I'll do it too. Why not? That won't prevent me from exterminating Christianity in Germany, with all its roots and branches, lock, stock, and barrel.' (Hermann Rauschning, *Gespräche mit Hitler* [New York: Europa, 1940], 50)

". . . The *Reich* Education Minister Friedrich Schmidt . . . who expressed the developing official line on the relationship between National Socialism and Christianity [and the speech was given in Hamburg in October 1941 or a pamphlet version of it, *"Das Reich als Aufgabe"*]:

"'. . . C) The fate of the people will be fulfilled in the here-and-now (not on the other side).

"'D) Germans must have the courage to extinguish "foreign" ideas, which have become a traditional burden. These include the "idea of humanity" and the "idea of the Christian Church."

"'E) The more radically Germans combat Christianity at home, the more success they will have in the War and the sooner other peoples will accept National Socialist *Weltanschauung* [world view].

"'F) Both Christian churches (Protestant and Catholic) have admitted their opposition to "germanic sensitivity" [*germanisches Empfinden*], thereby precluding any right to continued existence.

"'G) What will happen to the Church[es]? Today, the Churches are trying through their bishops to provoke the state.

"'At present, the party is silent, because the *Führer* has strictly ordered that nothing should be undertaken against the Churches. They can talk and write as they wish; we do not want to create any martyrs. After the war there will be a settling-up. Then we will have a case of either/or. Christianity is a New Eastern Jewish-saturated doctrine. There will be no reconciliation [*Versöhnung*] like that represented by those well-meaning fools, the German Christians.' (Hermelink, 504-505)"

Keele and Tobler in their essay cite the following:

"Bracher, *et al*, quote passages from Hitler's *Mein Kampf* (p. 506) and Rosenberg's *Weltanschauung v. Wissenschaft* 35 (Hlft 6) to demonstrate National Socialism's intent to coordinate" [*gleichschalten*] not only society, but each individual, to take over his soul. (Karl Dietrich Bracher, Wolfgang Sauer, Gerhard Schulz, *Die national sozialistische Machtergreifung*, 2nd ed. [Cologne: Westdeutscher Verlag, 1962], 262, 273-274. See also John Conway, *The Nazi Persecution of the Churches* [London: Weidenfeld and Nicolson, 1968c]; Friedrich Heer, *Der Glaube des Adolf Hitler: Anatomie einer politischer Religiosität* [Munich: Bechtle, 1968]; A slightly different twist is presented by Hans Buchheim, *Glaubens Krise im Dritten Reich: Drei Kapiteln national-sozialistischer Religionspotlitik* [Stuttgard: Deutsche Verlagsanstalt, 1953]."

The political influence of Karl Schnibbe's home life

Karl Schnibbe reports his father's attitude about the Nazis as he would turn on the radio:

"'Let's hear whether our enemies are finally fed up and have begged our *Führer*'s pardon.' That was how my father slandered and amused himself immensely while my mother looked anxiously to see if all of the windows were closed. Snappy march music resounded from the loudspeaker, and then some radio commentator blathered something about the marvelous providence and that an infallible *Führer* was sent to us. . . .

"The German troops continuously conquered on all fronts with few casualties. We were always victorious, of course, and the other guy was always completely destroyed.

"I had to laugh at the newscast. My father asked, 'Why are you grinning so stupidly? Don't you believe, you ruffian, what they are telling us there?' I joked of Goebbels being a billy goat and he laughed. 'You are too vulgar for me,' he said, and went into his bedroom to change clothes to go to church."[36]

Government agency mistakes

As to Helmuth's initial infatuation with the party, the Hamburg district office of the Hitler Youth says he joined "April 20, 1938," and the Superior Attorney General of the *Reich* also says 1938, but even though the sources are certainly credible, they are mistaken. He joined April 1939.

Another mistake of the Hitler Youth administration is misspelling his name "Hellmuth," which his church membership record also misspells the same way.[37]

Additionally, the Hitler Youth district office mistakes his birthdate as being in December 1925. If he had indeed entered the Hitler Youth according to that date, he would have been only 13, not the required minimum age of 14.

These government reports may have confused or grouped together the Hitler Youth with the German Young Folk (boys aged 10-14), since he did join the German Young Folk in 1938.[38] Similarly, in a later indictment from the Superior Attorney General of the *Reich*, an erroneous statement is made that Helmuth's friend at work, Gerhard Düwer, belonged to the Hitler Youth since 1933.[39] In 1933 Düwer would have been only nine.

Still, nothing can be taken away from their generally accurate record keeping, which is a German tendency more

than a Nazi one, and indeed can be viewed almost as a
national trait.

Helmuth's discretion

As for Helmuth's tendency toward discretion . . .

Interestingly, Helmuth never told Rudi or Karl of the revolutionaries. Karl admits, "He met these guys in the swimming pool . . . all those young people. . . . Helmuth never told me anything."[40] He summarizes, "There were a lot of people involved . . . a lot of people involved . . . but Helmuth kept it away from us."[41]

Rudi says this of the Bismarck group: "He never mentioned it to me,"[42] but learned later of Helmuth's involvement with them. (Actually, when first told of it, Rudi claimed it "absolutely not" true;[43] additionally, when asked if Helmuth had any Communist friends, Rudi replied, "Not that I know of."[44] These denials came in 1974. His reason for disavowing it: He believed Helmuth would have told him, since "we were very close . . . . Not only we saw each other in meetings three times a week, but we also visited each other."[45] But 18 years later when Rudi would publish his autobiography, he would have additional information and time to reflect — and at last admit that Helmuth had been associated with the Bismarck group.)

Similarly, Rudi admits to Helmuth's lack of openness when he confesses, "I really don't know his closest friend.

I thought we were real close, unless he had somebody else I didn't know of."[46]

All of which shows that Helmuth was extremely discreet about his friends, activities, political and social life. As another example, Helmuth likely never told Rudi of Giesela, just as he never told Karl Schnibbe[47] or Arthur Sommerfeld.[48]

APPENDIX H

Varying involvement memories

In his autobiography Karl remembers the three of them distributing leaflets. Similarly, in 1974 Rudi recalls all three of them meeting together and making plans. On one occasion Rudi asked Karl if he was "in with it," to which Karl said, "Yes."[49]

Fourteen years later, however, Rudi had forgotten Karl's involvement, as Rudi says of Karl, "He talked to me about the leaflets and the contents, and at that time he told me, 'I just took them home and burned them.' . . . I don't know if he [Karl] was afraid of me [telling others about his involvement] or if he actually did [distribute them]."[50]

Rudi believes only he (Rudi) helped Helmuth distribute the flyers.

Karl admits he did burn leftover flyers each night after distributing the bulk, so his family could not get in trouble.[51]

Their Sunday School classmate, Lieselotte Prüss Schmidt, confirms to an extent both Rudi's earlier version and Karl's version: She vividly recollects the boys whispering their "secret" plans at church week after week, which attests to the probability they did in fact work in unison.[52]

Announcement in church of Helmuth's arrest

Otto Berndt reports that the comment made by someone in church, saying they wanted to shoot Helmuth, was made six months after the arrest, when Helmuth's sentence was imposed.[53] But no one in the branch — except Helmuth's family — knew about Helmuth's sentence being imposed until many weeks after. Branch leaders likely knew when it was imposed, but said nothing: A number of members report not knowing Helmuth's outcome for a long time, which means their leaders never told them. Otto also believes it was Zander who made the comment,[54] while others believe it was Jacobi.

Jacobi and Bankowski were Zander's counselors in the branch. After Helmuth's arrest, either one of them — or Zander — could have made the announcement (including the comment) from the pulpit. Or, the comment could have been made offhandedly away from the pulpit, even after the meeting. Otto says he told Zander [or Jacobi], "Don't mention it. Please do me a favor and keep your mouth shut and say nothing. . . . His mother is here and his grandmother is here[55] . . . It's done and we feel sorry about it."[56] Otto continues, "But he didn't do it. He stood up in the meeting place and announced it . . . [including the shooting Helmuth comment]."[57] Otto adds that Zander's two counselors backed up the one making the comment. Otto says Bankowski "was one of my best friends. . . . I told him once, I said, 'How could you do that?'"[58] Otto does not report Bankowski's response.

All in all, it was likely Zander who made the announcement of Helmuth's arrest from the pulpit, followed by Jacobi making the comment (only possibly over the pulpit). Otto is probably confusing the incident and the person, but he undoubtedly attempted to stop the announcement being made at church, and remembers that attempt painfully.

Helmuth's membership record

Helmuth's church membership record, although altered only a year after the war's end, would read in its final state, five and a quarter years after his death:

"born 8 January 1925 at Hamburg

"Father unknown

"Mother Emma A. Gudat

"ordained Deacon 3 May 1937

"excommunicated 15 Feb 1942. Reason: Listening and spreading of news of foreign broadcasts.

"died (15 February 1942) [it should be 27 October 1942]

"violent death

"Notation on record: Excommunication was done by mistake. 11 November 1946.

"Entered by Pres. Max Zimmer and Elder Otto Berndt

"Decision of the excommunication reversed by the First Presidency of the Church of Jesus Christ of Latter Day Saints who ordered this notation placed upon the record of excommunication. January 24, 1948.

"Record of Members, Hamburg District #23403, #994[59]

APPENDIX K

Additional leaflet information

Rudi confessed to receiving only 15 small flyers from Helmuth,[60] and only in August 1941, then distributing them in Rothenburgsort, as ordered by Helmuth that same month.[61] But Helmuth reported that Rudi received 20.[62] The numbers were evidently close enough that the Gestapo apparently believed them.

The Gestapo figured Helmuth produced 60 copies of leaflets in August 1941, of which he mailed one to Horst van Treck in the National Labor Service, handed the aforementioned 20 to Rudi for distribution, and distributed the remaining 39 or so himself in mailboxes and on the street in Hammerbrook.[63]

Rudi recalls 60 copies each of three specific small flyers being made[64] and reports actually depositing them himself in telephone boxes.

They also knew Rudi "deposited them in the city district of Rothenburgsort, of which the preponderant part is also inhabited by blue collar workers," again in hallways and mailboxes, and that he "tacked some also on building bulletin boards."[65]

The papers drawn up by the Superior Attorney General of the *Reich* at the People's Court[66] and the report written by the Gestapo[67] claimed Helmuth distributed only 15 detailed leaflets personally,[68] rather than 39. He likely distributed far more. He only told them of one morning performing this distribution on his way to work, and one evening,[69] which they apparently believed. He did admit to coming up with the idea of placing them in hallways, and in one case a telephone booth.[70] As to mailboxes, the Gestapo would find leaflets in house mailboxes and in mailboxes of the German Post Office.[71] They were also found "on the street."[72] He confessed to entertaining the thought of sending them to Latter-day Saint soldiers whose addresses he obtained from his church clerical work, but he did not get around to carrying out this intention.[73]

In a cover-up, Rudi later told the Gestapo he received flyers from Helmuth only twice — one time it was the small flyers and on other occasion it was four or five large leaflets.[74] To further cover himself Rudi told them he read the large ones, then burned them.[75] He also told them he knew of no one else who received flyers from Helmuth.[76] He never admitted that they listened to the BBC, claiming he was often in Helmuth's apartment but that they never listened together. He says he only received flyers from him there. He did say he tried three or four times to listen to the BBC at home, but could not get it on their old radio set.[77]

Rudi also told them he received only four or five of the detailed leaflets to distribute and that after he had read them he merely burned them.

As mentioned earlier, the Gestapo also learned of flyers Helmuth sent by mail to acquaintances outside Hamburg.[78]

Specifically, they learned of Helmuth sending in the mail one copy of each leaflet to two friends: fellow apprentice Horst van Treck, who was in the Labor Service, as well as his school friend Prumnitz, who was attending the finance school in Thorn,[79] but these two friends refused to join him.

Karl Schnibbe recalls him making about 10 of each small flyer.[80]

The Gestapo believed Helmuth gave 15 to Horst "while he distributed the remainder in August 1941 in the districts of Hammerbrook in Hamburg by scattering them on the street or in hallways, as well as through tossing them in mailboxes."[81]

Two Gestapo documents[82] contrast this immaterial fact:

The Gestapo falsely believed Helmuth actually did receive the Remington with Zander's permission[83] to replace the portable one lent earlier. They further believed that in only one instance Helmuth used a typewriter at his place of employment.[84] They did not suspect Zander's complicity, and in fact the Chief State Counsel of the Hanseatic Higher Regional Court would later state, "Zander, the director of this Mormon sect, likewise allegedly said to have known nothing of the activity of Hübener."[85]

Karl told the Gestapo he received from Helmuth only on three occasions a single leaflet, which he read and then burned,[86] and they apparently believed his cover-up. In another report, Karl said the same, but added that he first saw the leaflets "around the fall of 1941."[87] He admits he became interested out of curiosity, and requested Helmuth to let him have a copy of his flyers in the future. In a second report, Karl admits to receiving not only the three detailed leaflets but a number of other flyers to "read in passing."[88] But he also admits to explaining some of the contents to Rudi,[89] specifically about the battles of Africa and the retreat of Rommel.[90] Karl convinced the Gestapo that he was present only once when Helmuth tried listening to the shortwave, and that reception was not possible at that time because of jamming.[91] The Germans put great effort into jamming the BBC.

Meanwhile Gerhard Düwer protested that he hadn't joined Helmuth until early January 1942.[92] Düwer also admitted that he occasionally heard the BBC on his parents' radio on the frequency of the German stations and could understand parts of the broadcasts,[93] but said he never attempted to tune in English stations.

Helmuth first talked with Düwer about the flyers in early January 1942 and in that conversation Helmuth told him he listened to the BBC and prepared leaflets. Helmuth then gave Düwer two leaflets, and soon after gave him more — "about 15 copies in all." (Düwer, by contrast, claims he only received nine leaflets.)

Düwer says he received the first leaflets in mid-January 1942, then four more on 30 January and the last ones on 4 February. (Düwer, in a later attempt to cover himself, claims he accepted them merely because he planned "at the proper time" to report Helmuth.)[94]

Düwer would later clarify that a private party was never held in the home of his parents, nor was a reading of the flyers on that occasion, nor did he participate in any private party, but he did state that he knew the neighbor children held a party when their parents were gone. Düwer also claimed to never show the flyers to anyone, except to the neighbor children, by the last name of Zumsande.[95]

Helmuth, under interrogation, said that he gave Düwer phonograph records for a party [that was obviously used for recruiting, unknown to the Gestapo] and that he did not know if Düwer had other records.[96]

These are all the known facts gathered by the Nazis about Helmuth's leaflets.

Differences between
Karl's and Rudi's accounts

According to Karl, Rudi's sentence was stiffer because he had confessed in prison to Rubinke, the "plant." Rudi however claims he was sentenced longer because he was "more involved." He says Karl burned his leaflets and that none were found in Karl's area — only in Hammerbrook and Rothenbergsort where Rudi distributed them.[97]

On the other hand, Rudi does admit to Karl explaining the meaning of certain flyers to him personally. Thus, if Karl "distributed" flyers to Rudi, he likely attempted to disseminate Helmuth's information to others, as well. And Karl did admit to Rudi to burning flyers — but only on occasions when he had some left over before going home on nights after he'd distributed the rest.[98] Nevertheless, because the burning is what Rudi remembers, he assumes that Karl did not distribute flyers at all. Karl was, after all, imprisoned for distribution of broadcast news after a thorough Gestapo investigation, even though the boys held back most of their information.

While remaining extremely close friends, it's possible that Rudi felt challenged when Karl stated in his first book, *The Price* (which is an out-of-print "rough draft" to Karl's later, expanded, fully documented autobiography, *When*

Truth Was Treason) that Rudi confessed more than he should have to Rubinke. (Karl also states it in a rather disparaging manner, saying that Rudi, "sang like a parakeet.") Rudi did confide more than he should have to Rubinke, so Karl could be correct in his assertion that Rudi's sentence was steeper because of that. However, Rudi's point is well taken — Rudi's sentence may have been steeper because the Gestapo figured Rudi was more involved than Karl was on the distribution level; still, Karl was evidently highly involved in distribution. Meanwhile, Rudi admits he did tell too much to Rubinke but that he also "held back" a lot of information; in his defense, Rudi adds, "There are some things I never mentioned to him, never," says Rudi.[99]

Rudi's version of the holding cell scene

Rudi reports of "the last time I saw him alive:" He says:

"In the same room was a Swiss spy. Also sentenced to die.[100] He said, 'Helmuth, this cannot be true – this must be a bad dream.'

"'Oh, no,' Helmuth says. 'They mean business.'

"He [the Swiss spy] says, 'Oh gosh, they could've given you five years.'

"'No,' he says. 'Look around you.'

"Only then I noticed the inscriptions on the walls:

"'Goodbye, Marie, take care of the kids, I shall never see you again.'

"'Freedom to Germany. Death to the Nazi Oppressors.' Their names scribbled under it. Others:

"'Mother, forgive me. But I believe what I'm doing is right.'

"'Germany forever, down with Hitler.'

"They meant business."[101]

In 1988 Rudi details more in their farewell scene: "'Helmuth, what is happening? I'm rattled. I don't know what's going on. They [the judges] don't mean it, that's just words. They'll just change it later on and send us home.'

"'No, Rudi,' he says, 'they meant it. Look around you.'"[102]

Other inscriptions Rudi reports are:

"'Louise, please take care of the children. I shall never see you again. I love you forever,' and 'Mother, I am too young to die,' and another one, 'This is Germany's darkest hour. God help us all,' stuff like that all over the wall . . .

Rudi states, "[Helmuth] said, 'When you read that you know they mean business.' And then this Swiss spy said, 'Ah, you're too young. They won't do anything to you.'"[103]

Rudi adds that he also saw "death dates" on the wall — a macabre addition to the farewells.[104]

In 1961 Rudi adds to the scene:

"I said to Helmuth: 'Gosh, how terrible.' All he could say was: 'They are all out of their minds.'"

Similarly, in 1974 Rudi reports he told his friend, "'Helmuth, how terrible this is!'"

Helmuth responded, "'They're all nuts. They don't even know what they're talking about.'"[105] . . . Rudi continues, "So we talked to this Swiss spy. 'What is happening . . . ?' 'Something terrible is happening in Europe.' That's what the Swiss spy said."[106]

Philosophical position of
The White Rose group

Rudi says of this group: "A short while after we had our trial and execution, another group came to light a year later. Called the White Rose. You might have heard, you might have seen the film. An educator by the name of Kurt Huber. I would like to read what his leaflet said. It is so good, it should be read.

"'In the name of the German youth, we are demanding from Adolf Hitler that our personal freedom, our most precious possession of all Germans, be returned to us that you so shamelessly took from us. We had to grow up in a police state that forbids the free expression of personal thoughts and desires. Hitler Youth, the SS and SA tried to change us in our most [formative] years into a uniformed, stereotyped and narcotic way, to think and act in a way the world's political schooling would permit — and this at a time when we tried to find our inner self, our self-esteem and self-worth, but instead you grinded us and our intellectual souls with a mist of phraseology and empty slogans. We believe in true signs and in true freedom of the intellect. No physical threat will intimidate us. Not even the closing of our high schools and universities. The German name will be blemished forever, unless the German youth will stand up and smash these evil men that tortured them, and rebuild a new intellectual youth. Everyone of us is needed in this fight for our future, our freedom and our honor, to restore the moral responsibility and integrity of Germany.'"[107]

Medals and emblems

Regarding the medals he received, Gerhard Kunkel later clarifies, "I received 6 medals: (1.) Exceptional Valor — it's the highest — for hand-to-hand combat in Russia; (2.) The Iron Cross — the highest for service beyond call; (3.) The Russia Blood Medal — for hand-to-hand combat and for being wounded; and (4-6.) three 'purple hearts' — two in Russia and one in Italy."[108]

Gerhard also explains, "The Nazi emblem was the swastika, while the military used the iron cross, an emblem left over from the Bismarck days, for their flags, airplanes, and everything military. The Iron Cross was also used as a medal of distinction and courage in battle. . . ."[109] The SS used an armband that was black with two silver streaks of lightning side by side. On the borders were silver designs, such as stars for certain ranks; for officers the border designs were gold."[110]

Arthur Sommerfeld's journey

Arthur Sommerfeld adds details after the July 1943 bombing raid on Hamburg:

"For those burns I was treated several months. Right after the bombing attack, my family went to the village Bergedorff for several days, to a shelter. Meanwhile I took a Red Cross train to a hospital in the same village. There, I stayed a week, then was transported to southern Germany where I stayed for five months. My treatments consisted of doctors scraping burned skin off my hand and perhaps off my neck.[111]

"My family . . . then took a train to Czechoslovakia. After my treatments in southern Germany, I took a train to Czechoslovakia to join them where my mother's sister lived. The village was Jungbuch, now Mladebuk, with a population of about 4,000. Marie Kuehnel, my future wife, lived in the same apartment building.[112]

APPENDIX Q

Otto Berndt's hindsight about Latter-day Saints opposing the Nazis

During the war, Otto Berndt's instincts had been to mainly help the Saints survive and to keep the Gestapo off their backs, but after the war he felt guilty. Especially when asked the question by occupation forces, "What did you do against Hitler?" During the Nazi reign, there was no clear word from Church headquarters — they were cut off from Salt Lake City and were left on their own. So Otto had made the best decision he could under the circumstances, not wanting to see the hundreds of Saints carted off to concentration camps. But after the war he had a change of heart, influenced greatly by his first mission president, Max Zimmer. He felt the Church should have come right out and opposed Hitler and taken the consequences.[113]

When Otto expressed this new perspective to his next mission president, Jean Wunderlich, Wunderluch calmed him down, saying it worked out for the members better the way it did. But in 1974 Otto reports that he still feels that Max Zimmer knew best.[114]

Otto also feels badly that the branch and the district did not do anything at the time Helmuth was arrested. He states that, although there was nothing to do to help Helmuth directly, they should have told the members after

375

the arrest to "wake up and see that what he did wasn't . . . criminal."[115]

Furthermore, he reveals his inner conflict when talking about the war years. In a tone consistent with Jean Wunderlich's philosophy, he states that since the Gestapo was always watching him and had interrogated him more than once, "The blame came always to me, so I had to tell the members to be careful. They could bring not only me, but the whole Church in danger. I said, 'We are glad we can hold our meetings. But the time could come that they . . . close our branch.' But it never happened. The members were wise enough to heed my counsel and we didn't have that happen.[116] . . . I even had to go to members who were a little bit too loudmouthed against the Nazis."[117]

Gerhard Kunkel and most members still agree with that philosophy.

"I really cannot blame the members that they didn't do any more because as you know, if you just said a little bit too much you were gone overnight, nobody knew where you went to. Everybody was afraid of the Gestapo."[118] Certainly had there been a directive from Church headquarters to German members to rise up against the *Reich*, the German saints would have obeyed and placed their lives on the line, as evidenced by their general faithfulness, obedience, and sacrifice during the war.

The fearless Max Zimmer

Otto reflects, "I remember one case as we traveled there [in Germany], we came from the French zone into the American zone in Limburg. I remember it very well, and we were stopped by a lieutenant with four or five soldiers there. And that lieutenant was very aggressive and mean. And we were sitting in the car and I recall Brother Zimmer had a piece of paper in his hand and was writing. He didn't listen to him at all, to that lieutenant. And then he turned around and asked his name, and he said, 'I'd like to see your name.' They wore a name tag. So he wrote the name down of the lieutenant. And the lieutenant asked him why he wanted his name. He said, 'I am a newspaper man, and I write articles for 26 newspapers in the United States, and I am a Swiss citizen. And your name and your seriel number will be in that paper and I'll write an article how a Swiss citizen was treated here from the occupation army.' And that lieutenant, he almost fainted. And he said, 'I didn't know that,' and tried to calm him down. And he said, 'No, you can't calm me down.' And Brother Zimmer spoke perfect English. Later on I asked him, I said, 'Is it true President Zimmer?' He said, 'No, it isn't true.' (Otto laughs) He said, 'I bluffed him.' He said, 'You see, Brother Berndt, it works.' And really it worked always. He wasn't afraid of anybody."[119]

Otto finds it amusing that Zimmer showed this human side to himself, a weakness that produced a laugh.

More analysis of the Church's survival in a totalitarian state

One may argue that Helmuth did the right thing by resisting an evil system. Another may admit he was heroic but, in the overall scheme of things, should have endured his own "Cold War" with the Nazis as did other religious peoples, since he almost got his Mormon people into inextricable trouble with the *Reich*, and may have brought about their entire extermination.

Mormons, Catholics, and various Protestant and non-Christian groups attempted to coexist much of the 20th entury with Communism, Naziism, and other totalitarian governments.

Witness the president of the Church of Jesus Christ of Latter-day Saints in 1973, Harold B. Lee, who declared to East German Latter-day Saints at the Munich Area Conference to return quietly to their homes in their country and refrain from agitating against Communism.[120]

President Lee certainly did not support Communism, but he did support survival — for both the individual and the Church — within totalitarian nations.

Mormon leaders possibly foresaw the downfall of the regime and wished its members to simply ride out the storm. Heber J. Grant, another president of the Church, visited prewar Nazi Germany in 1937 and counseled his members to not emigrate, for example,[121]

Why were they counseled to not emigrate?

Certainly not all Latter-day Saints in Germany had the health or finances to emigrate. Many Mormons opposed to Naziism were married to non-LDS spouses or had non-LDS family and loved ones who could not or would not emigrate. Furthermore, had most Latter-day Saints emigrated, the hundreds who could not have may have suffered retaliation by the Nazis.

When Mormon missionaries were removed in 1938, German members of the Church of Jesus Christ of Latter-day Saints were left on their own, and their overall experiences and trials prepared them for stronger, more vigilant citizenship in both the new Germany and in America. For example, the local German member missionaries continued to bring converts into the Church in Hamburg, going door to door, according to Rudi, baptizing all the way up to 1941.[122] although it was "a little bit restricted."

The heroism of those who suffered through the Nazi firestorm is a light for those of their own and of other faiths today. The heroes at that time may well include Helmuth's brothers, Hans and Gerhard, as well as Arthur Sommerfeld, Otto Berndt, Richard and Paul Prüss, Hans Guertler, Alfred Schmidt, and Karl's father, Johannes Schnibbe, all of whom were opposed to the Nazis but who obeyed the admonitions of church leaders and went about their duty quietly, serving their fellow man through church service. Some of these were called upon — even though they conscientiously objected to the purposes of the Nazis in power — to serve in the National Labor Service and even the army — and they did so.

To contrast the accommodating attitude of German Saints there is another side. One instance, outlined in *The Book of Mormon*, reveals Latter-day Saints believing resistance was inspired of God — when American colonists were inspired to rise up against British tyranny to establish a new nation where freedom of religion would flourish, allowing for the restored Church to be established and have a safe home. In such a case, however, involving modern-day resistance, Church leaders might have a say. Latter-day Saints are taught to follow the counsel of their Church leaders, not by blind obedience but through informed, confirmed, inspired obedience.

Further adventures of Rudi in the U.S.

Once in the U.S., Rudi faced additional adversity. One of his daughter's teachers, for example, was anti-German. "Finally I went to school and said, 'Back off. You can be replaced, but my children not.' So we kind of straightened it out."[123]

Additionally, besides the fellow who reported him to the FBI, Rudi found one fellow at work from his ward for whom he cosigned a loan and the fellow stopped paying the bank, leaving Rudi in the lurch. Rudi reports his confrontation: "Finally I grabbed him at work and put him in a corner and grabbed him by his throat and said, 'Okay mister, you either make your payments and get my name out from under it. In the first place I'm going to bash your head in. Secondly, I'll take you in to the vice-president and tell him what kind of a crook you are, that you're using and abusing the friendship of a fellow employee here. He'll probably fire you anyway. Then I take you as a step number three to the bishop and tell him. . . . Either you clear this up now or I'm going to start on you right now.' . . . It worked."[124]

He had another problem with an anti-German. One of his early bishops had been conned into a loan scheme with a dishonest German. So he took out his anger on Rudi and his brother-in-law, Werner Schmidt. Rudi reported the fellow, who was soon thereafter released.[125] Otherwise, Rudi was treated well in his new homeland and looked up to at work, plus he gave numerous talks and firesides about his experiences with Helmuth and Karl. At church he was patiently helped by church leaders, including by an elders quorum president who later became his bishop. He said to Rudi, "I noticed the way you reply and give the answers. You know the gospel well. You just have to study the language a little bit, but we'll help you with that." Rudi continues, "So that's how I learned to pick it up. And they were quite nice."[126] He taught elders quorum "a long time," then was ordained a Seventy and taught them.[127] He later became an instructor in the high priests quorum "many years, and was assigned as a high priest group leader," teaching them as well.[128]

Then he was assigned, for at least 10 years, to be the trainer instructor in his stake, involving the German name extraction program. Finally he was in the branch presidency of the Eva Dawn Branch, which served a rest home.[129]

At work he became the supervisor for almost 20 years,[130] then after retirement he was contracted to consult for his company.

He reports that in December 1953 he went through the temple the first time. "What the greatest part was, when our two children were brought up from the waiting room all dressed in white and sealed to us as husband and wife. It was a very emotional time, believe me. When those two little ones came they looked like little angels. They kneeled across from us and held our hands together . . . the children put their hands on top of ours, oh my. I wouldn't trade that for all the riches of the world. And the other two, of course were born under the covenant. . . . Even if we didn't understand it all, I said, 'That will come later.' But that was a great moment. So I had my sweetheart now for time and all eternity. That puts a special touch and a special feeling on it."[131]

His testimony ends with: "I lived a full and rich life. I'm kind of glad that in my youth I was shaken hard to come to my senses, to realize what life is all about. That there are more important things in life than just to be entertained, to have a good time. There are responsibilities. There are obligations. Especially when you start building and founding your own family. That's why it was probably so easy for me to oppose the German government, because I wasn't tied to anything. But as you asked before, if I would do it again, yes. I stand up for whatever is right and just and fair. Wherever there is anything of disrepute, I stand my ground. Oh yes, we demonstrated around those porno movie houses from our high priests quorum. And I believe in the mission of the Church or the 13th Article of Faith, the admonition of Paul — anything wholesome, trustworthy, and of good report, we seek after these things and incorporate them.

We look wherever there is something good. . . . I like to read, I like to study, I like to enlarge my outlook on life especially. I'm still seeking more spirituality, getting closer to the Lord, which this calling at the Eva Dawn Branch is quite an opportunity [for]. It humbles you and makes you realize how much disease and hurt and personal calamities there are to face and gives me a good feeling to help these poor brothers and sisters and to become their friend. Quite often they ask for a blessing, of course, which I gladly give. [I] share with them my testimony and I teach the lesson, too, on Sundays, of course. I have a strong testimony of the truth of the Church, the gospel of Jesus Christ. The assurance that Jesus Christ is my elder brother gives me a feeling of pride and humility at the same time, having such a great brother that loves me and gave his life for me, so whatever happens, if I repent, he will pay the price for me, has paid the price. I'm glad to be married in the temple to my wife for time and all eternity. I love my wife and my children very dearly, but above all I love the Lord and I love to serve. I love to spread the gospel wherever possible through word or example. Above all I like the opportunity to bear my testimony wherever possible."

NOTES

In addition to the author's own interview subjects cited below, credit is extended to the LDS Church Historian's Office for interviews conducted by Alan Keele, Douglas Tobler, and Matthew Heiss, cited in these notes; and to Blair Holmes for his exhaustive research and translation of documents and letters published in *When Truth Was Treason*, many of which are utilized as sources below.

CHAPTER 1

1. Gerhard Kunkel Oral History, interviewed by Douglas F. Tobler and Alan F. Keele, Salt Lake City, Utah, 1974, typescript, p.1. The James Moyle Oral History Program, Archives, Historical Department of the Church of Jesus Christ of Latter-day Saints, Salt Lake City, Utah.

2. Hans and Charlotte Kunkel interview with author, Salt Lake City, Utah, 18 October 1996, p. 2. Helmuth's brother Gerhard recalls him actually dying of bladder cancer 8 April 1917 on the German side of Tilsit, Gerhard Kunkel interview #2 with author, 25 February 2003, p. 2 but it's possible the date was 5 March

1920. "The Führer's New Clothes: Helmuth Hübener and the Dilemma of German Mormons in the Third Reich," unpublished essay by Alan F. Keele, Used by permission from Alan F. Keele. A shorter version of this essay was later published as an article in *Sunstone*, p. 2 [Tilsit is by the River Memel, and is split into Germany and Lithuania.]

3. Gerhard Kunkel interview #1 with author, 10 October 1996, p 10

4. Kunkel Oral History, p. 2

5. Gerhard Kunkel interview #1 with author, 10 October 1996, p 10

6. Kunkel Oral History, p. 24

7. Gerhard Kunkel interview #2 with author, 25 February 2003, p. 4

8. Gerhard Kunkel interview #2 with author, 25 February 2003

9. Gerhard Kunkel interview #2 with author, 25 February 2003, p.5

10. Gerhard Kunkel interview #2 with author, 25 February 2003; Kunkel Oral History, p. 3

11. Gerhard Kunkel interview #2 with author, 25 February 2003, p. 5

12. Gerhard Kunkel interview #1 with author, 10 October 1996, p. 10

13. *Ibid.*

14. "The Führer's New Clothes: Helmuth Hübener and the Dilemma of German Mormons in the Third Reich," unpublished essay by Alan F. Keele, Used by permission from Alan F. Keele. A shorter version of this essay was later published as an article in *Sunstone*, p. 2

15. Gerhard Kunkel interview #1 with author, 10 October 1996, p. 10. In a separate interview with the author, Gerhard Kunkel says his Mother took her two sons to Hamburg the spring of the following year, in 1924. "The Führer's New Clothes: Helmuth Hübener and the Dilemma of German Mormons in the Third Reich," unpublished essay by Alan F. Keele, Used by permission from Alan F. Keele. A shorter version of this essay was later published as an article in *Sunstone*, p. 2

16. 1923-1925

17. Gerhard Kunkel interview #2 with author, 25 February 2003, p. 7

18. Gerhard Kunkel interview #2 with author, 25 February 2003, p. 10

19. Gerhard Kunkel interview #2 with author, 25 February 2003, p. 7

20. Gerhard Kunkel interview #2 with author, 25 February 2003, p. 7. Specifically, they moved from the Suddrows' second story apartment at 137b which faced southward Gerhard Kunkel interview #2 with author, 25 February 2003, p. 5 into nearby 137c, which faced northward, in Wing C Gerhard Kunkel interview #2 with author, 25 February 2003, p. 7

21. Gerhard Kunkel interview #2 with author, 25 February 2003, pp. 4-5

22. Hans and Charlotte Kunkel interview with author, Salt Lake City, Utah, 18 October 1996, p. 3

23. Hans and Charlotte Kunkel interview with author, Salt Lake City, Utah, 18 October 1996, p. 2

24. Gerhard Kunkel interview #1 with author, 10 October 1996, p. 11

25. Gerhard Kunkel interview #1 with author, 10 October 1996; Statement of Hans Kunkel, Source: *Begleitheft zur Austellung um*

das kurze Leben und Wirken des Helmuth Hübener, Catalogue of the exhibit in the Hamburg Municipal District Archive (Stadtteilarchiv) of Hamm, 26 October – 10 December, 1992

26. "The Führer's New Clothes: Helmuth Hübener and the Dilemma of German Mormons in the Third Reich," unpublished essay by Alan F. Keele, Used by permission from Alan F. Keele. A shorter version of this essay was later published as an article in *Sunstone,* p.2

27. Gerhard Kunkel interview #1 with author, 10 October 1996, p. 3

28. "The Führer's New Clothes: Helmuth Hübener and the Dilemma of German Mormons in the Third Reich," unpublished essay by Alan F. Keele, Used by permission from Alan F. Keele. A shorter version of this essay was later published as an article in *Sunstone,* p. 3

29. Gerhard Kunkel interview #1 with author, 10 October 1996, p. 3

30. Gerhard Kunkel interview #1 with author, 10 October 1996, p. 3, Gerhard Kunkel interview #2 with author, p. 4

31. Document from Hamburg, 24 February 1942, Final Report: Gestapo's Final Report of 24 Feb 1942 by Criminal Commissioner Wangemann

32. Gerhard Kunkel interview #2 with author, 25 February 2003, p. 4

33. *Ibid.*

34. *Ibid.*

35. *Ibid.*

36. Gerhard Kunkel interview #1 with author, 10 October 1996, p. 6

37. Gerhard Kunkel interview #2 with author, 25 February 2003, p. 4

38. Gerhard Kunkel interview #2 with author, 25 February 2003, p. 4

39. Gerhard Kunkel interview #1 with author, 10 October 1996

40. Letter from Emma Hübener, Hamburg, 8 March 1942, To the General Public Prosecutor at the Hanseatic Higher Regional Court; and report from Chief of Police, Hamburg, Police Station at 43rd Police Precinct, No. 92/42, 4 February 1942

41. Statement of Hans Kunkel, Source: *Begleitheft zur Austellung um das kurze Leben und Wirken des Helmuth Hübener,* Catalogue of the exhibit in the Hamburg Municipal District Archive (Stadtteilarchiv) of Hamm, 26 October – 10 December, 1992

42. *Ibid.*

43. Gerhard Kunkel interview #1 with author, 10 October 1996, p. 11

44. Gerhard Kunkel interview #2 with author, 25 February 2003, p. 9. In another interview he estimated it as two miles away, ["The Führer's New Clothes: Helmuth Hübener and the Dilemma of German Mormons in the Third Reich," unpublished essay by Alan F. Keele, Used by permission from Alan F. Keele. A shorter version of this essay was later published as an article in *Sunstone*, p. 23]. Despite the mileage variance, Gerhard shows a remarkable consistency in interviews with hundreds of facts spread over 29 years - from 1974 to 2003.

45. Gerhard Kunkel interview #2 with author, 25 February 2003, pp. 3-4

46. "The Führer's New Clothes: Helmuth Hübener and the Dilemma of German Mormons in the Third Reich," unpublished essay by Alan F. Keele, Used by permission from Alan F. Keele. A shorter version of this essay was later published as an article in *Sunstone*, p. 3

47. Gerhard Kunkel interview #2 with author, 25 February 2003, p. 3

48. Gerhard Kunkel interview #2 with author, 25 February 2003, p. 3; Kunkel Oral History, p. 3. Johann Kunkel's next marriage was to Maria Schaefer in Bad Orb 22 June 1929. This is where he had moved after his separation from Emma - it was his birthplace and home before World War I Gerhard Kunkel interview #2 with author, 25 February 2003, p. 2

49. Gerhard Kunkel interview #1 with author, 10 October 1996, p. 11, "The Führer's New Clothes: Helmuth Hübener and the Dilemma of German Mormons in the Third Reich," unpublished essay by Alan F. Keele, Used by permission from Alan F. Keele. A shorter version of this essay was later published as an article in *Sunstone*, p. 12

50. Marie Friebel Sommerfeld 1897-1984, Interviewed in German by Douglas Tobler and Alan Keele, 1974 : (13 leaves in English) (Matthew K. Heiss later wrote Iris Schmidt on 17 Sep 1992 saying the Sommerfeld interview was never fully edited.) Typed ca. 1985 by Karen H. Pyper, p.1

51. Marie Friebel Sommerfeld 1897-1984, Interviewed in German by Douglas Tobler and Alan Keele, 1974 : (13 leaves in English; Matthew K. Heiss later wrote Iris Schmidt on 17 Sep 1992 saying the Sommerfeld interview was never fully edited; typed ca. 1985 by Karen H. Pyper), p. 1

52. Rudolf G. Wobbe Oral History, Doublas F. Tobler and Alan F. Keele, 1974, typescript, The James Moyle Oral History Program, Archives, Historical Department of the Church of Jesus Christ of Latter-day Saints, Salt Lake City, Utah, p. 29

53. Otto Berndt Oral History, interviewed by Douglas F. Tobler, Salt Lake City, Utah, 1974, typescript, The James Moyle Oral History Program, Archives, Historical Department of the Church of Jesus Christ of Latter-day Saints, Salt Lake City, Utah, p. 38

54. "The Führer's New Clothes: Helmuth Hübener and the Dilemma of German Mormons in the Third Reich," unpublished

essay by Alan F. Keele, Used by permission from Alan F. Keele. A shorter version of this essay was later published as an article in *Sunstone*, p. 24

55. Gerhard Kunkel interview #1 with author, 10 October 1996, p. 3

56. Kunkel Oral History, p. 25

57. Otto Berndt Oral History, interviewed by Douglas F. Tobler, Salt Lake City, Utah, 1974, typescript, The James Moyle Oral History Program, Archives, Historical Department of the Church of Jesus Christ of Latter-day Saints, Salt Lake City, Utah, p. 38

58. Otto Berndt Oral History, interviewed by Douglas F. Tobler, Salt Lake City, Utah, 1974, typescript, The James Moyle Oral History Program, Archives, Historical Department of the Church of Jesus Christ of Latter-day Saints, Salt Lake City, Utah, p. 38

59. Gerhard Kunkel interview #1 with author, 10 October 1996, p. 6

60. Kunkel

61. "The Führer's New Clothes: Helmuth Hübener and the Dilemma of German Mormons in the Third Reich," unpublished essay by Alan F. Keele, Used by permission from Alan F. Keele. A shorter version of this essay was later published as an article in Sunstone, p. 3

62. Guddat, also spelled Gudat

63. Marie Sommerfeld statement

64. Hübener

65. Blair Holmes, Alan Keele, and Karl-Heinz Schnibbe, *When Truth Was Treason*, Urbana and Chicago, Illinois: University of Illinois Press, 1995, p. 25

66. Hans and Charlotte Kunkel interview with author, Salt Lake City, Utah, 18 October 1996, p. 2

67. Gerhard Kunkel interview #1 with author, 10 October 1996; Gerhard Kunkel interview #2 with author, 25 February 2003

CHAPTER 2

1. "The Führer's New Clothes: Helmuth Hübener and the Dilemma of German Mormons in the Third Reich," unpublished essay by Alan F. Keele, Used by permission from Alan F. Keele. A shorter version of this essay was later published as an article in *Sunstone*, p. 5

2. *Der Stern*, Vol. 66 1934, 47, 142-143; and letter from Karl-Heinz Schnibbe to his family, 12 December 1948

3. who is often referred to by his friends as simply Karl, and which he shall be designated hereinafter in this text

4. Blair Holmes, Alan Keele, and Karl-Heinz Schnibbe, *When Truth Was Treason*, Urbana and Chicago, Illinois: University of Illinois Press, 1995, [Karl Schnibbe book], p. 8

5. Oppenheimer-Blum, Standard of Living, p. 15

6. Wolfram Fischer, *Deutsche Wirtschaftspolitik* 1918-1945, 3rd ed. [Opladen: C.W. Leske, 1968], p. 108

7. Rudi Wobbe Fireside [youth church lecture], 1987, transcribed by Richard Dewey and Heather Dewey, 1-4 February 2003, used by permission from Herta Wobbe, pp. 2-3. As for inflation, the Reichsmark had shrunk a billion times, causing people to wallpaper their homes with paper money and using it to light fires Rudi Wobbe Oral History, interviewed by Matthew K. Heiss, Salt Lake City, Utah, 1988, typescript, The James Moyle Oral History Program, Archives, Historical Department of the Church of Jesus Christ of Latter-day Saints, Salt Lake City, Utah, p. 3]

8. Rudi Wobbe Fireside [youth church lecture], 1987, transcribed by Richard Dewey and Heather Dewey, 1-4 February 2003, used by permission from Herta Wobbe, p. 3

9. Blair Holmes, Alan Keele, and Karl-Heinz Schnibbe, *When Truth Was Treason*, Urbana and Chicago, Illinois: University of Illinois Press, 1995, p. 13

10. Rudi Wobbe Oral History, interviewed by Matthew K. Heiss, Salt Lake City, Utah, 1988, typescript, The James Moyle Oral History Program, Archives, Historical Department of the Church of Jesus Christ of Latter-day Saints, Salt Lake City, Utah, p. 20

11. Rudolf G. Wobbe Oral History, Doublas F. Tobler and Alan F. Keele, 1974, typescript, The James Moyle Oral History Program, Archives, Historical Department of the Church of Jesus Christ of Latter-day Saints, Salt Lake City, Utah, p. 17

12. Blair Holmes, Alan Keele, and Karl-Heinz Schnibbe, *When Truth Was Treason*, Urbana and Chicago, Illinois: University of Illinois Press, 1995

13. Blair Holmes, Alan Keele, and Karl-Heinz Schnibbe, *When Truth Was Treason*, Urbana and Chicago, Illinois: University of Illinois Press, 1995, pp. 17-18

14. Blair Holmes, Alan Keele, and Karl-Heinz Schnibbe, *When Truth Was Treason*, Urbana and Chicago, Illinois: University of Illinois Press, 1995, p. 17

15. Blair Holmes, Alan Keele, and Karl-Heinz Schnibbe, *When Truth Was Treason*, Urbana and Chicago, Illinois: University of Illinois Press, 1995, p. 18

16. Pp 15-16, Blair Holmes, Alan Keele, and Karl-Heinz Schnibbe, *When Truth Was Treason*, Urbana and Chicago, Illinois: University of Illinois Press, 1995

17. Arthur and Marie Sommerfeld interview with author, 18 October 1996

18. Rudi Wobbe Fireside [youth church lecture], 1987, transcribed by Richard Dewey and Heather Dewey, 1-4 February 2003, used by permission from Herta Wobbe, p. 4

19. Blair Holmes, Alan Keele, and Karl-Heinz Schnibbe, *When Truth Was Treason*, Urbana and Chicago, Illinois: University of Illinois Press, 1995, p. 14

20. Pp 14-15 Blair Holmes, Alan Keele, and Karl-Heinz Schnibbe, *When Truth Was Treason*, Urbana and Chicago, Illinois: University of Illinois Press, 1995

21. P. 15 Blair Holmes, Alan Keele, and Karl-Heinz Schnibbe, *When Truth Was Treason*, Urbana and Chicago, Illinois: University of Illinois Press, 1995

22. Ditt, *Sozialdemokraten im Widerstand*, p. 72

23. Focke, *Altag unterm HakenKreuz*, p. 84

24. Schorer, *Als Hamburg unter den Nazis lebte*, pp. 21-22

25. Hans A. Schmitt, *Lucky Victim: An Ordinary Life in Extraordinary Times* 1933-1946 [Baton Rouge: Louisiana State University Press, 1989], Pp. 54-55

26. Rudi Wobbe Oral History, interviewed by Matthew K. Heiss, Salt Lake City, Utah, 1988, typescript, The James Moyle Oral History Program, Archives, Historical Department of the Church of Jesus Christ of Latter-day Saints, Salt Lake City, Utah, p. 54

27. H.W. Koch, *The Hitler Youth: Origins and Development*, 1922-45 [London: MacDonald and Jane's, 1975], pp. 172-73

28. Koch, *Ibid.*

29. Koch, *Ibid*

30. Leaflet written by Helmuth Hübener, "The Voice of the Homeland"

31. Jeremy Noakes, Social Outcasts in the Third Reich, in Bessel, *Life in the Third Reich*, pp. 83-84

32. Statement of Rudolf Wobbe, Rudolf Wobbe, Salt Lake City, Utah, 17 April 1961, Source: Historical Department, Church of Jesus Christ of Latter-day Saints, Salt Lake City, Utah Statement of Rudolf Wobbe, Rudolf Wobbe, Salt Lake City, Utah, 17 April 1961, Source: Historical Department, Church of Jesus Christ of Latter-day Saints, Salt Lake City, Utah

33. Rudi Wobbe Oral History, interviewed by Matthew K. Heiss, Salt Lake City, Utah, 1988, typescript, The James Moyle Oral History Program, Archives, Historical Department of the Church of Jesus Christ of Latter-day Saints, Salt Lake City, Utah, p. 12, andRudolf G. Wobbe Oral History, Doublas F. Tobler and Alan F. Keele, 1974, typescript, The James Moyle Oral History Program, Archives, Historical Department of the Church of Jesus Christ of Latter-day Saints, Salt Lake City, Utah, p. 38

34. Rudi Wobbe Oral History, interviewed by Matthew K. Heiss, Salt Lake City, Utah, 1988, typescript, The James Moyle Oral History Program, Archives, Historical Department of the Church of Jesus Christ of Latter-day Saints, Salt Lake City, Utah, p. 12

35. Statement of Friedrich Peters, born 1920, Source: *Begleitheft zur Austellung um das kurze Leben und Wirken des Helmuth Hübener,* Catalogue of the exhibit in the Hamburg Municipal District Archive (Stadtteilarchiv) of Hamm, 26 October – 10 December

36. Statement of Friedrich Peters, born 1920, Source: *Begleitheft zur Austellung um das kurze Leben und Wirken des Helmuth Hübener,* Catalogue of the exhibit in the Hamburg Municipal District Archive (Stadtteilarchiv) of Hamm, 26 October – 10 December

37. H.W. Koch, *Hitler Youth*, pp. 101, 113

38. H.W. Koch, *Hitler Youth*, pp. 101, 113

39. Delarues, *The Gestapo: A History of Horror* [New York: Paragon House, 1987], p. 80; also see Gellately, *Gestapo and German Society*; pp. 73-74; Grunberger, *Social History of the Third Reich*, p. 67; Behrend-Rosenfeld, *Ich stand nicht allein*, p. 64; Mackinnon, *Naked Years*, p. 196

40. Rudi Wobbe Oral History, interviewed by Matthew K. Heiss, Salt Lake City, Utah, 1988, typescript, The James Moyle Oral History Program, Archives, Historical Department of the Church of Jesus Christ of Latter-day Saints, Salt Lake City, Utah, p. 34

41. Ingo Müller, *Hitler's Justice*, pp. 74, 90-91, 111-115, 130-134

42. Leo Schwering, *In den Klauen der Gestapo, Tagebuchauf-zeichnungen der Jahre* 1944-1945 Koln: Verlag J.P. Bachem, 1988 p. 82

43. Rudi Wobbe Fireside [youth church lecture], 1987, transcribed by Richard Dewey and Heather Dewey, 1-4 February 2003, used by permission from Herta Wobbe, p. 4, also seeRudi Wobbe Oral History, interviewed by Matthew K. Heiss, Salt Lake City, Utah, 1988, typescript, The James Moyle Oral History Program, Archives, Historical Department of the Church of Jesus Christ of Latter-day Saints, Salt Lake City, Utah, p. 10

44. Rudi Wobbe Oral History, interviewed by Matthew K. Heiss, Salt Lake City, Utah, 1988, typescript, The James Moyle Oral History Program, Archives, Historical Department of the Church of Jesus Christ of Latter-day Saints, Salt Lake City, Utah, p. 10

45. Gerhard Kunkel interview #1 with author, 10 October 1996, p. 13

46. Gerhard Kunkel interview #1 with author, 10 October 1996, p. 13

47. Sanford M. bingham Oral History, interviewed by Douglas F. Tober and Alan F. Keele, typescript, P. 4, The James Moyle Oral History Program, Archives, Historical Department of the

Church of Jesus Christ of Latter-day Saints, Salt Lake City, Utah

48. Bingham Oral History, p. 30

49. Zentner and Bedurftig, Encyclopedia of the Third Reich, I: 715

50. Rudi Wobbe Fireside [youth church lecture], 1987, transcribed by Richard Dewey and Heather Dewey, 1-4 February 2003, used by permission from Herta Wobbe, p. 8

51. Blair Holmes, Alan Keele, and Karl-Heinz Schnibbe, *When Truth Was Treason*, Urbana and Chicago, Illinois: University of Illinois Press, 1995, p. 28

52. Encyclopedia: I: 298

53. Karl Schnibbe interview with author, Salt Lake City, Utah, 16 September 1996, transcribed by Don Ricks, p. 39

54. Gaeth Oral History, p. 19

55. Peter Hoffmann, *The History of the German Resistance, 1933-1945*, Cambridge, MA: MIT Press, 1977, p. 16

56. Arthur Gaeth Oral History, interviewed by Douglas F. Tobler, 1980, typescript, p. 18, The James Moyle Oral History Program, Archives, Historical Department of the Church of Jesus Christ of Latter-day Saints, Salt Lake City, Utah

CHAPTER 3

1. Rudi Wobbe Oral History, interviewed by Matthew K. Heiss, Salt Lake City, Utah, 1988, typescript, The James Moyle Oral History Program, Archives, Historical Department of the Church of Jesus Christ of Latter-day Saints, Salt Lake City, Utah, pp. 68-69

2. Rudi Wobbe Oral History, interviewed by Matthew K. Heiss, Salt Lake City, Utah, 1988, typescript, The James Moyle Oral History Program, Archives, Historical Department of the Church of Jesus Christ of Latter-day Saints, Salt Lake City, Utah, p. 9

3. "The Führer's New Clothes: Helmuth Hübener and the Dilemma of German Mormons in the Third Reich," unpublished essay by Alan F. Keele, Used by permission from Alan F. Keele. A shorter version of this essay was later published as an article in *Sunstone*, p. 8

4. Otto Berndt Oral History, interviewed by Douglas F. Tobler, Salt Lake City, Utah, 1974, typescript, The James Moyle Oral History Program, Archives, Historical Department of the Church of Jesus Christ of Latter-day Saints, Salt Lake City, Utah, p. 36. In 1974 district president Otto Berndt does not recall Helmuth as the branch clerk — only the district clerk — and that he had a key to my office. Otto Berndt Oral History, interviewed by Douglas F. Tobler, Salt Lake City, Utah, 1974, typescript, The James Moyle Oral History Program, Archives, Historical Department of the Church of Jesus Christ of Latter-day Saints, Salt Lake City, Utah, p. 36] But Gerhard Kunkel, Arthur Sommerfeld, Rudi Wobbe, Karl Schnibbe, and others state that Helmuth was the branch clerk. He was either both, or with the passage of time, Otto confused Helmuth's positons.

5. "The Führer's New Clothes: Helmuth Hübener and the Dilemma of German Mormons in the Third Reich," unpublished essay by Alan F. Keele, Used by permission from Alan F. Keele. A shorter version of this essay was later published as an article in *Sunstone*, p. 8

6. "The Führer's New Clothes: Helmuth Hübener and the Dilemma of German Mormons in the Third Reich," unpublished essay by Alan F. Keele, Used by permission from Alan F. Keele. A shorter version of this essay was later published as an article in *Sunstone*, p. 8

7. "The Führer's New Clothes: Helmuth Hübener and the Dilemma of German Mormons in the Third Reich," unpublished essay by Alan F. Keele, Used by permission from Alan F. Keele. A shorter version of this essay was later published as an article in *Sunstone*, p. 12

8. Arthur and Marie Sommerfeld interview with author, Salt Lake City, Utah, 18 October 1996, p. 12; see also Statement of Rudolf Wobbe, Rudolf Wobbe, Salt Lake City, Utah, 17 April 1961, Source: Historical Department, Church of Jesus Christ of Latter-day Saints, Salt Lake City, Utah Statement of Rudolf Wobbe, Rudolf Wobbe, Salt Lake City, Utah, 17 April 1961, Source: Historical Department, Church of Jesus Christ of Latter-day Saints, Salt Lake City, Utah, Statement of Marie Sommerfeld, Source: *Begleitheft zur Austellung um das kurze Leben und Wirken des Helmuth Hübener,* Catalogue of the exhibit in the Hamburg Municipal District Archive (Stadtteilarchiv) of Hamm, 26 October – 10 December, 1992; andRudolf G. Wobbe Oral History, Doublas F. Tobler and Alan F. Keele, 1974, typescript, The James Moyle Oral History Program, Archives, Historical Department of the Church of Jesus Christ of Latter-day Saints, Salt Lake City, Utah, p. 31

9. Otto Berndt Oral History, interviewed by Douglas F. Tobler, Salt Lake City, Utah, 1974, typescript, The James Moyle Oral History Program, Archives, Historical Department of the Church of Jesus Christ of Latter-day Saints, Salt Lake City, Utah, p. 46

10. Otto Berndt Oral History, interviewed by Douglas F. Tobler, Salt Lake City, Utah, 1974, typescript, The James Moyle Oral History Program, Archives, Historical Department of the Church of Jesus Christ of Latter-day Saints, Salt Lake City, Utah, p. 47

11. Arthur and Marie Sommerfeld interview with author, Salt Lake City, Utah, 18 October 1996, p. 13-14

12. Hilde Prüss Müller, interview with author 18 October 2003

13. "The Führer's New Clothes: Helmuth Hübener and the Dilemma of German Mormons in the Third Reich," unpublished

essay by Alan F. Keele, used by permission from Alan F. Keele. A shorter version of this essay was later published as an article in *Sunstone*, p. 15

14. MS 11881, Author: Vedder, Ana Marie, Title: Documents relating to Saloman Schwarz, 1942-1989

15. Blair Holmes, Alan Keele, and Karl-Heinz Schnibbe, *When Truth Was Treason*, Urbana and Chicago, Illinois: University of Illinois Press, 1995; Rudi Wobbe and Jerry Borrowman, *Three Against Hitler*, (American Fork, Utah: Covenant Communications, 1992); and Lieselotte Prüss Schmidt, 17 Oct 2003, and Hilde Prüss Müller 18 Oct 2003

16. Rudi Wobbe Oral History, interviewed by Matthew K. Heiss, Salt Lake City, Utah, 1988, typescript, The James Moyle Oral History Program, Archives, Historical Department of the Church of Jesus Christ of Latter-day Saints, Salt Lake City, Utah, p. 16. Despite some accounts saying Saloman Schwarz belonged to the St. Georg Branch and was expelled from it by Arthur Zander, Otto Berndt states that Saloman Schwarz actually belonged to the Barmbeck Branch, (Otto Berndt Oral History, interviewed by Douglas F. Tobler, Salt Lake City, Utah, 1974, typescript, The James Moyle Oral History Program, Archives, Historical Department of the Church of Jesus Christ of Latter-day Saints, Salt Lake City, Utah, p. 33), and Werner Schmidt, whose father was the branch president of Barmbeck, says that Salomon lived near the Barmbeck Branch and thus would have had his membership there (Werner Schmidt interview with author, 20 October 2003).

17. Rudi Wobbe Oral History, interviewed by Matthew K. Heiss, Salt Lake City, Utah, 1988, typescript, The James Moyle Oral History Program, Archives, Historical Department of the Church of Jesus Christ of Latter-day Saints, Salt Lake City, Utah, p. 17

18. "The Führer's New Clothes: Helmuth Hübener and the Dilemma of German Mormons in the Third Reich," unpublished essay by Alan F. Keele, used by permission from Alan F. Keele.

A shorter version of this essay was later published as an article in *Sunstone*, p. 15

19. "The Führer's New Clothes: Helmuth Hübener and the Dilemma of German Mormons in the Third Reich," unpublished essay by Alan F. Keele, used by permission from Alan F. Keele. A shorter version of this essay was later published as an article in *Sunstone*, p. 14 and Herta Wobbe conversation 27 April 1999

20. Rudi Wobbe Fireside [youth church lecture], 1987, transcribed by Richard Dewey and Heather Dewey, 1-4 February 2003, used by permission from Herta Wobbe, p.5

21. Rudolf G. Wobbe Oral History, Doublas F. Tobler and Alan F. Keele, 1974, typescript, The James Moyle Oral History Program, Archives, Historical Department of the Church of Jesus Christ of Latter-day Saints, Salt Lake City, Utah, p. 37

22. Werner Schmidt interview with author, 20 October 2003

23. Rudolf G. Wobbe Oral History, Doublas F. Tobler and Alan F. Keele, 1974, typescript, The James Moyle Oral History Program, Archives, Historical Department of the Church of Jesus Christ of Latter-day Saints, Salt Lake City, Utah, p. 37

24. Rudi Wobbe Fireside [youth church lecture], 1987, transcribed by Richard Dewey and Heather Dewey, 1-4 February 2003, used by permission from Herta Wobbe; and Rudolf G. Wobbe Oral History, Doublas F. Tobler and Alan F. Keele, 1974, typescript, The James Moyle Oral History Program, Archives, Historical Department of the Church of Jesus Christ of Latter-day Saints, Salt Lake City, Utah, p. 18

25. Otto Berndt Oral History, interviewed by Douglas F. Tobler, Salt Lake City, Utah, 1974, typescript, The James Moyle Oral History Program, Archives, Historical Department of the Church of Jesus Christ of Latter-day Saints, Salt Lake City, Utah, p. 33; see also Rudi Wobbe Oral History, interviewed by Matthew K. Heiss, Salt Lake City, Utah, 1988, typescript, The James Moyle Oral History Program, Archives, Historical Department

of the Church of Jesus Christ of Latter-day Saints, Salt Lake City, Utah, p. 23, in which Rudi also believes this held true for church socials and Sunday meetings as well, although Otto denies it occurred on Sundays

26. Blair Holmes, Alan Keele, and Karl-Heinz Schnibbe, *When Truth Was Treason*, Urbana and Chicago, Illinois: University of Illinois Press, 1995, p. 26

27. Karl Schnibbe interview with author, Salt Lake City, Utah, 16 September 1996, transcribed by Don Ricks, p. 43

28. Rudi Wobbe Oral History, interviewed by Matthew K. Heiss, Salt Lake City, Utah, 1988, typescript, The James Moyle Oral History Program, Archives, Historical Department of the Church of Jesus Christ of Latter-day Saints, Salt Lake City, Utah, p. 14

29. *Ibid.*

30. "The Führer's New Clothes: Helmuth Hübener and the Dilemma of German Mormons in the Third Reich," unpublished essay by Alan F. Keele, Used by permission from Alan F. Keele. A shorter version of this essay was later published as an article in *Sunstone*, pp. 15-16

31. Rudolf G. Wobbe Oral History, Doublas F. Tobler and Alan F. Keele, 1974, typescript, The James Moyle Oral History Program, Archives, Historical Department of the Church of Jesus Christ of Latter-day Saints, Salt Lake City, Utah, p. 16

32. Rudi Wobbe Oral History, interviewed by Matthew K. Heiss, Salt Lake City, Utah, 1988, typescript, The James Moyle Oral History Program, Archives, Historical Department of the Church of Jesus Christ of Latter-day Saints, Salt Lake City, Utah, p. 26

33. Rudolf G. Wobbe Oral History, Doublas F. Tobler and Alan F. Keele, 1974, typescript, The James Moyle Oral History Program, Archives, Historical Department of the Church of Jesus Christ of Latter-day Saints, Salt Lake City, Utah, p. 16

34. Herta Wobbe 9 April 1999 conversation with author

35. Karl Schnibbe interview with author, Salt Lake City, Utah, 16 September 1996, transcribed by Don Ricks, p. 35

36. Rudi Wobbe Oral History, interviewed by Matthew K. Heiss, Salt Lake City, Utah, 1988, typescript, The James Moyle Oral History Program, Archives, Historical Department of the Church of Jesus Christ of Latter-day Saints, Salt Lake City, Utah, p. 26

37. Blair Holmes, Alan Keele, and Karl-Heinz Schnibbe, *When Truth Was Treason*, Urbana and Chicago, Illinois: University of Illinois Press, 1995, p. 27

38. Karl Schnibbe interview with author, Salt Lake City, Utah, 16 September 1996, transcribed by Don Ricks, p. 43

39. Karl Schnibbe interview with author, Salt Lake City, Utah, 16 September 1996, transcribed by Don Ricks, p. 37

40. "The Führer's New Clothes: Helmuth Hübener and the Dilemma of German Mormons in the Third Reich," unpublished essay by Alan F. Keele, Used by permission from Alan F. Keele. A shorter version of this essay was later published as an article in *Sunstone*, p. 9

41. "The Führer's New Clothes: Helmuth Hübener and the Dilemma of German Mormons in the Third Reich," unpublished essay by Alan F. Keele, Used by permission from Alan F. Keele. A shorter version of this essay was later published as an article in *Sunstone*, pp. 9-10

42. Otto Berndt Oral History, interviewed by Douglas F. Tobler, Salt Lake City, Utah, 1974, typescript, The James Moyle Oral History Program, Archives, Historical Department of the Church of Jesus Christ of Latter-day Saints, Salt Lake City, Utah, p. 31. They made a product called Persil. "The Führer's New Clothes: Helmuth Hübener and the Dilemma of German Mormons in the Third Reich," unpublished essay by Alan F. Keele, Used by permission from Alan F. Keele. A shorter version of this

essay was later published as an article in *Sunstone*, pp. 9-10 Karl says it was a laundry detergent factory Blair Holmes, Alan Keele, and Karl-Heinz Schnibbe, *When Truth Was Treason*, Urbana and Chicago, Illinois: University of Illinois Press, 1995, p. 27

43. "The Führer's New Clothes: Helmuth Hübener and the Dilemma of German Mormons in the Third Reich," unpublished essay by Alan F. Keele, Used by permission from Alan F. Keele. A shorter version of this essay was later published as an article in *Sunstone*, p. 11

44. "The Führer's New Clothes: Helmuth Hübener and the Dilemma of German Mormons in the Third Reich," unpublished essay by Alan F. Keele, Used by permission from Alan F. Keele. A shorter version of this essay was later published as an article in *Sunstone*, p. 11

45. "The Führer's New Clothes: Helmuth Hübener and the Dilemma of German Mormons in the Third Reich," unpublished essay by Alan F. Keele, Used by permission from Alan F. Keele. A shorter version of this essay was later published as an article in *Sunstone*, p. 16

46. Marie Friebel Sommerfeld 1897-1984, Interviewed in German by Douglas Tobler and Alan Keele, 1974 : (13 leaves in English; Matthew K. Heiss later wrote Iris Schmidt on 17 Sep 1992 saying the Sommerfeld interview was never fully edited; typed ca. 1985 by Karen H. Pyper), p. 6

47. "The Führer's New Clothes: Helmuth Hübener and the Dilemma of German Mormons in the Third Reich," unpublished essay by Alan F. Keele, Used by permission from Alan F. Keele. A shorter version of this essay was later published as an article in *Sunstone*, p. 18

48. "The Führer's New Clothes: Helmuth Hübener and the Dilemma of German Mormons in the Third Reich," unpublished essay by Alan F. Keele, Used by permission from Alan F. Keele.

A shorter version of this essay was later published as an article in *Sunstone*, p. 19

49. Rudolf G. Wobbe Oral History, Doublas F. Tobler and Alan F. Keele, 1974, typescript, The James Moyle Oral History Program, Archives, Historical Department of the Church of Jesus Christ of Latter-day Saints, Salt Lake City, Utah, pp. 14-15

50. Rudolf G. Wobbe Oral History, Doublas F. Tobler and Alan F. Keele, 1974, typescript, The James Moyle Oral History Program, Archives, Historical Department of the Church of Jesus Christ of Latter-day Saints, Salt Lake City, Utah, p. 14

51. Rudolf G. Wobbe Oral History, Doublas F. Tobler and Alan F. Keele, 1974, typescript, The James Moyle Oral History Program, Archives, Historical Department of the Church of Jesus Christ of Latter-day Saints, Salt Lake City, Utah, p. 14

52. Rudi Wobbe Oral History, interviewed by Matthew K. Heiss, Salt Lake City, Utah, 1988, typescript, The James Moyle Oral History Program, Archives, Historical Department of the Church of Jesus Christ of Latter-day Saints, Salt Lake City, Utah, 0. 21

53. Otto Berndt Oral History, interviewed by Douglas F. Tobler, Salt Lake City, Utah, 1974, typescript, The James Moyle Oral History Program, Archives, Historical Department of the Church of Jesus Christ of Latter-day Saints, Salt Lake City, Utah, p. 36

54. Otto Berndt Oral History, interviewed by Douglas F. Tobler, Salt Lake City, Utah, 1974, typescript, The James Moyle Oral History Program, Archives, Historical Department of the Church of Jesus Christ of Latter-day Saints, Salt Lake City, Utah, p. 69

55. Rudolf G. Wobbe Oral History, Doublas F. Tobler and Alan F. Keele, 1974, typescript, The James Moyle Oral History Program, Archives, Historical Department of the Church of Jesus Christ of Latter-day Saints, Salt Lake City, Utah, p. 19

56. Rudolf G. Wobbe Oral History, Doublas F. Tobler and Alan F. Keele, 1974, typescript, The James Moyle Oral History Program, Archives, Historical Department of the Church of Jesus Christ of Latter-day Saints, Salt Lake City, Utah, p. 19

57. Rudolf G. Wobbe Oral History, Doublas F. Tobler and Alan F. Keele, 1974, typescript, The James Moyle Oral History Program, Archives, Historical Department of the Church of Jesus Christ of Latter-day Saints, Salt Lake City, Utah, pp. 21-22

58. Marie Friebel Sommerfeld 1897-1984, Interviewed in German by Douglas Tobler and Alan Keele, 1974 : (13 leaves in English; Matthew K. Heiss later wrote Iris Schmidt on 17 Sep 1992 saying the Sommerfeld interview was never fully edited; typed ca. 1985 by Karen H. Pyper), p. 11

59. Rudolf G. Wobbe Oral History, Doublas F. Tobler and Alan F. Keele, 1974, typescript, The James Moyle Oral History Program, Archives, Historical Department of the Church of Jesus Christ of Latter-day Saints, Salt Lake City, Utah, p. 36

60. Marie Friebel Sommerfeld 1897-1984, Interviewed in German by Douglas Tobler and Alan Keele, 1974 : (13 leaves in English; Matthew K. Heiss later wrote Iris Schmidt on 17 Sep 1992 saying the Sommerfeld interview was never fully edited; typed ca. 1985 by Karen H. Pyper), p. 11

61. "The Führer's New Clothes: Helmuth Hübener and the Dilemma of German Mormons in the Third Reich," unpublished essay by Alan F. Keele, Used by permission from Alan F. Keele. A shorter version of this essay was later published as an article in *Sunstone*, p. 10

62. Otto Berndt Oral History, interviewed by Douglas F. Tobler, Salt Lake City, Utah, 1974, typescript, The James Moyle Oral History Program, Archives, Historical Department of the Church of Jesus Christ of Latter-day Saints, Salt Lake City, Utah, p. 49

63. Marie Friebel Sommerfeld 1897-1984, Interviewed in German by Douglas Tobler and Alan Keele, 1974 : (13 leaves in English;

Matthew K. Heiss later wrote Iris Schmidt on 17 Sep 1992 saying the Sommerfeld interview was never fully edited; typed ca. 1985 by Karen H. Pyper), p. 7

64. Rudi Wobbe Oral History, interviewed by Matthew K. Heiss, Salt Lake City, Utah, 1988, typescript, The James Moyle Oral History Program, Archives, Historical Department of the Church of Jesus Christ of Latter-day Saints, Salt Lake City, Utah, p. 24

65. Marie Friebel Sommerfeld 1897-1984, Interviewed in German by Douglas Tobler and Alan Keele, 1974 : (13 leaves in English; Matthew K. Heiss later wrote Iris Schmidt on 17 Sep 1992 saying the Sommerfeld interview was never fully edited; typed ca. 1985 by Karen H. Pyper), p. 12

66. Rudolf G. Wobbe Oral History, Doublas F. Tobler and Alan F. Keele, 1974, typescript, The James Moyle Oral History Program, Archives, Historical Department of the Church of Jesus Christ of Latter-day Saints, Salt Lake City, Utah, p. 23 andRudi Wobbe Oral History, interviewed by Matthew K. Heiss, Salt Lake City, Utah, 1988, typescript, The James Moyle Oral History Program, Archives, Historical Department of the Church of Jesus Christ of Latter-day Saints, Salt Lake City, Utah, p. 24; and Otto Berndt Oral History, interviewed by Douglas F. Tobler, Salt Lake City, Utah, 1974, typescript, The James Moyle Oral History Program, Archives, Historical Department of the Church of Jesus Christ of Latter-day Saints, Salt Lake City, Utah, p. 36

67. "The Führer's New Clothes: Helmuth Hübener and the Dilemma of German Mormons in the Third Reich," unpublished essay by Alan F. Keele, Used by permission from Alan F. Keele. A shorter version of this essay was later published as an article in *Sunstone*, p. 20. Rudi Wobbe agrees Anton Huck merely leaned toward the party, Rudolf G. Wobbe Oral History, Doublas F. Tobler and Alan F. Keele, 1974, typescript, The James Moyle Oral History Program, Archives, Historical Department of the Church of Jesus Christ of Latter-day Saints, Salt Lake City, Utah, p. 22 although Otto Berndt's opinion

was that Huck really believed it. Otto Berndt Oral History, interviewed by Douglas F. Tobler, Salt Lake City, Utah, 1974, typescript, The James Moyle Oral History Program, Archives, Historical Department of the Church of Jesus Christ of Latter-day Saints, Salt Lake City, Utah, pp. 35

68. Rudi Wobbe Oral History, interviewed by Matthew K. Heiss, Salt Lake City, Utah, 1988, typescript, The James Moyle Oral History Program, Archives, Historical Department of the Church of Jesus Christ of Latter-day Saints, Salt Lake City, Utah, p. 24

69. Rudolf G. Wobbe Oral History, Doublas F. Tobler and Alan F. Keele, 1974, typescript, The James Moyle Oral History Program, Archives, Historical Department of the Church of Jesus Christ of Latter-day Saints, Salt Lake City, Utah, p. 16

70. Herta Wobbe conversations with author, 1996-2003

71. Resa Guertler Frey interview #1 with author, 17 Oct 2003

72. Rudi Wobbe Oral History, interviewed by Matthew K. Heiss, Salt Lake City, Utah, 1988, typescript, The James Moyle Oral History Program, Archives, Historical Department of the Church of Jesus Christ of Latter-day Saints, Salt Lake City, Utah, p. 21

73. Marie Friebel Sommerfeld 1897-1984, Interviewed in German by Douglas Tobler and Alan Keele, 1974 : (13 leaves in English; Matthew K. Heiss later wrote Iris Schmidt on 17 Sep 1992 saying the Sommerfeld interview was never fully edited; typed ca. 1985 by Karen H. Pyper), p. 7

74. Rudi Wobbe Oral History, interviewed by Matthew K. Heiss, Salt Lake City, Utah, 1988, typescript, The James Moyle Oral History Program, Archives, Historical Department of the Church of Jesus Christ of Latter-day Saints, Salt Lake City, Utah, p. 14

75. Otto Berndt Oral History, interviewed by Douglas F. Tobler, Salt Lake City, Utah, 1974, typescript, The James Moyle Oral History

Program, Archives, Historical Department of the Church of Jesus Christ of Latter-day Saints, Salt Lake City, Utah, p. 29

76. Otto Berndt Oral History, interviewed by Douglas F. Tobler, Salt Lake City, Utah, 1974, typescript, The James Moyle Oral History Program, Archives, Historical Department of the Church of Jesus Christ of Latter-day Saints, Salt Lake City, Utah, p. 68

77. Otto Berndt Oral History, interviewed by Douglas F. Tobler, Salt Lake City, Utah, 1974, typescript, The James Moyle Oral History Program, Archives, Historical Department of the Church of Jesus Christ of Latter-day Saints, Salt Lake City, Utah, p. 33

78. Otto Berndt Oral History, interviewed by Douglas F. Tobler, Salt Lake City, Utah, 1974, typescript, The James Moyle Oral History Program, Archives, Historical Department of the Church of Jesus Christ of Latter-day Saints, Salt Lake City, Utah, p. 5

79. "The Führer's New Clothes: Helmuth Hübener and the Dilemma of German Mormons in the Third Reich," unpublished essay by Alan F. Keele, Used by permission from Alan F. Keele. A shorter version of this essay was later published as an article in *Sunstone*, p. 12

80. "The Führer's New Clothes: Helmuth Hübener and the Dilemma of German Mormons in the Third Reich," unpublished essay by Alan F. Keele, Used by permission from Alan F. Keele. A shorter version of this essay was later published as an article in *Sunstone*, p. 13

81. Peter Prüss interview with author, 20 Oct 2003 and Klaus Guertler interview with the author, 18 October 2003

82. Resa Frey interview with author, 17 October 2003

83. Lieselotte Prüss Schmidt interview with author, 18 October 2003; see also Hilde Prüss Müller interview #1 with author, 18 October 2003 and HPM interview #2 with author 20 October 2003

84. Hilde Prüss Müller interview #1 with author, 18 October 2003

85. Hilde Prüss Müller interview #1 with author, 18 October 2003

86. Lieselotte Schmidt interview #1, 17 Oct 2003

87. Lieselotte Schmidt interview #1, 17 Oct 2003

88. Hilde Prüss Müller interview with the author, 18 October 2003

89. Hilde Prüss Müller, interview with author, 18 October 2003 [Despite their family's strong anti-Nazi views, Richard remained friends with Arthur Zander, just as his wife Rosalie stayed friends with Zander's wife, and Richard's daughter Hilde was friends with all the Zanders and actually visited their home regularly. Hilde Prüss Müller interview with the author, 18 October 2003]YYY

90. Hilde Prüss Müller interview with the author, 18 October 2003

91. Otto Berndt Oral History, interviewed by Douglas F. Tobler, Salt Lake City, Utah, 1974, typescript, The James Moyle Oral History Program, Archives, Historical Department of the Church of Jesus Christ of Latter-day Saints, Salt Lake City, Utah, p. 32

92. Rudi Wobbe Oral History, interviewed by Matthew K. Heiss, Salt Lake City, Utah, 1988, typescript, The James Moyle Oral History Program, Archives, Historical Department of the Church of Jesus Christ of Latter-day Saints, Salt Lake City, Utah, p. 25; and Otto Berndt Oral History, interviewed by Douglas F. Tobler, Salt Lake City, Utah, 1974, typescript, The James Moyle Oral History Program, Archives, Historical Department of the Church of Jesus Christ of Latter-day Saints, Salt Lake City, Utah, p. 56

93. Otto Berndt Oral History, interviewed by Douglas F. Tobler, Salt Lake City, Utah, 1974, typescript, The James Moyle Oral History

Program, Archives, Historical Department of the Church of Jesus Christ of Latter-day Saints, Salt Lake City, Utah, p. 57

94. Otto Berndt Oral History, interviewed by Douglas F. Tobler, Salt Lake City, Utah, 1974, typescript, The James Moyle Oral History Program, Archives, Historical Department of the Church of Jesus Christ of Latter-day Saints, Salt Lake City, Utah, p. 57

95. *Deseret News*, Church Section, 24 November 1945, letter from Max Zimmer

96. Rudi Wobbe Oral History, interviewed by Matthew K. Heiss, Salt Lake City, Utah, 1988, typescript, The James Moyle Oral History Program, Archives, Historical Department of the Church of Jesus Christ of Latter-day Saints, Salt Lake City, Utah, p. 5

97. Karl Schnibbe interview with author; see also p. 35

98. Karl Schnibbe interview with author, Salt Lake City, Utah, 16 September 1996, transcribed by Don Ricks, p. 33

99. Karl Schnibbe interview with author, Salt Lake City, Utah, 16 September 1996, transcribed by Don Ricks, pp. 33-34

100. Blair Holmes, Alan Keele, and Karl-Heinz Schnibbe, *When Truth Was Treason*, Urbana and Chicago, Illinois: University of Illinois Press, 1995, pp. 18-20

101. Karl Schnibbe interview with author, Salt Lake City, Utah, 16 September 1996, transcribed by Don Ricks, p. 33

102. Rudi Wobbe Oral History, interviewed by Matthew K. Heiss, Salt Lake City, Utah, 1988, typescript, The James Moyle Oral History Program, Archives, Historical Department of the Church of Jesus Christ of Latter-day Saints, Salt Lake City, Utah, p. 5

103. *Ibid.*

104. *Ibid.*

CHAPTER 4

1. Gerhard Kunkel interview #1 with author, 10 October 1996, p. 4

2. "He Was Always a Straight-A Student", Statement of Rolf Attin, born 1924, and Hans-Theo Rob, born 1925, Source: *Begleitheft zur Austellung um das kurze Leben und Wirken des Helmuth Hübener,* Catalogue of the exhibit in the Hamburg Court

3. Blair Holmes, Alan Keele, and Karl-Heinz Schnibbe, *When Truth Was Treason,* Urbana and Chicago, Illinois: University of Illinois Press, 1995. Karl also says He was their favorite.

4. Letter from Emma Hübener, Hamburg, 14 August 1942, Attorney General at the People's Court, Berlin w. 9, Bellevuestrasse, 15, File Reference 8j127/42g

5. Hans and Charlotte Kunkel interview with author, Salt Lake City, Utah, 18 October 1996, p. 2

6. Hans and Charlotte Kunkel interview with author, Salt Lake City, Utah, 18 October 1996, p. 2

7. Hans and Charlotte Kunkel interview with author, Salt Lake City, Utah, 18 October 1996, p. 2

8. Karl Schnibbe interview with author, Salt Lake City, Utah, 16 September 1996, transcribed by Don Ricks, p. 32

9. Karl Schnibbe interview with author, Salt Lake City, Utah, 16 September 1996, transcribed by Don Ricks, p. 32

10. Rudi Wobbe Oral History, interviewed by Matthew K. Heiss, Salt Lake City, Utah, 1988, typescript, The James Moyle Oral History Program, Archives, Historical Department of the Church of Jesus Christ of Latter-day Saints, Salt Lake City, Utah, p. 30

11. *Ibid.*

12. Rudi Wobbe Oral History, interviewed by Matthew K. Heiss, Salt Lake City, Utah, 1988, typescript, The James Moyle Oral History Program, Archives, Historical Department of the Church of Jesus Christ of Latter-day Saints, Salt Lake City, Utah, p. 31

13. State Police Agency Hamburg - Hamburg, 5, 9, 17, 20 February 1942,

14. "The Führer's New Clothes: Helmuth Hübener and the Dilemma of German Mormons in the Third Reich," unpublished essay by Alan F. Keele, Used by permission from Alan F. Keele. A shorter version of this essay was later published as an article in *Sunstone*, p. 4

15. "He Was Always a Straight-A Student", Statement of Rolf Attin, born 1924, and Hans-Theo Rob, born 1925, Source: *Begleitheft zur Austellung um das kurze Leben und Wirken des Helmuth Hübener,* Catalogue of the exhibit in the Hamburg Municipal District Archive (Stadtteilarchiv) of Hamm, 26 October – 10 December, 1992

16. BYU Special Collections

17. Arthur and Marie Sommerfeld interview with author, Salt Lake City, Utah, 18 October 1996, p. 21

18. Karl Schnibbe interview with author, Salt Lake City, Utah, 16 September 1996, transcribed by Don Ricks, p. 27

19. Gerhard Kunkel interview #1 with author, 10 October 1996, p. 7

20. Gerhard Kunkel interview #2 with author, 25 February 2003, p. 10

21. Gerhard Kunkel interview #2 with author, 25 February 2003, pp. 12-13

22. Arthur and Marie Sommerfeld interview with author, Salt Lake City, Utah, 18 October 1996

23. "He Was Always a Straight-A Student", Statement of Rolf Attin, born 1924, and Hans-Theo Rob, born 1925, Source: *Begleitheft zur Austellung um das kurze Leben und Wirken des Helmuth Hübener,* Catalogue of the exhibit in the Hamburg Municipal District Archive (Stadtteilarchiv) of Hamm, 26 October – 10 December, 1992

24. Hans and Charlotte Kunkel interview with author, Salt Lake City, Utah, 18 October 1996, p. 7

25. Arthur and Marie Sommerfeld interview with author, Salt Lake City, Utah, 18 October 1996, pp. 15-16

26. Gerhard Kunkel interview #2 with author, 25 February 2003, pp. 12-13

27. Hans and Charlotte Kunkel interview with author, Salt Lake City, Utah, 18 October 1996, p. 3

28. Statement of Marie Sommerfeld, Source: *Begleitheft zur Austellung um das kurze Leben und Wirken des Helmuth Hübener,* Catalogue of the exhibit in the Hamburg Municipal District Archive (Stadtteilarchiv) of Hamm, 26 October – 10 December, 1992

29. Statement of Hans Kunkel, Source: *Begleitheft zur Austellung um das kurze Leben und Wirken des Helmuth Hübener,* Catalogue of the exhibit in the Hamburg Municipal District Archive (Stadtteilarchiv) of Hamm, 26 October – 10 December, 1992

30. Arthur and Marie Sommerfeld interview with author, Salt Lake City, Utah, 18 October 1996, p. 22

31. Arthur and Marie Sommerfeld interview with author, Salt Lake City, Utah, 18 October 1996, pp. 22-23

32. Arthur and Marie Sommerfeld interview with author, 18 October 1996, pp. 2-3. Arthur Sommerfeld adds, Helmuth did not pair off with any of my sisters walking to and from church, but as a group sometimes they joined us walking, but not too often. Mostly just Helmuth and I walked together.

33. Arthur and Marie Sommerfeld interview with author, 18 October 1996, p. 24

34. Hans and Charlotte Kunkel interview with author, Salt Lake City, Utah, 18 October 1996, p. 3

35. Moyle interview of Marie Friebel Sommerfeld, 1897-1984, interviewed in German by Tobler and Keele, p. 2

36. Statement of Marie Sommerfeld, Source: *Begleitheft zur Austellung um das kurze Leben und Wirken des Helmuth Hübener,* Catalogue of the exhibit in the Hamburg Municipal District Archive (Stadtteilarchiv) of Hamm, 26 October – 10 December, 1992

37. Statement of Marie Sommerfeld, Source: *Begleitheft zur Austellung um das kurze Leben und Wirken des Helmuth Hübener,* Catalogue of the exhibit in the Hamburg Municipal District Archive (Stadtteilarchiv) of Hamm, 26 October – 10 December, 1992

38. Statement of Hedi Radtke Sommerfeld, Source: *Begleitheft zur Austellung um das kurze Leben und Wirken des Helmuth Hübener,* Catalogue of the exhibit in the Hamburg Municipal District Archive (Stadtteilarchiv) of Hamm, 26 October – 10 December

39. Arthur and Marie Sommerfeld interview with author, 18 October 1996

40. Marie Friebel Sommerfeld 1897-1984, Interviewed in German by Douglas Tobler and Alan Keele, 1974 : (13 leaves in English; Matthew K. Heiss later wrote Iris Schmidt on 17 Sep 1992 saying the Sommerfeld interview was never fully edited; typed ca. 1985 by Karen H. Pyper), p. 2

41. Marie Friebel Sommerfeld 1897-1984, Interviewed in German by Douglas Tobler and Alan Keele, 1974 : (13 leaves in English; Matthew K. Heiss later wrote Iris Schmidt on 17 Sep 1992 saying the Sommerfeld interview was never fully edited; typed ca. 1985 by Karen H. Pyper), p. 3

42. "The Führer's New Clothes: Helmuth Hübener and the Dilemma of German Mormons in the Third Reich," unpublished essay by Alan F. Keele, Used by permission from Alan F. Keele. A shorter version of this essay was later published as an article in *Sunstone*, p. 25

43. Gerhard Kunkel interview #1 with author, 10 October 1996, p. 3

44. Gerhard Kunkel interview #2 with author, 25 February 2003, p. 10

45. Hans and Charlotte Kunkel interview with author, Salt Lake City, Utah, 18 October 1996, p. 4

46. Statement of Friedrich Peters, born 1920, Source: *Begleitheft zur Austellung um das kurze Leben und Wirken des Helmuth Hübener,* Catalogue of the exhibit in the Hamburg Municipal District Archive (Stadtteilarchiv) of Hamm, 26 October – 10 December

CHAPTER 5

1. Record of Members, Hamburg District #23403, #994 and Statement of Friedrich Peters, born 1920, Source: *Begleitheft zur Austellung um das kurze Leben und Wirken des Helmuth Hübener,* Catalogue of the exhibit in the Hamburg Municipal District Archive (Stadtteilarchiv) of Hamm, 26 October – 10 December

2. Statement of Friedrich Peters, born 1920, Source: *Begleitheft zur Austellung um das kurze Leben und Wirken des Helmuth Hübener,* Catalogue of the exhibit in the Hamburg Municipal District Archive (Stadtteilarchiv) of Hamm, 26 October – 10 December

3. Statement of Friedrich Peters, born 1920, Source: *Begleitheft zur Austellung um das kurze Leben und Wirken des Helmuth Hübener,* Catalogue of the exhibit in the Hamburg Municipal

District Archive (Stadtteilarchiv) of Hamm, 26 October – 10 December

4. "The Führer's New Clothes: Helmuth Hübener and the Dilemma of German Mormons in the Third Reich," unpublished essay by Alan F. Keele, Used by permission from Alan F. Keele. A shorter version of this essay was later published as an article in *Sunstone*, p. 9

5. Rudolf G. Wobbe Oral History, Doublas F. Tobler and Alan F. Keele, 1974, typescript, The James Moyle Oral History Program, Archives, Historical Department of the Church of Jesus Christ of Latter-day Saints, Salt Lake City, Utah, p. 14

6. "I Knew Helmuth since 1928", Irmgard Becker, born 1916, recalls, Source: *Begleitheft zur Austellung um das kurze Leben und Wirken des Helmuth Hübener*, Catalogue of the exhibit in the Hamburg Municipal District Archive (Stadtteilarchiv) of Hamm; and Arthur and Marie Sommerfeld interview with author, Salt Lake City, Utah, 18 October 1996, p. 14

7. Arthur and Marie Sommerfeld interview with author, Salt Lake City, Utah, 18 October 1996, p. 14

8. Arthur and Marie Sommerfeld interview with author, 18 October 1996, p. 14

9. Blair Holmes, Alan Keele, and Karl-Heinz Schnibbe, *When Truth Was Treason*, Urbana and Chicago, Illinois: University of Illinois Press, 1995, pp. 12-13

10. Rudolf G. Wobbe Oral History, Doublas F. Tobler and Alan F. Keele, 1974, typescript, The James Moyle Oral History Program, Archives, Historical Department of the Church of Jesus Christ of Latter-day Saints, Salt Lake City, Utah, p. 14

11. "I Knew Helmuth since 1928", Irmgard Becker, born 1916, recalls, Source: *Begleitheft zur Austellung um das kurze Leben und Wirken des Helmuth Hübener*, Catalogue of the exhibit in the Hamburg Municipal District Archive (Stadtteilarchiv) of Hamm

12. Rudolf G. Wobbe Oral History, Doublas F. Tobler and Alan F. Keele, 1974, typescript, The James Moyle Oral History Program, Archives, Historical Department of the Church of Jesus Christ of Latter-day Saints, Salt Lake City, Utah, p. 13

13. "The Führer's New Clothes: Helmuth Hübener and the Dilemma of German Mormons in the Third Reich," unpublished essay by Alan F. Keele, Used by permission from Alan F. Keele. A shorter version of this essay was later published as an article in *Sunstone*, p. 4

14. "The Führer's New Clothes: Helmuth Hübener and the Dilemma of German Mormons in the Third Reich," unpublished essay by Alan F. Keele, Used by permission from Alan F. Keele. A shorter version of this essay was later published as an article in *Sunstone*, p. 4

15. "The Führer's New Clothes: Helmuth Hübener and the Dilemma of German Mormons in the Third Reich," unpublished essay by Alan F. Keele, Used by permission from Alan F. Keele. A shorter version of this essay was later published as an article in *Sunstone*, p. 4

16. "The Führer's New Clothes: Helmuth Hübener and the Dilemma of German Mormons in the Third Reich," unpublished essay by Alan F. Keele, Used by permission from Alan F. Keele. A shorter version of this essay was later published as an article in *Sunstone*, p. 5, Gerhard Kunkel interview #2 with author, 25 February 2003, p. 12

17. "The Führer's New Clothes: Helmuth Hübener and the Dilemma of German Mormons in the Third Reich," unpublished essay by Alan F. Keele, Used by permission from Alan F. Keele. A shorter version of this essay was later published as an article in *Sunstone*, p. 5

18. Marie Friebel Sommerfeld 1897-1984, Interviewed in German by Douglas Tobler and Alan Keele, 1974 : (13 leaves in English; Matthew K. Heiss later wrote Iris Schmidt on 17 Sep 1992

saying the Sommerfeld interview was never fully edited; typed ca. 1985 by Karen H. Pyper), p. 5

19. Marie Friebel Sommerfeld 1897-1984, Interviewed in German by Douglas Tobler and Alan Keele, 1974 : (13 leaves in English; Matthew K. Heiss later wrote Iris Schmidt on 17 Sep 1992 saying the Sommerfeld interview was never fully edited; typed ca. 1985 by Karen H. Pyper), p. 10

20. Karl Schnibbe interview with author, Salt Lake City, Utah, 16 September 1996, transcribed by Don Ricks, p. 30

21. Hans and Charlotte Kunkel interview with author, Salt Lake City, Utah, 18 October 1996, p. 2

22. "I Knew Helmuth since 1928", Irmgard Becker, born 1916, recalls, Source: *Begleitheft zur Austellung um das kurze Leben und Wirken des Helmuth Hübener,* Catalogue of the exhibit in the Hamburg Municipal District Archive (Stadtteilarchiv) of Hamm

23. Rudolf G. Wobbe Oral History, Doublas F. Tobler and Alan F. Keele, 1974, typescript, The James Moyle Oral History Program, Archives, Historical Department of the Church of Jesus Christ of Latter-day Saints, Salt Lake City, Utah, p. 13

24. Lieselotte Prüss Schkmidt interview with author, 17 October 2003

25. Rudolf G. Wobbe Oral History, Doublas F. Tobler and Alan F. Keele, 1974, typescript, The James Moyle Oral History Program, Archives, Historical Department of the Church of Jesus Christ of Latter-day Saints, Salt Lake City, Utah, p. 7

26. "The Führer's New Clothes: Helmuth Hübener and the Dilemma of German Mormons in the Third Reich," unpublished essay by Alan F. Keele, Used by permission from Alan F. Keele. A shorter version of this essay was later published as an article in *Sunstone*, p. 25

27. Rudi Wobbe Oral History, interviewed by Matthew K. Heiss, Salt Lake City, Utah, 1988, typescript, The James Moyle Oral History Program, Archives, Historical Department of the Church of Jesus Christ of Latter-day Saints, Salt Lake City, Utah, p. 33

28. Otto Berndt Oral History, interviewed by Douglas F. Tobler, Salt Lake City, Utah, 1974, typescript, The James Moyle Oral History Program, Archives, Historical Department of the Church of Jesus Christ of Latter-day Saints, Salt Lake City, Utah, p. 36

29. Rudi Wobbe Oral History, interviewed by Matthew K. Heiss, Salt Lake City, Utah, 1988, typescript, The James Moyle Oral History Program, Archives, Historical Department of the Church of Jesus Christ of Latter-day Saints, Salt Lake City, Utah, p. 33

30. Hilde Prüss Müller, interview with author 18 October 2003

31. Blair Holmes, Alan Keele, and Karl-Heinz Schnibbe, *When Truth Was Treason*, Urbana and Chicago, Illinois: University of Illinois Press, 1995, p. 24

32. "The Führer's New Clothes: Helmuth Hübener and the Dilemma of German Mormons in the Third Reich," unpublished essay by Alan F. Keele, Used by permission from Alan F. Keele. A shorter version of this essay was later published as an article in *Sunstone*, p. 10

33. Margaret Blair Young, "Doing Hübener," *Dialogue*, Winter 1988, p. 130

34. Karl Schnibbe interview with author, Salt Lake City, Utah, 16 September 1996, transcribed by Don Ricks, p. 29

35. Arthur and Marie Sommerfeld interview with author, 18 October 1996, p. 24

36. Gerhard Kunkel interview #2 with author, 25 February 2003, p. 12

37. Lieselotte Prüss Schkmidt interview with author, 17 October 2003

38. "The Führer's New Clothes: Helmuth Hübener and the Dilemma of German Mormons in the Third Reich," unpublished essay by Alan F. Keele, Used by permission from Alan F. Keele. A shorter version of this essay was later published as an article in *Sunstone*, p. 22

39. Statement of Marie Sommerfeld, Source: *Begleitheft zur Austellung um das kurze Leben und Wirken des Helmuth Hübener,* Catalogue of the exhibit in the Hamburg Municipal District Archive (Stadtteilarchiv) of Hamm, 26 October – 10 December, 1992

40. Rudolf G. Wobbe Oral History, Doublas F. Tobler and Alan F. Keele, 1974, typescript, The James Moyle Oral History Program, Archives, Historical Department of the Church of Jesus Christ of Latter-day Saints, Salt Lake City, Utah, p. 7

41. Otto Berndt Oral History, interviewed by Douglas F. Tobler, Salt Lake City, Utah, 1974, typescript, The James Moyle Oral History Program, Archives, Historical Department of the Church of Jesus Christ of Latter-day Saints, Salt Lake City, Utah, p. 37

42. Rudi Wobbe Oral History, interviewed by Matthew K. Heiss, Salt Lake City, Utah, 1988, typescript, The James Moyle Oral History Program, Archives, Historical Department of the Church of Jesus Christ of Latter-day Saints, Salt Lake City, Utah, p. 27

43. Rudi Wobbe Oral History, interviewed by Matthew K. Heiss, Salt Lake City, Utah, 1988, typescript, The James Moyle Oral History Program, Archives, Historical Department of the Church of Jesus Christ of Latter-day Saints, Salt Lake City, Utah, p. 27

44. Rudi Wobbe Oral History, interviewed by Matthew K. Heiss, Salt Lake City, Utah, 1988, typescript, The James Moyle Oral History Program, Archives, Historical Department of the

Church of Jesus Christ of Latter-day Saints, Salt Lake City, Utah, p. 28

45. Rudi Wobbe Oral History, interviewed by Matthew K. Heiss, Salt Lake City, Utah, 1988, typescript, The James Moyle Oral History Program, Archives, Historical Department of the Church of Jesus Christ of Latter-day Saints, Salt Lake City, Utah, pp. 27-28

46. Rudi Wobbe Oral History, interviewed by Matthew K. Heiss, Salt Lake City, Utah, 1988, typescript, The James Moyle Oral History Program, Archives, Historical Department of the Church of Jesus Christ of Latter-day Saints, Salt Lake City, Utah, p. 28

47. Otto Berndt Oral History, interviewed by Douglas F. Tobler, Salt Lake City, Utah, 1974, typescript, The James Moyle Oral History Program, Archives, Historical Department of the Church of Jesus Christ of Latter-day Saints, Salt Lake City, Utah, p. 19

48. Hans and Charlotte Kunkel interview with author, Salt Lake City, Utah, 18 October 1996, p. 3

49. Rudi Wobbe Oral History, interviewed by Matthew K. Heiss, Salt Lake City, Utah, 1988, typescript, The James Moyle Oral History Program, Archives, Historical Department of the Church of Jesus Christ of Latter-day Saints, Salt Lake City, Utah, p. 29

50. Rudi Wobbe Oral History, interviewed by Matthew K. Heiss, Salt Lake City, Utah, 1988, typescript, The James Moyle Oral History Program, Archives, Historical Department of the Church of Jesus Christ of Latter-day Saints, Salt Lake City, Utah, p. 12

51. Blair Holmes, Alan Keele, and Karl-Heinz Schnibbe, *When Truth Was Treason*, Urbana and Chicago, Illinois: University of Illinois Press, 1995, p. 25

52. Rudi Wobbe Oral History, interviewed by Matthew K. Heiss, Salt Lake City, Utah, 1988, typescript, The James Moyle Oral

History Program, Archives, Historical Department of the Church of Jesus Christ of Latter-day Saints, Salt Lake City, Utah, p. 33

53. Rudi Wobbe Oral History, interviewed by Matthew K. Heiss, Salt Lake City, Utah, 1988, typescript, The James Moyle Oral History Program, Archives, Historical Department of the Church of Jesus Christ of Latter-day Saints, Salt Lake City, Utah, p. 33

54. Rudolf G. Wobbe Oral History, Doublas F. Tobler and Alan F. Keele, 1974, typescript, The James Moyle Oral History Program, Archives, Historical Department of the Church of Jesus Christ of Latter-day Saints, Salt Lake City, Utah, p. 30

55. Otto Berndt, Jr. interview #1 with author, 20 October 2003

56. Resa Guertler Frey interview with author, 18 October 2003

57. Otto Berndt Oral History, interviewed by Douglas F. Tobler, Salt Lake City, Utah, 1974, typescript, The James Moyle Oral History Program, Archives, Historical Department of the Church of Jesus Christ of Latter-day Saints, Salt Lake City, Utah, p. 36

58. "The Führer's New Clothes: Helmuth Hübener and the Dilemma of German Mormons in the Third Reich," unpublished essay by Alan F. Keele, Used by permission from Alan F. Keele. A shorter version of this essay was later published as an article in *Sunstone*, p. 22

59. Otto Berndt Oral History, interviewed by Douglas F. Tobler, Salt Lake City, Utah, 1974, typescript, The James Moyle Oral History Program, Archives, Historical Department of the Church of Jesus Christ of Latter-day Saints, Salt Lake City, Utah, p. 37

60. Rudolf G. Wobbe Oral History, Doublas F. Tobler and Alan F. Keele, 1974, typescript, The James Moyle Oral History Program, Archives, Historical Department of the Church of Jesus Christ of Latter-day Saints, Salt Lake City, Utah, p. 30

61. Rudolf G. Wobbe Oral History, Doublas F. Tobler and Alan
    F. Keele, 1974, typescript, The James Moyle Oral History
    Program, Archives, Historical Department of the Church of
    Jesus Christ of Latter-day Saints, Salt Lake City, Utah, p. 29

CHAPTER 6

1. Gerhard Kunkel interview #1 with author, 10 October 1996,
   pp. 7-9

2. Gerhard Kunkel interview #2 with author, 25 February 2003,
   p. 16

3. Gerhard Kunkel interview #2 with author, 25 February 2003,
   pp. 18-20

4. Gerhard Kunkel interview #2 with author, 25 February 2003,
   pp. 18-20

5. Gerhard Kunkel interview #2 with author, 25 February 2003,
   p. 1

6. Gerhard Kunkel interview #1 with author, 10 October 1996,
   p. 9

7. Gerhard Kunkel interview #1 with author, 10 October 1996,
   p. 9

8. Statement of Hans Kunkel, Source: *Begleitheft zur Austellung um
   das kurze Leben und Wirken des Helmuth Hübener,* Catalogue
   of the exhibit in the Hamburg Municipal District Archive
   (Stadtteilarchiv) of Hamm, 26 October – 10 December, 1992

9. Arthur and Marie Sommerfeld interview with author, Salt Lake
   City, Utah, 18 October 1996, p. 22

10. Hans and Charlotte Kunkel interview with author, Salt Lake
    City, Utah, 18 October 1996, pp. 2-3

11. Karl Schnibbe interview with author, Salt Lake City, Utah, 16 September 1996, transcribed by Don Ricks, p. 33

12. Karl Schnibbe interview with author, Salt Lake City, Utah, 16 September 1996, transcribed by Don Ricks, p. 32

13. Rudi Wobbe Fireside [youth church lecture], 1987, transcribed by Richard Dewey and Heather Dewey, 1-4 February 2003, used by permission from Herta Wobbe, p. 8

14. Hans and Charlotte Kunkel interview with author, Salt Lake City, Utah, 18 October 1996, pp. 2-3

15. Statement of Hans Kunkel, Source: *Begleitheft zur Austellung um das kurze Leben und Wirken des Helmuth Hübener,* Catalogue of the exhibit in the Hamburg Municipal District Archive (Stadtteilarchiv) of Hamm, 26 October – 10 December, 1992 and Gerhard Kunkel interview #1 with author, 10 October 1996, p. 4

16. Gerhard Kunkel interview #1 with author, 10 October 1996, p. 4

17. "He Was Always a Straight-A Student", Statement of Rolf Attin, born 1924, and Hans-Theo Rob, born 1925, Source: *Begleitheft zur Austellung um das kurze Leben und Wirken des Helmuth Hübener,* Catalogue of the exhibit in the Hamburg Court

18. Helmuth Hübener secret, 1942

19. Statement of Hans Kunkel, Source: *Begleitheft zur Austellung um das kurze Leben und Wirken des Helmuth Hübener,* Catalogue of the exhibit in the Hamburg Municipal District Archive (Stadtteilarchiv) of Hamm, 26 October – 10 December, 1992

20. Verdict of the People's Court in the criminal case against Helmut Hübener, et al, on 11 August 1942, Findings, Part I

21. "He Was Always a Straight-A Student", Statement of Rolf Attin, born 1924, and Hans-Theo Rob, born 1925, Source: *Begleitheft*

zur Austellung um das kurze Leben und Wirken des Helmuth Hübener, Catalogue of the exhibit in the Hamburg Court

22. Document of Secret State Police — Hamburg, 11 May 1942, State Police Office Hamburg, B. No. II P - 126/42, Franz Walter Prumnitz: Franz Prumnitz in 11 May 1942 Gestapo Interrogation transcript, and "He Was Always a Straight-A Student", Statement of Rolf Attin, born 1924, and Hans-Theo Rob, born 1925, Source: *Begleitheft zur Austellung um das kurze Leben und Wirken des Helmuth Hübener,* Catalogue of the exhibit in the Hamburg Court

23. "He Was Always a Straight-A Student", Statement of Rolf Attin, born 1924, and Hans-Theo Rob, born 1925, Source: *Begleitheft zur Austellung um das kurze Leben und Wirken des Helmuth Hübener,* Catalogue of the exhibit in the Hamburg Court. According to classmates Attin and Rob, Helmuth began a year earlier than the government report states.

24. Gerhard Kunkel interview #1 with author, 10 October 1996, p. 5

25. Gerhard Kunkel interview #1 with author, 10 October 1996, pp. 4-5

26. "He Was Always a Straight-A Student", Statement of Rolf Attin, born 1924, and Hans-Theo Rob, born 1925, Source: *Begleitheft zur Austellung um das kurze Leben und Wirken des Helmuth Hübener,* Catalogue of the exhibit in the Hamburg Court

27. "He Was Always a Straight-A Student", Statement of Rolf Attin, born 1924, and Hans-Theo Rob, born 1925, Source: *Begleitheft zur Austellung um das kurze Leben und Wirken des Helmuth Hübener,* Catalogue of the exhibit in the Hamburg Court

28. Statement of August Meins, Helmuth's teacher, recalls: Source: *Begleitheft zur Austellung um das kurze Leben und Wirken des Helmuth Hübener,* Catalogue of the exhibit in the Hamburg Municipal District Archive (Stadtteilarchiv) of Hamm, 26 October

29. "He Was Always a Straight-A Student", Statement of Rolf Attin, born 1924, and Hans-Theo Rob, born 1925, Source: *Begleitheft zur Austellung um das kurze Leben und Wirken des Helmuth Hübener,* Catalogue of the exhibit in the Hamburg Court

30. Statement of August Meins, Helmuth's teacher, recalls: Source: *Begleitheft zur Austellung um das kurze Leben und Wirken des Helmuth Hübener,* Catalogue of the exhibit in the Hamburg Municipal District Archive (Stadtteilarchiv) of Hamm, 26 October

31. Letter from Emma Hübener, Hamburg, 8 March 1942, To the General Public Prosecutor at the Hanseatic Higher Regional Court.

32. Document of Secret State Police — Hamburg, 11 May 1942, State Police Office Hamburg, B. No. II P - 126/42, Franz Walter Prumnitz

33. "He Was Always a Straight-A Student", Statement of Rolf Attin, born 1924, and Hans-Theo Rob, born 1925, Source: *Begleitheft zur Austellung um das kurze Leben und Wirken des Helmuth Hübener,* Catalogue of the exhibit in the Hamburg Court

34. "He Was Always a Straight-A Student", Statement of Rolf Attin, born 1924, and Hans-Theo Rob, born 1925, Source: *Begleitheft zur Austellung um das kurze Leben und Wirken des Helmuth Hübener,* Catalogue of the exhibit in the Hamburg Court

35. Statement of August Meins, Helmuth's teacher, recalls: Source: *Begleitheft zur Austellung um das kurze Leben und Wirken des Helmuth Hübener,* Catalogue of the exhibit in the Hamburg Municipal District Archive (Stadtteilarchiv) of Hamm, 26 October

36. Statement of August Meins, Helmuth's teacher, recalls: Source: *Begleitheft zur Austellung um das kurze Leben und Wirken des Helmuth Hübener,* Catalogue of the exhibit in the Hamburg Municipal District Archive (Stadtteilarchiv) of Hamm, 26 October

37. Statement of August Meins, Helmuth's teacher, recalls: Source: *Begleitheft zur Austellung um das kurze Leben und Wirken des Helmuth Hübener*, Catalogue of the exhibit in the Hamburg Municipal District Archive (Stadtteilarchiv) of Hamm, 26 October

38. Statement of Marie Sommerfeld, Source: *Begleitheft zur Austellung um das kurze Leben und Wirken des Helmuth Hübener*, Catalogue of the exhibit in the Hamburg Municipal District Archive (Stadtteilarchiv) of Hamm, 26 October – 10 December, 1992

39. Marie Friebel Sommerfeld 1897-1984, Interviewed in German by Douglas Tobler and Alan Keele, 1974 : (13 leaves in English; Matthew K. Heiss later wrote Iris Schmidt on 17 Sep 1992 saying the Sommerfeld interview was never fully edited; typed ca. 1985 by Karen H. Pyper), p. 10

40. Karl Schnibbe interview with author, Salt Lake City, Utah, 16 September 1996, transcribed by Don Ricks, p. 38

41. Letter from Emma Hübener, Hamburg, 8 March 1942, To the General Public Prosecutor at the Hanseatic Higher Regional Court., Verdict of the People's Court in the criminal case against Helmut Hübener, et al, on 11 August 1942, under Findings, Part I

42. Gerhard Kunkel interview #2 with author, 25 February 2003, p. 8. Gerhard Kunkeland Marie Sommerfeld say he enjoyed the Hitler Youth, but their time frames were off: They do remember him enjoying a Nazi youth organization, but it would have been the German Young Folk because he was anti-Nazi by the time he joined the Hitler Youth

43. "Helmuth Hübener: Secret," Nazi document, 2 pp., 1942, BYU Library and Letter from Emma Hübener, Hamburg, 8 March 1942, To the General Public Prosecutor at the Hanseatic Higher Regional Court.: letter from Emma Hübener 8 March 1942 to the General Public Prosecutor at the Hanseatic Higher Regional Court

44. Document of Secret State Police — Hamburg, 11 May 1942, State Police Office Hamburg, B. No. II P - 126/42, Franz Walter Prumnitz

45. Service Certificate from Senior District Director Asmus, Hitler Youth, District Hamburg East, 17 August 1942; and Letter from National Socialist German Worker's Party, Hitler Youth/Youth Leadership of the Reich, Office of the Hitler Youth Jurisdiction, 182/42 G. 26 Gn. Ni./Ka., Berlin, 15 September 1942, To the Chancellery of the Führer of the NSDAP, Central Office, from the Senior District Leader and Hitler Youth Judge

46. Service Certificate from Senior District Director Asmus, Hitler Youth, District Hamburg East, 17 August 1942

47. Service Certificate from Senior District Director Asmus, Hitler Youth, District Hamburg East, 17 August 1942

48. Letter from National Socialist German Worker's Party, Hitler Youth/Youth Leadership of the Reich, Office of the Hitler Youth Jurisdiction, 182/42 G. 26 Gn. Ni./Ka., Berlin, 15 September 1942, To the Chancellery of the Führer of the NSDAP, Central Office

49. Statement of Hans Kunkel, Source: *Begleitheft zur Austellung um das kurze Leben und Wirken des Helmuth Hübener,* Catalogue of the exhibit in the Hamburg Municipal District Archive (Stadtteilarchiv) of Hamm, 26 October – 10 December, 1992

50. Letter from National Socialist German Worker's Party, Hitler Youth/Youth Leadership of the Reich, Office of the Hitler Youth Jurisdiction, 182/42 G. 26 Gn. Ni./Ka., Berlin, 15 September 1942, To the Chancellery of the Führer of the NSDAP, Central Office

CHAPTER 7

1. Blair Holmes, Alan Keele, and Karl-Heinz Schnibbe, *When Truth Was Treason*, Urbana and Chicago, Illinois: University of Illinois Press, 1995, pp. 22-23

2. *Salt Lake Tribune*, "Struggle Against Hitler Brought to Stage," Celia R. Baker, 13 May 2003

3. Blair Holmes, Alan Keele, and Karl-Heinz Schnibbe, *When Truth Was Treason*, Urbana and Chicago, Illinois: University of Illinois Press, 1995, p. 22

4. *BYU Today*, "Heubener's [sic] message haunts memories in remarkable drama," Dec 1976

5. P. 23, Blair Holmes, Alan Keele, and Karl-Heinz Schnibbe, *When Truth Was Treason*, Urbana and Chicago, Illinois: University of Illinois Press, 1995

6. Karl Schnibbe interview with author, Salt Lake City, Utah, 16 September 1996, transcribed by Don Ricks, p. 33

7. *Salt Lake Tribune* article, May 13, 2003

8. Rudi Wobbe Oral History, interviewed by Matthew K. Heiss, Salt Lake City, Utah, 1988, typescript, The James Moyle Oral History Program, Archives, Historical Department of the Church of Jesus Christ of Latter-day Saints, Salt Lake City, Utah, p. 9

9. Rudi Wobbe Oral History, interviewed by Matthew K. Heiss, Salt Lake City, Utah, 1988, typescript, The James Moyle Oral History Program, Archives, Historical Department of the Church of Jesus Christ of Latter-day Saints, Salt Lake City, Utah, p. 34

10. Rudi Wobbe Oral History, interviewed by Matthew K. Heiss, Salt Lake City, Utah, 1988, typescript, The James Moyle Oral History Program, Archives, Historical Department of the Church of Jesus Christ of Latter-day Saints, Salt Lake City,

Utah, p. 10. As for Krystallnacht itself, Rudi says he saw Jews paraded through the street with signs around their necks and being maligned, finding the scene awful. Rudi Wobbe Oral History, interviewed by Matthew K. Heiss, Salt Lake City, Utah, 1988, typescript, The James Moyle Oral History Program, Archives, Historical Department of the Church of Jesus Christ of Latter-day Saints, Salt Lake City, Utah, p. 34

11. Rudi Wobbe Fireside [youth church lecture], 1987, transcribed by Richard Dewey and Heather Dewey, 1-4 February 2003, used by permission from Herta Wobbe, p. 8

12. Rudi Wobbe Fireside [youth church lecture], 1987, transcribed by Richard Dewey and Heather Dewey, 1-4 February 2003, used by permission from Herta Wobbe, p. 19

13. Rudi Wobbe Oral History, interviewed by Matthew K. Heiss, Salt Lake City, Utah, 1988, typescript, The James Moyle Oral History Program, Archives, Historical Department of the Church of Jesus Christ of Latter-day Saints, Salt Lake City, Utah, p. 30

14. Rudi Wobbe Fireside [youth church lecture], 1987, transcribed by Richard Dewey and Heather Dewey, 1-4 February 2003, used by permission from Herta Wobbe, p. 19

15. Rudi Wobbe Oral History, interviewed by Matthew K. Heiss, Salt Lake City, Utah, 1988, typescript, The James Moyle Oral History Program, Archives, Historical Department of the Church of Jesus Christ of Latter-day Saints, Salt Lake City, Utah, p. 30

16. Statement of Friedrich Peters, born 1920, Source: Begleitheft zur Austellung um das kurze Leben und Wirken des Helmuth Hübener, Catalogue of the exhibit in the Hamburg Municipal District Archive (Stadtteilarchiv) of Hamm, 26 October – 10 December

17. Rudi Wobbe Oral History, interviewed by Matthew K. Heiss, Salt Lake City, Utah, 1988, typescript, The James Moyle Oral History Program, Archives, Historical Department of the

Church of Jesus Christ of Latter-day Saints, Salt Lake City, Utah, p. 34-35

18. Rudi Wobbe and Jerry Borrowman, *Three Against Hitler,* (American Fork, Utah: Covenant Communications, 1992), p. 21

19. Rudi Wobbe and Jerry Borrowman, *Three Against Hitler,* (American Fork, Utah: Covenant Communications, 1992), p. 21

20. Blair Holmes, Alan Keele, and Karl-Heinz Schnibbe, *When Truth Was Treason*, Urbana and Chicago, Illinois: University of Illinois Press, 1995, p. 26

21. Blair Holmes, Alan Keele, and Karl-Heinz Schnibbe, *When Truth Was Treason*, Urbana and Chicago, Illinois: University of Illinois Press, 1995, p. 26

22. Karl Schnibbe interview with author, Salt Lake City, Utah, 16 September 1996, transcribed by Don Ricks, p. 39

23. Rudolf G. Wobbe Oral History, Doublas F. Tobler and Alan F. Keele, 1974, typescript, The James Moyle Oral History Program, Archives, Historical Department of the Church of Jesus Christ of Latter-day Saints, Salt Lake City, Utah, p. 3

24. Rudi Wobbe Oral History, interviewed by Matthew K. Heiss, Salt Lake City, Utah, 1988, typescript, The James Moyle Oral History Program, Archives, Historical Department of the Church of Jesus Christ of Latter-day Saints, Salt Lake City, Utah, p. 11

25. Rudi Wobbe and Jerry Borrowman, *Three Against Hitler,* (American Fork, Utah: Covenant Communications, 1992), pp. 7-8; andRudi Wobbe Oral History, interviewed by Matthew K. Heiss, Salt Lake City, Utah, 1988, typescript, The James Moyle Oral History Program, Archives, Historical Department of the Church of Jesus Christ of Latter-day Saints, Salt Lake City, Utah, p. 11

26. Rudolf G. Wobbe Oral History, Doublas F. Tobler and Alan
    F. Keele, 1974, typescript, The James Moyle Oral History
    Program, Archives, Historical Department of the Church of
    Jesus Christ of Latter-day Saints, Salt Lake City, Utah, p. 4
    andRudi Wobbe Oral History, interviewed by Matthew K.
    Heiss, Salt Lake City, Utah, 1988, typescript, The James Moyle
    Oral History Program, Archives, Historical Department of the
    Church of Jesus Christ of Latter-day Saints, Salt Lake City,
    Utah, p. 35

27. Rudolf G. Wobbe Oral History, Doublas F. Tobler and Alan
    F. Keele, 1974, typescript, The James Moyle Oral History
    Program, Archives, Historical Department of the Church of
    Jesus Christ of Latter-day Saints, Salt Lake City, Utah, p. 4

28. Rudi Wobbe Fireside [youth church lecture], 1987, transcribed
    by Richard Dewey and Heather Dewey, 1-4 February 2003, used
    by permission from Herta Wobbe, pp. 9-10; see also Rudolf G.
    Wobbe Oral History, Doublas F. Tobler and Alan F. Keele, 1974,
    typescript, The James Moyle Oral History Program, Archives,
    Historical Department of the Church of Jesus Christ of Latter-
    day Saints, Salt Lake City, Utah, p. 4

29. Rudi Wobbe and Jerry Borrowman, *Three Against Hitler,*
    (American Fork, Utah: Covenant Communications, 1992), p.
    13

30. Rudi Wobbe Oral History, interviewed by Matthew K. Heiss,
    Salt Lake City, Utah, 1988, typescript, The James Moyle Oral
    History Program, Archives, Historical Department of the
    Church of Jesus Christ of Latter-day Saints, Salt Lake City,
    Utah, p. 35

31. Karl Schnibbe interview with author, Salt Lake City, Utah, 16
    September 1996, transcribed by Don Ricks, p. 40

32. Blair Holmes, Alan Keele, and Karl-Heinz Schnibbe, *When
    Truth Was Treason*, Urbana and Chicago, Illinois: University
    of Illinois Press, 1995

33. Blair Holmes, Alan Keele, and Karl-Heinz Schnibbe, *When Truth Was Treason*, Urbana and Chicago, Illinois: University of Illinois Press, 1995, pp. 18-20

34. Karl Schnibbe interview with author, Salt Lake City, Utah, 16 September 1996, transcribed by Don Ricks, p. 34

35. Document of Chief State Counsel of the Hanseatic Higher Regional Court, Hamburg 36, 25 March 1942, Criminal Case! Juveniles!; letter to Chief State Counsel; Document of The Superior Attorney General of the Reich, Berlin 28 May 1942 at the People's Court, 8J 127/42g, In Custody!: III-2; Verdict of the People's Court in the criminal case against Helmut Hübener, et al, on 11 August 1942: Findings, pt. I

36. Rudolf G. Wobbe Oral History, Doublas F. Tobler and Alan F. Keele, 1974, typescript, The James Moyle Oral History Program, Archives, Historical Department of the Church of Jesus Christ of Latter-day Saints, Salt Lake City, Utah, p. 3

37. Statement of Rudolf Wobbe, Rudolf Wobbe, Salt Lake City, Utah, 17 April 1961, Source: Historical Department, Church of Jesus Christ of Latter-day Saints, Salt Lake City, Utah Statement of Rudolf Wobbe, Rudolf Wobbe, Salt Lake City, Utah, 17 April 1961, Source: Historical Department, Church of Jesus Christ of Latter-day Saints, Salt Lake City, Utah

38. *Hitler Youth*, pp. 130, 168, 220

39. Blair Holmes, Alan Keele, and Karl-Heinz Schnibbe, *When Truth Was Treason*, Urbana and Chicago, Illinois: University of Illinois Press, 1995, p. 27

40. Blair Holmes, Alan Keele, and Karl-Heinz Schnibbe, *When Truth Was Treason*, Urbana and Chicago, Illinois: University of Illinois Press, 1995, p. 27

41. Blair Holmes, Alan Keele, and Karl-Heinz Schnibbe, *When Truth Was Treason*, Urbana and Chicago, Illinois: University of Illinois Press, 1995, p. 29. Rudi, on the other hand, does not recall them talking about it in any depth or detail, and

says they knew more or less instinctively that something is wrong. Rudolf G. Wobbe Oral History, Doublas F. Tobler and Alan F. Keele, 1974, typescript, The James Moyle Oral History Program, Archives, Historical Department of the Church of Jesus Christ of Latter-day Saints, Salt Lake City, Utah, p. 4 although he later does remember talking quite a bit about history with Helmuth. Rudolf G. Wobbe Oral History, Doublas F. Tobler and Alan F. Keele, 1974, typescript, The James Moyle Oral History Program, Archives, Historical Department of the Church of Jesus Christ of Latter-day Saints, Salt Lake City, Utah, p. 6

42. Blair Holmes, Alan Keele, and Karl-Heinz Schnibbe, *When Truth Was Treason*, Urbana and Chicago, Illinois: University of Illinois Press, 1995

C H A P T E R   8

1. Arthur and Marie Sommerfeld interview with author, Salt Lake City, Utah, 18 October 1996, pp. 20-21

2. Hans and Charlotte Kunkel interview with author, Salt Lake City, Utah, 18 October 1996, p. 3

3. Ulrich Sander, *"Helmuth-Hübener Gruppe,"* in Hochmuth and Meyer, *Streiflichter,* pp. 328-29

4. Franz Ahrenz interview of Ida & Jupp Wieczorek, source: *Begleitheft zur Austellung um das kurze Leben und Wirken des Helmuth Hübener,* Catalogue of the exhibit in the Hamburg Municipal District Archive (Stadtteilarchiv) of Hamm, 26 October - 10 December 1992

5. Rudi Wobbe and Jerry Borrowman, *Three Against Hitler,* (American Fork, Utah: Covenant Communications, 1992), p. 39

6. Blair Holmes, Alan Keele, and Karl-Heinz Schnibbe, *When Truth Was Treason*, Urbana and Chicago, Illinois: University of Illinois Press, 1995

7. Herta Wobbe interview with author, 27 April 1999

8. Gerhard Kunkel interview #1 with author, 10 October 1996, p. 4

9. Rudi Wobbe Oral History, interviewed by Matthew K. Heiss, Salt Lake City, Utah, 1988, typescript, The James Moyle Oral History Program, Archives, Historical Department of the Church of Jesus Christ of Latter-day Saints, Salt Lake City, Utah, pp. 26-27

10. Liesolotte Prüss Müller interview with author 18 October 2003

11. Rudi Wobbe Oral History, interviewed by Matthew K. Heiss, Salt Lake City, Utah, 1988, typescript, The James Moyle Oral History Program, Archives, Historical Department of the Church of Jesus Christ of Latter-day Saints, Salt Lake City, Utah, p. 27

12. Arthur and Marie Sommerfeld interview with author, Salt Lake City, Utah, 18 October 1996, p. 17

13. Rudi Wobbe Oral History, interviewed by Matthew K. Heiss, Salt Lake City, Utah, 1988, typescript, The James Moyle Oral History Program, Archives, Historical Department of the Church of Jesus Christ of Latter-day Saints, Salt Lake City, Utah, p. 22

14. Rudi Wobbe Oral History, interviewed by Matthew K. Heiss, Salt Lake City, Utah, 1988, typescript, The James Moyle Oral History Program, Archives, Historical Department of the Church of Jesus Christ of Latter-day Saints, Salt Lake City, Utah, p. 22

15. Rudi Wobbe Oral History, interviewed by Matthew K. Heiss, Salt Lake City, Utah, 1988, typescript, The James Moyle Oral

History Program, Archives, Historical Department of the Church of Jesus Christ of Latter-day Saints, Salt Lake City, Utah, p. 27

16. Arthur and Marie Sommerfeld interview with author, Salt Lake City, Utah, 18 October 1996, p. 18

17. Rudi Wobbe Oral History, interviewed by Matthew K. Heiss, Salt Lake City, Utah, 1988, typescript, The James Moyle Oral History Program, Archives, Historical Department of the Church of Jesus Christ of Latter-day Saints, Salt Lake City, Utah, 0. 22

18. *Before the Blood Tribunal*, p. 20

19. Rudi Wobbe and Jerry Borrowman, *Three Against Hitler,* (American Fork, Utah: Covenant Communications, 1992), p. 20. Arthur Sommerfeld does not recall Worbs or the radio present at the scene, but remembers pulling guard duty that night with Rudi and Helmuth. Arthur and Marie Sommerfeld interview with author, Salt Lake City, Utah, 18 October 1996, pp. 17-18

20. Statement of Friedrich Peters, born 1920, Source: *Begleitheft zur Austellung um das kurze Leben und Wirken des Helmuth Hübener,* Catalogue of the exhibit in the Hamburg Municipal District Archive (Stadtteilarchiv) of Hamm, 26 October – 10 December

CHAPTER 9

1. Rudi Wobbe Oral History, interviewed by Matthew K. Heiss, Salt Lake City, Utah, 1988, typescript, The James Moyle Oral History Program, Archives, Historical Department of the Church of Jesus Christ of Latter-day Saints, Salt Lake City, Utah, p. 31

2. Statement of Hans Kunkel, Source: *Begleitheft zur Austellung um das kurze Leben und Wirken des Helmuth Hübener,* Catalogue

of the exhibit in the Hamburg Municipal District Archive (Stadtteilarchiv) of Hamm, 26 October – 10 December, 1992

3. Karl Schnibbe interview with author, Salt Lake City, Utah, 16 September 1996, transcribed by Don Ricks, p. 39

4. Hans and Charlotte Kunkel interview with author, Salt Lake City, Utah, 18 October 1996, p. 3

5. Karl Schnibbe interview with author, Salt Lake City, Utah, 16 September 1996, transcribed by Don Ricks, p. 36

6. Rudi Wobbe Oral History, interviewed by Matthew K. Heiss, Salt Lake City, Utah, 1988, typescript, The James Moyle Oral History Program, Archives, Historical Department of the Church of Jesus Christ of Latter-day Saints, Salt Lake City, Utah, p. 31

7. Document of Nazi government, "Helmuth Hübener: Secret," 1942

8. Rudi Wobbe Fireside [youth church lecture], 1987, transcribed by Richard Dewey and Heather Dewey, 1-4 February 2003, used by permission from Herta Wobbe, p. 11

9. Rudolf G. Wobbe Oral History, Doublas F. Tobler and Alan F. Keele, 1974, typescript, The James Moyle Oral History Program, Archives, Historical Department of the Church of Jesus Christ of Latter-day Saints, Salt Lake City, Utah, p. 6

10. Statement of Hans Kunkel, Source: *Begleitheft zur Austellung um das kurze Leben und Wirken des Helmuth Hübener,* Catalogue of the exhibit in the Hamburg Municipal District Archive (Stadtteilarchiv) of Hamm, 26 October – 10 December, 1992

11. Document of Nazi government, "Helmuth Hübener: Secret," 1942

12. Document of The Superior Attorney General of the Reich, Berlin 28 May 1942 at the People's Court, 8J 127/42g, In Custody! IId

13. Document from Hamburg, 24 February 1942, Final Report: Gestapo's Final Report of 24 Feb 1942 by Criminal Commissioner Wangemann

14. Document of District Court Hamburg, 27 February 1942, File Number 120. Gs. 60/42, Criminal Case against Hübener, et al; Gestapo's Warrant of Arrest of 27 Feb 1942 and Document of The Superior Attorney General of the Reich, Berlin 28 May 1942 at the People's Court, 8J 127/42g, In Custody!, Indictment introduction

15. Document of Nazi government, "Helmuth Hübener: Secret," 1942

16. Statement of Hans Kunkel, Source: *Begleitheft zur Austellung um das kurze Leben und Wirken des Helmuth Hübener,* Catalogue of the exhibit in the Hamburg Municipal District Archive (Stadtteilarchiv) of Hamm, 26 October – 10 December, 1992

17. Gerhard Kunkel interview #1 with author, 10 October 1996, p. 27

18. Gerhard Kunkel interview #1 with author, 10 October 1996, p. 6

19. Hans and Charlotte Kunkel interview with author, Salt Lake City, Utah, 18 October 1996, p. 1

20. Hans and Charlotte Kunkel interview with author, Salt Lake City, Utah, 18 October 1996, p. 1

21. Hans and Charlotte Kunkel interview with author, Salt Lake City, Utah, 18 October 1996, p. 1

22. "The Führer's New Clothes: Helmuth Hübener and the Dilemma of German Mormons in the Third Reich," unpublished essay by Alan F. Keele, Used by permission from Alan F. Keele. A shorter version of this essay was later published as an article in *Sunstone*, p. 11

23. "The Führer's New Clothes: Helmuth Hübener and the Dilemma of German Mormons in the Third Reich," unpublished essay by Alan F. Keele, Used by permission from Alan F. Keele. A shorter version of this essay was later published as an article in *Sunstone*, p. 11

24. Document of Nazi government, "Helmuth Hübener: Secret," 1942

25. Statement of Hans Kunkel, Source: *Begleitheft zur Austellung um das kurze Leben und Wirken des Helmuth Hübener,* Catalogue of the exhibit in the Hamburg Municipal District Archive (Stadtteilarchiv) of Hamm, 26 October – 10 December, 1992, Rudi Wobbe Fireside [youth church lecture], 1987, transcribed by Richard Dewey and Heather Dewey, 1-4 February 2003, used by permission from Herta Wobbe, p. 11

26. Statement of Hans Kunkel, Source: *Begleitheft zur Austellung um das kurze Leben und Wirken des Helmuth Hübener,* Catalogue of the exhibit in the Hamburg Municipal District Archive (Stadtteilarchiv) of Hamm, 26 October – 10 December, 1992

27. Rudi Wobbe Fireside [youth church lecture], 1987, transcribed by Richard Dewey and Heather Dewey, 1-4 February 2003, used by permission from Herta Wobbe, p. 11

28. Rudolf G. Wobbe Oral History, Doublas F. Tobler and Alan F. Keele, 1974, typescript, The James Moyle Oral History Program, Archives, Historical Department of the Church of Jesus Christ of Latter-day Saints, Salt Lake City, Utah, p. 6

29. "The Führer's New Clothes: Helmuth Hübener and the Dilemma of German Mormons in the Third Reich," unpublished essay by Alan F. Keele, Used by permission from Alan F. Keele. A shorter version of this essay was later published as an article in *Sunstone*, p. 29

30. P. 29, Blair Holmes, Alan Keele, and Karl-Heinz Schnibbe, *When Truth Was Treason*, Urbana and Chicago, Illinois: University of Illinois Press, 1995

31. Blair Holmes, Alan Keele, and Karl-Heinz Schnibbe, *When Truth Was Treason*, Urbana and Chicago, Illinois: University of Illinois Press, 1995, p. 29

32. 12 March 1942 Political Judgement [a background check] of District Personnel Office Leader from Hamburg Region, Hamburg District 4 of National Socialist German Workers' Party to Secret State Police of Hamburg; Gerhard Kunkel interview, p. 11

33. "The Führer's New Clothes: Helmuth Hübener and the Dilemma of German Mormons in the Third Reich," unpublished essay by Alan F. Keele, Used by permission from Alan F. Keele. A shorter version of this essay was later published as an article in *Sunstone*, p. 12

34. 12 March 1942 Political Judgement [a background check] of District Personnel Office Leader from Hamburg Region, Hamburg District 4 of National Socialist German Workers' Party to Secret State Police of Hamburg

35. 12 March 1942 Political Judgement [a background check] of District Personnel Office Leader from Hamburg Region, Hamburg District 4 of National Socialist German Workers' Party to Secret State Police of Hamburg

36. 12 March 1942 Political Judgement [a background check] of District Personnel Office Leader from Hamburg Region, Hamburg District 4 of National Socialist German Workers' Party to Secret State Police of Hamburg

37. Gerhard Kunkel interview #2 with author, 25 February 2003, p. 9

38. *Ibid.*

39. *Ibid.*

40. P. 2, Charlotte and Hans Kunkel interview

41. *Op. Cit.*

42. "The Führer's New Clothes: Helmuth Hübener and the Dilemma of German Mormons in the Third Reich," unpublished essay by Alan F. Keele, Used by permission from Alan F. Keele. A shorter version of this essay was later published as an article in *Sunstone*, pp. 23-24

43. *Op. Cit;.* and"The Führer's New Clothes: Helmuth Hübener and the Dilemma of German Mormons in the Third Reich," unpublished essay by Alan F. Keele, Used by permission from Alan F. Keele. A shorter version of this essay was later published as an article in *Sunstone*, p. 23

44. Gerhard Kunkel interview #1 with author, 10 October 1996, p. 11

45. "The Führer's New Clothes: Helmuth Hübener and the Dilemma of German Mormons in the Third Reich," unpublished essay by Alan F. Keele, Used by permission from Alan F. Keele. A shorter version of this essay was later published as an article in *Sunstone*, p. 23

46. Gerhard Kunkel interview #2 with author, 25 February 2003, p.7

47. Gerhard Kunkel interview #1 with author, 10 October 1996, p. 11 and Gerhard Kunkel interview #2 with author, 25 February 2003, p. 7

48. Gerhard Kunkel interview #1 with author, 10 October 1996, p. 11, also"The Führer's New Clothes: Helmuth Hübener and the Dilemma of German Mormons in the Third Reich," unpublished essay by Alan F. Keele, Used by permission from Alan F. Keele. A shorter version of this essay was later published as an article in *Sunstone*, p. 24

49. Karl Schnibbe interview with author, Salt Lake City, Utah, 16 September 1996, transcribed by Don Ricks, p. 29

50. Rudolf G. Wobbe Oral History, Douglas F. Tobler and Alan F. Keele, 1974, p. 29

51. "The Führer's New Clothes: Helmuth Hübener and the Dilemma of German Mormons in the Third Reich," unpublished essay by Alan F. Keele, Used by permission from Alan F. Keele. A shorter version of this essay was later published as an article in *Sunstone*, p. 25

52. Rudolf G. Wobbe Oral History, Doublas F. Tobler and Alan F. Keele, 1974, typescript, The James Moyle Oral History Program, Archives, Historical Department of the Church of Jesus Christ of Latter-day Saints, Salt Lake City, Utah, p. 29

53. Gerhard Kunkel interview #2 with author, 25 February 2003, p. 9

54. See also Letter from Emma Hübener, Hamburg, 8 March 1942, To the General Public Prosecutor at the Hanseatic Higher Regional Court.

55. Also Hans and Charlotte Kunkel interview with author, Salt Lake City, Utah, 18 October 1996, p. 2

56. Hans and Charlotte Kunkel interview with author, Salt Lake City, Utah, 18 October 1996, p. 2

57. "The Führer's New Clothes: Helmuth Hübener and the Dilemma of German Mormons in the Third Reich," unpublished essay by Alan F. Keele, Used by permission from Alan F. Keele. A shorter version of this essay was later published as an article in *Sunstone*, p. 24

58. Gerhard Kunkel interview #2 with author, 25 February 2003

59. Hans and Charlotte Kunkel interview with author, Salt Lake City, Utah, 18 October 1996, p. 2

60. Hans and Charlotte Kunkel interview with author, Salt Lake City, Utah, 18 October 1996, p. 1

61. Document from Hamburg, 24 February 1942, Final Report. However, another government report contradicts this one,

stating Helmuth's mother is at home. Document of Nazi government, "Helmuth Hübener: Secret," 1942

62. Letter from Emma Hübener, Hamburg, 8 March 1942, To the General Public Prosecutor at the Hanseatic Higher Regional Court.

CHAPTER 10

1. Gerhard Kunkel interview #2 with author, 25 February 2003, p. 10. Gerhard was actually in France beginning 20 August 1940, Gerhard Kunkel interview #2 with author, 25 February 2003, p. 7

2. Gerhard Kunkel interview #1 with author, 10 October 1996, pp. 11-12

3. *Ibid.*

4. *Ibid.* In a 1974 interview he recalls the size of the shortwave radio as somewhat smaller. "The Führer's New Clothes: Helmuth Hübener and the Dilemma of German Mormons in the Third Reich," unpublished essay by Alan F. Keele, Used by permission from Alan F. Keele. A shorter version of this essay was later published as an article in *Sunstone*, p. 17

5. Gerhard Kunkel interview #1 with author, 10 October 1996, pp. 11-12

6. *Ibid.*

7. "The Führer's New Clothes: Helmuth Hübener and the Dilemma of German Mormons in the Third Reich," unpublished essay by Alan F. Keele, Used by permission from Alan F. Keele. A shorter version of this essay was later published as an article in *Sunstone*, p. 17

8. Gerhard Kunkel interview #1 with author, 10 October 1996, pp. 11-12

9. Gerhard Kunkel interview #2 with author, 25 February 2003, pp. 10-11

10. Verdict of the People's Court in the criminal case against Helmut Hübener, et al, on 11 August 1942, Findings, Pt. I

11. Gerhard Kunkel interview #1 with author, 10 October 1996. Gerhard recalls coming home from France in April 1941. Gerhard Kunkel interview #1 with author, 10 October 1996, p. 11 and Gerhard Kunkel interview #2 with author, 25 February 2003, p. 11 The government says he was home two days before leaving again. Helmuth also stated later it was two or three days that Gerhard was home. Document of 5 Feb 1942 Gestapo interrogation transcript with Helmuth Hübener and Verdict of the People's Court in the criminal case against Helmut Hübener, et al, on 11 August 1942

12. Verdict of the People's Court in the criminal case against Helmut Hübener, et al, on 11 August 1942: The court orders; Gerhard Kunkel interview #1 with author, 10 October 1996, p. 11

13. Gerhard Kunkel interview #1 with author, 10 October 1996, p. 11

14. Else R. Behrend-Rosenfeld, *Ich stand nicht allein. Erlebnisse einer Judin in Deutschland*, 1933-1944 [Frankfurt am Main: Europaische Verlagsantalt, 1963], p. 235

15. "The Führer's New Clothes: Helmuth Hübener and the Dilemma of German Mormons in the Third Reich," unpublished essay by Alan F. Keele, Used by permission from Alan F. Keele. A shorter version of this essay was later published as an article in *Sunstone*, p. 17

16. Gerhard Kunkel interview #1 with author, 10 October 1996, p. 12. In 2003 Gerhard does not recall telling Helmuth about it, but says he could have told him Gerhard Kunkel interview #2 with author, 25 February 2003, pp. 9-10, thinking his youngest brother found the radio on his own.

17. Gerhard Kunkel interview #2 with author, 25 February 2003, pp. 9-10

18. "The Führer's New Clothes: Helmuth Hübener and the Dilemma of German Mormons in the Third Reich," unpublished essay by Alan F. Keele, Used by permission from Alan F. Keele. A shorter version of this essay was later published as an article in *Sunstone*, p. 24

19. Gerhard Kunkel interview #1 with author, 10 October 1996, p. 12

20. Gerhard Kunkel interview #1 with author, 10 October 1996, pp. 7-9

21. Gerhard Kunkel interview #1 with author, 10 October 1996, pp. 12-13

22. "The Führer's New Clothes: Helmuth Hübener and the Dilemma of German Mormons in the Third Reich," unpublished essay by Alan F. Keele, Used by permission from Alan F. Keele. A shorter version of this essay was later published as an article in *Sunstone*, 27

23. Verdict of the People's Court in the criminal case against Helmut Hübener, et al, on 11 August 1942: Findings, Pt. II, sec. 1, and Document of State Police Agency Hamburg — Hamburg, 5, 9, 17, 20 February 1942

24. Rudi Wobbe Oral History, interviewed by Matthew K. Heiss, Salt Lake City, Utah, 1988, typescript, The James Moyle Oral History Program, Archives, Historical Department of the Church of Jesus Christ of Latter-day Saints, Salt Lake City, Utah, p. 35

25. Karl Schnibbe interview with author, Salt Lake City, Utah, 16 September 1996, transcribed by Don Ricks, p. 41

26. Document of State Police Agency Hamburg — Hamburg, 5, 9, 17, 20 February 1942, Document of The Superior Attorney

General of the Reich, Berlin 28 May 1942 at the People's Court, 8J 127/42g, In Custody!: section IIa

27. Document of State Police Agency Hamburg — Hamburg, 5, 9, 17, 20 February 1942

28. Document of State Police Agency Hamburg — Hamburg, 5, 9, 17, 20 February 1942, 27, 52

29. Verdict of the People's Court in the criminal case against Helmut Hübener, et al, on 11 August 1942; Document of The Superior Attorney General of the Reich, Berlin 28 May 1942 at the People's Court, 8J 127/42g, In Custody!, and Document of State Police Agency Hamburg — Hamburg, 5, 9, 17, 20 February 1942. 9 Feb 1942 Gestapo interrogation transcript with Helmuth Hübener

30. Document of The Superior Attorney General of the Reich, Berlin 28 May 1942 at the People's Court, 8J 127/42g, In Custody!: sec IIa, Document of State Police Agency Hamburg — Hamburg, 5, 9, 17, 20 February 1942, Verdict of the People's Court in the criminal case against Helmut Hübener, et al, on 11 August 1942

31. Statement of Marie Sommerfeld, Source: *Begleitheft zur Austellung um das kurze Leben und Wirken des Helmuth Hübener*, Catalogue of the exhibit in the Hamburg Municipal District Archive (Stadtteilarchiv) of Hamm, 26 October – 10 December, 1992; Document of Chief State Counsel of the Hanseatic Higher Regional Court, Hamburg 36, 25 March 1942, Criminal Case! Juveniles!

32. Document of State Police Agency Hamburg — Hamburg, 5, 9, 17, 20 February 1942, Document of The Superior Attorney General of the Reich, Berlin 28 May 1942 at the People's Court, 8J 127/42g, In Custody!; and Rudi Wobbe Fireside [youth church lecture], 1987, transcribed by Richard Dewey and Heather Dewey, 1-4 February 2003, used by permission from Herta Wobbe, p. 8

33. Rudi Wobbe Fireside [youth church lecture], 1987, transcribed by Richard Dewey and Heather Dewey, 1-4 February 2003, used by permission from Herta Wobbe, p. 8 and Karl Schnibbe interview with author, Salt Lake City, Utah, 16 September 1996, transcribed by Don Ricks, p. 41

34. Karl Schnibbe interview with author, Salt Lake City, Utah, 16 September 1996, transcribed by Don Ricks, p. 41

35. Rudi Wobbe Fireside [youth church lecture], 1987, transcribed by Richard Dewey and Heather Dewey, 1-4 February 2003, used by permission from Herta Wobbe, p. 8

36. Deutschkron, *Outcast*, p. 63

37. Document from Hamburg, 24 February 1942, Final Report: Gestapo's Final Report of 24 Feb 1942 by Criminal Commissioner Wangemann; and Document of The Superior Attorney General of the Reich, Berlin 28 May 1942 at the People's Court, 8J 127/42g, In Custody!: sec Iia, Document of State Police Agency Hamburg — Hamburg, 5, 9, 17, 20 February 1942 Verdict of the People's Court in the criminal case against Helmut Hübener, et al, on 11 August 1942

38. Rudi Wobbe Fireside [youth church lecture], 1987, transcribed by Richard Dewey and Heather Dewey, 1-4 February 2003, used by permission from Herta Wobbe, p. 8

39. Rudi Wobbe Fireside [youth church lecture], 1987, transcribed by Richard Dewey and Heather Dewey, 1-4 February 2003, used by permission from Herta Wobbe, p. 9

40. Rudi Wobbe Fireside [youth church lecture], 1987, transcribed by Richard Dewey and Heather Dewey, 1-4 February 2003, used by permission from Herta Wobbe, p. 8

41. Helmuth Hübener flyer regarding German losses

42. Blair Holmes, Alan Keele, and Karl-Heinz Schnibbe, *When Truth Was Treason*, Urbana and Chicago, Illinois: University of Illinois Press, 1995

CHAPTER 11

1. Arthur and Marie Sommerfeld interview with author, Salt Lake City, Utah, 18 October 1996

2. Arthur and Marie Sommerfeld interview with author, Salt Lake City, Utah, 18 October 1996, p. 15

3. Arthur and Marie Sommerfeld interview with author, 18 October 1996, pp. 18-20

4. Arthur and Marie Sommerfeld interview with author, Salt Lake City, Utah, 18 October 1996, pp. 23-24

5. Arthur and Marie Sommerfeld interview with author, 18 October 1996, pp. 18-19

6. Blair Holmes, Alan Keele, and Karl-Heinz Schnibbe, *When Truth Was Treason*, Urbana and Chicago, Illinois: University of Illinois Press, 1995

7. Arthur and Marie Sommerfeld interview with author, Salt Lake City, Utah, 18 October 1996, pp. 18-19

8. Statement of Marie Sommerfeld, Source: *Begleitheft zur Austellung um das kurze Leben und Wirken des Helmuth Hübener*, Catalogue of the exhibit in the Hamburg Municipal District Archive (Stadtteilarchiv) of Hamm, 26 October – 10 December, 1992

9. Arthur and Marie Sommerfeld interview with author, Salt Lake City, Utah, 18 October 1996, p. 24

10. MS 133277, Archives, LDS Church Historian's Office, p. 8

11. Otto Berndt, Jr. Interview #2 with author, 20 October 2003; see also Otto Berndt Oral History, interviewed by Douglas F. Tobler, Salt Lake City, Utah, 1974, typescript, The James Moyle Oral History Program, Archives, Historical Department of the Church of Jesus Christ of Latter-day Saints, Salt Lake City, Utah, p. 33 Thirty-two years later Otto, Sr. believes all

three boys - Karl, Rudi and Helmuth weren't too active in the church, unlike the testimony of all others who spoke of the boys; Otto was in the air force during part of this period and was gone on assignments for the district during much of his other years he knew the boys; in any case, due to the preponderance of evidence, he is in error.

12. Rudi Wobbe Oral History, interviewed by Matthew K. Heiss, Salt Lake City, Utah, 1988, typescript, The James Moyle Oral History Program, Archives, Historical Department of the Church of Jesus Christ of Latter-day Saints, Salt Lake City, Utah, p. 4

13. Document of The Superior Attorney General of the Reich, Berlin 28 May 1942 at the People's Court, 8J 127/42g, In Custody!: Indictment introduction

14. Gestapo Warrant of Arrest of 27 Feb 1942 and Verdict of the People's Court in the criminal case against Helmut Hübener, et al, on 11 August 1942: Findings, Pt. I

15. Rudi Wobbe Oral History, interviewed by Matthew K. Heiss, Salt Lake City, Utah, 1988, typescript, The James Moyle Oral History Program, Archives, Historical Department of the Church of Jesus Christ of Latter-day Saints, Salt Lake City, Utah, p. 3

16. Rudi Wobbe Oral History, interviewed by Matthew K. Heiss, Salt Lake City, Utah, 1988, typescript, The James Moyle Oral History Program, Archives, Historical Department of the Church of Jesus Christ of Latter-day Saints, Salt Lake City, Utah, p. 3

17. Rudi Wobbe Oral History, interviewed by Matthew K. Heiss, Salt Lake City, Utah, 1988, typescript, The James Moyle Oral History Program, Archives, Historical Department of the Church of Jesus Christ of Latter-day Saints, Salt Lake City, Utah, p. 4

18. Rudi Wobbe Oral History, interviewed by Matthew K. Heiss, Salt Lake City, Utah, 1988, typescript, The James Moyle Oral

History Program, Archives, Historical Department of the Church of Jesus Christ of Latter-day Saints, Salt Lake City, Utah, p. 10

19. Rudi Wobbe Oral History, interviewed by Matthew K. Heiss, Salt Lake City, Utah, 1988, typescript, The James Moyle Oral History Program, Archives, Historical Department of the Church of Jesus Christ of Latter-day Saints, Salt Lake City, Utah, p. 12

20. Report from District Personnel Office Director of Personnel Office Division, Hamburg Region, Hamburg District 4 of National Socialist German Workers' Party of 10 March 1942 to Secret State Police of Hamburg

21. Rudi Wobbe Oral History, interviewed by Matthew K. Heiss, Salt Lake City, Utah, 1988, typescript, The James Moyle Oral History Program, Archives, Historical Department of the Church of Jesus Christ of Latter-day Saints, Salt Lake City, Utah, p. 4

22. *Ibid*, p. 12

23. *Ibid.*

24. Rudi Wobbe Oral History, interviewed by Matthew K. Heiss, Salt Lake City, Utah, 1988, typescript, The James Moyle Oral History Program, Archives, Historical Department of the Church of Jesus Christ of Latter-day Saints, Salt Lake City, Utah, p. 8

25. Rudi Wobbe Oral History, interviewed by Matthew K. Heiss, Salt Lake City, Utah, 1988, typescript, The James Moyle Oral History Program, Archives, Historical Department of the Church of Jesus Christ of Latter-day Saints, Salt Lake City, Utah, p. 1

26. Rudi Wobbe Oral History, interviewed by Matthew K. Heiss, Salt Lake City, Utah, 1988, typescript, The James Moyle Oral History Program, Archives, Historical Department of the Church of Jesus Christ of Latter-day Saints, Salt Lake

City, Utah, pp. 1-2 and Hamburg District Record of Members, number 23403

27. Rudi Wobbe Oral History, interviewed by Matthew K. Heiss, Salt Lake City, Utah, 1988, typescript, The James Moyle Oral History Program, Archives, Historical Department of the Church of Jesus Christ of Latter-day Saints, Salt Lake City, Utah, p. 1

28. Rudi Wobbe Oral History, interviewed by Matthew K. Heiss, Salt Lake City, Utah, 1988, typescript, The James Moyle Oral History Program, Archives, Historical Department of the Church of Jesus Christ of Latter-day Saints, Salt Lake City, Utah, p. 2

29. Rudi Wobbe Oral History, interviewed by Matthew K. Heiss, Salt Lake City, Utah, 1988, typescript, The James Moyle Oral History Program, Archives, Historical Department of the Church of Jesus Christ of Latter-day Saints, Salt Lake City, Utah, pp. 3-4

30. Rudi Wobbe Oral History, interviewed by Matthew K. Heiss, Salt Lake City, Utah, 1988, typescript, The James Moyle Oral History Program, Archives, Historical Department of the Church of Jesus Christ of Latter-day Saints, Salt Lake City, Utah, p. 8

31. Rudi Wobbe Oral History, interviewed by Matthew K. Heiss, Salt Lake City, Utah, 1988, typescript, The James Moyle Oral History Program, Archives, Historical Department of the Church of Jesus Christ of Latter-day Saints, Salt Lake City, Utah, p. 25

32. Rudi Wobbe Oral History, interviewed by Matthew K. Heiss, Salt Lake City, Utah, 1988, typescript, The James Moyle Oral History Program, Archives, Historical Department of the Church of Jesus Christ of Latter-day Saints, Salt Lake City, Utah, p. 9

33. Rudi Wobbe Oral History, interviewed by Matthew K. Heiss, Salt Lake City, Utah, 1988, typescript, The James Moyle Oral

History Program, Archives, Historical Department of the Church of Jesus Christ of Latter-day Saints, Salt Lake City, Utah, p. 9

34. Hamburg membership record 994

35. Rudi Wobbe Oral History, interviewed by Matthew K. Heiss, Salt Lake City, Utah, 1988, typescript, The James Moyle Oral History Program, Archives, Historical Department of the Church of Jesus Christ of Latter-day Saints, Salt Lake City, Utah, p. 13

36. Rudi Wobbe Oral History, interviewed by Matthew K. Heiss, Salt Lake City, Utah, 1988, typescript, The James Moyle Oral History Program, Archives, Historical Department of the Church of Jesus Christ of Latter-day Saints, Salt Lake City, Utah, pp. 14-15

37. Rudi Wobbe Oral History, interviewed by Matthew K. Heiss, Salt Lake City, Utah, 1988, typescript, The James Moyle Oral History Program, Archives, Historical Department of the Church of Jesus Christ of Latter-day Saints, Salt Lake City, Utah, p. 15

38. *Ibid.*

39. Verdict of the People's Court in the criminal case against Helmut Hübener, et al, on 11 August 1942: Findings, Part I

40. Rudi Wobbe Oral History, interviewed by Matthew K. Heiss, Salt Lake City, Utah, 1988, typescript, The James Moyle Oral History Program, Archives, Historical Department of the Church of Jesus Christ of Latter-day Saints, Salt Lake City, Utah, p. 26

41. Rudi Wobbe Oral History, interviewed by Matthew K. Heiss, Salt Lake City, Utah, 1988, typescript, The James Moyle Oral History Program, Archives, Historical Department of the Church of Jesus Christ of Latter-day Saints, Salt Lake City, Utah, p. 28

42. Rudi Wobbe Oral History, interviewed by Matthew K. Heiss, Salt Lake City, Utah, 1988, typescript, The James Moyle Oral History Program, Archives, Historical Department of the Church of Jesus Christ of Latter-day Saints, Salt Lake City, Utah, p. 29

43. Rudi Wobbe Oral History, interviewed by Matthew K. Heiss, Salt Lake City, Utah, 1988, typescript, The James Moyle Oral History Program, Archives, Historical Department of the Church of Jesus Christ of Latter-day Saints, Salt Lake City, Utah, p. 12

44. Rudi Wobbe Oral History, interviewed by Matthew K. Heiss, Salt Lake City, Utah, 1988, typescript, The James Moyle Oral History Program, Archives, Historical Department of the Church of Jesus Christ of Latter-day Saints, Salt Lake City, Utah, pp. 28-29

45. Rudolf G. Wobbe Oral History, Doublas F. Tobler and Alan F. Keele, 1974, typescript, The James Moyle Oral History Program, Archives, Historical Department of the Church of Jesus Christ of Latter-day Saints, Salt Lake City, Utah, p. 13

46. Rudi Wobbe Oral History, interviewed by Matthew K. Heiss, Salt Lake City, Utah, 1988, typescript, The James Moyle Oral History Program, Archives, Historical Department of the Church of Jesus Christ of Latter-day Saints, Salt Lake City, Utah, pp. 31-32

47. Rudi Wobbe Oral History, interviewed by Matthew K. Heiss, Salt Lake City, Utah, 1988, typescript, The James Moyle Oral History Program, Archives, Historical Department of the Church of Jesus Christ of Latter-day Saints, Salt Lake City, Utah, p. 32

48. Rudi Wobbe Oral History, interviewed by Matthew K. Heiss, Salt Lake City, Utah, 1988, typescript, The James Moyle Oral History Program, Archives, Historical Department of the Church of Jesus Christ of Latter-day Saints, Salt Lake City, Utah, p. 32

49. Rudolf G. Wobbe Oral History, Doublas F. Tobler and Alan F. Keele, 1974, typescript, The James Moyle Oral History Program, Archives, Historical Department of the Church of Jesus Christ of Latter-day Saints, Salt Lake City, Utah, p. 13

50. Rudi Wobbe Oral History, interviewed by Matthew K. Heiss, Salt Lake City, Utah, 1988, typescript, The James Moyle Oral History Program, Archives, Historical Department of the Church of Jesus Christ of Latter-day Saints, Salt Lake City, Utah, p. 32

51. Rudi Wobbe Oral History, interviewed by Matthew K. Heiss, Salt Lake City, Utah, 1988, typescript, The James Moyle Oral History Program, Archives, Historical Department of the Church of Jesus Christ of Latter-day Saints, Salt Lake City, Utah, p. 33

52. Document of The Superior Attorney General of the Reich, Berlin 28 May 1942 at the People's Court, 8J 127/42g, In Custody!: Indictment introduction

53. Statement of Marie Sommerfeld, Source: *Begleitheft zur Austellung um das kurze Leben und Wirken des Helmuth Hübener*, Catalogue of the exhibit in the Hamburg Municipal District Archive (Stadtteilarchiv) of Hamm, 26 October – 10 December, 1992

54. Statement of Hans Kunkel, Source: *Begleitheft zur Austellung um das kurze Leben und Wirken des Helmuth Hübener*, Catalogue of the exhibit in the Hamburg Municipal District Archive (Stadtteilarchiv) of Hamm, 26 October – 10 December, 1992

55. Karl Schnibbe interview with author, Salt Lake City, Utah, 16 September 1996, transcribed by Don Ricks, p. 31

56. P. 2, Karl Schnibbe interview with author, Salt Lake City, Utah, 16 September 1996, transcribed by Don Ricks

57. Karl Schnibbe interview with author, Salt Lake City, Utah, 16 September 1996, transcribed by Don Ricks, p. 31

58. Document of The Superior Attorney General of the Reich, Berlin 28 May 1942 at the People's Court, 8J 127/42g, In Custody!, *Ibid*; Document of District Court Hamburg, 27 February 1942, File Number 120. Gs. 60/42, Criminal Case against Hübener, et al

59. Karl Schnibbe interview with author, Salt Lake City, Utah, 16 September 1996, transcribed by Don Ricks, p. 31

60. Document of District Court Hamburg, 27 February 1942, File Number 120. Gs. 60/42, Criminal Case against Hübener, et al; and Document of The Superior Attorney General of the Reich, Berlin 28 May 1942 at the People's Court, 8J 127/42g, In Custody!

61. Letter from Johann Schnibbe to government officials, 21 March 1942 [source: Berlin Document Center]

62. Blair Holmes, Alan Keele, and Karl-Heinz Schnibbe, *When Truth Was Treason*, Urbana and Chicago, Illinois: University of Illinois Press, 1995, p. 24

63. Gerhard Kunkel interview #2 with author, 25 February 2003, p. 12

64. Blair Holmes, Alan Keele, and Karl-Heinz Schnibbe, *When Truth Was Treason*, Urbana and Chicago, Illinois: University of Illinois Press, 1995, p. 24

65. Karl Schnibbe interview with author, Salt Lake City, Utah, 16 September 1996, transcribed by Don Ricks, p. 2

66. Karl Schnibbe interview with author, Salt Lake City, Utah, 16 September 1996, transcribed by Don Ricks, p. 29

67. Blair Holmes, Alan Keele, and Karl-Heinz Schnibbe, *When Truth Was Treason*, Urbana and Chicago, Illinois: University of Illinois Press, 1995, p. 25

68. Karl Schnibbe interview with author, Salt Lake City, Utah, 16 September 1996, transcribed by Don Ricks, p. 29

69. Rudolf G. Wobbe Oral History, Doublas F. Tobler and Alan F. Keele, 1974, typescript, The James Moyle Oral History Program, Archives, Historical Department of the Church of Jesus Christ of Latter-day Saints, Salt Lake City, Utah, p. 26

70. Karl Schnibbe interview with author, Salt Lake City, Utah, 16 September 1996, transcribed by Don Ricks, p. 2

71. Karl Schnibbe interview with author, Salt Lake City, Utah, 16 September 1996, transcribed by Don Ricks, p. 27

72. Arthur and Marie Sommerfeld interview with author, 18 October 1996 pp. 15-16

C H A P T E R   1 2

1. Blair Holmes, Alan Keele, and Karl-Heinz Schnibbe, *When Truth Was Treason*, Urbana and Chicago, Illinois: University of Illinois Press, 1995

2. Gerhard Kunkel interview #1 with author, 10 October 1996, p. 13

3. "The Führer's New Clothes: Helmuth Hübener and the Dilemma of German Mormons in the Third Reich," unpublished essay by Alan F. Keele, Used by permission from Alan F. Keele. A shorter version of this essay was later published as an article in *Sunstone*, p. 5

4. "The Führer's New Clothes: Helmuth Hübener and the Dilemma of German Mormons in the Third Reich," unpublished essay by Alan F. Keele, Used by permission from Alan F. Keele. A shorter version of this essay was later published as an article in *Sunstone*, p. 5-6

5. Gerhard Kunkel interview #1 with author, 10 October 1996, p. 12

6. Otto Berndt Oral History, interviewed by Douglas F. Tobler, Salt Lake City, Utah, 1974, typescript, The James Moyle Oral History Program, Archives, Historical Department of the Church of Jesus Christ of Latter-day Saints, Salt Lake City, Utah, p. 52

7. "The Führer's New Clothes: Helmuth Hübener and the Dilemma of German Mormons in the Third Reich," unpublished essay by Alan F. Keele, Used by permission from Alan F. Keele. A shorter version of this essay was later published as an article in *Sunstone*, p. 30

8. "The Führer's New Clothes: Helmuth Hübener and the Dilemma of German Mormons in the Third Reich," unpublished essay by Alan F. Keele, Used by permission from Alan F. Keele. A shorter version of this essay was later published as an article in *Sunstone*, p. 30

9. Blair Holmes, Alan Keele, and Karl-Heinz Schnibbe, *When Truth Was Treason*, Urbana and Chicago, Illinois: University of Illinois Press, 1995

10. Blair Holmes, Alan Keele, and Karl-Heinz Schnibbe, *When Truth Was Treason*, Urbana and Chicago, Illinois: University of Illinois Press, 1995

11. Blair Holmes, Alan Keele, and Karl-Heinz Schnibbe, *When Truth Was Treason*, Urbana and Chicago, Illinois: University of Illinois Press, 1995

12. Karl Schnibbe interview with author, Salt Lake City, Utah, 16 September 1996, transcribed by Don Ricks, p. 30

13. Blair Holmes, Alan Keele, and Karl-Heinz Schnibbe, *When Truth Was Treason*, Urbana and Chicago, Illinois: University of Illinois Press, 1995

14. *Truth & Conviction*, documentary film produced by Brigham Young University, produced by Rick McFarland and Matt Whitaker, written and directed by Matt Whitaker, December 2003, one hour length

15. Blair Holmes, Alan Keele, and Karl-Heinz Schnibbe, *When Truth Was Treason*, Urbana and Chicago, Illinois: University of Illinois Press, 1995

16. Blair Holmes, Alan Keele, and Karl-Heinz Schnibbe, *When Truth Was Treason*, Urbana and Chicago, Illinois: University of Illinois Press, 1995

17. Blair Holmes, Alan Keele, and Karl-Heinz Schnibbe, *When Truth Was Treason*, Urbana and Chicago, Illinois: University of Illinois Press, 1995

18. Blair Holmes, Alan Keele, and Karl-Heinz Schnibbe, *When Truth Was Treason*, Urbana and Chicago, Illinois: University of Illinois Press, 1995

19. Blair Holmes, Alan Keele, and Karl-Heinz Schnibbe, *When Truth Was Treason*, Urbana and Chicago, Illinois: University of Illinois Press, 1995

CHAPTER 13

1. Rudi Wobbe Oral History, interviewed by Matthew K. Heiss, Salt Lake City, Utah, 1988, typescript, The James Moyle Oral History Program, Archives, Historical Department of the Church of Jesus Christ of Latter-day Saints, Salt Lake City, Utah, p. 36

2. Rudi Wobbe Oral History, interviewed by Matthew K. Heiss, Salt Lake City, Utah, 1988, typescript, The James Moyle Oral History Program, Archives, Historical Department of the Church of Jesus Christ of Latter-day Saints, Salt Lake City, Utah, p. 35

3. Rudi Wobbe Oral History, interviewed by Matthew K. Heiss, Salt Lake City, Utah, 1988, typescript, The James Moyle Oral History Program, Archives, Historical Department of the Church of Jesus Christ of Latter-day Saints, Salt Lake City, Utah, p. 36. In 1987 Rudi recalled Helmuth actually spilling

the beans about the BBC before Rudi had gone to his place, with Helmuth saying right up front, "Why, come on over and let's listen to some of the BBC London broadcasts." Rudolf G. Wobbe Oral History, Doublas F. Tobler and Alan F. Keele, 1974, typescript, The James Moyle Oral History Program, Archives, Historical Department of the Church of Jesus Christ of Latter-day Saints, Salt Lake City, Utah, p. 2

4. Rudi Wobbe Fireside [youth church lecture], 1987, transcribed by Richard Dewey and Heather Dewey, 1-4 February 2003, used by permission from Herta Wobbe, p. 8

5. Rudi Wobbe Oral History, interviewed by Matthew K. Heiss, Salt Lake City, Utah, 1988, typescript, The James Moyle Oral History Program, Archives, Historical Department of the Church of Jesus Christ of Latter-day Saints, Salt Lake City, Utah, p. 36

6. Rudolf G. Wobbe Oral History, Doublas F. Tobler and Alan F. Keele, 1974, typescript, The James Moyle Oral History Program, Archives, Historical Department of the Church of Jesus Christ of Latter-day Saints, Salt Lake City, Utah, p. 2

7. Rudolf G. Wobbe Oral History, Doublas F. Tobler and Alan F. Keele, 1974, typescript, The James Moyle Oral History Program, Archives, Historical Department of the Church of Jesus Christ of Latter-day Saints, Salt Lake City, Utah, pp. 25-26

8. Rudolf G. Wobbe Oral History, Doublas F. Tobler and Alan F. Keele, 1974, typescript, The James Moyle Oral History Program, Archives, Historical Department of the Church of Jesus Christ of Latter-day Saints, Salt Lake City, Utah, p. 26

9. Rudolf G. Wobbe Oral History, Doublas F. Tobler and Alan F. Keele, 1974, typescript, The James Moyle Oral History Program, Archives, Historical Department of the Church of Jesus Christ of Latter-day Saints, Salt Lake City, Utah, p. 2

10. Rudolf G. Wobbe Oral History, Doublas F. Tobler and Alan F. Keele, 1974, typescript, The James Moyle Oral History

Program, Archives, Historical Department of the Church of Jesus Christ of Latter-day Saints, Salt Lake City, Utah, p. 3

11. Otto Berndt Oral History, interviewed by Douglas F. Tobler, Salt Lake City, Utah, 1974, typescript, The James Moyle Oral History Program, Archives, Historical Department of the Church of Jesus Christ of Latter-day Saints, Salt Lake City, Utah, p. 37

12. Otto Berndt Oral History, interviewed by Douglas F. Tobler, Salt Lake City, Utah, 1974, typescript, The James Moyle Oral History Program, Archives, Historical Department of the Church of Jesus Christ of Latter-day Saints, Salt Lake City, Utah, p. 39

13. Rudi Wobbe Oral History, interviewed by Matthew K. Heiss, Salt Lake City, Utah, 1988, typescript, The James Moyle Oral History Program, Archives, Historical Department of the Church of Jesus Christ of Latter-day Saints, Salt Lake City, Utah, p. 37

14. Rudi Wobbe Oral History, interviewed by Matthew K. Heiss, Salt Lake City, Utah, 1988, typescript, The James Moyle Oral History Program, Archives, Historical Department of the Church of Jesus Christ of Latter-day Saints, Salt Lake City, Utah, p. 37

15. Rudolf G. Wobbe Oral History, Doublas F. Tobler and Alan F. Keele, 1974, typescript, The James Moyle Oral History Program, Archives, Historical Department of the Church of Jesus Christ of Latter-day Saints, Salt Lake City, Utah, p. 4

16. Rudolf G. Wobbe Oral History, Doublas F. Tobler and Alan F. Keele, 1974, typescript, The James Moyle Oral History Program, Archives, Historical Department of the Church of Jesus Christ of Latter-day Saints, Salt Lake City, Utah, p. 6

17. Rudolf G. Wobbe Oral History, Doublas F. Tobler and Alan F. Keele, 1974, typescript, The James Moyle Oral History Program, Archives, Historical Department of the Church of Jesus Christ of Latter-day Saints, Salt Lake City, Utah, p. 4

18. Rudolf G. Wobbe Oral History, Doublas F. Tobler and Alan F. Keele, 1974, typescript, The James Moyle Oral History Program, Archives, Historical Department of the Church of Jesus Christ of Latter-day Saints, Salt Lake City, Utah, p. 28

19. Rudi Wobbe Fireside [youth church lecture], 1987, transcribed by Richard Dewey and Heather Dewey, 1-4 February 2003, used by permission from Herta Wobbe, p. 20

20. Rudolf G. Wobbe Oral History, Doublas F. Tobler and Alan F. Keele, 1974, typescript, The James Moyle Oral History Program, Archives, Historical Department of the Church of Jesus Christ of Latter-day Saints, Salt Lake City, Utah, p. 13

21. Blair Holmes, Alan Keele, and Karl-Heinz Schnibbe, *When Truth Was Treason*, Urbana and Chicago, Illinois: University of Illinois Press, 1995

22. C. F. Latour, "Goebbels' Außerordentliche Rundfunkmaßnahmen, 1939 - 1942," *Vierteljahresheft fur Zeitgeschichte* II, no. 4 [1963]; pp. 418-19; Balfour, Withstanding Hitler, Pp. 62-62

23. Blair Holmes, Alan Keele, and Karl-Heinz Schnibbe, *When Truth Was Treason*, Urbana and Chicago, Illinois: University of Illinois Press, 1995

24. Lieselotte Puress Schmidt interview #1 with author, 17 October 2003

25. Lieselotte Prüss Schmidt interview #1 with author, 17 October 2003

26. Lieselotte Prüss Schmidt interview #2 with author, 18 October 2003

27. Lieselotte Puress Schmidt interview #1 with author, 17 October 2003

28. Lieselotte Puress Schmidt interview #2 with author, 18 October 2003

29. Lieselotte Prüss Schmidt interview with author, 17 October 2003. A side note Gerhard Kunkel points out is that a larger number, if not a majority, of the St Georg Branch members were elderly, which also held true for the people generally in the Hamburg area. "The Führer's New Clothes: Helmuth Hübener and the Dilemma of German Mormons in the Third Reich," unpublished essay by Alan F. Keele, Used by permission from Alan F. Keele. A shorter version of this essay was later published as an article in *Sunstone*, p. 19 Some elements of this more conservative, older population were less favorable to national socialism, but at the same time were more fearful to do anything about it, looking for security at that point in their lives, compared to the more tempestuous younger generation, who, ironically, were more inclined to favor Hitler. Obviously, this combination of factors did not open the way for a large resistance element.

30. Blair Holmes, Alan Keele, and Karl-Heinz Schnibbe, *When Truth Was Treason*, Urbana and Chicago, Illinois: University of Illinois Press, 1995

31. Rudi Wobbe Fireside [youth church lecture], 1987, transcribed by Richard Dewey and Heather Dewey, 1-4 February 2003, used by permission from Herta Wobbe, p. 9

32. Blair Holmes, Alan Keele, and Karl-Heinz Schnibbe, *When Truth Was Treason*, Urbana and Chicago, Illinois: University of Illinois Press, 1995

33. Blair Holmes, Alan Keele, and Karl-Heinz Schnibbe, *When Truth Was Treason*, Urbana and Chicago, Illinois: University of Illinois Press, 1995

34. Blair Holmes, Alan Keele, and Karl-Heinz Schnibbe, *When Truth Was Treason*, Urbana and Chicago, Illinois: University of Illinois Press, 1995

35. Rudi Wobbe Oral History, interviewed by Matthew K. Heiss, Salt Lake City, Utah, 1988, typescript, The James Moyle Oral History Program, Archives, Historical Department of the

Church of Jesus Christ of Latter-day Saints, Salt Lake City, Utah, p. 36

36. Rudi Wobbe and Jerry Borrowman, *Three Against Hitler,* (American Fork, Utah: Covenant Communications, 1992)

37. Rudi Wobbe Oral History, interviewed by Matthew K. Heiss, Salt Lake City, Utah, 1988, typescript, The James Moyle Oral History Program, Archives, Historical Department of the Church of Jesus Christ of Latter-day Saints, Salt Lake City, Utah, p. 37

38. Blair Holmes, Alan Keele, and Karl-Heinz Schnibbe, *When Truth Was Treason*, Urbana and Chicago, Illinois: University of Illinois Press, 1995

CHAPTER 14

1. 18 Feb 1942 Gestapo interrogation affidavit from Rudi Wobbe

2. Rudi Wobbe Fireside [youth church lecture], 1987, transcribed by Richard Dewey and Heather Dewey, 1-4 February 2003, used by permission from Herta Wobbe, p. 9

3. Document of The Superior Attorney General of the Reich, Berlin 28 May 1942 at the People's Court, 8J 127/42g, In Custody!: III-1

4. Verdict of the People's Court in the criminal case against Helmut Hübener, et al, on 11 August 1942: Findings, Pt. II, sec. 1; Document of Chief State Counsel of the Hanseatic Higher Regional Court, Hamburg 36, 25 March 1942, Criminal Case! Juveniles!; Document of The Superior Attorney General of the Reich, Berlin 28 May 1942 at the People's Court, 8J 127/42g, In Custody!: III-1

5. Rudi Wobbe Oral History, interviewed by Matthew K. Heiss, Salt Lake City, Utah, 1988, typescript, The James Moyle Oral History Program, Archives, Historical Department of the

Church of Jesus Christ of Latter-day Saints, Salt Lake City, Utah, p. 37

6. Rudi Wobbe Fireside [youth church lecture], 1987, transcribed by Richard Dewey and Heather Dewey, 1-4 February 2003, used by permission from Herta Wobbe, p. 10

7. Rudi Wobbe Fireside [youth church lecture], 1987, transcribed by Richard Dewey and Heather Dewey, 1-4 February 2003, used by permission from Herta Wobbe, p. 10

8. Blair Holmes, Alan Keele, and Karl-Heinz Schnibbe, *When Truth Was Treason*, Urbana and Chicago, Illinois: University of Illinois Press, 1995

9. Rudi Wobbe Fireside [youth church lecture], 1987, transcribed by Richard Dewey and Heather Dewey, 1-4 February 2003, used by permission from Herta Wobbe, p. 10

10. Blair Holmes, Alan Keele, and Karl-Heinz Schnibbe, *When Truth Was Treason*, Urbana and Chicago, Illinois: University of Illinois Press, 1995

11. Rudi Wobbe Fireside [youth church lecture], 1987, transcribed by Richard Dewey and Heather Dewey, 1-4 February 2003, used by permission from Herta Wobbe, p. 20

12. Rudi Wobbe Oral History, interviewed by Matthew K. Heiss, Salt Lake City, Utah, 1988, typescript, The James Moyle Oral History Program, Archives, Historical Department of the Church of Jesus Christ of Latter-day Saints, Salt Lake City, Utah, p. 37

13. Document of The Superior Attorney General of the Reich, Berlin 28 May 1942 at the People's Court, 8J 127/42g, In Custody!IIb

14. Blair Holmes, Alan Keele, and Karl-Heinz Schnibbe, *When Truth Was Treason*, Urbana and Chicago, Illinois: University of Illinois Press, 1995

15. Statement of Rudolf Wobbe, Rudolf Wobbe, Salt Lake City, Utah, 17 April 1961, Source: Historical Department, Church of Jesus Christ of Latter-day Saints, Salt Lake City, Utah Statement of Rudolf Wobbe, Rudolf Wobbe, Salt Lake City, Utah, 17 April 1961, Source: Historical Department, Church of Jesus Christ of Latter-day Saints, Salt Lake City, Utah

16. Helmuth Hübener flyer, "Down with Hitler"

17. See also Verdict of the People's Court in the criminal case against Helmut Hübener, et al, on 11 August 1942; and Statement of Rudolf Wobbe, Rudolf Wobbe, Salt Lake City, Utah, 17 April 1961, Source: Historical Department, Church of Jesus Christ of Latter-day Saints, Salt Lake City, Utah Statement of Rudolf Wobbe, Rudolf Wobbe, Salt Lake City, Utah, 17 April 1961, Source: Historical Department, Church of Jesus Christ of Latter-day Saints, Salt Lake City, Utah

18. Rudi Wobbe Fireside [youth church lecture], 1987, transcribed by Richard Dewey and Heather Dewey, 1-4 February 2003, used by permission from Herta Wobbe, p. 9, also Statement of Rudolf Wobbe, Rudolf Wobbe, Salt Lake City, Utah, 17 April 1961, Source: Historical Department, Church of Jesus Christ of Latter-day Saints, Salt Lake City, Utah Statement of Rudolf Wobbe, Rudolf Wobbe, Salt Lake City, Utah, 17 April 1961, Source: Historical Department, Church of Jesus Christ of Latter-day Saints, Salt Lake City, Utah

19. Rudi Wobbe Oral History, interviewed by Matthew K. Heiss, Salt Lake City, Utah, 1988, typescript, The James Moyle Oral History Program, Archives, Historical Department of the Church of Jesus Christ of Latter-day Saints, Salt Lake City, Utah, p. 39

20. Document of The Superior Attorney General of the Reich, Berlin 28 May 1942 at the People's Court, 8J 127/42g, In Custody!: sec IIc

21. Blair Holmes, Alan Keele, and Karl-Heinz Schnibbe, *When Truth Was Treason*, Urbana and Chicago, Illinois: University of Illinois Press, 1995

22. Verdict of the People's Court in the criminal case against Helmut Hübener, et al, on 11 August 1942: Findings, Pt II, sec 2

23. Verdict of the People's Court in the criminal case against Helmut Hübener, et al, on 11 August 1942: Findings, Pt. II, sec 2

24. Document of The Superior Attorney General of the Reich, Berlin 28 May 1942 at the People's Court, 8J 127/42g, In Custody!: part II sect. c, Rudi Wobbe Fireside [youth church lecture], 1987, transcribed by Richard Dewey and Heather Dewey, 1-4 February 2003, used by permission from Herta Wobbe, p. 10

25. Statement of Hans Kunkel, Source: *Begleitheft zur Austellung um das kurze Leben und Wirken des Helmuth Hübener,* Catalogue of the exhibit in the Hamburg Municipal District Archive (Stadtteilarchiv) of Hamm, 26 October – 10 December, 1992

26. Rudolf G. Wobbe Oral History, Doublas F. Tobler and Alan F. Keele, 1974, typescript, The James Moyle Oral History Program, Archives, Historical Department of the Church of Jesus Christ of Latter-day Saints, Salt Lake City, Utah, p. 26

27. Rudolf G. Wobbe Oral History, Doublas F. Tobler and Alan F. Keele, 1974, typescript, The James Moyle Oral History Program, Archives, Historical Department of the Church of Jesus Christ of Latter-day Saints, Salt Lake City, Utah, p. 26

28. Helmut Hübener leaflet, "Hitler Youth"

29. Helmut Hübener leaflet, "Weekend Incarceration"

30. Rudi Wobbe Fireside [youth church lecture], 1987, transcribed by Richard Dewey and Heather Dewey, 1-4 February 2003, used by permission from Herta Wobbe, p. 10

31. Rudi Wobbe Fireside [youth church lecture], 1987, transcribed by Richard Dewey and Heather Dewey, 1-4 February 2003, used by permission from Herta Wobbe, p. 10

32. Document of The Superior Attorney General of the Reich, Berlin 28 May 1942 at the People's Court, 8J 127/42g, In Custody!: IV

33. Rudi Wobbe Fireside [youth church lecture], 1987, transcribed by Richard Dewey and Heather Dewey, 1-4 February 2003, used by permission from Herta Wobbe, p. 10

34. Rudi Wobbe Fireside [youth church lecture], 1987, transcribed by Richard Dewey and Heather Dewey, 1-4 February 2003, used by permission from Herta Wobbe, p. 10

35. Document of Chief State Counsel of the Hanseatic Higher Regional Court, Hamburg 36, 25 March 1942, Criminal Case! Juveniles!; 25 Mar 1942 letter regarding criminal case against Hübener from Chief State Counsel of the Hanseatic Higher Court to the Attorney General at the People's Court

36. Statement of Hans Kunkel, Source: *Begleitheft zur Austellung um das kurze Leben und Wirken des Helmuth Hübener,* Catalogue of the exhibit in the Hamburg Municipal District Archive (Stadtteilarchiv) of Hamm, 26 October – 10 December, 1992

37. Hans and Charlotte Kunkel interview with author, Salt Lake City, Utah, 18 October 1996, p. 3

38. Document of The Superior Attorney General of the Reich, Berlin 28 May 1942 at the People's Court, 8J 127/42g, In Custody!: sec IIc; Verdict of the People's Court in the criminal case against Helmut Hübener, et al, on 11 August 1942: Findings, Pt 1 sec 2; Pt II, sec 2

39. Document of The Superior Attorney General of the Reich, Berlin 28 May 1942 at the People's Court, 8J 127/42g, In Custody!: sec IIb

40. Document of The Superior Attorney General of the Reich, Berlin 28 May 1942 at the People's Court, 8J 127/42g, In Custody!, sec lib

41. Letter from Otto Berndt, Church of Jesus Christ of Latter-day Saints, West German Mission, District: Hamburg 6 April 1942, To the Secret State Police in Hamburg, Stadthausbrucke; Statement of Marie Sommerfeld, Source: *Begleitheft zur Austellung um das kurze Leben und Wirken des Helmuth Hübener,* Catalogue of the exhibit in the Hamburg Municipal District Archive (Stadtteilarchiv) of Hamm, 26 October – 10 December, 1992

42. Document of The Superior Attorney General of the Reich, Berlin 28 May 1942 at the People's Court, 8J 127/42g, In Custody!: sec IIb and Verdict of the People's Court in the criminal case against Helmut Hübener, et al, on 11 August 1942: Part II sec 1

43. Statement of Marie Sommerfeld, Source: *Begleitheft zur Austellung um das kurze Leben und Wirken des Helmuth Hübener,* Catalogue of the exhibit in the Hamburg Municipal District Archive (Stadtteilarchiv) of Hamm, 26 October – 10 December, 1992

44. Document of Chief State Counsel of the Hanseatic Higher Regional Court, Hamburg 36, 25 March 1942, Criminal Case! Juveniles!

45. Letter from Otto Berndt, Church of Jesus Christ of Latter-day Saints, West German Mission, District: Hamburg 6 April 1942, To the Secret State Police in Hamburg, Stadthausbrucke

46. Letter from Otto Berndt, Church of Jesus Christ of Latter-day Saints, West German Mission, District: Hamburg 6 April 1942, To the Secret State Police in Hamburg, Stadthausbrucke

47. Letter from Otto Berndt, Church of Jesus Christ of Latter-day Saints, West German Mission, District: Hamburg 6 April 1942, To the Secret State Police in Hamburg, Stadthausbrucke

48. Blair Holmes, Alan Keele, and Karl-Heinz Schnibbe, *When Truth Was Treason*, Urbana and Chicago, Illinois: University of Illinois Press, 1995, p. 39

49. Document of The Superior Attorney General of the Reich, Berlin 28 May 1942 at the People's Court, 8J 127/42g, In Custody!, sec II-c

50. Statement of Rudolf Wobbe, Rudolf Wobbe, Salt Lake City, Utah, 17 April 1961, Source: Historical Department, Church of Jesus Christ of Latter-day Saints, Salt Lake City, Utah Statement of Rudolf Wobbe, Rudolf Wobbe, Salt Lake City, Utah, 17 April 1961, Source: Historical Department, Church of Jesus Christ of Latter-day Saints, Salt Lake City, Utah

51. Blair Holmes, Alan Keele, and Karl-Heinz Schnibbe, *When Truth Was Treason*, Urbana and Chicago, Illinois: University of Illinois Press, 1995, p. 39

52. Statement of Rudolf Wobbe, Rudolf Wobbe, Salt Lake City, Utah, 17 April 1961, Source: Historical Department, Church of Jesus Christ of Latter-day Saints, Salt Lake City, Utah Statement of Rudolf Wobbe, Rudolf Wobbe, Salt Lake City, Utah, 17 April 1961, Source: Historical Department, Church of Jesus Christ of Latter-day Saints, Salt Lake City, Utah

53. Blair Holmes, Alan Keele, and Karl-Heinz Schnibbe, *When Truth Was Treason*, Urbana and Chicago, Illinois: University of Illinois Press, 1995, p. 39

54. Document of The Superior Attorney General of the Reich, Berlin 28 May 1942 at the People's Court, 8J 127/42g, In Custody!IIC

55. Verdict of the People's Court in the criminal case against Helmut Hübener, et al, on 11 August 1942: II-c

56. Verdict of the People's Court in the criminal case against Helmut Hübener, et al, on 11 August 1942: II-2c

57. Document of The Superior Attorney General of the Reich, Berlin 28 May 1942 at the People's Court, 8J 127/42g, In Custody!: sect II-c; and Verdict of the People's Court in the criminal case against Helmut Hübener, et al, on 11 August 1942: Part II, sec 2

58. Document of The Superior Attorney General of the Reich, Berlin 28 May 1942 at the People's Court, 8J 127/42g, In Custody!: II-c and Verdict of the People's Court in the criminal case against Helmut Hübener, et al, on 11 August 1942: Findings, pt II, sec 2

59. Blair Holmes, Alan Keele, and Karl-Heinz Schnibbe, *When Truth Was Treason*, Urbana and Chicago, Illinois: University of Illinois Press, 1995, p. 39

60. Document of State Police Agency Hamburg — Hamburg, 5, 9, 17, 20 February 1942; 17 Feb 1942 Gestapo analysis of Criminal Secretary Mussener

CHAPTER 15

1. *Truth & Conviction*, documentary film produced by Brigham Young University, produced by Rick McFarland and Matt Whitaker, written and directed by Matt Whitaker, December 2003, one hour length

2. Statement of Hans Kunkel, Source: *Begleitheft zur Austellung um das kurze Leben und Wirken des Helmuth Hübener,* Catalogue of the exhibit in the Hamburg Municipal District Archive (Stadtteilarchiv) of Hamm, 26 October – 10 December, 1992

3. Blair Holmes, Alan Keele, and Karl-Heinz Schnibbe, *When Truth Was Treason*, Urbana and Chicago, Illinois: University of Illinois Press, 1995

4. Karl Schnibbe interview with author, Salt Lake City, Utah, 16 September 1996, transcribed by Don Ricks, p. 4

5. Karl Schnibbe interview with author, Salt Lake City, Utah, 16 September 1996, transcribed by Don Ricks, Pp. 4-5

6. Karl Schnibbe interview with author, Salt Lake City, Utah, 16 September 1996, transcribed by Don Ricks, p. 5

7. Karl Schnibbe interview with author, Salt Lake City, Utah, 16 September 1996, transcribed by Don Ricks, p. 4

8. Blair Holmes, Alan Keele, and Karl-Heinz Schnibbe, *When Truth Was Treason*, Urbana and Chicago, Illinois: University of Illinois Press, 1995, p. 42

9. Statement of Rudolf Wobbe, Rudolf Wobbe, Salt Lake City, Utah, 17 April 1961, Source: Historical Department, Church of Jesus Christ of Latter-day Saints, Salt Lake City, Utah Statement of Rudolf Wobbe, Rudolf Wobbe, Salt Lake City, Utah, 17 April 1961, Source: Historical Department, Church of Jesus Christ of Latter-day Saints, Salt Lake City, Utah

10. Rudi Wobbe Oral History, interviewed by Matthew K. Heiss, Salt Lake City, Utah, 1988, typescript, The James Moyle Oral History Program, Archives, Historical Department of the Church of Jesus Christ of Latter-day Saints, Salt Lake City, Utah, p. 37

11. Blair Holmes, Alan Keele, and Karl-Heinz Schnibbe, *When Truth Was Treason*, Urbana and Chicago, Illinois: University of Illinois Press, 1995, p. 42

12. Statement of Hans Kunkel, Source: *Begleitheft zur Austellung um das kurze Leben und Wirken des Helmuth Hübener,* Catalogue of the exhibit in the Hamburg Municipal District Archive (Stadtteilarchiv) of Hamm, 26 October – 10 December, 1992. Gerhard Kunkel was away in the army at this point, so he could only speculate that a great number of the branch members knew what was going on, but they kept quiet about it, and that in the city generally, only the Mormons knew about it. "The Führer's New Clothes: Helmuth Hübener and the Dilemma of German Mormons in the Third Reich," unpublished essay by Alan F. Keele, Used by permission from Alan F. Keele.

A shorter version of this essay was later published as an article in *Sunstone*, p. 26 Certainly that latter observation is correct, until Helmuth would enlarge his resistance group, but all evidence points to just five actually knowing.

13. In Rudi Wobbe's 1974 interview he thought Helmuth only probably told Arthur Sommerfeld about his activities, since Arthur had gone to Helmuth's apartment quite often and visited. Rudolf G. Wobbe Oral History, Doublas F. Tobler and Alan F. Keele, 1974, typescript, The James Moyle Oral History Program, Archives, Historical Department of the Church of Jesus Christ of Latter-day Saints, Salt Lake City, Utah, p. 12 But in his 1992 autobiography, Rudi says that Arthur was also involved and knew [Helmuth's] plans to some extent, Rudi Wobbe and Jerry Borrowman, *Three Against Hitler,* (American Fork, Utah: Covenant Communications, 1992), p. 39

14. Gerhard Kunkel interview #1 with author, 10 October 1996, pp. 5-6

15. Arthur and Marie Sommerfeld interview with author, Salt Lake City, Utah, 18 October 1996, p. 21

16. Rudi Wobbe Oral History, interviewed by Matthew K. Heiss, Salt Lake City, Utah, 1988, typescript, The James Moyle Oral History Program, Archives, Historical Department of the Church of Jesus Christ of Latter-day Saints, Salt Lake City, Utah, p. 22

17. *Ibid.*

18. Karl Schnibbe interview with author, Salt Lake City, Utah, 16 September 1996, transcribed by Don Ricks

19. Statement of Otto Berndt, Ca. 1961, Source: Historical Department, Church of Jesus Christ of Latter-day Saints, Salt Lake City, Utah

20. Otto Berndt Oral History, interviewed by Douglas F. Tobler, Salt Lake City, Utah, 1974, typescript, The James Moyle Oral History

Program, Archives, Historical Department of the Church of Jesus Christ of Latter-day Saints, Salt Lake City, Utah, p. 54

21. Statement of Otto Berndt, Ca. 1961, Source: Historical Department, Church of Jesus Christ of Latter-day Saints, Salt Lake City, Utah

22. Otto Berndt Oral History, interviewed by Douglas F. Tobler, Salt Lake City, Utah, 1974, typescript, The James Moyle Oral History Program, Archives, Historical Department of the Church of Jesus Christ of Latter-day Saints, Salt Lake City, Utah, p. 54

23. Otto Berndt Oral History, interviewed by Douglas F. Tobler, Salt Lake City, Utah, 1974, typescript, The James Moyle Oral History Program, Archives, Historical Department of the Church of Jesus Christ of Latter-day Saints, Salt Lake City, Utah, p. 53

24. Statement of Otto Berndt, Ca. 1961, Source: Historical Department, Church of Jesus Christ of Latter-day Saints, Salt Lake City, Utah andRudi Wobbe Oral History, interviewed by Matthew K. Heiss, Salt Lake City, Utah, 1988, typescript, The James Moyle Oral History Program, Archives, Historical Department of the Church of Jesus Christ of Latter-day Saints, Salt Lake City, Utah, p. 22

25. Rudi Wobbe Oral History, interviewed by Matthew K. Heiss, Salt Lake City, Utah, 1988, typescript, The James Moyle Oral History Program, Archives, Historical Department of the Church of Jesus Christ of Latter-day Saints, Salt Lake City, Utah, p. 22

26. Otto Berndt Oral History, interviewed by Douglas F. Tobler, Salt Lake City, Utah, 1974, typescript, The James Moyle Oral History Program, Archives, Historical Department of the Church of Jesus Christ of Latter-day Saints, Salt Lake City, Utah, p. 54

27. Karl Schnibbe interview with author, Salt Lake City, Utah, 16 September 1996, transcribed by Don Ricks, p. 44

28. Rudi Wobbe Oral History, interviewed by Matthew K. Heiss, Salt Lake City, Utah, 1988, typescript, The James Moyle Oral

History Program, Archives, Historical Department of the Church of Jesus Christ of Latter-day Saints, Salt Lake City, Utah, p. 22

29. Statement of Otto Berndt, Ca. 1961, Source: Historical Department, Church of Jesus Christ of Latter-day Saints, Salt Lake City, Utah and OP, p. 54

30. Rudi Wobbe Oral History, interviewed by Matthew K. Heiss, Salt Lake City, Utah, 1988, typescript, The James Moyle Oral History Program, Archives, Historical Department of the Church of Jesus Christ of Latter-day Saints, Salt Lake City, Utah, p. 22

31. Otto Berndt Oral History, interviewed by Douglas F. Tobler, Salt Lake City, Utah, 1974, typescript, The James Moyle Oral History Program, Archives, Historical Department of the Church of Jesus Christ of Latter-day Saints, Salt Lake City, Utah, Statement of Otto Berndt, Ca. 1961, Source: Historical Department, Church of Jesus Christ of Latter-day Saints, Salt Lake City, Utah; Rudi Wobbe Fireside [youth church lecture], 1987, transcribed by Richard Dewey and Heather Dewey, 1-4 February 2003, used by permission from Herta Wobbe, p. 6; andRudolf G. Wobbe Oral History, Doublas F. Tobler and Alan F. Keele, 1974, typescript, The James Moyle Oral History Program, Archives, Historical Department of the Church of Jesus Christ of Latter-day Saints, Salt Lake City, Utah, p. 5, andRudi Wobbe Oral History, interviewed by Matthew K. Heiss, Salt Lake City, Utah, 1988, typescript, The James Moyle Oral History Program, Archives, Historical Department of the Church of Jesus Christ of Latter-day Saints, Salt Lake City, Utah, p. 23

32. Rudolf G. Wobbe Oral History, Doublas F. Tobler and Alan F. Keele, 1974, typescript, The James Moyle Oral History Program, Archives, Historical Department of the Church of Jesus Christ of Latter-day Saints, Salt Lake City, Utah, p. 5

33. Rudi Wobbe Fireside [youth church lecture], 1987, transcribed by Richard Dewey and Heather Dewey, 1-4 February 2003, used by permission from Herta Wobbe, p. 6

34. Rudi Wobbe Oral History, interviewed by Matthew K. Heiss, Salt Lake City, Utah, 1988, typescript, The James Moyle Oral History Program, Archives, Historical Department of the Church of Jesus Christ of Latter-day Saints, Salt Lake City, Utah, p. 23

35. Rudolf G. Wobbe Oral History, Doublas F. Tobler and Alan F. Keele, 1974, typescript, The James Moyle Oral History Program, Archives, Historical Department of the Church of Jesus Christ of Latter-day Saints, Salt Lake City, Utah, p. 5

36. Rudi Wobbe Fireside [youth church lecture], 1987, transcribed by Richard Dewey and Heather Dewey, 1-4 February 2003, used by permission from Herta Wobbe, p. 6

37. Rudi Wobbe Oral History, interviewed by Matthew K. Heiss, Salt Lake City, Utah, 1988, typescript, The James Moyle Oral History Program, Archives, Historical Department of the Church of Jesus Christ of Latter-day Saints, Salt Lake City, Utah, p. 23

38. Rudi Wobbe Fireside [youth church lecture], 1987, transcribed by Richard Dewey and Heather Dewey, 1-4 February 2003, used by permission from Herta Wobbe, p. 6

39. Rudi Wobbe Oral History, interviewed by Matthew K. Heiss, Salt Lake City, Utah, 1988, typescript, The James Moyle Oral History Program, Archives, Historical Department of the Church of Jesus Christ of Latter-day Saints, Salt Lake City, Utah, p. 23

40. Statement of Otto Berndt, Ca. 1961, Source: Historical Department, Church of Jesus Christ of Latter-day Saints, Salt Lake City, Utah

41. Rudi Wobbe Fireside [youth church lecture], 1987, transcribed by Richard Dewey and Heather Dewey, 1-4 February 2003, used by permission from Herta Wobbe, p. 6

42. Otto Berndt Oral History, interviewed by Douglas F. Tobler, Salt Lake City, Utah, 1974, typescript, The James Moyle Oral History Program, Archives, Historical Department of the Church of Jesus Christ of Latter-day Saints, Salt Lake City, Utah, p. 54

43. Rudi Wobbe Fireside [youth church lecture], 1987, transcribed by Richard Dewey and Heather Dewey, 1-4 February 2003, used by permission from Herta Wobbe, p. 6note

44. Rudi Wobbe Oral History, interviewed by Matthew K. Heiss, Salt Lake City, Utah, 1988, typescript, The James Moyle Oral History Program, Archives, Historical Department of the Church of Jesus Christ of Latter-day Saints, Salt Lake City, Utah, p. 23

45. Rudolf G. Wobbe Oral History, Doublas F. Tobler and Alan F. Keele, 1974, typescript, The James Moyle Oral History Program, Archives, Historical Department of the Church of Jesus Christ of Latter-day Saints, Salt Lake City, Utah, p. 5

46. Rudi Wobbe Fireside [youth church lecture], 1987, transcribed by Richard Dewey and Heather Dewey, 1-4 February 2003, used by permission from Herta Wobbe, p. 6. As a fairly insignificant detail, the length of time from Heinrich Worbs' interview with Helmuth until Worb's death has differing numbers - Karl tells the author it was three months later, Karl Schnibbe interview with author, Salt Lake City, Utah, 16 September 1996, transcribed by Don Ricks, p. 44 while in his autobiography he says four months later. Blair Holmes, Alan Keele, and Karl-Heinz Schnibbe, *When Truth Was Treason*, Urbana and Chicago, Illinois: University of Illinois Press, 1995. Otto Berndt says in one report that he died soon thereafter, Statement of Otto Berndt, Ca. 1961, Source: Historical Department, Church of Jesus Christ of Latter-day Saints, Salt Lake City, Utah and in another, about six weeks later. Otto Berndt Oral History, interviewed by Douglas F. Tobler, Salt Lake City, Utah, 1974,

typescript, The James Moyle Oral History Program, Archives, Historical Department of the Church of Jesus Christ of Latter-day Saints, Salt Lake City, Utah, 54

47. Rudi Wobbe Oral History, interviewed by Matthew K. Heiss, Salt Lake City, Utah, 1988, typescript, The James Moyle Oral History Program, Archives, Historical Department of the Church of Jesus Christ of Latter-day Saints, Salt Lake City, Utah. Many years after the fact, Otto Berndt recalls the Heinrich Worbs incident occurring late 1942 or early 1943 Statement of Otto Berndt, Ca. 1961, Source: Historical Department, Church of Jesus Christ of Latter-day Saints, Salt Lake City, Utah, but from Karl and Rudi's accounts it had to have taken place in late 1941 or early 1942.

48. Otto Berndt Oral History, interviewed by Douglas F. Tobler, Salt Lake City, Utah, 1974, typescript, The James Moyle Oral History Program, Archives, Historical Department of the Church of Jesus Christ of Latter-day Saints, Salt Lake City, Utah, p. 55

49. Otto Berndt Oral History, interviewed by Douglas F. Tobler, Salt Lake City, Utah, 1974, typescript, The James Moyle Oral History Program, Archives, Historical Department of the Church of Jesus Christ of Latter-day Saints, Salt Lake City, Utah, p. 55

50. Otto Berndt Oral History, interviewed by Douglas F. Tobler, Salt Lake City, Utah, 1974, typescript, The James Moyle Oral History Program, Archives, Historical Department of the Church of Jesus Christ of Latter-day Saints, Salt Lake City, Utah, p. 58

51. Otto Berndt Oral History, interviewed by Douglas F. Tobler, Salt Lake City, Utah, 1974, typescript, The James Moyle Oral History Program, Archives, Historical Department of the Church of Jesus Christ of Latter-day Saints, Salt Lake City, Utah, p. 58

52. Otto Berndt Oral History, interviewed by Douglas F. Tobler, Salt Lake City, Utah, 1974, typescript, The James Moyle Oral History Program, Archives, Historical Department of the Church of Jesus Christ of Latter-day Saints, Salt Lake City, Utah, p. 55

53. Blair Holmes, Alan Keele, and Karl-Heinz Schnibbe, *When Truth Was Treason*, Urbana and Chicago, Illinois: University of Illinois Press, 1995

CHAPTER 16

1. "He Was Always a Straight-A Student", Statement of Rolf Attin, born 1924, and Hans-Theo Rob, born 1925, Source: *Begleitheft zur Austellung um das kurze Leben und Wirken des Helmuth Hübener,* Catalogue of the exhibit in the Hamburg Court

2. Document of State Police Agency Hamburg — Hamburg, 5, 9, 17, 20 February 1942

3. Document of State Police Agency Hamburg — Hamburg, 5, 9, 17, 20 February 1942; Gestapo's 9 Feb 1942 interrogation transcript with Helmuth Hübener

4. Document of State Police Agency Hamburg - Hamburg, 5, 9, 17, 20 February 1942,

5. Document of State Police Agency Hamburg — Hamburg, 5, 9, 17, 20 February 1942; Document of The Superior Attorney General of the Reich, Berlin 28 May 1942 at the People's Court, 8J 127/42g, In Custody!: sec III-3, Document of State Police Agency Hamburg - Hamburg, 5, 9, 17, 20 February 1942,

6. Document of The Superior Attorney General of the Reich, Berlin 28 May 1942 at the People's Court, 8J 127/42g, In Custody!

7. Document of State Police Agency Hamburg — Hamburg, 5, 9, 17, 20 February 1942, Helmuth Hübener affidavit; Document of The Superior Attorney General of the Reich, Berlin 28 May 1942 at the People's Court, 8J 127/42g, In Custody!: III-3

8. Document of The Superior Attorney General of the Reich, Berlin 28 May 1942 at the People's Court, 8J 127/42g, In Custody!: III-3

9. Document of State Police Agency Hamburg — Hamburg, 5, 9, 17, 20 February 1942; Helmuth Hübener affidavit; Document of The Superior Attorney General of the Reich, Berlin 28 May 1942 at the People's Court, 8J 127/42g, In Custody!: III-3

10. Verdict of the People's Court in the criminal case against Helmut Hübener, et al, on 11 August 1942

11. Document of The Superior Attorney General of the Reich, Berlin 28 May 1942 at the People's Court, 8J 127/42g, In Custody!: Indictment introduction

12. Verdict of the People's Court in the criminal case against Helmut Hübener, et al, on 11 August 1942: Findings, Pt I

13. Verdict of the People's Court in the criminal case against Helmut Hübener, et al, on 11 August 1942: Findings, Sec. 1. Gerhard Düwer's father, ironically, was with the Security Service of the SS, Document of State Police Agency Hamburg - Hamburg, 5, 9, 17, 20 February 1942,, part II but only saw his father every third day when he came home from work. Document of State Police Agency Hamburg - Hamburg, 5, 9, 17, 20 February 1942,, part II

14. Sander, *"Helmuth-Hübener Gruppe,"* in Hochmuth and Meyer, *Streiflichter,* pp. 234-235

15. *Ibid.*

16. Rudolf G. Wobbe Oral History, Doublas F. Tobler and Alan F. Keele, 1974, typescript, The James Moyle Oral History Program, Archives, Historical Department of the Church of Jesus Christ of Latter-day Saints, Salt Lake City, Utah, p. 24, and Blair Holmes, Alan Keele, and Karl-Heinz Schnibbe, *When Truth Was Treason*, Urbana and Chicago, Illinois: University of Illinois Press, 1995

17. Rudolf G. Wobbe Oral History, Doublas F. Tobler and Alan F. Keele, 1974, typescript, The James Moyle Oral History Program, Archives, Historical Department of the Church of Jesus Christ of Latter-day Saints, Salt Lake City, Utah, p. 24

18. Document of State Police Agency Hamburg - Hamburg, 5, 9, 17, 20 February 1942,; Document of The Superior Attorney General of the Reich, Berlin 28 May 1942 at the People's Court, 8J 127/42g, In Custody!:   II-C

19. Verdict of the People's Court in the criminal case against Helmut Hübener, et al, on 11 August 1942: pt III sec 2

20. Statement of Hans Kunkel, Source: *Begleitheft zur Austellung um das kurze Leben und Wirken des Helmuth Hübener,* Catalogue of the exhibit in the Hamburg Municipal District Archive (Stadtteilarchiv) of Hamm, 26 October – 10 December, 1992

21. Blair Holmes, Alan Keele, and Karl-Heinz Schnibbe, *When Truth Was Treason,* Urbana and Chicago, Illinois: University of Illinois Press, 1995; see also Karl Schnibbe interview with author, Salt Lake City, Utah, 16 September 1996, transcribed by Don Ricks, p. 21

22. Rudolf G. Wobbe Oral History, Doublas F. Tobler and Alan F. Keele, 1974, typescript, The James Moyle Oral History Program, Archives, Historical Department of the Church of Jesus Christ of Latter-day Saints, Salt Lake City, Utah, p. 24

23. Helmuth actually wrote the letter to Franz Walter Prumnitz sometime before Christmas Day, during the vacation. Document of Secret State Police - Hamburg, 11 May 1942, State Police Office Hamburg, B. No. II P - 126/42, Franz Walter Prumnitz

24. Document of Secret State Police - Hamburg, 11 May 1942, State Police Office Hamburg, B. No. II P - 126/42, Franz Walter Prumnitz: 11 May 1942 Gestapo interrogation transcript of Franz Prumnitz

25. Document of Gestapo's 19 - 20 May 1942 Horst van Treck interrogation transcript

CHAPTER 17

1. Statement of Hans Kunkel, Source: *Begleitheft zur Austellung um das kurze Leben und Wirken des Helmuth Hübener,* Catalogue of the exhibit in the Hamburg Municipal District Archive (Stadtteilarchiv) of Hamm, 26 October – 10 December, 1992

2. Statement of Hans Kunkel, Source: *Begleitheft zur Austellung um das kurze Leben und Wirken des Helmuth Hübener,* Catalogue of the exhibit in the Hamburg Municipal District Archive (Stadtteilarchiv) of Hamm, 26 October – 10 December, 1992

3. Statement of Hans Kunkel, Source: *Begleitheft zur Austellung um das kurze Leben und Wirken des Helmuth Hübener,* Catalogue of the exhibit in the Hamburg Municipal District Archive (Stadtteilarchiv) of Hamm, 26 October – 10 December, 1992

4. Statement of Hans Kunkel, Source: *Begleitheft zur Austellung um das kurze Leben und Wirken des Helmuth Hübener,* Catalogue of the exhibit in the Hamburg Municipal District Archive (Stadtteilarchiv) of Hamm, 26 October – 10 December, 1992

5. Document of State Police Agency Hamburg — Hamburg, 5, 9, 17, 20 February 1942

6. Document of State Police Agency Hamburg — Hamburg, 5, 9, 17, 20 February 1942; Gestapo interrogation transcript of 9 Feb 1942 with Helmuth Hübener

7. Document of State Police Agency Hamburg — Hamburg, 5, 9, 17, 20 February 1942

8. Klaus-Jorg Siegfried, Das Leben der Zwangsarbeiter im Volkswagenwerk 1939-1945 [New York: Campus Verlag, 1988], Pp. 124-25

9. Document of State Police Agency Hamburg - Hamburg, 5, 9, 17, 20 February 1942,; Document of The Superior Attorney General of the Reich, Berlin 28 May 1942 at the People's Court, 8J 127/42g, In Custody!: Iic

10. Sander, *"Helmuth-Hübener Gruppe,"* in Hochmuth and Meyer, *Streiflichter,* p. 335

11. Document of State Police Agency Hamburg - Hamburg, 5, 9, 17, 20 February 1942,

12. Document of State Police Agency Hamburg - Hamburg, 5, 9, 17, 20 February 1942,

13. Verdict of the People's Court in the criminal case against Helmut Hübener, et al, on 11 August 1942: pt I sec 2Doc 9 State Police Agency Hamburg - Hamburg, 5, 9, 17, 20 February 1942,: 6 Feb 1942 Werner Kranz investigative affidavit to the Gestapo

14. Document of State Police Agency Hamburg - Hamburg, 5, 9, 17, 20 February 1942,: 6 Feb 1942 Werner Kranz investigative affidavit; Verdict of the People's Court in the criminal case against Helmut Hübener, et al, on 11 August 1942: Findings, Pt II sec 2

15. Document of State Police Agency — Hamburg, 10 February 1942, About the Person: Schnibbe, Karl-Heinz; Hamburg, 11 February 1942; Kurt Heinrich Martin Mohns; Kurt and Horst Zumsande

CHAPTER 18

1. Verdict of the People's Court in the criminal case against Helmut Hübener, et al, on 11 August 1942: pt II sec 2

2. Zentner and Bedurftig, *Encyclopedia of the Third Reich*, 2: 1064

3. Document of State Police Agency — Hamburg, 10 February 1942, About the Person: Schnibbe, Karl-Heinz; Hamburg, 11 February 1942; Kurt Heinrich Martin Mohns; Kurt and Horst Zumsande; Mohns section

4. Document of State Police Agency — Hamburg, 10 February 1942, About the Person: Schnibbe, Karl-Heinz; Hamburg, 11 February 1942; Kurt Heinrich Martin Mohns; Kurt and Horst Zumsande; Mohns section

5. Document of The Superior Attorney General of the Reich, Berlin 28 May 1942 at the People's Court, 8J 127/42g, In Custody!: III-3; Verdict of the People's Court in the criminal case against Helmut Hübener, et al, on 11 August 1942: pt II sec 2

6. Verdict of the People's Court in the criminal case against Helmut Hübener, et al, on 11 August 1942: Pt IV, sec 2; Pt II, sec 2

7. Verdict of the People's Court in the criminal case against Helmut Hübener, et al, on 11 August 1942: part II sec 2, and Document of State Police Agency — Hamburg, 10 February 1942, About the Person: Schnibbe, Karl-Heinz; Hamburg, 11 February 1942; Kurt Heinrich Martin Mohns; Kurt and Horst Zumsande: Mohns affidavit to Gestapo; Document of The Superior Attorney General of the Reich, Berlin 28 May 1942 at the People's Court, 8J 127/42g, In Custody!: III-3

8. Document of The Superior Attorney General of the Reich, Berlin 28 May 1942 at the People's Court, 8J 127/42g, In Custody!: III-3; Verdict of the People's Court in the criminal case against Helmut Hübener, et al, on 11 August 1942: pt II sec 2

9. Document of State Police Agency — Hamburg, 10 February 1942, About the Person: Schnibbe, Karl-Heinz; Hamburg, 11 February 1942; Kurt Heinrich Martin Mohns; Kurt and Horst Zumsande; Mohns section

C H A P T E R   1 9

1. Statement of Marie Sommerfeld, Source: *Begleitheft zur Austellung um das kurze Leben und Wirken des Helmuth Hübener,* Catalogue of the exhibit in the Hamburg Municipal District Archive (Stadtteilarchiv) of Hamm, 26 October – 10 December, 1992; and Hans and Charlotte Kunkel interview with author, Salt Lake City, Utah, 18 October 1996, p. 5, Rudi Wobbe Fireside [youth church lecture], 1987, transcribed by Richard Dewey and Heather Dewey, 1-4 February 2003, used by permission from Herta Wobbe, p. 11

2. "The Führer's New Clothes: Helmuth Hübener and the Dilemma of German Mormons in the Third Reich," unpublished essay by Alan F. Keele, Used by permission from Alan F. Keele. A shorter version of this essay was later published as an article in *Sunstone,* p. 14

3. Rudi Wobbe Oral History, interviewed by Matthew K. Heiss, Salt Lake City, Utah, 1988, typescript, The James Moyle Oral History Program, Archives, Historical Department of the Church of Jesus Christ of Latter-day Saints, Salt Lake City, Utah, pp. 43-44. Gerhard Düwer would later get to know Rudi, and possibly reported this to him.

4. Hans and Charlotte Kunkel interview with author, Salt Lake City, Utah, 18 October 1996, p. 5

5. Hans and Charlotte Kunkel interview with author, Salt Lake City, Utah, 18 October 1996, p. 5

6. Statement of Marie Sommerfeld, Source: *Begleitheft zur Austellung um das kurze Leben und Wirken des Helmuth Hübener,* Catalogue of the exhibit in the Hamburg Municipal District Archive (Stadtteilarchiv) of Hamm, 26 October – 10 December, 1992

7. Hans and Charlotte Kunkel interview with author, Salt Lake City, Utah, 18 October 1996, p. 5

8. Document of The Superior Attorney General of the Reich, Berlin 28 May 1942 at the People's Court, 8J 127/42g, In Custody! II-C

9. "The Führer's New Clothes: Helmuth Hübener and the Dilemma of German Mormons in the Third Reich," unpublished essay by Alan F. Keele, Used by permission from Alan F. Keele. A shorter version of this essay was later published as an article in *Sunstone*, p. 27

10. Statement of Marie Sommerfeld, Source: *Begleitheft zur Austellung um das kurze Leben und Wirken des Helmuth Hübener,* Catalogue of the exhibit in the Hamburg Municipal District Archive (Stadtteilarchiv) of Hamm, 26 October – 10 December, 1992, p. 1

11. "The Führer's New Clothes: Helmuth Hübener and the Dilemma of German Mormons in the Third Reich," unpublished essay by Alan F. Keele, Used by permission from Alan F. Keele. A shorter version of this essay was later published as an article in *Sunstone*, pp. 14-15

12. Statement of Marie Sommerfeld, Source: *Begleitheft zur Austellung um das kurze Leben und Wirken des Helmuth Hübener,* Catalogue of the exhibit in the Hamburg Municipal District Archive (Stadtteilarchiv) of Hamm, 26 October – 10 December, 1992

13. Statement of Marie Sommerfeld, Source: *Begleitheft zur Austellung um das kurze Leben und Wirken des Helmuth Hübener,* Catalogue of the exhibit in the Hamburg Municipal District Archive (Stadtteilarchiv) of Hamm, 26 October – 10 December, 1992

14. Marie Friebel Sommerfeld 1897-1984, Interviewed in German by Douglas Tobler and Alan Keele, 1974 : (13 leaves in English; Matthew K. Heiss later wrote Iris Schmidt on 17 Sep 1992 saying the Sommerfeld interview was never fully edited; typed ca. 1985 by Karen H. Pyper), p. 3

15. Statement of Marie Sommerfeld, Source: *Begleitheft zur Austellung um das kurze Leben und Wirken des Helmuth Hübener,* Catalogue of the exhibit in the Hamburg Municipal District Archive (Stadtteilarchiv) of Hamm, 26 October – 10 December, 1992

16. Marie Friebel Sommerfeld 1897-1984, Interviewed in German by Douglas Tobler and Alan Keele, 1974 : (13 leaves in English; Matthew K. Heiss later wrote Iris Schmidt on 17 Sep 1992 saying the Sommerfeld interview was never fully edited; typed ca. 1985 by Karen H. Pyper), p. 3

17. Statement of Marie Sommerfeld, Source: *Begleitheft zur Austellung um das kurze Leben und Wirken des Helmuth Hübener,* Catalogue of the exhibit in the Hamburg Municipal District Archive (Stadtteilarchiv) of Hamm, 26 October – 10 December, 1992

18. Marie Friebel Sommerfeld 1897-1984, Interviewed in German by Douglas Tobler and Alan Keele, 1974 : (13 leaves in English; Matthew K. Heiss later wrote Iris Schmidt on 17 Sep 1992 saying the Sommerfeld interview was never fully edited; typed ca. 1985 by Karen H. Pyper), p. 3

19. "The Führer's New Clothes: Helmuth Hübener and the Dilemma of German Mormons in the Third Reich," unpublished essay by Alan F. Keele, Used by permission from Alan F. Keele. A shorter version of this essay was later published as an article in *Sunstone*, p. 14

20. Blair Holmes, Alan Keele, and Karl-Heinz Schnibbe, *When Truth Was Treason*, Urbana and Chicago, Illinois: University of Illinois Press, 1995

21. Blair Holmes, Alan Keele, and Karl-Heinz Schnibbe, *When Truth Was Treason*, Urbana and Chicago, Illinois: University of Illinois Press, 1995. Rudi says that Zander added a comment that, And how dar he did this, bringing in jeopardyi the branch, putting the Church in a bad light. Rudi Wobbe Oral History, interviewed by Matthew K. Heiss, Salt Lake City, Utah, 1988,

typescript, The James Moyle Oral History Program, Archives, Historical Department of the Church of Jesus Christ of Latter-day Saints, Salt Lake City, Utah, p. 38

22. Rudolf G. Wobbe Oral History, Doublas F. Tobler and Alan F. Keele, 1974, typescript, The James Moyle Oral History Program, Archives, Historical Department of the Church of Jesus Christ of Latter-day Saints, Salt Lake City, Utah, p. 28

23. Blair Holmes, Alan Keele, and Karl-Heinz Schnibbe, *When Truth Was Treason*, Urbana and Chicago, Illinois: University of Illinois Press, 1995

24. Rudi Wobbe Oral History, interviewed by Matthew K. Heiss, Salt Lake City, Utah, 1988, typescript, The James Moyle Oral History Program, Archives, Historical Department of the Church of Jesus Christ of Latter-day Saints, Salt Lake City, Utah, p. 38. This comment was made in 1988, yet in 1974 Rudi says Helmuth's arrest was not announced in church, but rather he was told by Helmuth's grandmother, Sister Sudrow, Rudolf G. Wobbe Oral History, Doublas F. Tobler and Alan F. Keele, 1974, typescript, The James Moyle Oral History Program, Archives, Historical Department of the Church of Jesus Christ of Latter-day Saints, Salt Lake City, Utah, pp. 28-29 presumably at church. With the passage of years, Rudi's memory in this instance apparently improved.

25. Rudi Wobbe Oral History, interviewed by Matthew K. Heiss, Salt Lake City, Utah, 1988, typescript, The James Moyle Oral History Program, Archives, Historical Department of the Church of Jesus Christ of Latter-day Saints, Salt Lake City, Utah, p. 38; see also p. 15; "The Führer's New Clothes: Helmuth Hübener and the Dilemma of German Mormons in the Third Reich," unpublished essay by Alan F. Keele, Used by permission from Alan F. Keele. A shorter version of this essay was later published as an article in *Sunstone*, quoting interviews with Wobbe, Schnibbe, Otto Berndt, and Hans Kunkel

26. Otto Berndt Oral History, interviewed by Douglas F. Tobler, Salt Lake City, Utah, 1974, typescript, The James Moyle Oral History Program, Archives, Historical Department of the Church of Jesus Christ of Latter-day Saints, Salt Lake City, Utah, p. 49

27. Rudolf G. Wobbe Oral History, Doublas F. Tobler and Alan F. Keele, 1974, typescript, The James Moyle Oral History Program, Archives, Historical Department of the Church of Jesus Christ of Latter-day Saints, Salt Lake City, Utah, p. 30

28. Rudolf G. Wobbe Oral History, Doublas F. Tobler and Alan F. Keele, 1974, typescript, The James Moyle Oral History Program, Archives, Historical Department of the Church of Jesus Christ of Latter-day Saints, Salt Lake City, Utah, p. 9

29. Rudi Wobbe Oral History, interviewed by Matthew K. Heiss, Salt Lake City, Utah, 1988, typescript, The James Moyle Oral History Program, Archives, Historical Department of the Church of Jesus Christ of Latter-day Saints, Salt Lake City, Utah, p. 40

30. Statement of Rudolf Wobbe, Rudolf Wobbe, Salt Lake City, Utah, 17 April 1961, Source: Historical Department, Church of Jesus Christ of Latter-day Saints, Salt Lake City, Utah Statement of Rudolf Wobbe, Rudolf Wobbe, Salt Lake City, Utah, 17 April 1961, Source: Historical Department, Church of Jesus Christ of Latter-day Saints, Salt Lake City, Utah

31. Rudi Wobbe Oral History, interviewed by Matthew K. Heiss, Salt Lake City, Utah, 1988, typescript, The James Moyle Oral History Program, Archives, Historical Department of the Church of Jesus Christ of Latter-day Saints, Salt Lake City, Utah, p. 40

32. Rudi Wobbe Oral History, interviewed by Matthew K. Heiss, Salt Lake City, Utah, 1988, typescript, The James Moyle Oral History Program, Archives, Historical Department of the Church of Jesus Christ of Latter-day Saints, Salt Lake City, Utah, p. 40

33. Rothfels, *German Opposition to Hitler,* p. 11

34. Rudolf G. Wobbe Oral History, Doublas F. Tobler and Alan F. Keele, 1974, typescript, The James Moyle Oral History Program, Archives, Historical Department of the Church of Jesus Christ of Latter-day Saints, Salt Lake City, Utah, p. 28

CHAPTER 20

1. Blair Holmes, Alan Keele, and Karl-Heinz Schnibbe, *When Truth Was Treason*, Urbana and Chicago, Illinois: University of Illinois Press, 1995

2. *Truth & Conviction*, documentary film produced by Brigham Young University, produced by Rick McFarland and Matt Whitaker, written and directed by Matt Whitaker, December 2003, one hour length

3. Blair Holmes, Alan Keele, and Karl-Heinz Schnibbe, *When Truth Was Treason*, Urbana and Chicago, Illinois: University of Illinois Press, 1995

4. *Truth & Conviction*, documentary film produced by Brigham Young University, produced by Rick McFarland and Matt Whitaker, written and directed by Matt Whitaker, December 2003, one hour length

5. Blair Holmes, Alan Keele, and Karl-Heinz Schnibbe, *When Truth Was Treason*, Urbana and Chicago, Illinois: University of Illinois Press, 1995

6. Statement of Rudolf Wobbe, Rudolf Wobbe, Salt Lake City, Utah, 17 April 1961, Source: Historical Department, Church of Jesus Christ of Latter-day Saints, Salt Lake City, Utah Statement of Rudolf Wobbe, Rudolf Wobbe, Salt Lake City, Utah, 17 April 1961, Source: Historical Department, Church of Jesus Christ of Latter-day Saints, Salt Lake City, Utah and Rudi Wobbe Fireside [youth church lecture], 1987, transcribed by Richard Dewey and Heather Dewey, 1-4 February 2003, used by permission from Herta Wobbe, p. 11

7. Rudolf G. Wobbe Oral History, Doublas F. Tobler and Alan F. Keele, 1974, typescript, The James Moyle Oral History Program, Archives, Historical Department of the Church of Jesus Christ of Latter-day Saints, Salt Lake City, Utah, p. 30

8. Rudi Wobbe Fireside, 1987 (youth church lecture), transcribed by Richard Dewey and Heather Dewey, 1-4 February 2003. Used by permission from Herta Wobbe. p. 30

9. Rudi Wobbe Oral History, interviewed by Matthew K. Heiss, Salt Lake City, Utah, 1988, typescript, The James Moyle Oral History Program, Archives, Historical Department of the Church of Jesus Christ of Latter-day Saints, Salt Lake City, Utah, p. 39

10. Rudi Wobbe Oral History, interviewed by Matthew K. Heiss, Salt Lake City, Utah, 1988, typescript, The James Moyle Oral History Program, Archives, Historical Department of the Church of Jesus Christ of Latter-day Saints, Salt Lake City, Utah, p. 40

11. Statement of Rudolf Wobbe, Rudolf Wobbe, Salt Lake City, Utah, 17 April 1961, Source: Historical Department, Church of Jesus Christ of Latter-day Saints, Salt Lake City, Utah Statement of Rudolf Wobbe, Rudolf Wobbe, Salt Lake City, Utah, 17 April 1961, Source: Historical Department, Church of Jesus Christ of Latter-day Saints, Salt Lake City, Utah

12. Rudi Wobbe Oral History, interviewed by Matthew K. Heiss, Salt Lake City, Utah, 1988, typescript, The James Moyle Oral History Program, Archives, Historical Department of the Church of Jesus Christ of Latter-day Saints, Salt Lake City, Utah, pp. 40

13. Rudi Wobbe Oral History, interviewed by Matthew K. Heiss, Salt Lake City, Utah, 1988, typescript, The James Moyle Oral History Program, Archives, Historical Department of the Church of Jesus Christ of Latter-day Saints, Salt Lake City, Utah, p. 40

14. Rudi Wobbe Fireside [youth church lecture], 1987, transcribed by Richard Dewey and Heather Dewey, 1-4 February 2003, used by permission from Herta Wobbe, p. 12

15. Rudi Wobbe Oral History, interviewed by Matthew K. Heiss, Salt Lake City, Utah, 1988, typescript, The James Moyle Oral History Program, Archives, Historical Department of the Church of Jesus Christ of Latter-day Saints, Salt Lake City, Utah, pp. 40-41

16. Rudi Wobbe Oral History, interviewed by Matthew K. Heiss, Salt Lake City, Utah, 1988, typescript, The James Moyle Oral History Program, Archives, Historical Department of the Church of Jesus Christ of Latter-day Saints, Salt Lake City, Utah, pp. 40-41

17. Statement of Rudolf Wobbe, Rudolf Wobbe, Salt Lake City, Utah, 17 April 1961, Source: Historical Department, Church of Jesus Christ of Latter-day Saints, Salt Lake City, Utah Statement of Rudolf Wobbe, Rudolf Wobbe, Salt Lake City, Utah, 17 April 1961, Source: Historical Department, Church of Jesus Christ of Latter-day Saints, Salt Lake City, Utah

18. Rudi Wobbe Oral History, interviewed by Matthew K. Heiss, Salt Lake City, Utah, 1988, typescript, The James Moyle Oral History Program, Archives, Historical Department of the Church of Jesus Christ of Latter-day Saints, Salt Lake City, UtahandRudolf G. Wobbe Oral History, Doublas F. Tobler and Alan F. Keele, 1974, typescript, The James Moyle Oral History Program, Archives, Historical Department of the Church of Jesus Christ of Latter-day Saints, Salt Lake City, Utah

19. Rudi Wobbe Oral History, interviewed by Matthew K. Heiss, Salt Lake City, Utah, 1988, typescript, The James Moyle Oral History Program, Archives, Historical Department of the Church of Jesus Christ of Latter-day Saints, Salt Lake City, Utah, pp. 40-41

20. *Ibid.*

21. Rudi Wobbe Fireside [youth church lecture], 1987, transcribed by Richard Dewey and Heather Dewey, 1-4 February 2003, used by permission from Herta Wobbe, p. 12

22. Rudi Wobbe and Jerry Borrowman, *Three Against Hitler,* (American Fork, Utah: Covenant Communications, 1992), p.. 50

23. Rudi Wobbe Oral History, interviewed by Matthew K. Heiss, Salt Lake City, Utah, 1988, typescript, The James Moyle Oral History Program, Archives, Historical Department of the Church of Jesus Christ of Latter-day Saints, Salt Lake City, Utah, pp. 40-41

24. Rudi Wobbe Oral History, interviewed by Matthew K. Heiss, Salt Lake City, Utah, 1988, typescript, The James Moyle Oral History Program, Archives, Historical Department of the Church of Jesus Christ of Latter-day Saints, Salt Lake City, Utah, pp. 40-41

25. Rudi Wobbe and Jerry Borrowman, *Three Against Hitler,* (American Fork, Utah: Covenant Communications, 1992), p. 50

26. Rudi Wobbe Oral History, interviewed by Matthew K. Heiss, Salt Lake City, Utah, 1988, typescript, The James Moyle Oral History Program, Archives, Historical Department of the Church of Jesus Christ of Latter-day Saints, Salt Lake City, Utah, pp. 40-41

27. Rudi Wobbe Fireside [youth church lecture], 1987, transcribed by Richard Dewey and Heather Dewey, 1-4 February 2003, used by permission from Herta Wobbe, p. 12

28. Rudi Wobbe Fireside [youth church lecture], 1987, transcribed by Richard Dewey and Heather Dewey, 1-4 February 2003, used by permission from Herta Wobbe, p. 19

29. The Diary of Gerhard Düwer; Document of The Superior Attorney General of the Reich, Berlin 28 May 1942 at the People's Court, 8J 127/42g, In Custody!: Indictment section

30. Document of The Superior Attorney General of the Reich, Berlin 28 May 1942 at the People's Court, 8J 127/42g, In Custody!: Indictment section

31. Document of The Superior Attorney General of the Reich, Berlin 28 May 1942 at the People's Court, 8J 127/42g, In Custody!: Indictment section

32. Statement of Hans Kunkel, Source: *Begleitheft zur Austellung um das kurze Leben und Wirken des Helmuth Hübener,* Catalogue of the exhibit in the Hamburg Municipal District Archive (Stadtteilarchiv) of Hamm, 26 October – 10 December, 1992

33. Rudi Wobbe Oral History, interviewed by Matthew K. Heiss, Salt Lake City, Utah, 1988, typescript, The James Moyle Oral History Program, Archives, Historical Department of the Church of Jesus Christ of Latter-day Saints, Salt Lake City, Utah, p. 42-43

34. Gerhard Kunkel interview #2 with author, 25 February 2003

35. "The Führer's New Clothes: Helmuth Hübener and the Dilemma of German Mormons in the Third Reich," unpublished essay by Alan F. Keele, Used by permission from Alan F. Keele. A shorter version of this essay was later published as an article in *Sunstone*, p. 17, which utilizes Alan Keele interview with Otto Berndt; also: Otto Berndt Letter to *Improvement Era*, May 1969, pp. 100-101

36. Letter from Otto Berndt to Improvement Era, May 1969; Otto Berndt Oral History, interviewed by Douglas F. Tobler, Salt Lake City, Utah, 1974, typescript, The James Moyle Oral History Program, Archives, Historical Department of the Church of Jesus Christ of Latter-day Saints, Salt Lake City, Utah, p. 44

37. Otto Berndt Oral History, interviewed by Douglas F. Tobler, Salt Lake City, Utah, 1974, typescript, The James Moyle Oral History Program, Archives, Historical Department of the Church of Jesus Christ of Latter-day Saints, Salt Lake City, Utah, p. 39

38. Rudi Wobbe Fireside [youth church lecture], 1987, transcribed by Richard Dewey and Heather Dewey, 1-4 February 2003, used by permission from Herta Wobbe, p. 21

39. Rudi Wobbe Fireside [youth church lecture], 1987, transcribed by Richard Dewey and Heather Dewey, 1-4 February 2003, used by permission from Herta Wobbe, p. 21

40. Otto Berndt Oral History, interviewed by Douglas F. Tobler, Salt Lake City, Utah, 1974, typescript, The James Moyle Oral History Program, Archives, Historical Department of the Church of Jesus Christ of Latter-day Saints, Salt Lake City, Utah, pp. 61-62

41. Rudi Wobbe Fireside [youth church lecture], 1987, transcribed by Richard Dewey and Heather Dewey, 1-4 February 2003, used by permission from Herta Wobbe, p. 21

42. Otto Berndt Oral History, interviewed by Douglas F. Tobler, Salt Lake City, Utah, 1974, typescript, The James Moyle Oral History Program, Archives, Historical Department of the Church of Jesus Christ of Latter-day Saints, Salt Lake City, Utah, p. 44

43. Rudi Wobbe Fireside [youth church lecture], 1987, transcribed by Richard Dewey and Heather Dewey, 1-4 February 2003, used by permission from Herta Wobbe, p. 21

44. Karl Schnibbe interview with author, Salt Lake City, Utah, 16 September 1996, transcribed by Don Ricks, p.12

45. Statement of Otto Berndt, Ca. 1961, Source: Historical Department, Church of Jesus Christ of Latter-day Saints, Salt Lake City, Utah

46. Otto Berndt Oral History, interviewed by Douglas F. Tobler, Salt Lake City, Utah, 1974, typescript, The James Moyle Oral History Program, Archives, Historical Department of the Church of Jesus Christ of Latter-day Saints, Salt Lake City, Utah, p. 40

47. Karl Schnibbe interview with author, Salt Lake City, Utah, 16 September 1996, transcribed by Don Ricks, p. 12

48. Karl Schnibbe interview with author, Salt Lake City, Utah, 16 September 1996, transcribed by Don Ricks, p. 12

49. Otto Berndt Oral History, interviewed by Douglas F. Tobler, Salt Lake City, Utah, 1974, typescript, The James Moyle Oral History Program, Archives, Historical Department of the Church of Jesus Christ of Latter-day Saints, Salt Lake City, Utah, p. 38

50. Otto Berndt Oral History, interviewed by Douglas F. Tobler, Salt Lake City, Utah, 1974, typescript, The James Moyle Oral History Program, Archives, Historical Department of the Church of Jesus Christ of Latter-day Saints, Salt Lake City, Utah, p. 43

51. "The Führer's New Clothes: Helmuth Hübener and the Dilemma of German Mormons in the Third Reich," unpublished essay by Alan F. Keele, Used by permission from Alan F. Keele. A shorter version of this essay was later published as an article in *Sunstone*, p. 17; also Karl Schnibbe interview with author, Salt Lake City, Utah, 16 September 1996, transcribed by Don Ricks, and Rudi Wobbe Fireside [youth church lecture], 1987, transcribed by Richard Dewey and Heather Dewey, 1-4 February 2003, used by permission from Herta Wobbe

52. Otto Berndt Oral History, interviewed by Douglas F. Tobler, Salt Lake City, Utah, 1974, typescript, The James Moyle Oral History Program, Archives, Historical Department of the Church of Jesus Christ of Latter-day Saints, Salt Lake City, Utah, pp. 60-61

53. Otto Berndt Oral History, interviewed by Douglas F. Tobler, Salt Lake City, Utah, 1974, typescript, The James Moyle Oral History Program, Archives, Historical Department of the Church of Jesus Christ of Latter-day Saints, Salt Lake City, Utah, p. 44

54. *Sonderbericht uber die Lage in den Protestantischen Kirchen und in den Verschiendenen Sekten und deren staatsfeindliche Wirkung*, National Archives, Washington, D.C., also Statement of Friedrich Peters, born 1920, Source: *Begleitheft zur Austellung um das kurze Leben und Wirken des Helmuth Hübener*, Catalogue

of the exhibit in the Hamburg Municipal District Archive (Stadtteilarchiv) of Hamm, 26 October – 10 December

55. "The Führer's New Clothes: Helmuth Hübener and the Dilemma of German Mormons in the Third Reich," unpublished essay by Alan F. Keele, Used by permission from Alan F. Keele. A shorter version of this essay was later published as an article in *Sunstone*, p. 17, citing Alan Keele's interviews with Otto Berndt

56. Letter from Rosa Bohringer to Albert R. Bowen, 19 June 1948, Max Zimmer file, LDS Church archives

57. Otto Berndt Oral History, interviewed by Douglas F. Tobler, Salt Lake City, Utah, 1974, typescript, The James Moyle Oral History Program, Archives, Historical Department of the Church of Jesus Christ of Latter-day Saints, Salt Lake City, Utah

58. Otto Berndt Oral History, interviewed by Douglas F. Tobler, Salt Lake City, Utah, 1974, typescript, The James Moyle Oral History Program, Archives, Historical Department of the Church of Jesus Christ of Latter-day Saints, Salt Lake City, Utah

59. Otto Berndt Oral History, interviewed by Douglas F. Tobler, Salt Lake City, Utah, 1974, typescript, The James Moyle Oral History Program, Archives, Historical Department of the Church of Jesus Christ of Latter-day Saints, Salt Lake City, Utah

60. Statement of Marie Sommerfeld, Source: *Begleitheft zur Austellung um das kurze Leben und Wirken des Helmuth Hübener,* Catalogue of the exhibit in the Hamburg Municipal District Archive (Stadtteilarchiv) of Hamm, 26 October – 10 December, 1992

61. Karl Schnibbe interview with author, Salt Lake City, Utah, 16 September 1996, transcribed by Don Ricks, p.13

62. Marie Friebel Sommerfeld 1897-1984, Interviewed in German by Douglas Tobler and Alan Keele, 1974 : (13 leaves in English; Matthew K. Heiss later wrote Iris Schmidt on 17 Sep 1992

saying the Sommerfeld interview was never fully edited; typed ca. 1985 by Karen H. Pyper), p. 5

63. Marie Friebel Sommerfeld 1897-1984, Interviewed in German by Douglas Tobler and Alan Keele, 1974 : (13 leaves in English; Matthew K. Heiss later wrote Iris Schmidt on 17 Sep 1992 saying the Sommerfeld interview was never fully edited; typed ca. 1985 by Karen H. Pyper), p. 6

64. Otto Berndt Oral History, interviewed by Douglas F. Tobler, Salt Lake City, Utah, 1974, typescript, The James Moyle Oral History Program, Archives, Historical Department of the Church of Jesus Christ of Latter-day Saints, Salt Lake City, Utah, p. 32

65. MS History of West German Mission

66. Otto Berndt Oral History, interviewed by Douglas F. Tobler, Salt Lake City, Utah, 1974, typescript, The James Moyle Oral History Program, Archives, Historical Department of the Church of Jesus Christ of Latter-day Saints, Salt Lake City, Utah, p. 40

67. Otto Berndt Oral History, interviewed by Douglas F. Tobler, Salt Lake City, Utah, 1974, typescript, The James Moyle Oral History Program, Archives, Historical Department of the Church of Jesus Christ of Latter-day Saints, Salt Lake City, Utah, p. 40

68. Statement of Friedrich Peters, born 1920, Source: *Begleitheft zur Austellung um das kurze Leben und Wirken des Helmuth Hübener,* Catalogue of the exhibit in the Hamburg Municipal District Archive (Stadtteilarchiv) of Hamm, 26 October – 10 December

69. Statement of Otto Berndt, Ca. 1961, Source: Historical Department, Church of Jesus Christ of Latter-day Saints, Salt Lake City, Utah; Statement of Friedrich Peters, born 1920, Source: *Begleitheft zur Austellung um das kurze Leben und Wirken des Helmuth Hübener,* Catalogue of the exhibit in the Hamburg Municipal District Archive (Stadtteilarchiv) of Hamm, 26 October – 10 December

70. Statement of Friedrich Peters, born 1920, Source: *Begleitheft zur Austellung um das kurze Leben und Wirken des Helmuth Hübener,* Catalogue of the exhibit in the Hamburg Municipal District Archive (Stadtteilarchiv) of Hamm, 26 October – 10 December

71. "The Führer's New Clothes: Helmuth Hübener and the Dilemma of German Mormons in the Third Reich," unpublished essay by Alan F. Keele, Used by permission from Alan F. Keele. A shorter version of this essay was later published as an article in *Sunstone*, p. 16

72. Statement of Friedrich Peters, born 1920, Source: *Begleitheft zur Austellung um das kurze Leben und Wirken des Helmuth Hübener,* Catalogue of the exhibit in the Hamburg Municipal District Archive (Stadtteilarchiv) of Hamm, 26 October – 10 December

73. "The Führer's New Clothes: Helmuth Hübener and the Dilemma of German Mormons in the Third Reich," unpublished essay by Alan F. Keele, Used by permission from Alan F. Keele. A shorter version of this essay was later published as an article in *Sunstone*, p. 21, see also Letter from Matthew K. Heiss, LDS Historical Dept. 11 Aug 1992 to Iris Schmidt, MSR Frankfurt, Europe Area office LDS

74. "The Führer's New Clothes: Helmuth Hübener and the Dilemma of German Mormons in the Third Reich," unpublished essay by Alan F. Keele, Used by permission from Alan F. Keele. A shorter version of this essay was later published as an article in *Sunstone*, p 16

75. Statement of Otto Berndt, Ca. 1961, Source: Historical Department, Church of Jesus Christ of Latter-day Saints, Salt Lake City, Utah

76. Rudi Wobbe Oral History, interviewed by Matthew K. Heiss, Salt Lake City, Utah, 1988, typescript, The James Moyle Oral History Program, Archives, Historical Department of the

Church of Jesus Christ of Latter-day Saints, Salt Lake City, Utah, pp. 39-40

CHAPTER 21

1. Statement of Rudolf Wobbe, Rudolf Wobbe, Salt Lake City, Utah, 17 April 1961, Source: Historical Department, Church of Jesus Christ of Latter-day Saints, Salt Lake City, Utah Statement of Rudolf Wobbe, Rudolf Wobbe, Salt Lake City, Utah, 17 April 1961, Source: Historical Department, Church of Jesus Christ of Latter-day Saints, Salt Lake City, Utah

2. Rudolf G. Wobbe Oral History, Doublas F. Tobler and Alan F. Keele, 1974, typescript, The James Moyle Oral History Program, Archives, Historical Department of the Church of Jesus Christ of Latter-day Saints, Salt Lake City, Utah, p. 9

3. Rudi Wobbe Oral History, interviewed by Matthew K. Heiss, Salt Lake City, Utah, 1988, typescript, The James Moyle Oral History Program, Archives, Historical Department of the Church of Jesus Christ of Latter-day Saints, Salt Lake City, Utah, p. 41

4. Rudi Wobbe Oral History, interviewed by Matthew K. Heiss, Salt Lake City, Utah, 1988, typescript, The James Moyle Oral History Program, Archives, Historical Department of the Church of Jesus Christ of Latter-day Saints, Salt Lake City, Utah, pp. 41-42

5. Rudi Wobbe Oral History, interviewed by Matthew K. Heiss, Salt Lake City, Utah, 1988, typescript, The James Moyle Oral History Program, Archives, Historical Department of the Church of Jesus Christ of Latter-day Saints, Salt Lake City, Utah, pp. 41-42

6. Rudi Wobbe Fireside [youth church lecture], 1987, transcribed by Richard Dewey and Heather Dewey, 1-4 February 2003, used by permission from Herta Wobbe, p. 12

7. Blair Holmes, Alan Keele, and Karl-Heinz Schnibbe, *When Truth Was Treason*, Urbana and Chicago, Illinois: University of Illinois Press, 1995

8. Rudi Wobbe Oral History, interviewed by Matthew K. Heiss, Salt Lake City, Utah, 1988, typescript, The James Moyle Oral History Program, Archives, Historical Department of the Church of Jesus Christ of Latter-day Saints, Salt Lake City, Utah, pp. 41-42

9. Zorn, *Aus dem Leben Charlotte Gross*, in Zorn and Meyer, *Frauen gegen Hitler,* p. 13

10. Blair Holmes, Alan Keele, and Karl-Heinz Schnibbe, *When Truth Was Treason*, Urbana and Chicago, Illinois: University of Illinois Press, 1995; also see Meyer, Nacht uber Hamburg, pp. 20-21; Gerda Zorn, Aus dem Leben der Charlotte Gross, in Zorn and Meyer, Frauen gegen Hitler, pp. 13-14; Lucie Suhling, Aufmachen -- Polizei! in *Ibid.*, p. 37

11. Blair Holmes, Alan Keele, and Karl-Heinz Schnibbe, *When Truth Was Treason*, Urbana and Chicago, Illinois: University of Illinois Press, 1995

12. Karl Schnibbe interview with author, Salt Lake City, Utah, 16 September 1996, transcribed by Don Ricks, p. 23

13. *Salt Lake Tribune*, 13 May 2003

14. Rudi Wobbe Oral History, interviewed by Matthew K. Heiss, Salt Lake City, Utah, 1988, typescript, The James Moyle Oral History Program, Archives, Historical Department of the Church of Jesus Christ of Latter-day Saints, Salt Lake City, Utah, p. 42-43

15. Rudi Wobbe Oral History, interviewed by Matthew K. Heiss, Salt Lake City, Utah, 1988, typescript, The James Moyle Oral History Program, Archives, Historical Department of the Church of Jesus Christ of Latter-day Saints, Salt Lake City, Utah, p. 43

16. Rudi Wobbe Oral History, interviewed by Matthew K. Heiss, Salt Lake City, Utah, 1988, typescript, The James Moyle Oral History Program, Archives, Historical Department of the Church of Jesus Christ of Latter-day Saints, Salt Lake City, Utah, p. 8

17. Rudi Wobbe Oral History, interviewed by Matthew K. Heiss, Salt Lake City, Utah, 1988, typescript, The James Moyle Oral History Program, Archives, Historical Department of the Church of Jesus Christ of Latter-day Saints, Salt Lake City, Utah, p. 43

18. Rudi Wobbe Oral History, interviewed by Matthew K. Heiss, Salt Lake City, Utah, 1988, typescript, The James Moyle Oral History Program, Archives, Historical Department of the Church of Jesus Christ of Latter-day Saints, Salt Lake City, Utah, p. 8

19. Rudi Wobbe Oral History, interviewed by Matthew K. Heiss, Salt Lake City, Utah, 1988, typescript, The James Moyle Oral History Program, Archives, Historical Department of the Church of Jesus Christ of Latter-day Saints, Salt Lake City, Utah, p. 43

20. Rudi Wobbe Oral History, interviewed by Matthew K. Heiss, Salt Lake City, Utah, 1988, typescript, The James Moyle Oral History Program, Archives, Historical Department of the Church of Jesus Christ of Latter-day Saints, Salt Lake City, Utah, p. 32

21. Rudi Wobbe Oral History, interviewed by Matthew K. Heiss, Salt Lake City, Utah, 1988, typescript, The James Moyle Oral History Program, Archives, Historical Department of the Church of Jesus Christ of Latter-day Saints, Salt Lake City, Utah, p. 43

22. Rudi Wobbe Oral History, interviewed by Matthew K. Heiss, Salt Lake City, Utah, 1988, typescript, The James Moyle Oral History Program, Archives, Historical Department of the

Church of Jesus Christ of Latter-day Saints, Salt Lake City, Utah, p. 41

23. Rudi Wobbe Oral History, interviewed by Matthew K. Heiss, Salt Lake City, Utah, 1988, typescript, The James Moyle Oral History Program, Archives, Historical Department of the Church of Jesus Christ of Latter-day Saints, Salt Lake City, Utah, p. 41

24. Ditt, *Sozialdemokraten*, p. 93

25. Rudi Wobbe Oral History, interviewed by Matthew K. Heiss, Salt Lake City, Utah, 1988, typescript, The James Moyle Oral History Program, Archives, Historical Department of the Church of Jesus Christ of Latter-day Saints, Salt Lake City, Utah, p. 41

26. Rudi Wobbe Oral History, interviewed by Matthew K. Heiss, Salt Lake City, Utah, 1988, typescript, The James Moyle Oral History Program, Archives, Historical Department of the Church of Jesus Christ of Latter-day Saints, Salt Lake City, Utah, p. 41

27. Statement of Rudolf Wobbe, Rudolf Wobbe, Salt Lake City, Utah, 17 April 1961, Source: Historical Department, Church of Jesus Christ of Latter-day Saints, Salt Lake City, Utah Statement of Rudolf Wobbe, Rudolf Wobbe, Salt Lake City, Utah, 17 April 1961, Source: Historical Department, Church of Jesus Christ of Latter-day Saints, Salt Lake City, Utah, paragraph 10

28. Blair Holmes, Alan Keele, and Karl-Heinz Schnibbe, *When Truth Was Treason*, Urbana and Chicago, Illinois: University of Illinois Press, 1995

29. Karl Schnibbe interview with author, Salt Lake City, Utah, 16 September 1996, transcribed by Don Ricks, p. 22

30. Karl Schnibbe interview with author, Salt Lake City, Utah, 16 September 1996, transcribed by Don Ricks, p. 22

31. Blair Holmes, Alan Keele, and Karl-Heinz Schnibbe, *When Truth Was Treason*, Urbana and Chicago, Illinois: University of Illinois Press, 1995

32. Sander, Helmuth-Hübener Gruppe, in Hochmuth and Meyer, Streiflichter, p. 336

33. Rudi Wobbe Oral History, interviewed by Matthew K. Heiss, Salt Lake City, Utah, 1988, typescript, The James Moyle Oral History Program, Archives, Historical Department of the Church of Jesus Christ of Latter-day Saints, Salt Lake City, Utah, p. 44

34. Document of State Police Agency Hamburg — Hamburg, 5, 9, 17, 20 February 1942

35. Statement of Rudolf Wobbe, Rudolf Wobbe, Salt Lake City, Utah, 17 April 1961, Source: Historical Department, Church of Jesus Christ of Latter-day Saints, Salt Lake City, Utah Statement of Rudolf Wobbe, Rudolf Wobbe, Salt Lake City, Utah, 17 April 1961, Source: Historical Department, Church of Jesus Christ of Latter-day Saints, Salt Lake City, Utah

36. Bericht von Walter Schmedemann, in Ditt, SozialdemoKraten im Widerstand, p. 145; and Lucie Suhling, Aufmachen - Polizei! in Zorn and Meyer, Frauen gegen Hitler, p. 35; and Meyer, Nacht uber Hamburg, p. 22

37. Karl Schnibbe interview with author, Salt Lake City, Utah, 16 September 1996, transcribed by Don Ricks, p. 6

38. Rudolf G. Wobbe Oral History, Doublas F. Tobler and Alan F. Keele, 1974, typescript, The James Moyle Oral History Program, Archives, Historical Department of the Church of Jesus Christ of Latter-day Saints, Salt Lake City, Utah, p. 27

39. Rudi Wobbe Oral History, interviewed by Matthew K. Heiss, Salt Lake City, Utah, 1988, typescript, The James Moyle Oral History Program, Archives, Historical Department of the Church of Jesus Christ of Latter-day Saints, Salt Lake City, Utah, p. 41

40. Karl Schnibbe interview with author, Salt Lake City, Utah, 16 September 1996, transcribed by Don Ricks, p. 6

41. Rudi Wobbe and Jerry Borrowman, *Three Against Hitler,* (American Fork, Utah: Covenant Communications, 1992), p. 60

42. Karl Schnibbe interview with author, Salt Lake City, Utah, 16 September 1996, transcribed by Don Ricks, p. 5

43. Karl Schnibbe interview with author, Salt Lake City, Utah, 16 September 1996, transcribed by Don Ricks, p. 6

C H A P T E R 2 2

1. Document of Chief State Counsel of the Hanseatic Higher Regional Court, Hamburg 36, 25 March 1942, Criminal Case! Juveniles!; Document of The Superior Attorney General of the Reich, Berlin 28 May 1942 at the People's Court, 8J 127/42g, In Custody!: Indictment section

2. Karl Schnibbe interview with author, Salt Lake City, Utah, 16 September 1996, transcribed by Don Ricks, p. 23

3. Blair Holmes, Alan Keele, and Karl-Heinz Schnibbe, *When Truth Was Treason*, Urbana and Chicago, Illinois: University of Illinois Press, 1995

4. Rudi Wobbe Oral History, interviewed by Matthew K. Heiss, Salt Lake City, Utah, 1988, typescript, The James Moyle Oral History Program, Archives, Historical Department of the Church of Jesus Christ of Latter-day Saints, Salt Lake City, Utah, p. 45

5. Blair Holmes, Alan Keele, and Karl-Heinz Schnibbe, *When Truth Was Treason*, Urbana and Chicago, Illinois: University of Illinois Press, 1995

6. Blair Holmes, Alan Keele, and Karl-Heinz Schnibbe, *When Truth Was Treason*, Urbana and Chicago, Illinois: University of Illinois Press, 1995

7. "I Knew Helmuth since 1928", Irmgard Becker, born 1916, recalls, Source: *Begleitheft zur Austellung um das kurze Leben und Wirken des Helmuth Hübener,* Catalogue of the exhibit in the Hamburg Municipal District Archive (Stadtteilarchiv) of Hamm

8. Blair Holmes, Alan Keele, and Karl-Heinz Schnibbe, *When Truth Was Treason*, Urbana and Chicago, Illinois: University of Illinois Press, 1995

9. Statement of Rudolf Wobbe, Rudolf Wobbe, Salt Lake City, Utah, 17 April 1961, Source: Historical Department, Church of Jesus Christ of Latter-day Saints, Salt Lake City, Utah Statement of Rudolf Wobbe, Rudolf Wobbe, Salt Lake City, Utah, 17 April 1961, Source: Historical Department, Church of Jesus Christ of Latter-day Saints, Salt Lake City, Utah

10. Rudi Wobbe Oral History, interviewed by Matthew K. Heiss, Salt Lake City, Utah, 1988, typescript, The James Moyle Oral History Program, Archives, Historical Department of the Church of Jesus Christ of Latter-day Saints, Salt Lake City, Utah, p. 46

11. Blair Holmes, Alan Keele, and Karl-Heinz Schnibbe, *When Truth Was Treason*, Urbana and Chicago, Illinois: University of Illinois Press, 1995

12. Statement of Rudolf Wobbe, Rudolf Wobbe, Salt Lake City, Utah, 17 April 1961, Source: Historical Department, Church of Jesus Christ of Latter-day Saints, Salt Lake City, Utah Statement of Rudolf Wobbe, Rudolf Wobbe, Salt Lake City, Utah, 17 April 1961, Source: Historical Department, Church of Jesus Christ of Latter-day Saints, Salt Lake City, Utah

13. Rudi Wobbe Oral History, interviewed by Matthew K. Heiss, Salt Lake City, Utah, 1988, typescript, The James Moyle Oral History Program, Archives, Historical Department of the

Church of Jesus Christ of Latter-day Saints, Salt Lake City, Utah, p. 46

14. Blair Holmes, Alan Keele, and Karl-Heinz Schnibbe, *When Truth Was Treason*, Urbana and Chicago, Illinois: University of Illinois Press, 1995

15. Rudi Wobbe Oral History, interviewed by Matthew K. Heiss, Salt Lake City, Utah, 1988, typescript, The James Moyle Oral History Program, Archives, Historical Department of the Church of Jesus Christ of Latter-day Saints, Salt Lake City, Utah, p. 46

16. Rudi Wobbe Oral History, interviewed by Matthew K. Heiss, Salt Lake City, Utah, 1988, typescript, The James Moyle Oral History Program, Archives, Historical Department of the Church of Jesus Christ of Latter-day Saints, Salt Lake City, Utah, p. 46

17. Rudi Wobbe Fireside [youth church lecture], 1987, transcribed by Richard Dewey and Heather Dewey, 1-4 February 2003, used by permission from Herta Wobbe, p. 21

18. Rudi Wobbe Oral History, interviewed by Matthew K. Heiss, Salt Lake City, Utah, 1988, typescript, The James Moyle Oral History Program, Archives, Historical Department of the Church of Jesus Christ of Latter-day Saints, Salt Lake City, Utah, p. 46

19. Ditt, *SozialdemoKraten im Widerstand*, pp. 97-98

20. Rudi Wobbe Oral History, interviewed by Matthew K. Heiss, Salt Lake City, Utah, 1988, typescript, The James Moyle Oral History Program, Archives, Historical Department of the Church of Jesus Christ of Latter-day Saints, Salt Lake City, Utah, p. 45 also Document of Secret State Police, Hamburg 10 July 1942, State Police Office Hamburg, B. No. II P - 126/42, Rudolf Gustav Wobbe, Upon interrogation andRudolf G. Wobbe Oral History, Doublas F. Tobler and Alan F. Keele, 1974, typescript, The James Moyle Oral History Program, Archives,

Historical Department of the Church of Jesus Christ of Latter-day Saints, Salt Lake City, Utah, p. 1

21. Blair Holmes, Alan Keele, and Karl-Heinz Schnibbe, *When Truth Was Treason*, Urbana and Chicago, Illinois: University of Illinois Press, 1995; see also Certified Copy, on the subject of Rudolf Wobbe, Hamburg Investigatory Prison 5, Cell 54, /s/ Bernhard Rubinke, 4 July 1942

22. Rudi Wobbe Oral History, interviewed by Matthew K. Heiss, Salt Lake City, Utah, 1988, typescript, The James Moyle Oral History Program, Archives, Historical Department of the Church of Jesus Christ of Latter-day Saints, Salt Lake City, Utah, p. 45

23. Rudi Wobbe Oral History, interviewed by Matthew K. Heiss, Salt Lake City, Utah, 1988, typescript, The James Moyle Oral History Program, Archives, Historical Department of the Church of Jesus Christ of Latter-day Saints, Salt Lake City, Utah, p. 45

24. Author's analysis of Certified Copy, On the subject of Rudolf Wobbe, Hamburg Investigatory Prison 5 Cell 54, /s/ Bernhard Rubinke, 4 July 1942

25. Document of Secret State Police, Hamburg 10 July 1942, State Police Office Hamburg, B. No. II P - 126/42, Rudolf Gustav Wobbe, Upon interrogation

26. Verdict of the People's Court in the criminal case against Helmut Hübener, et al, on 11 August 1942: part II sec 2

27. Blair Holmes, Alan Keele, and Karl-Heinz Schnibbe, *When Truth Was Treason*, Urbana and Chicago, Illinois: University of Illinois Press, 1995

28. Rudi Wobbe Oral History, interviewed by Matthew K. Heiss, Salt Lake City, Utah, 1988, typescript, The James Moyle Oral History Program, Archives, Historical Department of the Church of Jesus Christ of Latter-day Saints, Salt Lake City, Utah, pp. 45-46

29. Letter from Helmuth Hübener, Excerpted Copy, Investigatory Prison, Js 11/42, Sender: Hübener, Helmuth; Recipient: Parents, Hamburg, 5 April 1942

30. Letter from Helmuth Hübener, Excerpted Copy, Investigatory Prison, Js 11/42, Sender: Hübener, Helmuth; Recipient: Parents, Hamburg, 5 April 1942

31. Letter from Helmuth Hübener, Excerpted Copy, Investigatory Prison, Js 11/42, Sender: Hübener, Helmuth; Recipient: Parents, Hamburg, 5 April 1942

32. "The Führer's New Clothes: Helmuth Hübener and the Dilemma of German Mormons in the Third Reich," unpublished essay by Alan F. Keele, Used by permission from Alan F. Keele. A shorter version of this essay was later published as an article in *Sunstone*, p. 36

33. Statement of Marie Sommerfeld, Source: *Begleitheft zur Austellung um das kurze Leben und Wirken des Helmuth Hübener*, Catalogue of the exhibit in the Hamburg Municipal District Archive (Stadtteilarchiv) of Hamm, 26 October – 10 December, 1992

34. Arthur and Marie Sommerfeld interview with author, 18 October 1996, p. 1

35. Statement of Hedi Radtke Sommerfeld, Source: *Begleitheft zur Austellung um das kurze Leben und Wirken des Helmuth Hübener*, Catalogue of the exhibit in the Hamburg Municipal District Archive (Stadtteilarchiv) of Hamm, 26 October – 10 December

36. MS13277, p. 5

37. Marie Friebel Sommerfeld 1897-1984, Interviewed in German by Douglas Tobler and Alan Keele, 1974 : (13 leaves in English; Matthew K. Heiss later wrote Iris Schmidt on 17 Sep 1992 saying the Sommerfeld interview was never fully edited; typed ca. 1985 by Karen H. Pyper), p. 5

38. Marie Friebel Sommerfeld 1897-1984, Interviewed in German by Douglas Tobler and Alan Keele, 1974 : (13 leaves in English; Matthew K. Heiss later wrote Iris Schmidt on 17 Sep 1992 saying the Sommerfeld interview was never fully edited; typed ca. 1985 by Karen H. Pyper), p. 5

39. Marie Friebel Sommerfeld 1897-1984, Interviewed in German by Douglas Tobler and Alan Keele, 1974 : (13 leaves in English; Matthew K. Heiss later wrote Iris Schmidt on 17 Sep 1992 saying the Sommerfeld interview was never fully edited; typed ca. 1985 by Karen H. Pyper), p. 12. Elsewhere Mary Sommerfeld recalls the conversation with her son, Arthur, somewhat differently at the Berlin hospital: "We told him everything, and he was able to calm us: He did not belong to it and he knew nothing about it."; Statement of Marie Sommerfeld, Source: *Begleitheft zur Austellung um das kurze Leben und Wirken des Helmuth Hübener,* Catalogue of the exhibit in the Hamburg Municipal District Archive (Stadtteilarchiv) of Hamm, 26 October – 10 December, 1992. But Arthur verifies her first report: I was in the Berlin hospital when my mother came to visit me to inquire if I were involved in Helmuth's resistance work. Arthur and Marie Sommerfeld interview with author, 18 October 1996, p. 1 . . . I told her we listened together but I assured her I didn't distribute the flyers. Arthur and Marie Sommerfeld interview with author, Salt Lake City, Utah, 18 October 1996, p. 17

40. Statement of Hedi Radtke Sommerfeld, Source: *Begleitheft zur Austellung um das kurze Leben und Wirken des Helmuth Hübener,* Catalogue of the exhibit in the Hamburg Municipal District Archive (Stadtteilarchiv) of Hamm, 26 October – 10 December

41. Statement of Hedi Radtke Sommerfeld, Source: *Begleitheft zur Austellung um das kurze Leben und Wirken des Helmuth Hübener,* Catalogue of the exhibit in the Hamburg Municipal District Archive (Stadtteilarchiv) of Hamm, 26 October – 10 December

42. Marie Friebel Sommerfeld 1897-1984, Interviewed in German by Douglas Tobler and Alan Keele, 1974 : (13 leaves in English; Matthew K. Heiss later wrote Iris Schmidt on 17 Sep 1992 saying the Sommerfeld interview was never fully edited; typed ca. 1985 by Karen H. Pyper), p. 4

43. Letter of Rudi Wobbe 1 March 1942 from Investigatory Prison, Hamburg City, to Mrs. Wobbe

44. Blair Holmes, Alan Keele, and Karl-Heinz Schnibbe, *When Truth Was Treason*, Urbana and Chicago, Illinois: University of Illinois Press, 1995

45. Blair Holmes, Alan Keele, and Karl-Heinz Schnibbe, *When Truth Was Treason*, Urbana and Chicago, Illinois: University of Illinois Press, 1995

46. Document of Chief State Counsel of the Hanseatic Higher Regional Court, Hamburg 36, 25 March 1942, Criminal Case! Juveniles!

47. Blair Holmes, Alan Keele, and Karl-Heinz Schnibbe, *When Truth Was Treason*, Urbana and Chicago, Illinois: University of Illinois Press, 1995

CHAPTER 23

1. Ingo Müller, *Hitler's Justice*, pp. 140-52

2. Blair Holmes, Alan Keele, and Karl-Heinz Schnibbe, *When Truth Was Treason*, Urbana and Chicago, Illinois: University of Illinois Press, 1995

3. Letter from: Johannes Schnibbe, Hamburg 24, 7 May 1942, Rossausweg 32 I, To the Attorney General at the People's Court, Berlin - W9, Bellevuestrabe 15

4. Letter from Marie Wobbe, Hamburg, 17 June 1942, Subject: The Criminal Case of Hübener et al. 87, 127/42 Juvenile

5. Letter from Joh. Schnibbe, Hamburg, 30 June 1942, Rossausweg 32 I, To the Attorney General of the People's Court, Berlin -W9, Bellevuestrabe 15, Re: In the Case of Hübener et al. (juveniles), Document Number JS: 11/42

6. Gerhard Kunkel interview #2 with author, 25 February 2003, p. 11

7. Gerhard Kunkel interview #2 with author, 25 February 2003, p. 11

8. Gerhard Kunkel interview #2 with author, 25 February 2003, p. 12, "The Führer's New Clothes: Helmuth Hübener and the Dilemma of German Mormons in the Third Reich," unpublished essay by Alan F. Keele, Used by permission from Alan F. Keele. A shorter version of this essay was later published as an article in *Sunstone*, p. 5

9. "The Führer's New Clothes: Helmuth Hübener and the Dilemma of German Mormons in the Third Reich," unpublished essay by Alan F. Keele, Used by permission from Alan F. Keele. A shorter version of this essay was later published as an article in *Sunstone*, p. 5

10. Gerhard Kunkel interview #2 with author, 25 February 2003, p. 17

11. Karl Schnibbe interview with author, Salt Lake City, Utah, 16 September 1996, transcribed by Don Ricks, p. 23

12. Blair Holmes, Alan Keele, and Karl-Heinz Schnibbe, *When Truth Was Treason*, Urbana and Chicago, Illinois: University of Illinois Press, 1995

13. Karl Schnibbe interview with author, Salt Lake City, Utah, 16 September 1996, transcribed by Don Ricks, p. 21

14. Rudolf G. Wobbe Oral History, Doublas F. Tobler and Alan F. Keele, 1974, typescript, The James Moyle Oral History Program, Archives, Historical Department of the Church of Jesus Christ of Latter-day Saints, Salt Lake City, Utahp. 25.

In his 1988 interview Rudi says he only met him at the trial, Rudi Wobbe Oral History, interviewed by Matthew K. Heiss, Salt Lake City, Utah, 1988, typescript, The James Moyle Oral History Program, Archives, Historical Department of the Church of Jesus Christ of Latter-day Saints, Salt Lake City, Utah, p. 48 forgetting or failing to mention the van and train ride with Düwer from Hamburg to Berlin.

15. Blair Holmes, Alan Keele, and Karl-Heinz Schnibbe, *When Truth Was Treason*, Urbana and Chicago, Illinois: University of Illinois Press, 1995

16. Karl Schnibbe interview with author, Salt Lake City, Utah, 16 September 1996, transcribed by Don Ricks, p. 21

17. Karl Schnibbe interview with author, Salt Lake City, Utah, 16 September 1996, transcribed by Don Ricks, p. 21 andRudi Wobbe Oral History, interviewed by Matthew K. Heiss, Salt Lake City, Utah, 1988, typescript, The James Moyle Oral History Program, Archives, Historical Department of the Church of Jesus Christ of Latter-day Saints, Salt Lake City, Utah, p. 47

18. Karl Schnibbe interview with author, Salt Lake City, Utah, 16 September 1996, transcribed by Don Ricks, p. 21

19. Rudi Wobbe Oral History, interviewed by Matthew K. Heiss, Salt Lake City, Utah, 1988, typescript, The James Moyle Oral History Program, Archives, Historical Department of the Church of Jesus Christ of Latter-day Saints, Salt Lake City, Utah, p. 47

20. Rudolf G. Wobbe Oral History, Doublas F. Tobler and Alan F. Keele, 1974, typescript, The James Moyle Oral History Program, Archives, Historical Department of the Church of Jesus Christ of Latter-day Saints, Salt Lake City, Utah, p. 27

21. Rudi Wobbe Oral History, interviewed by Matthew K. Heiss, Salt Lake City, Utah, 1988, typescript, The James Moyle Oral History Program, Archives, Historical Department of the

Church of Jesus Christ of Latter-day Saints, Salt Lake City, Utah, p. 47

22. Blair Holmes, Alan Keele, and Karl-Heinz Schnibbe, *When Truth Was Treason*, Urbana and Chicago, Illinois: University of Illinois Press, 1995

23. Rudolf G. Wobbe Oral History, Doublas F. Tobler and Alan F. Keele, 1974, typescript, The James Moyle Oral History Program, Archives, Historical Department of the Church of Jesus Christ of Latter-day Saints, Salt Lake City, Utah, p. 25

24. Rudi Wobbe Oral History, interviewed by Matthew K. Heiss, Salt Lake City, Utah, 1988, typescript, The James Moyle Oral History Program, Archives, Historical Department of the Church of Jesus Christ of Latter-day Saints, Salt Lake City, Utah, p. 47

25. Statement of Rudolf Wobbe, Rudolf Wobbe, Salt Lake City, Utah, 17 April 1961, Source: Historical Department, Church of Jesus Christ of Latter-day Saints, Salt Lake City, Utah Statement of Rudolf Wobbe, Rudolf Wobbe, Salt Lake City, Utah, 17 April 1961, Source: Historical Department, Church of Jesus Christ of Latter-day Saints, Salt Lake City, Utah

26. Reichsjustizministerium, Prison System, p. 33

27. Rudi Wobbe Oral History, interviewed by Matthew K. Heiss, Salt Lake City, Utah, 1988, typescript, The James Moyle Oral History Program, Archives, Historical Department of the Church of Jesus Christ of Latter-day Saints, Salt Lake City, Utah, p. 47

28. Blair Holmes, Alan Keele, and Karl-Heinz Schnibbe, *When Truth Was Treason*, Urbana and Chicago, Illinois: University of Illinois Press, 1995

29. Rudi Wobbe Oral History, interviewed by Matthew K. Heiss, Salt Lake City, Utah, 1988, typescript, The James Moyle Oral History Program, Archives, Historical Department of the

Church of Jesus Christ of Latter-day Saints, Salt Lake City, Utah, p. 47

30. Blair Holmes, Alan Keele, and Karl-Heinz Schnibbe, *When Truth Was Treason*, Urbana and Chicago, Illinois: University of Illinois Press, 1995

31. Rudi Wobbe Oral History, interviewed by Matthew K. Heiss, Salt Lake City, Utah, 1988, typescript, The James Moyle Oral History Program, Archives, Historical Department of the Church of Jesus Christ of Latter-day Saints, Salt Lake City, Utah, p. 48

32. Rudi Wobbe Oral History, interviewed by Matthew K. Heiss, Salt Lake City, Utah, 1988, typescript, The James Moyle Oral History Program, Archives, Historical Department of the Church of Jesus Christ of Latter-day Saints, Salt Lake City, Utah, p. 48

33. Schwering, *In den Klauen der Gestapo*, pp 148-49

34. Blair Holmes, Alan Keele, and Karl-Heinz Schnibbe, *When Truth Was Treason*, Urbana and Chicago, Illinois: University of Illinois Press, 1995

35. Statement of Rudolf Wobbe, Rudolf Wobbe, Salt Lake City, Utah, 17 April 1961, Source: Historical Department, Church of Jesus Christ of Latter-day Saints, Salt Lake City, Utah Statement of Rudolf Wobbe, Rudolf Wobbe, Salt Lake City, Utah, 17 April 1961, Source: Historical Department, Church of Jesus Christ of Latter-day Saints, Salt Lake City, Utah

36. Statement of Marie Sommerfeld, Source: *Begleitheft zur Austellung um das kurze Leben und Wirken des Helmuth Hübener,* Catalogue of the exhibit in the Hamburg Municipal District Archive (Stadtteilarchiv) of Hamm, 26 October – 10 December, 1992

C H A P T E R   2 4

1. Blair Holmes, Alan Keele, and Karl-Heinz Schnibbe, *When Truth Was Treason*, Urbana and Chicago, Illinois: University of Illinois Press, 1995

2. Karl Schnibbe interview with author, Salt Lake City, Utah, 16 September 1996, transcribed by Don Ricks, p. 10

3. Karl Schnibbe interview with author, Salt Lake City, Utah, 16 September 1996, transcribed by Don Ricks, p. 7

4. Karl Schnibbe interview with author, Salt Lake City, Utah, 16 September 1996, transcribed by Don Ricks, 7

5. Karl Schnibbe interview with author, Salt Lake City, Utah, 16 September 1996, transcribed by Don Ricks, p. 7

6. Karl Schnibbe interview with author, Salt Lake City, Utah, 16 September 1996, transcribed by Don Ricks, p. 7

7. Rudi Wobbe Oral History, interviewed by Matthew K. Heiss, Salt Lake City, Utah, 1988, typescript, The James Moyle Oral History Program, Archives, Historical Department of the Church of Jesus Christ of Latter-day Saints, Salt Lake City, Utah, p. 48

8. Karl Schnibbe interview with author, Salt Lake City, Utah, 16 September 1996, transcribed by Don Ricks p. 9

9. Karl Schnibbe interview with author, Salt Lake City, Utah, 16 September 1996, transcribed by Don Ricks, p. 7

10. Verdict of the People's Court in the criminal case against Helmut Hübener, et al, on 11 August 1942: introduction to court orders

11. Rudi Wobbe Oral History, interviewed by Matthew K. Heiss, Salt Lake City, Utah, 1988, typescript, The James Moyle Oral History Program, Archives, Historical Department of the

Church of Jesus Christ of Latter-day Saints, Salt Lake City, Utah, p. 49

12. Statement of Rudolf Wobbe, Rudolf Wobbe, Salt Lake City, Utah, 17 April 1961, Source: Historical Department, Church of Jesus Christ of Latter-day Saints, Salt Lake City, Utah Statement of Rudolf Wobbe, Rudolf Wobbe, Salt Lake City, Utah, 17 April 1961, Source: Historical Department, Church of Jesus Christ of Latter-day Saints, Salt Lake City, Utah

13. Statement of Rudolf Wobbe, Rudolf Wobbe, Salt Lake City, Utah, 17 April 1961, Source: Historical Department, Church of Jesus Christ of Latter-day Saints, Salt Lake City, Utah Statement of Rudolf Wobbe, Rudolf Wobbe, Salt Lake City, Utah, 17 April 1961, Source: Historical Department, Church of Jesus Christ of Latter-day Saints, Salt Lake City, Utah; Statement of Hans Kunkel, Source: *Begleitheft zur Austellung um das kurze Leben und Wirken des Helmuth Hübener,* Catalogue of the exhibit in the Hamburg Municipal District Archive (Stadtteilarchiv) of Hamm, 26 October – 10 December, 1992, Karl Schnibbe interview with author, Salt Lake City, Utah, 16 September 1996, transcribed by Don Ricks, p. 8

14. Statement of Rudolf Wobbe, Rudolf Wobbe, Salt Lake City, Utah, 17 April 1961, Source: Historical Department, Church of Jesus Christ of Latter-day Saints, Salt Lake City, Utah Statement of Rudolf Wobbe, Rudolf Wobbe, Salt Lake City, Utah, 17 April 1961, Source: Historical Department, Church of Jesus Christ of Latter-day Saints, Salt Lake City, Utah

15. Rudi Wobbe Fireside [youth church lecture], 1987, transcribed by Richard Dewey and Heather Dewey, 1-4 February 2003, used by permission from Herta Wobbe, p. 13

16. Document of Nazi government, "Helmuth Hübener: Secret," 1942

17. Rudi Wobbe Oral History, interviewed by Matthew K. Heiss, Salt Lake City, Utah, 1988, typescript, The James Moyle Oral History Program, Archives, Historical Department of the

Church of Jesus Christ of Latter-day Saints, Salt Lake City, Utah, p. 48

18. *Ibid.*

19. *Ibid.*

20. Rudi Wobbe and Jerry Borrowman, *Three Against Hitler,* (American Fork, Utah: Covenant Communications, 1992), p. 69; also Rudi Wobbe Oral History, interviewed by Matthew K. Heiss, Salt Lake City, Utah, 1988, typescript, The James Moyle Oral History Program, Archives, Historical Department of the Church of Jesus Christ of Latter-day Saints, Salt Lake City, Utah, p. 49

21. Karl Schnibbe interview with author, Salt Lake City, Utah, 16 September 1996, transcribed by Don Ricks, p. 9

22. Karl Schnibbe interview with author, Salt Lake City, Utah, 16 September 1996, transcribed by Don Ricks, p. 10

23. Statement of Rudolf Wobbe, Rudolf Wobbe, Salt Lake City, Utah, 17 April 1961, Source: Historical Department, Church of Jesus Christ of Latter-day Saints, Salt Lake City, Utah Statement of Rudolf Wobbe, Rudolf Wobbe, Salt Lake City, Utah, 17 April 1961, Source: Historical Department, Church of Jesus Christ of Latter-day Saints, Salt Lake City, Utah

24. Blair Holmes, Alan Keele, and Karl-Heinz Schnibbe, *When Truth Was Treason*, Urbana and Chicago, Illinois: University of Illinois Press, 1995

25. Karl Schnibbe interview with author, Salt Lake City, Utah, 16 September 1996, transcribed by Don Ricks, p. 10

26. Rudi Wobbe Oral History, interviewed by Matthew K. Heiss, Salt Lake City, Utah, 1988, typescript, The James Moyle Oral History Program, Archives, Historical Department of the Church of Jesus Christ of Latter-day Saints, Salt Lake City, Utah, p. 48

27. Rudi Wobbe Oral History, interviewed by Matthew K. Heiss, Salt Lake City, Utah, 1988, typescript, The James Moyle Oral History Program, Archives, Historical Department of the Church of Jesus Christ of Latter-day Saints, Salt Lake City, Utah, p. 49

28. Rudi Wobbe Fireside [youth church lecture], 1987, transcribed by Richard Dewey and Heather Dewey, 1-4 February 2003, used by permission from Herta Wobbe, p. 13

29. Rudi Wobbe Oral History, interviewed by Matthew K. Heiss, Salt Lake City, Utah, 1988, typescript, The James Moyle Oral History Program, Archives, Historical Department of the Church of Jesus Christ of Latter-day Saints, Salt Lake City, Utah, p. 45

30. Statement of Rudolf Wobbe, Rudolf Wobbe, Salt Lake City, Utah, 17 April 1961, Source: Historical Department, Church of Jesus Christ of Latter-day Saints, Salt Lake City, Utah Statement of Rudolf Wobbe, Rudolf Wobbe, Salt Lake City, Utah, 17 April 1961, Source: Historical Department, Church of Jesus Christ of Latter-day Saints, Salt Lake City, Utah

31. Rudi Wobbe Oral History, interviewed by Matthew K. Heiss, Salt Lake City, Utah, 1988, typescript, The James Moyle Oral History Program, Archives, Historical Department of the Church of Jesus Christ of Latter-day Saints, Salt Lake City, Utah, p. 49

32. Rudi Wobbe Fireside [youth church lecture], 1987, transcribed by Richard Dewey and Heather Dewey, 1-4 February 2003, used by permission from Herta Wobbe, p. 13

33. Blair Holmes, Alan Keele, and Karl-Heinz Schnibbe, *When Truth Was Treason*, Urbana and Chicago, Illinois: University of Illinois Press, 1995

34. Blair Holmes, Alan Keele, and Karl-Heinz Schnibbe, *When Truth Was Treason*, Urbana and Chicago, Illinois: University of Illinois Press, 1995

35. Rudi Wobbe Oral History, interviewed by Matthew K. Heiss, Salt Lake City, Utah, 1988, typescript, The James Moyle Oral History Program, Archives, Historical Department of the Church of Jesus Christ of Latter-day Saints, Salt Lake City, Utah, p. 50

36. Rudi Wobbe Oral History, interviewed by Matthew K. Heiss, Salt Lake City, Utah, 1988, typescript, The James Moyle Oral History Program, Archives, Historical Department of the Church of Jesus Christ of Latter-day Saints, Salt Lake City, Utah, p. 50

37. Blair Holmes, Alan Keele, and Karl-Heinz Schnibbe, *When Truth Was Treason*, Urbana and Chicago, Illinois: University of Illinois Press, 1995

38. Blair Holmes, Alan Keele, and Karl-Heinz Schnibbe, *When Truth Was Treason*, Urbana and Chicago, Illinois: University of Illinois Press, 1995

39. Statement of Hans Kunkel, Source: *Begleitheft zur Austellung um das kurze Leben und Wirken des Helmuth Hübener,* Catalogue of the exhibit in the Hamburg Municipal District Archive (Stadtteilarchiv) of Hamm, 26 October – 10 December, 1992

40. Karl Schnibbe interview with author, Salt Lake City, Utah, 16 September 1996, transcribed by Don Ricks, p. 9

41. Document of State Police Agency Hamburg - Hamburg, 5, 9, 17, 20 February 1942,

42. Indictment from The Superior Attorney General of the Reich, Berlin 28 May 1942 at the People's Court, 8J 127/42g, In Custody!: II-3

43. Verdict of the People's Court in the criminal case against Helmut Hübener, et al, on 11 August 1942, pt II sec 2

44. Document of The Superior Attorney General of the Reich, Berlin 28 May 1942 at the People's Court, 8J 127/42g, In Custody!: III-3; and Verdict of the People's Court in the criminal

case against Helmut Hübener, et al, on 11 August 1942: pt II sec 2; and Document of State Police Agency Hamburg - Hamburg, 5, 9, 17, 20 February 1942,

45. Verdict of the People's Court in the criminal case against Helmut Hübener, et al, on 11 August 1942, pt. II, sec 2

46. Document of The Superior Attorney General of the Reich, Berlin 28 May 1942 at the People's Court, 8J 127/42g, In Custody!: III-3

47. Document of The Superior Attorney General of the Reich, Berlin 28 May 1942 at the People's Court, 8J 127/42g, In Custody!: III-3

CHAPTER 25

1. Rudi Wobbe Oral History, interviewed by Matthew K. Heiss, Salt Lake City, Utah, 1988, typescript, The James Moyle Oral History Program, Archives, Historical Department of the Church of Jesus Christ of Latter-day Saints, Salt Lake City, Utah, p. 50

2. Rudi Wobbe Oral History, interviewed by Matthew K. Heiss, Salt Lake City, Utah, 1988, typescript, The James Moyle Oral History Program, Archives, Historical Department of the Church of Jesus Christ of Latter-day Saints, Salt Lake City, Utah, p. 56

3. Verdict of the People's Court in the criminal case against Helmut Hübener, et al, on 11 August 1942: Findings, Pt II sec 2

4. Document of The Superior Attorney General of the Reich, Berlin 28 May 1942 at the People's Court, 8J 127/42g, In Custody!: part IV

5. Document of The Superior Attorney General of the Reich, Berlin 28 May 1942 at the People's Court, 8J 127/42g, In Custody!: II-c

6. Helmut Hübener leaflet, "The Nazi Reichsmarshall"

7. Statement of Rudolf Wobbe, Rudolf Wobbe, Salt Lake City, Utah, 17 April 1961, Source: Historical Department, Church of Jesus Christ of Latter-day Saints, Salt Lake City, Utah Statement of Rudolf Wobbe, Rudolf Wobbe, Salt Lake City, Utah, 17 April 1961, Source: Historical Department, Church of Jesus Christ of Latter-day Saints, Salt Lake City, Utah

8. Rudi Wobbe Oral History, interviewed by Matthew K. Heiss, Salt Lake City, Utah, 1988, typescript, The James Moyle Oral History Program, Archives, Historical Department of the Church of Jesus Christ of Latter-day Saints, Salt Lake City, Utah, p. 50

9. Blair Holmes, Alan Keele, and Karl-Heinz Schnibbe, *When Truth Was Treason*, Urbana and Chicago, Illinois: University of Illinois Press, 1995, p. 69

10. Blair Holmes, Alan Keele, and Karl-Heinz Schnibbe, *When Truth Was Treason*, Urbana and Chicago, Illinois: University of Illinois Press, 1995, p. 69

11. Blair Holmes, Alan Keele, and Karl-Heinz Schnibbe, *When Truth Was Treason*, Urbana and Chicago, Illinois: University of Illinois Press, 1995, p. 69; Rudi Wobbe Fireside [youth church lecture], 1987, transcribed by Richard Dewey and Heather Dewey, 1-4 February 2003, used by permission from Herta Wobbe, p. 13, see also Statement of Hans Kunkel, Source: *Begleitheft zur Austellung um das kurze Leben und Wirken des Helmuth Hübener,* Catalogue of the exhibit in the Hamburg Municipal District Archive (Stadtteilarchiv) of Hamm, 26 October – 10 December, 1992

12. Blair Holmes, Alan Keele, and Karl-Heinz Schnibbe, *When Truth Was Treason*, Urbana and Chicago, Illinois: University of Illinois Press, 1995, p. 69

13. "The Führer's New Clothes: Helmuth Hübener and the Dilemma of German Mormons in the Third Reich," unpublished essay by Alan F. Keele, Used by permission from Alan F. Keele. A shorter version of this essay was later published as an article in *Sunstone*, p. 43, citing interviews with Schnibbe and Wobbe

14. Rudi Wobbe Fireside [youth church lecture], 1987, transcribed by Richard Dewey and Heather Dewey, 1-4 February 2003, used by permission from Herta Wobbe, p. 13

15. Rudi Wobbe Fireside [youth church lecture], 1987, transcribed by Richard Dewey and Heather Dewey, 1-4 February 2003, used by permission from Herta Wobbe, p. 13

16. Rudi Wobbe Oral History, interviewed by Matthew K. Heiss, Salt Lake City, Utah, 1988, typescript, The James Moyle Oral History Program, Archives, Historical Department of the Church of Jesus Christ of Latter-day Saints, Salt Lake City, Utah, p. 49

17. Rudi Wobbe Fireside [youth church lecture], 1987, transcribed by Richard Dewey and Heather Dewey, 1-4 February 2003, used by permission from Herta Wobbe, P. 13

18. Statement of Rudolf Wobbe, Rudolf Wobbe, Salt Lake City, Utah, 17 April 1961, Source: Historical Department, Church of Jesus Christ of Latter-day Saints, Salt Lake City, Utah Statement of Rudolf Wobbe, Rudolf Wobbe, Salt Lake City, Utah, 17 April 1961, Source: Historical Department, Church of Jesus Christ of Latter-day Saints, Salt Lake City, Utah

19. Statement of Rudolf Wobbe, Rudolf Wobbe, Salt Lake City, Utah, 17 April 1961, Source: Historical Department, Church of Jesus Christ of Latter-day Saints, Salt Lake City, Utah Statement of Rudolf Wobbe, Rudolf Wobbe, Salt Lake City, Utah, 17 April 1961, Source: Historical Department, Church of Jesus Christ of Latter-day Saints, Salt Lake City, Utah

20. Rudi Wobbe Fireside [youth church lecture], 1987, transcribed by Richard Dewey and Heather Dewey, 1-4 February 2003, used by permission from Herta Wobbe, p. 13

21. Rudi Wobbe Oral History, interviewed by Matthew K. Heiss, Salt Lake City, Utah, 1988, typescript, The James Moyle Oral History Program, Archives, Historical Department of the Church of Jesus Christ of Latter-day Saints, Salt Lake City, Utah, p. 49

22. Rudi Wobbe Oral History, interviewed by Matthew K. Heiss, Salt Lake City, Utah, 1988, typescript, The James Moyle Oral History Program, Archives, Historical Department of the Church of Jesus Christ of Latter-day Saints, Salt Lake City, Utah, p. 56

23. Rudi Wobbe Fireside [youth church lecture], 1987, transcribed by Richard Dewey and Heather Dewey, 1-4 February 2003, used by permission from Herta Wobbe, p. 13

24. Blair Holmes, Alan Keele, and Karl-Heinz Schnibbe, *When Truth Was Treason*, Urbana and Chicago, Illinois: University of Illinois Press, 1995

25. Statement of Hans Kunkel, Source: *Begleitheft zur Austellung um das kurze Leben und Wirken des Helmuth Hübener,* Catalogue of the exhibit in the Hamburg Municipal District Archive (Stadtteilarchiv) of Hamm, 26 October – 10 December, 1992

26. Rudi Wobbe Oral History, interviewed by Matthew K. Heiss, Salt Lake City, Utah, 1988, typescript, The James Moyle Oral History Program, Archives, Historical Department of the Church of Jesus Christ of Latter-day Saints, Salt Lake City, Utah, p. 56

27. Rudi Wobbe Oral History, interviewed by Matthew K. Heiss, Salt Lake City, Utah, 1988, typescript, The James Moyle Oral History Program, Archives, Historical Department of the Church of Jesus Christ of Latter-day Saints, Salt Lake City, Utah, p. 49

28. Rudi Wobbe Fireside [youth church lecture], 1987, transcribed by Richard Dewey and Heather Dewey, 1-4 February 2003, used by permission from Herta Wobbe, p. 13

29. Rudi Wobbe Oral History, interviewed by Matthew K. Heiss, Salt Lake City, Utah, 1988, typescript, The James Moyle Oral History Program, Archives, Historical Department of the Church of Jesus Christ of Latter-day Saints, Salt Lake City, Utah, p. 48

30. Rudi Wobbe Oral History, interviewed by Matthew K. Heiss, Salt Lake City, Utah, 1988, typescript, The James Moyle Oral History Program, Archives, Historical Department of the Church of Jesus Christ of Latter-day Saints, Salt Lake City, Utah, p. 50

31. Rudi Wobbe Oral History, interviewed by Matthew K. Heiss, Salt Lake City, Utah, 1988, typescript, The James Moyle Oral History Program, Archives, Historical Department of the Church of Jesus Christ of Latter-day Saints, Salt Lake City, Utah, p. 50

32. Rudi Wobbe Oral History, interviewed by Matthew K. Heiss, Salt Lake City, Utah, 1988, typescript, The James Moyle Oral History Program, Archives, Historical Department of the Church of Jesus Christ of Latter-day Saints, Salt Lake City, Utah, p. 50

33. Karl Schnibbe interview with author, Salt Lake City, Utah, 16 September 1996, transcribed by Don Ricks, p. 10

34. Rudi Wobbe Fireside [youth church lecture], 1987, transcribed by Richard Dewey and Heather Dewey, 1-4 February 2003, used by permission from Herta Wobbe, p. 13, Rudi Wobbe and Jerry Borrowman, *Three Against Hitler*, (American Fork, Utah: Covenant Communications, 1992), p. 74; andRudi Wobbe Oral History, interviewed by Matthew K. Heiss, Salt Lake City, Utah, 1988, typescript, The James Moyle Oral History Program, Archives, Historical Department of the Church of Jesus Christ of Latter-day Saints, Salt Lake City, Utah, pp. 50-51

35. Rudi Wobbe Fireside [youth church lecture], 1987, transcribed by Richard Dewey and Heather Dewey, 1-4 February 2003, used by permission from Herta Wobbe, p.13

36. Rudi Wobbe and Jerry Borrowman, *Three Against Hitler,* (American Fork, Utah: Covenant Communications, 1992), p. 74

37. Werner, Johe, Die gleichgeschaltete Justiz [Stuttgart: Europaische Verlagsanstalt, 1967] p. 187, cited in Grunberger, Social History of the Third Reich, p. 126 and *When Truth Was Treason*, p. 347

CHAPTER 26

1. Verdict of the People's Court in the criminal case against Helmut Hübener, et al, on 11 August 1942: pt IV sec 1

2. Verdict of the People's Court in the criminal case against Helmut Hübener, et al, on 11 August 1942: pt V sec 1

3. Statement of Rudolf Wobbe, Rudolf Wobbe, Salt Lake City, Utah, 17 April 1961, Source: Historical Department, Church of Jesus Christ of Latter-day Saints, Salt Lake City, Utah Statement of Rudolf Wobbe, Rudolf Wobbe, Salt Lake City, Utah, 17 April 1961, Source: Historical Department, Church of Jesus Christ of Latter-day Saints, Salt Lake City, Utah

4. Rudolf G. Wobbe Oral History, Doublas F. Tobler and Alan F. Keele, 1974, typescript, The James Moyle Oral History Program, Archives, Historical Department of the Church of Jesus Christ of Latter-day Saints, Salt Lake City, Utah, p. 7

5. Rudi Wobbe Fireside [youth church lecture], 1987, transcribed by Richard Dewey and Heather Dewey, 1-4 February 2003, used by permission from Herta Wobbe, p. 11

6. Alan Keele, in 1996 conversation with author; *Truth & Conviction*, documentary film produced by Brigham Young

University, produced by Rick McFarland and Matt Whitaker, written and directed by Matt Whitaker, December 2003, one hour length

7. Rudolf G. Wobbe Oral History, Doublas F. Tobler and Alan F. Keele, 1974, typescript, The James Moyle Oral History Program, Archives, Historical Department of the Church of Jesus Christ of Latter-day Saints, Salt Lake City, Utah, p. 7

8. Verdict of the People's Court in the criminal case against Helmut Hübener, et al, on 11 August 1942: Findings and Sentencing of the Court, Part V, Section 1

9. Blair Holmes, Alan Keele, and Karl-Heinz Schnibbe, *When Truth Was Treason*, Urbana and Chicago, Illinois: University of Illinois Press, 1995

10. Rudi Wobbe Oral History, interviewed by Matthew K. Heiss, Salt Lake City, Utah, 1988, typescript, The James Moyle Oral History Program, Archives, Historical Department of the Church of Jesus Christ of Latter-day Saints, Salt Lake City, Utah, pp. 50-51

11. Verdict of the People's Court in the criminal case against Helmut Hübener, et al, on 11 August 1942: pt V sec 3

12. Verdict of the People's Court in the criminal case against Helmut Hübener, et al, on 11 August 1942: pt V sec 3

13. Rudi Wobbe Fireside [youth church lecture], 1987, transcribed by Richard Dewey and Heather Dewey, 1-4 February 2003, used by permission from Herta Wobbe, p. 14

14. Blair Holmes, Alan Keele, and Karl-Heinz Schnibbe, *When Truth Was Treason*, Urbana and Chicago, Illinois: University of Illinois Press, 1995

15. Rudi Wobbe Fireside [youth church lecture], 1987, transcribed by Richard Dewey and Heather Dewey, 1-4 February 2003, used by permission from Herta Wobbe, p. 14

16. Rudi Wobbe Oral History, interviewed by Matthew K. Heiss, Salt Lake City, Utah, 1988, typescript, The James Moyle Oral History Program, Archives, Historical Department of the Church of Jesus Christ of Latter-day Saints, Salt Lake City, Utah, p. 51

17. *Truth & Conviction*, documentary film produced by Brigham Young University, produced by Rick McFarland and Matt Whitaker, written and directed by Matt Whitaker, December 2003, one hour length

18. *Begleitheft zur Austellung um das kurze Leben und Wirken des Helmuth Hübener,* Catalogue of the exhibit in the Hamburg Municipal District Archive (Stadtteilarchiv) of Hamm, 26 October – 10 December, 1992

19. Statement of Marie Sommerfeld, Source: *Begleitheft zur Austellung um das kurze Leben und Wirken des Helmuth Hübener,* Catalogue of the exhibit in the Hamburg Municipal District Archive (Stadtteilarchiv) of Hamm, 26 October – 10 December, 1992

20. Statement of Rudolf Wobbe, Rudolf Wobbe, Salt Lake City, Utah, 17 April 1961, Source: Historical Department, Church of Jesus Christ of Latter-day Saints, Salt Lake City, Utah Statement of Rudolf Wobbe, Rudolf Wobbe, Salt Lake City, Utah, 17 April 1961, Source: Historical Department, Church of Jesus Christ of Latter-day Saints, Salt Lake City, Utah

21. Blair Holmes, Alan Keele, and Karl-Heinz Schnibbe, *When Truth Was Treason*, Urbana and Chicago, Illinois: University of Illinois Press, 1995

22. *Erster Deutscher Rundfunk*, Oct 27, 1992, *Jungendfunk: Aktuelle Erinnerung an jugendliche Hitlergegner*

23. *Verordnung zum Schutz gegen jugendliche Schwerverbrecher, Reichsgesetzblatt* [Oct 4, 1939], I, pt I, p. 2000

24. *Stadtblatt der Frankfurter Zeitung*, January 20, 1935, cited in Hellfeld and Klonne, *Die betrogene Generation*, p. 237

25. Blair Holmes, Alan Keele, and Karl-Heinz Schnibbe, *When Truth Was Treason*, Urbana and Chicago, Illinois: University of Illinois Press, 1995. In an interview with the author in 1996 Karl says the trial lasted one hour, ending at 10 A.M., but his autobiography is likely correct. Karl Schnibbe interview with author, Salt Lake City, Utah, 16 September 1996, transcribed by Don Ricks Rudi corroborates the report that it lasted all day.

26. Rudi Wobbe Fireside [youth church lecture], 1987, transcribed by Richard Dewey and Heather Dewey, 1-4 February 2003, used by permission from Herta Wobbe, p. 14

27. Rudi Wobbe Fireside [youth church lecture], 1987, transcribed by Richard Dewey and Heather Dewey, 1-4 February 2003, used by permission from Herta Wobbe, p. 14; see also Rudi Wobbe Oral History, interviewed by Matthew K. Heiss, Salt Lake City, Utah, 1988, typescript, The James Moyle Oral History Program, Archives, Historical Department of the Church of Jesus Christ of Latter-day Saints, Salt Lake City, Utah, p. 51

28. Blair Holmes, Alan Keele, and Karl-Heinz Schnibbe, *When Truth Was Treason*, Urbana and Chicago, Illinois: University of Illinois Press, 1995

29. Rudi Wobbe Oral History, interviewed by Matthew K. Heiss, Salt Lake City, Utah, 1988, typescript, The James Moyle Oral History Program, Archives, Historical Department of the Church of Jesus Christ of Latter-day Saints, Salt Lake City, Utah, p. 51

30. Rudi Wobbe Oral History, interviewed by Matthew K. Heiss, Salt Lake City, Utah, 1988, typescript, The James Moyle Oral History Program, Archives, Historical Department of the Church of Jesus Christ of Latter-day Saints, Salt Lake City, Utah, p. 51

31. Rudi Wobbe Oral History, interviewed by Matthew K. Heiss, Salt Lake City, Utah, 1988, typescript, The James Moyle Oral History Program, Archives, Historical Department of the

Church of Jesus Christ of Latter-day Saints, Salt Lake City, Utah, p. 51

32. Rudolf G. Wobbe Oral History, Doublas F. Tobler and Alan F. Keele, 1974, typescript, The James Moyle Oral History Program, Archives, Historical Department of the Church of Jesus Christ of Latter-day Saints, Salt Lake City, Utah, p. 8

33. Statement of Rudolf Wobbe, Rudolf Wobbe, Salt Lake City, Utah, 17 April 1961, Source: Historical Department, Church of Jesus Christ of Latter-day Saints, Salt Lake City, Utah Statement of Rudolf Wobbe, Rudolf Wobbe, Salt Lake City, Utah, 17 April 1961, Source: Historical Department, Church of Jesus Christ of Latter-day Saints, Salt Lake City, Utah

34. Blair Holmes, Alan Keele, and Karl-Heinz Schnibbe, *When Truth Was Treason*, Urbana and Chicago, Illinois: University of Illinois Press, 1995

35. Rudolf G. Wobbe Oral History, Doublas F. Tobler and Alan F. Keele, 1974, typescript, The James Moyle Oral History Program, Archives, Historical Department of the Church of Jesus Christ of Latter-day Saints, Salt Lake City, Utah, p. 8

36. Statement of Rudolf Wobbe, Rudolf Wobbe, Salt Lake City, Utah, 17 April 1961, Source: Historical Department, Church of Jesus Christ of Latter-day Saints, Salt Lake City, Utah Statement of Rudolf Wobbe, Rudolf Wobbe, Salt Lake City, Utah, 17 April 1961, Source: Historical Department, Church of Jesus Christ of Latter-day Saints, Salt Lake City, Utah

37. Blair Holmes, Alan Keele, and Karl-Heinz Schnibbe, *When Truth Was Treason*, Urbana and Chicago, Illinois: University of Illinois Press, 1995

38. *Truth & Conviction*, documentary film produced by Brigham Young University, produced by Rick McFarland and Matt Whitaker, written and directed by Matt Whitaker, December 2003, one hour length

39. Blair Holmes, Alan Keele, and Karl-Heinz Schnibbe, *When Truth Was Treason*, Urbana and Chicago, Illinois: University of Illinois Press, 1995

40. Rudi Wobbe Fireside [youth church lecture], 1987, transcribed by Richard Dewey and Heather Dewey, 1-4 February 2003, used by permission from Herta Wobbe, p. 14

41. *Truth & Conviction*, Brigham Young University documentary film produced by Matt Whitaker, written and directed by Rick McFarland, December 2002, 60 minutes

42. Rudi Wobbe Oral History, interviewed by Matthew K. Heiss, Salt Lake City, Utah, 1988, typescript, The James Moyle Oral History Program, Archives, Historical Department of the Church of Jesus Christ of Latter-day Saints, Salt Lake City, Utah, p. 51

43. Blair Holmes, Alan Keele, and Karl-Heinz Schnibbe, *When Truth Was Treason*, Urbana and Chicago, Illinois: University of Illinois Press, 1995

44. *Truth & Conviction*, documentary film produced by Brigham Young University, produced by Rick McFarland and Matt Whitaker, written and directed by Matt Whitaker, December 2003, one hour length

45. *Salt Lake Tribune*, 13 May 2003

46. Rudi Wobbe Oral History, interviewed by Matthew K. Heiss, Salt Lake City, Utah, 1988, typescript, The James Moyle Oral History Program, Archives, Historical Department of the Church of Jesus Christ of Latter-day Saints, Salt Lake City, Utah, p. 51

47. Rudi Wobbe Fireside [youth church lecture], 1987, transcribed by Richard Dewey and Heather Dewey, 1-4 February 2003, used by permission from Herta Wobbe, p. 14

48. Blair Holmes, Alan Keele, and Karl-Heinz Schnibbe, *When Truth Was Treason*, Urbana and Chicago, Illinois: University of Illinois Press, 1995

49. *Truth & Conviction*, documentary film produced by Brigham Young University, produced by Rick McFarland and Matt Whitaker, written and directed by Matt Whitaker, December 2003, one hour length

50. Rudi Wobbe Oral History, interviewed by Matthew K. Heiss, Salt Lake City, Utah, 1988, typescript, The James Moyle Oral History Program, Archives, Historical Department of the Church of Jesus Christ of Latter-day Saints, Salt Lake City, Utah, p. 51

CHAPTER 27

1. Rudolf G. Wobbe Oral History, Doublas F. Tobler and Alan F. Keele, 1974, typescript, The James Moyle Oral History Program, Archives, Historical Department of the Church of Jesus Christ of Latter-day Saints, Salt Lake City, Utah, p. 8

2. Rudolf G. Wobbe Oral History, Doublas F. Tobler and Alan F. Keele, 1974, typescript, The James Moyle Oral History Program, Archives, Historical Department of the Church of Jesus Christ of Latter-day Saints, Salt Lake City, Utah, p. 8

3. Blair Holmes, Alan Keele, and Karl-Heinz Schnibbe, *When Truth Was Treason*, Urbana and Chicago, Illinois: University of Illinois Press, 1995

4. Statement of Rudolf Wobbe, Rudolf Wobbe, Salt Lake City, Utah, 17 April 1961, Source: Historical Department, Church of Jesus Christ of Latter-day Saints, Salt Lake City, Utah Statement of Rudolf Wobbe, Rudolf Wobbe, Salt Lake City, Utah, 17 April 1961, Source: Historical Department, Church of Jesus Christ of Latter-day Saints, Salt Lake City, Utah

5. Statement of Rudolf Wobbe, Rudolf Wobbe, Salt Lake City, Utah, 17 April 1961, Source: Historical Department, Church of Jesus Christ of Latter-day Saints, Salt Lake City, Utah Statement of Rudolf Wobbe, Rudolf Wobbe, Salt Lake City, Utah, 17 April 1961, Source: Historical Department, Church of Jesus Christ of Latter-day Saints, Salt Lake City, Utah

6. Rudi Wobbe Oral History, interviewed by Matthew K. Heiss, Salt Lake City, Utah, 1988, typescript, The James Moyle Oral History Program, Archives, Historical Department of the Church of Jesus Christ of Latter-day Saints, Salt Lake City, Utah, p. 52

7. Statement of Rudolf Wobbe, Rudolf Wobbe, Salt Lake City, Utah, 17 April 1961, Source: Historical Department, Church of Jesus Christ of Latter-day Saints, Salt Lake City, Utah Statement of Rudolf Wobbe, Rudolf Wobbe, Salt Lake City, Utah, 17 April 1961, Source: Historical Department, Church of Jesus Christ of Latter-day Saints, Salt Lake City, Utah

8. Rudi Wobbe Oral History, interviewed by Matthew K. Heiss, Salt Lake City, Utah, 1988, typescript, The James Moyle Oral History Program, Archives, Historical Department of the Church of Jesus Christ of Latter-day Saints, Salt Lake City, Utah, p. 52

9. Rudi Wobbe Oral History, interviewed by Matthew K. Heiss, Salt Lake City, Utah, 1988, typescript, The James Moyle Oral History Program, Archives, Historical Department of the Church of Jesus Christ of Latter-day Saints, Salt Lake City, Utah, p. 55

10. Statement of Rudolf Wobbe, Rudolf Wobbe, Salt Lake City, Utah, 17 April 1961, Source: Historical Department, Church of Jesus Christ of Latter-day Saints, Salt Lake City, Utah Statement of Rudolf Wobbe, Rudolf Wobbe, Salt Lake City, Utah, 17 April 1961, Source: Historical Department, Church of Jesus Christ of Latter-day Saints, Salt Lake City, Utah

11. Rudi Wobbe Oral History, interviewed by Matthew K. Heiss, Salt Lake City, Utah, 1988, typescript, The James Moyle Oral History Program, Archives, Historical Department of the Church of Jesus Christ of Latter-day Saints, Salt Lake City, Utah, p. 52

12. Statement of Rudolf Wobbe, Rudolf Wobbe, Salt Lake City, Utah, 17 April 1961, Source: Historical Department, Church of Jesus Christ of Latter-day Saints, Salt Lake City, Utah Statement of Rudolf Wobbe, Rudolf Wobbe, Salt Lake City, Utah, 17 April 1961, Source: Historical Department, Church of Jesus Christ of Latter-day Saints, Salt Lake City, Utah

13. Rudi Wobbe Oral History, interviewed by Matthew K. Heiss, Salt Lake City, Utah, 1988, typescript, The James Moyle Oral History Program, Archives, Historical Department of the Church of Jesus Christ of Latter-day Saints, Salt Lake City, Utah, p. 52

14. Statement of Rudolf Wobbe, Rudolf Wobbe, Salt Lake City, Utah, 17 April 1961, Source: Historical Department, Church of Jesus Christ of Latter-day Saints, Salt Lake City, Utah Statement of Rudolf Wobbe, Rudolf Wobbe, Salt Lake City, Utah, 17 April 1961, Source: Historical Department, Church of Jesus Christ of Latter-day Saints, Salt Lake City, Utah

15. Rudi Wobbe Oral History, interviewed by Matthew K. Heiss, Salt Lake City, Utah, 1988, typescript, The James Moyle Oral History Program, Archives, Historical Department of the Church of Jesus Christ of Latter-day Saints, Salt Lake City, Utah, p. 55

16. Rudi Wobbe Oral History, interviewed by Matthew K. Heiss, Salt Lake City, Utah, 1988, typescript, The James Moyle Oral History Program, Archives, Historical Department of the Church of Jesus Christ of Latter-day Saints, Salt Lake City, Utah, p. 52

17. Rudi Wobbe Oral History, interviewed by Matthew K. Heiss, Salt Lake City, Utah, 1988, typescript, The James Moyle Oral

History Program, Archives, Historical Department of the Church of Jesus Christ of Latter-day Saints, Salt Lake City, Utah, p. 55

18. Statement of Rudolf Wobbe, Rudolf Wobbe, Salt Lake City, Utah, 17 April 1961, Source: Historical Department, Church of Jesus Christ of Latter-day Saints, Salt Lake City, Utah Statement of Rudolf Wobbe, Rudolf Wobbe, Salt Lake City, Utah, 17 April 1961, Source: Historical Department, Church of Jesus Christ of Latter-day Saints, Salt Lake City, Utah

19. Rudi Wobbe Oral History, interviewed by Matthew K. Heiss, Salt Lake City, Utah, 1988, typescript, The James Moyle Oral History Program, Archives, Historical Department of the Church of Jesus Christ of Latter-day Saints, Salt Lake City, Utah, p. 55

20. Rudolf G. Wobbe Oral History, Doublas F. Tobler and Alan F. Keele, 1974, typescript, The James Moyle Oral History Program, Archives, Historical Department of the Church of Jesus Christ of Latter-day Saints, Salt Lake City, Utah, p. 8

21. Rudi Wobbe Oral History, interviewed by Matthew K. Heiss, Salt Lake City, Utah, 1988, typescript, The James Moyle Oral History Program, Archives, Historical Department of the Church of Jesus Christ of Latter-day Saints, Salt Lake City, Utah, p. 73

22. Rudi Wobbe and Jerry Borrowman, *Three Against Hitler,* (American Fork, Utah: Covenant Communications, 1992), p. 81

23. Blair Holmes, Alan Keele, and Karl-Heinz Schnibbe, *When Truth Was Treason,* Urbana and Chicago, Illinois: University of Illinois Press, 1995, p. 66

24. Blair Holmes, Alan Keele, and Karl-Heinz Schnibbe, *When Truth Was Treason,* Urbana and Chicago, Illinois: University of Illinois Press, 1995, p. 71

25. Rudi Wobbe and Jerry Borrowman, *Three Against Hitler,* (American Fork, Utah: Covenant Communications, 1992), p. 81

26. Rudi Wobbe and Jerry Borrowman, *Three Against Hitler,* (American Fork, Utah: Covenant Communications, 1992), p. 81

27. Rudi Wobbe and Jerry Borrowman, *Three Against Hitler,* (American Fork, Utah: Covenant Communications, 1992), p. 82

28. Blair Holmes, Alan Keele, and Karl-Heinz Schnibbe, *When Truth Was Treason,* Urbana and Chicago, Illinois: University of Illinois Press, 1995, p. 73

29. Rudi Wobbe and Jerry Borrowman, *Three Against Hitler,* (American Fork, Utah: Covenant Communications, 1992), p. 83

30. Statement of Marie Sommerfeld, Source: *Begleitheft zur Austellung um das kurze Leben und Wirken des Helmuth Hübener,* Catalogue of the exhibit in the Hamburg Municipal District Archive (Stadtteilarchiv) of Hamm, 26 October – 10 December, 1992

31. Letter from Emma Hübener, Hamburg, 14 August 1942, Attorney General at the People's Court, Berlin w. 9, Bellevuestrasse, 15, File Reference 8j127/42g

32. Statement of Marie Sommerfeld, Source: *Begleitheft zur Austellung um das kurze Leben und Wirken des Helmuth Hübener,* Catalogue of the exhibit in the Hamburg Municipal District Archive (Stadtteilarchiv) of Hamm, 26 October – 10 December, 1992

33. Statement of Marie Sommerfeld, Source: *Begleitheft zur Austellung um das kurze Leben und Wirken des Helmuth Hübener,* Catalogue of the exhibit in the Hamburg Municipal District Archive (Stadtteilarchiv) of Hamm, 26 October – 10 December, 1992

34. Statement of Marie Sommerfeld, Source: *Begleitheft zur Austellung um das kurze Leben und Wirken des Helmuth Hübener,* Catalogue of the exhibit in the Hamburg Municipal District Archive (Stadtteilarchiv) of Hamm, 26 October – 10 December, 1992

35. Statement of Hans Kunkel, Source: *Begleitheft zur Austellung um das kurze Leben und Wirken des Helmuth Hübener,* Catalogue of the exhibit in the Hamburg Municipal District Archive (Stadtteilarchiv) of Hamm, 26 October – 10 December, 1992

36. Statement of Marie Sommerfeld, Source: *Begleitheft zur Austellung um das kurze Leben und Wirken des Helmuth Hübener,* Catalogue of the exhibit in the Hamburg Municipal District Archive (Stadtteilarchiv) of Hamm, 26 October – 10 December, 1992

37. Letter from Dr. Knie (Helmuth's attorney) to The Attorney General of the People's Court, 17 August 1942

38. Letter from Secret State Police, Secret State Police Office, IV A t c-8185/42, Berlin SW II, 28 August 1942, Prinz-Albrecht-Strabe 8, Express Letter, To the Attorney General at the People's Court in Berlin W 9, Bellevuestrabe 15

39. Letter from Notary Judicial Counsel W. Grotefend to The Attorney General at the People's Court, 15 August 1942; Statement of Marie Sommerfeld, Source: *Begleitheft zur Austellung um das kurze Leben und Wirken des Helmuth Hübener,* Catalogue of the exhibit in the Hamburg Municipal District Archive (Stadtteilarchiv) of Hamm, 26 October – 10 December, 1992; Statement of Hans Kunkel, Source: *Begleitheft zur Austellung um das kurze Leben und Wirken des Helmuth Hübener,* Catalogue of the exhibit in the Hamburg Municipal District Archive (Stadtteilarchiv) of Hamm, 26 October – 10 December, 1992

40. Statement of Marie Sommerfeld, Source: *Begleitheft zur Austellung um das kurze Leben und Wirken des Helmuth Hübener,* Catalogue of the exhibit in the Hamburg Municipal

District Archive (Stadtteilarchiv) of Hamm, 26 October – 10 December, 1992; and Statement of Hans Kunkel, Source: *Begleitheft zur Austellung um das kurze Leben und Wirken des Helmuth Hübener,* Catalogue of the exhibit in the Hamburg Municipal District Archive (Stadtteilarchiv) of Hamm, 26 October – 10 December, 1992

41. Statement of Marie Sommerfeld, Source: *Begleitheft zur Austellung um das kurze Leben und Wirken des Helmuth Hübener,* Catalogue of the exhibit in the Hamburg Municipal District Archive (Stadtteilarchiv) of Hamm, 26 October – 10 December, 1992

42. *Versuch einer Familiengeschichte in Begleitheft,* p. 3

43. "The Führer's New Clothes: Helmuth Hübener and the Dilemma of German Mormons in the Third Reich," unpublished essay by Alan F. Keele, Used by permission from Alan F. Keele. A shorter version of this essay was later published as an article in *Sunstone,* p. 12

44. "The Führer's New Clothes: Helmuth Hübener and the Dilemma of German Mormons in the Third Reich," unpublished essay by Alan F. Keele, Used by permission from Alan F. Keele. A shorter version of this essay was later published as an article in *Sunstone,* p. 12, 23

45. "The Führer's New Clothes: Helmuth Hübener and the Dilemma of German Mormons in the Third Reich," unpublished essay by Alan F. Keele, Used by permission from Alan F. Keele. A shorter version of this essay was later published as an article in *Sunstone,* p. 12

46. Letter from National Socialist German Worker's Party, Hitler Youth/Youth Leadership of the Reich, Office of the Hitler Youth Jurisdiction, 182/42 G. 26 Gn. Ni./Ka., Berlin, 15 September 1942, To the Chancellery of the Führer of the NSDAP, Central Office

47. Blair Holmes, Alan Keele, and Karl-Heinz Schnibbe, *When Truth Was Treason*, Urbana and Chicago, Illinois: University of Illinois Press, 1995

48. Karl Schnibbe comment to Alan Keele, told to Richard Dewey Oct 1995

49. Letter from The National Minister of Justice, Berlin 19 October 1942, Ivg 10A 916/42g, SECRET Urgent!, To the Attorney General at the People's Court in Berlin, Personally or his official representative

50. Letter from The Attorney General of the People's Court, Berlin, 27 October 1942, SJ 127/42 [source: Institut für Marxismus-Leninismus]

C H A P T E R   2 8

1. Statement of Otto Berndt, Ca. 1961, Source: Historical Department, Church of Jesus Christ of Latter-day Saints, Salt Lake City, Utah

2. Statement of Otto Berndt, Ca. 1961, Source: Historical Department, Church of Jesus Christ of Latter-day Saints, Salt Lake City, Utah and Statement of Marie Sommerfeld, Source: *Begleitheft zur Austellung um das kurze Leben und Wirken des Helmuth Hübener*, Catalogue of the exhibit in the Hamburg Municipal District Archive (Stadtteilarchiv) of Hamm, 26 October – 10 December, 1992

3. Statement of Marie Sommerfeld, Source: *Begleitheft zur Austellung um das kurze Leben und Wirken des Helmuth Hübener*, Catalogue of the exhibit in the Hamburg Municipal District Archive (Stadtteilarchiv) of Hamm, 26 October – 10 December, 1992; Gerhard Kunkel interview #1 with author, 10 October 1996

4. Hans and Charlotte Kunkel interview with author, Salt Lake City, Utah, 18 October 1996, p. 4 and Statement of

Marie Sommerfeld, Source: *Begleitheft zur Austellung um das kurze Leben und Wirken des Helmuth Hübener,* Catalogue of the exhibit in the Hamburg Municipal District Archive (Stadtteilarchiv) of Hamm, 26 October – 10 December, 1992

5. Letter from Helmuth Hübener to Marie Sommerfeld and family, 27 October 1942; and Statement of Marie Sommerfeld, Source: *Begleitheft zur Austellung um das kurze Leben und Wirken des Helmuth Hübener,* Catalogue of the exhibit in the Hamburg Municipal District Archive (Stadtteilarchiv) of Hamm, 26 October – 10 December, 1992

6. Arthur and Marie Sommerfeld interview with author, Salt Lake City, Utah, 18 October 1996, p. 16

7. Statement of Marie Sommerfeld, Source: *Begleitheft zur Austellung um das kurze Leben und Wirken des Helmuth Hübener,* Catalogue of the exhibit in the Hamburg Municipal District Archive (Stadtteilarchiv) of Hamm, 26 October – 10 December, 1992

8. Statement of Rudolf Wobbe, Rudolf Wobbe, Salt Lake City, Utah, 17 April 1961, Source: Historical Department, Church of Jesus Christ of Latter-day Saints, Salt Lake City, Utah Statement of Rudolf Wobbe, Rudolf Wobbe, Salt Lake City, Utah, 17 April 1961, Source: Historical Department, Church of Jesus Christ of Latter-day Saints, Salt Lake City, Utah

9. Arthur and Marie Sommerfeld interview with author, Salt Lake City, Utah, 18 October 1996, p.14

10. Arthur and Marie Sommerfeld interview with author, Salt Lake City, Utah, 18 October 1996

11. Statement of Marie Sommerfeld, Source: *Begleitheft zur Austellung um das kurze Leben und Wirken des Helmuth Hübener,* Catalogue of the exhibit in the Hamburg Municipal District Archive (Stadtteilarchiv) of Hamm, 26 October – 10 December, 1992

12. Statement of Hedi Radtke Sommerfeld, Source: *Begleitheft zur Austellung um das kurze Leben und Wirken des Helmuth Hübener*, Catalogue of the exhibit in the Hamburg Municipal District Archive (Stadtteilarchiv) of Hamm, 26 October – 10 December

13. Statement of Marie Sommerfeld, Source: *Begleitheft zur Austellung um das kurze Leben und Wirken des Helmuth Hübener*, Catalogue of the exhibit in the Hamburg Municipal District Archive (Stadtteilarchiv) of Hamm, 26 October – 10 December, 1992

14. *Truth & Conviction*, documentary film produced by Brigham Young University, produced by Rick McFarland and Matt Whitaker, written and directed by Matt Whitaker, December 2003, one hour length

15. Letter from Helmuth Hübener to Marie Sommerfeld and family, 27 October 1942; Statement of Marie Sommerfeld, Source: *Begleitheft zur Austellung um das kurze Leben und Wirken des Helmuth Hübener*, Catalogue of the exhibit in the Hamburg Municipal District Archive (Stadtteilarchiv) of Hamm, 26 October – 10 December, 1992

16. Letter from Helmuth Hübener to Marie Sommerfeld and family, 27 October 1942

17. *Truth & Conviction*, documentary film produced by Brigham Young University, produced by Rick McFarland and Matt Whitaker, written and directed by Matt Whitaker, December 2003, one hour length

18. Gerhard Kunkel interview #1 with author, 10 October 1996, p. 14

19. Gerhard Kunkel interview #2 with author, 25 February 2003, p. 13

20. Gerhard Kunkel interview #1 with author, 10 October 1996, p. 14

21. Gerhard Kunkel interview #1 with author, 10 October 1996, p. 15

22. Statement of Otto Berndt, Ca. 1961, Source: Historical Department, Church of Jesus Christ of Latter-day Saints, Salt Lake City, Utah

23. Statement of Hans Kunkel, Source: *Begleitheft zur Austellung um das kurze Leben und Wirken des Helmuth Hübener,* Catalogue of the exhibit in the Hamburg Municipal District Archive (Stadtteilarchiv) of Hamm, 26 October – 10 December, 1992

24. Hans and Charlotte Kunkel interview with author, Salt Lake City, Utah, 18 October 1996, p. 4

25. Hans and Charlotte Kunkel interview with author, Salt Lake City, Utah, 18 October 1996p. 5

26. Hans and Charlotte Kunkel interview with author, Salt Lake City, Utah, 18 October 1996, p. 4

27. Hans and Charlotte Kunkel interview with author, Salt Lake City, Utah, 18 October 1996, p. 5

28. Statement of Marie Sommerfeld, Source: *Begleitheft zur Austellung um das kurze Leben und Wirken des Helmuth Hübener,* Catalogue of the exhibit in the Hamburg Municipal District Archive (Stadtteilarchiv) of Hamm, 26 October – 10 December, 1992

29. Statement of Marie Sommerfeld, Source: *Begleitheft zur Austellung um das kurze Leben und Wirken des Helmuth Hübener,* Catalogue of the exhibit in the Hamburg Municipal District Archive (Stadtteilarchiv) of Hamm, 26 October – 10 December, 1992

30. Marie Friebel Sommerfeld 1897-1984, Interviewed in German by Douglas Tobler and Alan Keele, 1974 : (13 leaves in English; Matthew K. Heiss later wrote Iris Schmidt on 17 Sep 1992 saying the Sommerfeld interview was never fully edited; typed ca. 1985 by Karen H. Pyper), p. 4

31. Statement of Marie Sommerfeld, Source: *Begleitheft zur Austellung um das kurze Leben und Wirken des Helmuth Hübener,* Catalogue of the exhibit in the Hamburg Municipal District Archive (Stadtteilarchiv) of Hamm, 26 October – 10 December, 1992

32. Letter from The Attorney General Berlin 27 October 1942, of the People's Court, 8J 127/42, Source: Institut fur Marxismus-Leninismus

33. Letter from The National Minister of Justice, Berlin 19 October 1942, Ivg 10A 916/42g, SECRET Urgent!, To the Attorney General at the People's Court in Berlin, Personally or his official representative

34. No. 39 of the Reichs Ordinance of February 19, 1939

35. Statement of Hans Kunkel, Source: *Begleitheft zur Austellung um das kurze Leben und Wirken des Helmuth Hübener,* Catalogue of the exhibit in the Hamburg Municipal District Archive (Stadtteilarchiv) of Hamm, 26 October – 10 December, 1992

36. Statement of Hans Kunkel, Source: *Begleitheft zur Austellung um das kurze Leben und Wirken des Helmuth Hübener,* Catalogue of the exhibit in the Hamburg Municipal District Archive (Stadtteilarchiv) of Hamm, 26 October – 10 December, 1992

C H A P T E R   2 9

1. "The Führer's New Clothes: Helmuth Hübener and the Dilemma of German Mormons in the Third Reich," unpublished essay by Alan F. Keele, Used by permission from Alan F. Keele. A shorter version of this essay was later published as an article in *Sunstone*, p. 23

2. Hans and Charlotte Kunkel interview with author, Salt Lake City, Utah, 18 October 1996p. 4

3. Statement of Hans Kunkel, Source: *Begleitheft zur Austellung um das kurze Leben und Wirken des Helmuth Hübener,* Catalogue of the exhibit in the Hamburg Municipal District Archive (Stadtteilarchiv) of Hamm, 26 October – 10 December, 1992

4. *Ibid.* Hans Kunkel' wife Charlotte was present at the time he received word of Helmuth's death and agrees with this version. Hans and Charlotte Kunkel interview with author, Salt Lake City, Utah, 18 October 1996, p. 2] Another version has it that a red placard jumped out at him on 28 October, while his mother learned about it through the newspaper, Statement of Hans Kunkel, Source: *Begleitheft zur Austellung um das kurze Leben und Wirken des Helmuth Hübener,* Catalogue of the exhibit in the Hamburg Municipal District Archive (Stadtteilarchiv) of Hamm, 26 October – 10 December, 1992 which would have also been 28 October.

5. MS 3245, Author: Sander, Ulrich; title: Letter, 1962, Oct 2, Hamburg, Germany to *Die Presse und die Jugendorganisationen* in Germany, which includes the newspaper cited plus 3 other newspaper articles dated 5 June 1948, 31 July 1948, 6 Jan 1960, all of which are one-half to one page in length.

6. Otto Berndt Oral History, interviewed by Douglas F. Tobler, Salt Lake City, Utah, 1974, typescript, The James Moyle Oral History Program, Archives, Historical Department of the Church of Jesus Christ of Latter-day Saints, Salt Lake City, Utah, p. 40

7. Statement of Hans Kunkel, Source: *Begleitheft zur Austellung um das kurze Leben und Wirken des Helmuth Hübener,* Catalogue of the exhibit in the Hamburg Municipal District Archive (Stadtteilarchiv) of Hamm, 26 October – 10 December, 1992

8. Statement of Marie Sommerfeld, Source: *Begleitheft zur Austellung um das kurze Leben und Wirken des Helmuth Hübener,* Catalogue of the exhibit in the Hamburg Municipal District Archive (Stadtteilarchiv) of Hamm, 26 October – 10 December, 1992

9. Statement of Friedrich Peters, born 1920, Source: *Begleitheft zur Austellung um das kurze Leben und Wirken des Helmuth Hübener,* Catalogue of the exhibit in the Hamburg Municipal District Archive (Stadtteilarchiv) of Hamm, 26 October – 10 December

10. Rudi Wobbe and Jerry Borrowman, *Three Against Hitler,* (American Fork, Utah: Covenant Communications, 1992), p. 83

11. Rudi Wobbe and Jerry Borrowman, *Three Against Hitler,* (American Fork, Utah: Covenant Communications, 1992), p. 83

12. Rudi Wobbe and Jerry Borrowman, *Three Against Hitler,* (American Fork, Utah: Covenant Communications, 1992), pp. 83-84

13. Rudi Wobbe Fireside [youth church lecture], 1987, transcribed by Richard Dewey and Heather Dewey, 1-4 February 2003, used by permission from Herta Wobbe, p. 15

14. MS 15335, starting on from 515 of microfilm copy at church archives; author: Dahl, John Albert; title: Book Review, 1997, Oct 14; Dahl points out that this treatment of an LDS male who refused to join the SA goes against the norm since the SA brigade was voluntary.

C H A P T E R   3 0

1. *Truth & Conviction,* documentary film produced by Brigham Young University, produced by Rick McFarland and Matt Whitaker, written and directed by Matt Whitaker, December 2003, one hour length

2. *Truth & Conviction,* documentary film produced by Brigham Young University, produced by Rick McFarland and Matt Whitaker, written and directed by Matt Whitaker, December 2003, one hour length

3. Gerhard Kunkel interview #1 with author, 10 October 1996, p. 15

4. "The Führer's New Clothes: Helmuth Hübener and the Dilemma of German Mormons in the Third Reich," unpublished essay by Alan F. Keele, Used by permission from Alan F. Keele. A shorter version of this essay was later published as an article in *Sunstone*, p. 16

5. Statement of Hans Kunkel, Source: *Begleitheft zur Austellung um das kurze Leben und Wirken des Helmuth Hübener,* Catalogue of the exhibit in the Hamburg Municipal District Archive (Stadtteilarchiv) of Hamm, 26 October – 10 December, 1992

6. Gerhard Kunkel interview #1 with author, 10 October 1996

7. Also Statement of Hans Kunkel, Source: *Begleitheft zur Austellung um das kurze Leben und Wirken des Helmuth Hübener,* Catalogue of the exhibit in the Hamburg Municipal District Archive (Stadtteilarchiv) of Hamm, 26 October – 10 December, 1992

8. Gerhard Kunkel interview #2 with author, 25 February 2003, pp. 13-14

9. Gerhard Kunkel interview #1 with author, 10 October 1996, p. 15

10. "The Führer's New Clothes: Helmuth Hübener and the Dilemma of German Mormons in the Third Reich," unpublished essay by Alan F. Keele, Used by permission from Alan F. Keele. A shorter version of this essay was later published as an article in *Sunstone*, p. 16

11. Gerhard Kunkel interview #2 with author, 25 February 2003, p. 14

12. Gerhard Kunkel interview #1 with author, 10 October 1996, pp. 15-16

13. "The Führer's New Clothes: Helmuth Hübener and the Dilemma of German Mormons in the Third Reich," unpublished essay by Alan F. Keele, Used by permission from Alan F. Keele. A shorter version of this essay was later published as an article in *Sunstone*, p. 16

14. Gerhard Kunkel interview #1 with author, 10 October 1996, pp. 15-16

15. Gerhard Kunkel interview #1 with author, 10 October 1996, p. 14

16. Gerhard Kunkel interview #1 with author, 10 October 1996, p. 18

17. Gerhard Kunkel interview #2 with author, 25 February 2003, p. 17

18. Gerhard Kunkel interview #1 with author, 10 October 1996, p. 18

19. Gerhard Kunkel interview #1 with author, 10 October 1996, pp. 16-17

20. Gerhard Kunkel interview #1 with author, 10 October 1996, p. 14

21. *Ibid.*

22. Gerhard Kunkel interview #1 with author, 10 October 1996, pp. 16-17

23. Gerhard Kunkel interview #2 with author, 25 February 2003, p. 14

24. Gerhard Kunkel interview #2 with author, 25 February 2003, p. 15

25. Gerhard Kunkel interview #2 with author, 25 February 2003, p. 15

26. Gerhard Kunkel interview #2 with author, 25 February 2003, p. 15

27. Gerhard Kunkel interview #1 with author, 10 October 1996, p. 18

28. Hans and Charlotte Kunkel interview with author, Salt Lake City, Utah, 18 October 1996, p. 6

29. Gerhard Kunkel interview #1 with author, 10 October 1996, pp. 18-20

CHAPTER 31

1. Noble Frankland, *Bomber Offensive: The Devastation of Europe* [New York: Random House, 1970], p. 69

2. Hilde Prüss Müller, interview #2 with author, 20 October 2003

3. Rudi Wobbe and Jerry Borrowman, *Three Against Hitler,* (American Fork, Utah: Covenant Communications, 1992), p. 101

4. Rudi Wobbe and Jerry Borrowman, *Three Against Hitler,* (American Fork, Utah: Covenant Communications, 1992), p. 101

5. Blair Holmes, Alan Keele, and Karl-Heinz Schnibbe, *When Truth Was Treason*, Urbana and Chicago, Illinois: University of Illinois Press, 1995, p. 74

6. Hans and Charlotte Kunkel interview with author, Salt Lake City, Utah, 18 October 1996, p. 6

7. Blair Holmes, Alan Keele, and Karl-Heinz Schnibbe, *When Truth Was Treason*, Urbana and Chicago, Illinois: University of Illinois Press, 1995, p. 74

8. Rudi Wobbe Oral History, interviewed by Matthew K. Heiss, Salt Lake City, Utah, 1988, typescript, The James Moyle Oral History Program, Archives, Historical Department of the Church of Jesus Christ of Latter-day Saints, Salt Lake City, Utah, p. 57

9. Noble Frankland, *Bomber Offensive: The Devastation of Europe* [New York: Random House, 1970], p. 69

10. Gerhard Kunkel interview #1 with author, 10 October 1996, p. 25

11. Arthur and Marie Sommerfeld interview with author, Salt Lake City, Utah, 18 October 1996, p. 3

12. Arthur and Marie Sommerfeld interview with author, Salt Lake City, Utah, 18 October 1996, p.3

13. Hans and Charlotte Kunkel interview with author, Salt Lake City, Utah, 18 October 1996, p. 6

14. Hilde Prüss Müller interview #2 with author 20 Oct 2003

15. Hilde Prüss Müller interview #2 with author 20 Oct 2003

16. Hilde Prüss Müller interview #3 with author 8 November 2003

17. Werner Schmidt interview with author, 20 October 2003

18. Werner Schmidt interview with author, 20 October 2003

19. Werner Schmidt interview with author, 20 October 2003

20. Herta Schmidt Wobbe conversations 1996 - 2003, and Werner Schmidt interview with author, 20 October 2003

CHAPTER 32

1. Also Statement of Hans Kunkel, Source: *Begleitheft zur Austellung um das kurze Leben und Wirken des Helmuth Hübener,* Catalogue of the exhibit in the Hamburg Municipal District Archive (Stadtteilarchiv) of Hamm, 26 October – 10 December, 1992

2. Gerhard Kunkel interview #1 with author, 10 October 1996, pp. 20-21

3. Gerhard Kunkel interview #2 with author, 25 February 2003, p. 9

4. Gerhard Kunkel interview #2 with author, 25 February 2003, p. 17

5. Gerhard Kunkel interview #1 with author, 10 October 1996, p. 21

6. Hans and Charlotte Kunkel interview with author, Salt Lake City, Utah, 18 October 1996, p. 6

7. Hans and Charlotte Kunkel interview with author, Salt Lake City, Utah, 18 October 1996, p. 6

8. Hans and Charlotte Kunkel interview with author, Salt Lake City, Utah, 18 October 1996, p. 6

9. Hans and Charlotte Kunkel interview with author, Salt Lake City, Utah, 18 October 1996, p. 6

10. Hans and Charlotte Kunkel interview with author, Salt Lake City, Utah, 18 October 1996, p. 6

11. Hans and Charlotte Kunkel interview with author, Salt Lake City, Utah, 18 October 1996, pp. 6-7

12. Arthur and Marie Sommerfeld interview with author, 18 October 1996, p. 4

13. Arthur and Marie Sommerfeld interview with author, Salt Lake City, Utah, 18 October 1996, p. 5

14. Arthur and Marie Sommerfeld interview with author, Salt Lake City, Utah, 18 October 1996, p. 5

15. Arthur and Marie Sommerfeld interview with author, Salt Lake City, Utah, 18 October 1996, p. 4

16. Arthur and Marie Sommerfeld interview with author, Salt Lake City, Utah, 18 October 1996, p. 5

17. Arthur and Marie Sommerfeld interview with author, Salt Lake City, Utah, 18 October 1996, p. 6

18. Arthur and Marie Sommerfeld interview with author, Salt Lake City, Utah, 18 October 1996, p. 5

19. Hilde Prüss Müller interviews with author 18 October 2003 and 8 November 2003

20. Otto Berndt Oral History, interviewed by Douglas F. Tobler, Salt Lake City, Utah, 1974, typescript, The James Moyle Oral History Program, Archives, Historical Department of the Church of Jesus Christ of Latter-day Saints, Salt Lake City, Utah, p. 50

21. Otto Berndt Oral History, interviewed by Douglas F. Tobler, Salt Lake City, Utah, 1974, typescript, The James Moyle Oral History Program, Archives, Historical Department of the Church of Jesus Christ of Latter-day Saints, Salt Lake City, Utah, p. 51

22. Otto Berndt Oral History, interviewed by Douglas F. Tobler, Salt Lake City, Utah, 1974, typescript, The James Moyle Oral History Program, Archives, Historical Department of the Church of Jesus Christ of Latter-day Saints, Salt Lake City, Utah, p. 51

23. Otto Berndt Oral History, interviewed by Douglas F. Tobler, Salt Lake City, Utah, 1974, typescript, The James Moyle Oral History Program, Archives, Historical Department of the Church of Jesus Christ of Latter-day Saints, Salt Lake City, Utah, p. 51

24. Otto Berndt Oral History, interviewed by Douglas F. Tobler, Salt Lake City, Utah, 1974, typescript, The James Moyle Oral History Program, Archives, Historical Department of the Church of Jesus Christ of Latter-day Saints, Salt Lake City, Utah, p. 51

25. Otto Berndt Oral History, interviewed by Douglas F. Tobler, Salt Lake City, Utah, 1974, typescript, The James Moyle Oral History Program, Archives, Historical Department of the Church of Jesus Christ of Latter-day Saints, Salt Lake City, Utah, p. 52 and Otto Berndt, Jr. Interview #1 with author, 20 Oct 2003

26. Otto Berndt, Jr. Interview #1 with author, 20 Oct 2003

27. Karl Schnibbe interview with author, Salt Lake City, Utah, 16 September 1996, transcribed by Don Ricks, pp. 15-16

28. Karl Schnibbe interview with author, Salt Lake City, Utah, 16 September 1996, transcribed by Don Ricks, p. 16

29. Karl Schnibbe interview with author, Salt Lake City, Utah, 16 September 1996, transcribed by Don Ricks, p. 16-17

30. Karl Schnibbe interview with author, Salt Lake City, Utah, 16 September 1996, transcribed by Don Ricks, pp. 17-18

31. Rudi Wobbe Fireside [youth church lecture], 1987, transcribed by Richard Dewey and Heather Dewey, 1-4 February 2003, used by permission from Herta Wobbe pp. 15-18

32. Rudi Wobbe Oral History, interviewed by Matthew K. Heiss, Salt Lake City, Utah, 1988, typescript, The James Moyle Oral History Program, Archives, Historical Department of the Church of Jesus Christ of Latter-day Saints, Salt Lake City, Utah, p. 64

33. Rudi Wobbe Oral History, interviewed by Matthew K. Heiss, Salt Lake City, Utah, 1988, typescript, The James Moyle Oral History Program, Archives, Historical Department of the Church of Jesus Christ of Latter-day Saints, Salt Lake City, Utah, p. 64

34. Rudi Wobbe Fireside [youth church lecture], 1987, transcribed by Richard Dewey and Heather Dewey, 1-4 February 2003, used by permission from Herta Wobbe, pp. 15-18

35. Rudi Wobbe Fireside [youth church lecture], 1987, transcribed by Richard Dewey and Heather Dewey, 1-4 February 2003, used by permission from Herta Wobbe, pp. 15-18

36. Rudi Wobbe Oral History, interviewed by Matthew K. Heiss, Salt Lake City, Utah, 1988, typescript, The James Moyle Oral History Program, Archives, Historical Department of the Church of Jesus Christ of Latter-day Saints, Salt Lake City, Utah, p. 64

37. Rudi Wobbe Fireside [youth church lecture], 1987, transcribed by Richard Dewey and Heather Dewey, 1-4 February 2003, used by permission from Herta Wobbe, pp. 15-18

38. Rudi Wobbe Oral History, interviewed by Matthew K. Heiss, Salt Lake City, Utah, 1988, typescript, The James Moyle Oral History Program, Archives, Historical Department of the Church of Jesus Christ of Latter-day Saints, Salt Lake City, Utah, p. 64

C H A P T E R   3 3

1. Rudi Wobbe Fireside [youth church lecture], 1987, transcribed by Richard Dewey and Heather Dewey, 1-4 February 2003, used by permission from Herta Wobbe, pp. 15-18

2. Rudi Wobbe Oral History, interviewed by Matthew K. Heiss, Salt Lake City, Utah, 1988, typescript, The James Moyle Oral History Program, Archives, Historical Department of the Church of Jesus Christ of Latter-day Saints, Salt Lake City, Utah, p. 73

3. Rudi Wobbe Fireside [youth church lecture], 1987, transcribed by Richard Dewey and Heather Dewey, 1-4 February 2003, used by permission from Herta Wobbe, pp. 15-18

4. Rudi Wobbe Oral History, interviewed by Matthew K. Heiss, Salt Lake City, Utah, 1988, typescript, The James Moyle Oral History Program, Archives, Historical Department of the Church of Jesus Christ of Latter-day Saints, Salt Lake City, Utah, p. 73

5. Rudi Wobbe Oral History, interviewed by Matthew K. Heiss, Salt Lake City, Utah, 1988, typescript, The James Moyle Oral History Program, Archives, Historical Department of the Church of Jesus Christ of Latter-day Saints, Salt Lake City, Utah, p. 57

6. Rudi Wobbe Fireside [youth church lecture], 1987, transcribed by Richard Dewey and Heather Dewey, 1-4 February 2003, used by permission from Herta Wobbe, pp. 15-18

7. Rudi Wobbe Fireside [youth church lecture], 1987, transcribed by Richard Dewey and Heather Dewey, 1-4 February 2003, used by permission from Herta Wobbe, pp. 18-19

8. Karl Schnibbe interview with author, Salt Lake City, Utah, 16 September 1996, transcribed by Don Ricks, p. 19

9. Karl Schnibbe interview with author, Salt Lake City, Utah, 16 September 1996, transcribed by Don Ricks, p. 18

10. Karl Schnibbe interview with author, Salt Lake City, Utah, 16 September 1996, transcribed by Don Ricks, pp. 18-19

11. Karl Schnibbe interview with author, Salt Lake City, Utah, 16 September 1996, transcribed by Don Ricks, p. 19

12. *Truth & Conviction*, documentary film produced by Brigham Young University, produced by Rick McFarland and Matt Whitaker, written and directed by Matt Whitaker, December 2003, one hour length

13. Karl Schnibbe interview with author, Salt Lake City, Utah, 16 September 1996, transcribed by Don Ricks, p. 19

CHAPTER 34

1. Gerhard Kunkel interview #1 with author, 10 October 1996

2. Rudi Wobbe Oral History, interviewed by Matthew K. Heiss, Salt Lake City, Utah, 1988, typescript, The James Moyle Oral History Program, Archives, Historical Department of the Church of Jesus Christ of Latter-day Saints, Salt Lake City, Utah, p. 76

3. Rudi Wobbe Oral History, interviewed by Matthew K. Heiss, Salt Lake City, Utah, 1988, typescript, The James Moyle Oral History Program, Archives, Historical Department of the Church of Jesus Christ of Latter-day Saints, Salt Lake City, Utah, p. 76

4. Herta Wobbe conversations with author

5. Rudi Wobbe Oral History, interviewed by Matthew K. Heiss, Salt Lake City, Utah, 1988, typescript, The James Moyle Oral History Program, Archives, Historical Department of the Church of Jesus Christ of Latter-day Saints, Salt Lake City, Utah, p. 81

6. Rudi Wobbe Oral History, interviewed by Matthew K. Heiss, Salt Lake City, Utah, 1988, typescript, The James Moyle Oral History Program, Archives, Historical Department of the Church of Jesus Christ of Latter-day Saints, Salt Lake City, Utah, pp. 77-78

7. Rudi Wobbe Oral History, interviewed by Matthew K. Heiss, Salt Lake City, Utah, 1988, typescript, The James Moyle Oral History Program, Archives, Historical Department of the Church of Jesus Christ of Latter-day Saints, Salt Lake City, Utah, p. 78

8. Rudi Wobbe Oral History, interviewed by Matthew K. Heiss, Salt Lake City, Utah, 1988, typescript, The James Moyle Oral History Program, Archives, Historical Department of the

Church of Jesus Christ of Latter-day Saints, Salt Lake City,
Utah, p. 86

9. Rudi Wobbe Oral History, interviewed by Matthew K. Heiss,
   Salt Lake City, Utah, 1988, typescript, The James Moyle Oral
   History Program, Archives, Historical Department of the
   Church of Jesus Christ of Latter-day Saints, Salt Lake City,
   Utah, p.90

10. Rudi Wobbe Oral History, interviewed by Matthew K. Heiss,
    Salt Lake City, Utah, 1988, typescript, The James Moyle Oral
    History Program, Archives, Historical Department of the
    Church of Jesus Christ of Latter-day Saints, Salt Lake City,
    Utah, p. 90

11. Werner Schmidt interview with author, 20 October 2003

12. Rudi Wobbe Oral History, interviewed by Matthew K. Heiss,
    Salt Lake City, Utah, 1988, typescript, The James Moyle Oral
    History Program, Archives, Historical Department of the
    Church of Jesus Christ of Latter-day Saints, Salt Lake City,
    Utah, p. 88

13. Rudi Wobbe Oral History, interviewed by Matthew K. Heiss,
    Salt Lake City, Utah, 1988, typescript, The James Moyle Oral
    History Program, Archives, Historical Department of the
    Church of Jesus Christ of Latter-day Saints, Salt Lake City,
    Utah, p. 92

14. Rudi Wobbe Oral History, interviewed by Matthew K. Heiss,
    Salt Lake City, Utah, 1988, typescript, The James Moyle Oral
    History Program, Archives, Historical Department of the
    Church of Jesus Christ of Latter-day Saints, Salt Lake City,
    Utah, p. 92

15. Rudi Wobbe Oral History, interviewed by Matthew K. Heiss,
    Salt Lake City, Utah, 1988, typescript, The James Moyle Oral
    History Program, Archives, Historical Department of the
    Church of Jesus Christ of Latter-day Saints, Salt Lake City,
    Utah, p. 94

16. Rudi Wobbe Oral History, interviewed by Matthew K. Heiss, Salt Lake City, Utah, 1988, typescript, The James Moyle Oral History Program, Archives, Historical Department of the Church of Jesus Christ of Latter-day Saints, Salt Lake City, Utah, p. 93

CHAPTER 35

1. Otto Berndt Oral History, interviewed by Douglas F. Tobler, Salt Lake City, Utah, 1974, typescript, The James Moyle Oral History Program, Archives, Historical Department of the Church of Jesus Christ of Latter-day Saints, Salt Lake City, Utah, p. 70

2. Otto Berndt Oral History, interviewed by Douglas F. Tobler, Salt Lake City, Utah, 1974, typescript, The James Moyle Oral History Program, Archives, Historical Department of the Church of Jesus Christ of Latter-day Saints, Salt Lake City, Utah, p. 70

3. Otto Berndt Oral History, interviewed by Douglas F. Tobler, Salt Lake City, Utah, 1974, typescript, The James Moyle Oral History Program, Archives, Historical Department of the Church of Jesus Christ of Latter-day Saints, Salt Lake City, Utah, p. 75

4. Otto Berndt Oral History, interviewed by Douglas F. Tobler, Salt Lake City, Utah, 1974, typescript, The James Moyle Oral History Program, Archives, Historical Department of the Church of Jesus Christ of Latter-day Saints, Salt Lake City, Utah, p. 75

5. Otto Berndt Oral History, interviewed by Douglas F. Tobler, Salt Lake City, Utah, 1974, typescript, The James Moyle Oral History Program, Archives, Historical Department of the Church of Jesus Christ of Latter-day Saints, Salt Lake City, Utah, p. 76

6. Otto Berndt Oral History, interviewed by Douglas F. Tobler, Salt Lake City, Utah, 1974, typescript, The James Moyle Oral History Program, Archives, Historical Department of the Church of Jesus Christ of Latter-day Saints, Salt Lake City, Utah, p. 77

7. Otto Berndt Oral History, interviewed by Douglas F. Tobler, Salt Lake City, Utah, 1974, typescript, The James Moyle Oral History Program, Archives, Historical Department of the Church of Jesus Christ of Latter-day Saints, Salt Lake City, Utah, p. 77

8. Otto Berndt Oral History, interviewed by Douglas F. Tobler, Salt Lake City, Utah, 1974, typescript, The James Moyle Oral History Program, Archives, Historical Department of the Church of Jesus Christ of Latter-day Saints, Salt Lake City, Utah, p. 78

9. Otto Berndt Oral History, interviewed by Douglas F. Tobler, Salt Lake City, Utah, 1974, typescript, The James Moyle Oral History Program, Archives, Historical Department of the Church of Jesus Christ of Latter-day Saints, Salt Lake City, Utah, p. 78

10. Otto Berndt Oral History, interviewed by Douglas F. Tobler, Salt Lake City, Utah, 1974, typescript, The James Moyle Oral History Program, Archives, Historical Department of the Church of Jesus Christ of Latter-day Saints, Salt Lake City, Utah, 79

11. Otto Berndt Oral History, interviewed by Douglas F. Tobler, Salt Lake City, Utah, 1974, typescript, The James Moyle Oral History Program, Archives, Historical Department of the Church of Jesus Christ of Latter-day Saints, Salt Lake City, Utah, p. 79

12. Otto Berndt Oral History, interviewed by Douglas F. Tobler, Salt Lake City, Utah, 1974, typescript, The James Moyle Oral History Program, Archives, Historical Department of the Church of Jesus Christ of Latter-day Saints, Salt Lake City, Utah, p. 79

13. Otto Berndt Oral History, interviewed by Douglas F. Tobler, Salt Lake City, Utah, 1974, typescript, The James Moyle Oral History Program, Archives, Historical Department of the Church of Jesus Christ of Latter-day Saints, Salt Lake City, Utah, pp. 80-81

14. Otto Berndt Oral History, interviewed by Douglas F. Tobler, Salt Lake City, Utah, 1974, typescript, The James Moyle Oral History Program, Archives, Historical Department of the Church of Jesus Christ of Latter-day Saints, Salt Lake City, Utah, p. 51

15. Otto Berndt Oral History, interviewed by Douglas F. Tobler, Salt Lake City, Utah, 1974, typescript, The James Moyle Oral History Program, Archives, Historical Department of the Church of Jesus Christ of Latter-day Saints, Salt Lake City, Utah, p. 51

16. Otto Berndt Oral History, interviewed by Douglas F. Tobler, Salt Lake City, Utah, 1974, typescript, The James Moyle Oral History Program, Archives, Historical Department of the Church of Jesus Christ of Latter-day Saints, Salt Lake City, Utah, p. 51

17. Otto Berndt Oral History, interviewed by Douglas F. Tobler, Salt Lake City, Utah, 1974, typescript, The James Moyle Oral History Program, Archives, Historical Department of the Church of Jesus Christ of Latter-day Saints, Salt Lake City, Utah, p. 82 - 83

18. Otto Berndt Oral History, interviewed by Douglas F. Tobler, Salt Lake City, Utah, 1974, typescript, The James Moyle Oral History Program, Archives, Historical Department of the Church of Jesus Christ of Latter-day Saints, Salt Lake City, Utah, p. 84

19. Otto Berndt Oral History, interviewed by Douglas F. Tobler, Salt Lake City, Utah, 1974, typescript, The James Moyle Oral History Program, Archives, Historical Department of the Church of Jesus Christ of Latter-day Saints, Salt Lake City, Utah, p. 84

20. Otto Berndt Oral History, interviewed by Douglas F. Tobler, Salt Lake City, Utah, 1974, typescript, The James Moyle Oral History Program, Archives, Historical Department of the Church of Jesus Christ of Latter-day Saints, Salt Lake City, Utah, p. 84

21. Otto Berndt Oral History, interviewed by Douglas F. Tobler, Salt Lake City, Utah, 1974, typescript, The James Moyle Oral History Program, Archives, Historical Department of the Church of Jesus Christ of Latter-day Saints, Salt Lake City, Utah, p. 83

22. Otto Berndt Oral History, interviewed by Douglas F. Tobler, Salt Lake City, Utah, 1974, typescript, The James Moyle Oral History Program, Archives, Historical Department of the Church of Jesus Christ of Latter-day Saints, Salt Lake City, Utah, p. 83

23. Otto Berndt Oral History, interviewed by Douglas F. Tobler, Salt Lake City, Utah, 1974, typescript, The James Moyle Oral History Program, Archives, Historical Department of the Church of Jesus Christ of Latter-day Saints, Salt Lake City, Utah, pp. 86-87

24. Otto Berndt Oral History, interviewed by Douglas F. Tobler, Salt Lake City, Utah, 1974, typescript, The James Moyle Oral History Program, Archives, Historical Department of the Church of Jesus Christ of Latter-day Saints, Salt Lake City, Utah, p. 88

25. Otto Berndt Oral History, interviewed by Douglas F. Tobler, Salt Lake City, Utah, 1974, typescript, The James Moyle Oral History Program, Archives, Historical Department of the Church of Jesus Christ of Latter-day Saints, Salt Lake City, Utah, p. 86

26. Otto Berndt Oral History, interviewed by Douglas F. Tobler, Salt Lake City, Utah, 1974, typescript, The James Moyle Oral History Program, Archives, Historical Department of the Church of Jesus Christ of Latter-day Saints, Salt Lake City, Utah, p. 87

27. Otto Berndt Oral History, interviewed by Douglas F. Tobler, Salt Lake City, Utah, 1974, typescript, The James Moyle Oral History Program, Archives, Historical Department of the Church of Jesus Christ of Latter-day Saints, Salt Lake City, Utah, pp. 88

28. Otto Berndt Oral History, interviewed by Douglas F. Tobler, Salt Lake City, Utah, 1974, typescript, The James Moyle Oral History Program, Archives, Historical Department of the Church of Jesus Christ of Latter-day Saints, Salt Lake City, Utah, p. 88

29. Otto Berndt Oral History, interviewed by Douglas F. Tobler, Salt Lake City, Utah, 1974, typescript, The James Moyle Oral History Program, Archives, Historical Department of the Church of Jesus Christ of Latter-day Saints, Salt Lake City, Utah, pp. 90-91

30. Otto Berndt Oral History, interviewed by Douglas F. Tobler, Salt Lake City, Utah, 1974, typescript, The James Moyle Oral History Program, Archives, Historical Department of the Church of Jesus Christ of Latter-day Saints, Salt Lake City, Utah, p. 93

31. Otto Berndt Oral History, interviewed by Douglas F. Tobler, Salt Lake City, Utah, 1974, typescript, The James Moyle Oral History Program, Archives, Historical Department of the Church of Jesus Christ of Latter-day Saints, Salt Lake City, Utah, p. 93

CHAPTER 36

1. Gerhard Kunkel interview, p. 25

2. Otto Berndt Oral History, interviewed by Douglas F. Tobler, Salt Lake City, Utah, 1974, typescript, The James Moyle Oral History Program, Archives, Historical Department of the Church of Jesus Christ of Latter-day Saints, Salt Lake City, Utah, p. 47

3. Otto Berndt Oral History, interviewed by Douglas F. Tobler, Salt Lake City, Utah, 1974, typescript, The James Moyle Oral History Program, Archives, Historical Department of the Church of Jesus Christ of Latter-day Saints, Salt Lake City, Utah, p. 47

4. Otto Berndt Oral History, interviewed by Douglas F. Tobler, Salt Lake City, Utah, 1974, typescript, The James Moyle Oral History Program, Archives, Historical Department of the Church of Jesus Christ of Latter-day Saints, Salt Lake City, Utah, p. 48

5. Otto Berndt Oral History, interviewed by Douglas F. Tobler, Salt Lake City, Utah, 1974, typescript, The James Moyle Oral History Program, Archives, Historical Department of the Church of Jesus Christ of Latter-day Saints, Salt Lake City, Utah, p. 48

6. Rudi Wobbe Oral History, interviewed by Matthew K. Heiss, Salt Lake City, Utah, 1988, typescript, The James Moyle Oral History Program, Archives, Historical Department of the Church of Jesus Christ of Latter-day Saints, Salt Lake City, Utah, p. 15

7. Arthur and Marie Sommerfeld interview with author, 18 October 1996

8. Rudi Wobbe Oral History, interviewed by Matthew K. Heiss, Salt Lake City, Utah, 1988, typescript, The James Moyle Oral History Program, Archives, Historical Department of the Church of Jesus Christ of Latter-day Saints, Salt Lake City, Utah, p. 77

9. Rudi Wobbe Oral History, interviewed by Matthew K. Heiss, Salt Lake City, Utah, 1988, typescript, The James Moyle Oral History Program, Archives, Historical Department of the Church of Jesus Christ of Latter-day Saints, Salt Lake City, Utah, p. 77

10. Otto Berndt Oral History, interviewed by Douglas F. Tobler, Salt Lake City, Utah, 1974, typescript, The James Moyle Oral History Program, Archives, Historical Department of the Church of Jesus Christ of Latter-day Saints, Salt Lake City, Utah, p. 43

11. Otto Berndt Oral History, interviewed by Douglas F. Tobler, Salt Lake City, Utah, 1974, typescript, The James Moyle Oral History Program, Archives, Historical Department of the Church of Jesus Christ of Latter-day Saints, Salt Lake City, Utah, p. 45

12. Otto Berndt Oral History, interviewed by Douglas F. Tobler, Salt Lake City, Utah, 1974, typescript, The James Moyle Oral History Program, Archives, Historical Department of the Church of Jesus Christ of Latter-day Saints, Salt Lake City, Utah, p. 49

13. Otto Berndt Oral History, interviewed by Douglas F. Tobler, Salt Lake City, Utah, 1974, typescript, The James Moyle Oral History Program, Archives, Historical Department of the Church of Jesus Christ of Latter-day Saints, Salt Lake City, Utah, p. 61

14. Otto Berndt Oral History, interviewed by Douglas F. Tobler, Salt Lake City, Utah, 1974, typescript, The James Moyle Oral History Program, Archives, Historical Department of the Church of Jesus Christ of Latter-day Saints, Salt Lake City, Utah, p. 61

15. Gerhard Kunkel interview #1 with author, 10 October 1996, pp. 25-26

16. Karl Schnibbe interview with author, Salt Lake City, Utah, 16 September 1996, transcribed by Don Ricks, p. 13

17. Karl Schnibbe interview with author, Salt Lake City, Utah, 16 September 1996, transcribed by Don Ricks, p. 12

18. Karl Schnibbe interview with author, Salt Lake City, Utah, 16 September 1996, transcribed by Don Ricks, p. 15

19. Karl Schnibbe interview with author, Salt Lake City, Utah, 16 September 1996, transcribed by Don Ricks, p. 15

20. Karl Schnibbe interview with author, Salt Lake City, Utah, 16 September 1996, transcribed by Don Ricks, p. 21

21. Karl Schnibbe interview with author, Salt Lake City, Utah, 16 September 1996, transcribed by Don Ricks, pp. 24-25

22. P. 12, Archive MS 15335, starting on frame 515 of microfilm copy. Title: Book Review, 1997 Oct 14.

23. Otto Berndt, Jr. interview #2 with author 20 October 2003

24. Otto Berndt, Jr. Interview #1 with author 20 October 2003

25. Arthur and Marie Sommerfeld interview with author, 18 October 1996, pp. 12-13

26. Arthur and Marie Sommerfeld interview with author, Salt Lake City, Utah, 18 October 1996, p. 6

27. Arthur and Marie Sommerfeld interview with author, Salt Lake City, Utah, 18 October 1996, p. 6

28. Arthur and Marie Sommerfeld interview with author, 18 October 1996, p. 9

29. Arthur and Marie Sommerfeld interview with author, 18 October 1996, p. 6

30. Arthur and Marie Sommerfeld interview with author, 18 October 1996, p. 10

31. Gerhard Kunkel interview #1 with author, 10 October 1996

C H A P T E R   3 7

1. Rudi Wobbe Oral History, interviewed by Matthew K. Heiss, Salt Lake City, Utah, 1988, typescript, The James Moyle Oral History Program, Archives, Historical Department of the Church of Jesus Christ of Latter-day Saints, Salt Lake City, Utah, pp. 97-98

2. Rudi Wobbe Oral History, interviewed by Matthew K. Heiss, Salt Lake City, Utah, 1988, typescript, The James Moyle Oral History Program, Archives, Historical Department of the Church of Jesus Christ of Latter-day Saints, Salt Lake City, Utah, pp. 97-98

3. Rudi Wobbe Fireside [youth church lecture], 1987, transcribed by Richard Dewey and Heather Dewey, 1-4 February 2003, used by permission from Herta Wobbe, p. 2

4. Rudi Wobbe Oral History, interviewed by Matthew K. Heiss, Salt Lake City, Utah, 1988, typescript, The James Moyle Oral History Program, Archives, Historical Department of the Church of Jesus Christ of Latter-day Saints, Salt Lake City, Utah, p. 99

5. Rudi Wobbe Oral History, interviewed by Matthew K. Heiss, Salt Lake City, Utah, 1988, typescript, The James Moyle Oral History Program, Archives, Historical Department of the Church of Jesus Christ of Latter-day Saints, Salt Lake City, Utah, p. 101

6. Rudi Wobbe Oral History, interviewed by Matthew K. Heiss, Salt Lake City, Utah, 1988, typescript, The James Moyle Oral History Program, Archives, Historical Department of the

Church of Jesus Christ of Latter-day Saints, Salt Lake City, Utah, p. 101

7. Rudi Wobbe Oral History, interviewed by Matthew K. Heiss, Salt Lake City, Utah, 1988, typescript, The James Moyle Oral History Program, Archives, Historical Department of the Church of Jesus Christ of Latter-day Saints, Salt Lake City, Utah, p. 102

8. Rudi Wobbe Oral History, interviewed by Matthew K. Heiss, Salt Lake City, Utah, 1988, typescript, The James Moyle Oral History Program, Archives, Historical Department of the Church of Jesus Christ of Latter-day Saints, Salt Lake City, Utah, p. 102

9. Rudi Wobbe Oral History, interviewed by Matthew K. Heiss, Salt Lake City, Utah, 1988, typescript, The James Moyle Oral History Program, Archives, Historical Department of the Church of Jesus Christ of Latter-day Saints, Salt Lake City, Utah, p. 102

10. Arthur and Marie Sommerfeld interview with author, 18 October 1996, p. 13

11. Werner Schmidt interview with author, 20 Oct 2003

12. Rudi Wobbe Oral History, interviewed by Matthew K. Heiss, Salt Lake City, Utah, 1988, typescript, The James Moyle Oral History Program, Archives, Historical Department of the Church of Jesus Christ of Latter-day Saints, Salt Lake City, Utah

13. Rudi Wobbe Oral History, interviewed by Matthew K. Heiss, Salt Lake City, Utah, 1988, typescript, The James Moyle Oral History Program, Archives, Historical Department of the Church of Jesus Christ of Latter-day Saints, Salt Lake City, Utah, p. 101

14. Rudi Wobbe Oral History, interviewed by Matthew K. Heiss, Salt Lake City, Utah, 1988, typescript, The James Moyle Oral History Program, Archives, Historical Department of the

Church of Jesus Christ of Latter-day Saints, Salt Lake City, Utah, p. 104

15. Rudi Wobbe Oral History, interviewed by Matthew K. Heiss, Salt Lake City, Utah, 1988, typescript, The James Moyle Oral History Program, Archives, Historical Department of the Church of Jesus Christ of Latter-day Saints, Salt Lake City, Utah, p. 106

16. Rudi Wobbe Oral History, interviewed by Matthew K. Heiss, Salt Lake City, Utah, 1988, typescript, The James Moyle Oral History Program, Archives, Historical Department of the Church of Jesus Christ of Latter-day Saints, Salt Lake City, Utah, p. 104

17. Herta Wobbe interview with author 9 April 1999

18. Herta Wobbe interview with author 9 April 1999

19. Herta Wobbe interview with author 9 April 1999

20. Rudi Wobbe Oral History, interviewed by Matthew K. Heiss, Salt Lake City, Utah, 1988, typescript, The James Moyle Oral History Program, Archives, Historical Department of the Church of Jesus Christ of Latter-day Saints, Salt Lake City, Utah, p. 75

21. Rudi Wobbe Oral History, interviewed by Matthew K. Heiss, Salt Lake City, Utah, 1988, typescript, The James Moyle Oral History Program, Archives, Historical Department of the Church of Jesus Christ of Latter-day Saints, Salt Lake City, Utah, p. 75

22. Rudolf G. Wobbe Oral History, Doublas F. Tobler and Alan F. Keele, 1974, typescript, The James Moyle Oral History Program, Archives, Historical Department of the Church of Jesus Christ of Latter-day Saints, Salt Lake City, Utah, p. 32

23. Rudolf G. Wobbe Oral History, Doublas F. Tobler and Alan F. Keele, 1974, typescript, The James Moyle Oral History

Program, Archives, Historical Department of the Church of Jesus Christ of Latter-day Saints, Salt Lake City, Utah, p. 33

24. Rudi Wobbe Oral History, interviewed by Matthew K. Heiss, Salt Lake City, Utah, 1988, typescript, The James Moyle Oral History Program, Archives, Historical Department of the Church of Jesus Christ of Latter-day Saints, Salt Lake City, Utah, p. 105

25. Rudi Wobbe Oral History, interviewed by Matthew K. Heiss, Salt Lake City, Utah, 1988, typescript, The James Moyle Oral History Program, Archives, Historical Department of the Church of Jesus Christ of Latter-day Saints, Salt Lake City, Utah, p. 105

26. Herta Wobbe interviews with author, April-June 1999

27. Arthur and Marie Sommerfeld interview with author, 18 October 1996, p. 11

28. Arthur and Marie Sommerfeld interview with author, 18 October 1996, p. 10

29. Arthur and Marie Sommerfeld interview with author, 18 October 1996, p. 13

30. Hans and Charlotte Kunkel interview with author, Salt Lake City, Utah, 18 October 1996, p. 4

31. Gerhard Kunkel interview #1 with author, 10 October 1996, p. 26

32. Resa Guertler Frey interview with author, 17 October 2003

33. Hilde Prüss Müller, interview with author 18 October 2003

34. Lieselotte Prüss Werner interview with author, 21 Oct 2003

35. Otto Berndt, Jr. Interview #3 with author, 8 November 2003; and Otto Berndt Oral History, interviewed by Douglas F. Tobler, Salt Lake City, Utah, 1974, typescript, The James Moyle Oral History Program, Archives, Historical Department of the

Church of Jesus Christ of Latter-day Saints, Salt Lake City, Utah, p. 93

36. Karl Schnibbe interview with author, Salt Lake City, Utah, 16 September 1996, transcribed by Don Ricks, pp. 19-20

37. Karl Schnibbe interview with author, Salt Lake City, Utah, 16 September 1996, transcribed by Don Ricks, p. 20

38. Karl Schnibbe interview with author, Salt Lake City, Utah, 16 September 1996, transcribed by Don Ricks, p. 14

39. Karl Schnibbe interview with author, Salt Lake City, Utah, 16 September 1996, transcribed by Don Ricks, pp. 14-15

40. Karl Schnibbe interview with author, Salt Lake City, Utah, 16 September 1996, transcribed by Don Ricks, p. 15

C H A P T E R   3 8

1. *Truth & Conviction*, documentary film produced by Brigham Young University, produced by Rick McFarland and Matt Whitaker, written and directed by Matt Whitaker, December 2003, one hour length

2. *Truth & Conviction*, documentary film produced by Brigham Young University, produced by Rick McFarland and Matt Whitaker, written and directed by Matt Whitaker, December 2003, one hour length

3. *Truth & Conviction*, documentary film produced by Brigham Young University, produced by Rick McFarland and Matt Whitaker, written and directed by Matt Whitaker, December 2003, one hour length

4. Rudi Wobbe Oral History, interviewed by Matthew K. Heiss, Salt Lake City, Utah, 1988, typescript, The James Moyle Oral History Program, Archives, Historical Department of the

Church of Jesus Christ of Latter-day Saints, Salt Lake City, Utah, p.70 and Karl Scnibbe interview with author

5. Rudi Wobbe Oral History, interviewed by Matthew K. Heiss, Salt Lake City, Utah, 1988, typescript, The James Moyle Oral History Program, Archives, Historical Department of the Church of Jesus Christ of Latter-day Saints, Salt Lake City, Utah, p. 70

6. Rudi Wobbe Oral History, interviewed by Matthew K. Heiss, Salt Lake City, Utah, 1988, typescript, The James Moyle Oral History Program, Archives, Historical Department of the Church of Jesus Christ of Latter-day Saints, Salt Lake City, Utah, pp. 70-72

7. "The Führer's New Clothes: Helmuth Hübener and the Dilemma of German Mormons in the Third Reich," unpublished essay by Alan F. Keele, Used by permission from Alan F. Keele. A shorter version of this essay was later published as an article in *Sunstone*, p. 24

8. "The Führer's New Clothes: Helmuth Hübener and the Dilemma of German Mormons in the Third Reich," unpublished essay by Alan F. Keele, Used by permission from Alan F. Keele. A shorter version of this essay was later published as an article in *Sunstone*, p. 24

9. "The Führer's New Clothes: Helmuth Hübener and the Dilemma of German Mormons in the Third Reich," unpublished essay by Alan F. Keele, Used by permission from Alan F. Keele. A shorter version of this essay was later published as an article in *Sunstone*, p. 44

CHAPTER 39

1. Herta Wobbe conversations with author

2. Karl Schnibbe interview with author, Salt Lake City, Utah, 16 September 1996, transcribed by Don Ricks, pp. 2-3

3. Rudi Wobbe Oral History, interviewed by Matthew K. Heiss, Salt Lake City, Utah, 1988, typescript, The James Moyle Oral History Program, Archives, Historical Department of the Church of Jesus Christ of Latter-day Saints, Salt Lake City, Utah, p. 106

4. Rudi Wobbe Fireside [youth church lecture], 1987, transcribed by Richard Dewey and Heather Dewey, 1-4 February 2003, used by permission from Herta Wobbe, p. 13

5. Rudolf G. Wobbe Oral History, Doublas F. Tobler and Alan F. Keele, 1974, typescript, The James Moyle Oral History Program, Archives, Historical Department of the Church of Jesus Christ of Latter-day Saints, Salt Lake City, Utah, p. 27

6. Blair Holmes, Alan Keele, and Karl-Heinz Schnibbe, *When Truth Was Treason*, Urbana and Chicago, Illinois: University of Illinois Press, 1995

7. Karl Schnibbe interview with author, Salt Lake City, Utah, 16 September 1996, transcribed by Don Ricks, pp. 10-11

8. Hans and Charlotte Kunkel interview with author, Salt Lake City, Utah, 18 October 1996, p. 6

9. Hans and Charlotte Kunkel interview with author, Salt Lake City, Utah, 18 October 1996, p. 5

10. Hans and Charlotte Kunkel interview with author, Salt Lake City, Utah, 18 October 1996, p. 6

11. Gerhard Kunkel interview #2 with author, 25 February 2003, p. 15

12. Gerhard Kunkel interview #1 with author, 10 October 1996, p. 2

13. Gerhard Kunkel interview #2 with author, 25 February 2003, p. 15

14. Gerhard Kunkel interview #2 with author, 25 February 2003, p. 15

15. Gerhard Kunkel interview #1 with author, 10 October 1996, p. 27

C H A P T E R 4 0

1. Herta Wobbe interview 30 June 1999

2. Marie Friebel Sommerfeld 1897-1984, Interviewed in German by Douglas Tobler and Alan Keele, 1974 : (13 leaves in English) (Matthew K. Heiss later wrote Iris Schmidt on 17 Sep 1992 saying the Sommerfeld interview was never fully edited.) Typed ca. 1985 by Karen H. Pyper, p. 12

3. Statement of Marie Sommerfeld, Source: *Begleitheft zur Austellung um das kurze Leben und Wirken des Helmuth Hübener,* Catalogue of the exhibit in the Hamburg Municipal District Archive (Stadtteilarchiv) of Hamm, 26 October – 10 December, 1992

4. Cited in *When Truth Was Treason*, p. 346

5. *Wie bewaltigen wir das schwerste Kapitel deutscher Geschichte? Beiheft*, p. 50

6. "The Führer's New Clothes: Helmuth Hübener and the Dilemma of German Mormons in the Third Reich," unpublished essay by Alan F. Keele, Used by permission from Alan F. Keele. A shorter version of this essay was later published as an article in *Sunstone*, p. 35, citing interview in Hamburg 29 March 1974

7. Karl Schnibbe interview with author, Salt Lake City, Utah, 16 September 1996, transcribed by Don Ricks, p. 30

8. Archives MS 13271, MS Record Access #203188-Arch 91. Title: Firesides file 1962; 1988.

9. Marie Friebel Sommerfeld 1897-1984, Interviewed in German by Douglas Tobler and Alan Keele, 1974 : (13 leaves in English) (Matthew K. Heiss later wrote Iris Schmidt on 17 Sep 1992 saying the Sommerfeld interview was never fully edited.) Typed ca. 1985 by Karen H. Pyper

10. "The Führer's New Clothes: Helmuth Hübener and the Dilemma of German Mormons in the Third Reich," unpublished essay by Alan F. Keele, Used by permission from Alan F. Keele. A shorter version of this essay was later published as an article in *Sunstone*, p. 12

11. "The Führer's New Clothes: Helmuth Hübener and the Dilemma of German Mormons in the Third Reich," unpublished essay by Alan F. Keele, Used by permission from Alan F. Keele. A shorter version of this essay was later published as an article in *Sunstone*, p. 12

12. "The Führer's New Clothes: Helmuth Hübener and the Dilemma of German Mormons in the Third Reich," unpublished essay by Alan F. Keele, Used by permission from Alan F. Keele. A shorter version of this essay was later published as an article in *Sunstone*, p. 13

13. Rudolf G. Wobbe Oral History, Doublas F. Tobler and Alan F. Keele, 1974, typescript, The James Moyle Oral History Program, Archives, Historical Department of the Church of Jesus Christ of Latter-day Saints, Salt Lake City, Utah, pp. 27-28

14. "The Führer's New Clothes: Helmuth Hübener and the Dilemma of German Mormons in the Third Reich," unpublished essay by Alan F. Keele, Used by permission from Alan F. Keele. A shorter version of this essay was later published as an article in *Sunstone*, pp. 21-22

15. "The Führer's New Clothes: Helmuth Hübener and the Dilemma of German Mormons in the Third Reich," unpublished essay by Alan F. Keele, Used by permission from Alan F. Keele.

A shorter version of this essay was later published as an article in *Sunstone*, pp. 23-24, 29-32

16. *BYU Today*, "Heubener's [sic] message haunts memories in remarkable drama," Dec 1976

17. Rudolf G. Wobbe Oral History, Doublas F. Tobler and Alan F. Keele, 1974, typescript, The James Moyle Oral History Program, Archives, Historical Department of the Church of Jesus Christ of Latter-day Saints, Salt Lake City, Utah, p. 39

18. Rudolf G. Wobbe Oral History, Doublas F. Tobler and Alan F. Keele, 1974, typescript, The James Moyle Oral History Program, Archives, Historical Department of the Church of Jesus Christ of Latter-day Saints, Salt Lake City, Utah, p. 39

19. Otto Berndt Oral History, interviewed by Douglas F. Tobler, Salt Lake City, Utah, 1974, typescript, The James Moyle Oral History Program, Archives, Historical Department of the Church of Jesus Christ of Latter-day Saints, Salt Lake City, Utah, p. 41

20. Rudi Wobbe Oral History, interviewed by Matthew K. Heiss, Salt Lake City, Utah, 1988, typescript, The James Moyle Oral History Program, Archives, Historical Department of the Church of Jesus Christ of Latter-day Saints, Salt Lake City, Utah, pp. 68-69

21. Rudolf G. Wobbe Oral History, Doublas F. Tobler and Alan F. Keele, 1974, typescript, The James Moyle Oral History Program, Archives, Historical Department of the Church of Jesus Christ of Latter-day Saints, Salt Lake City, Utah, p. 40

22. Rudolf G. Wobbe Oral History, Doublas F. Tobler and Alan F. Keele, 1974, typescript, The James Moyle Oral History Program, Archives, Historical Department of the Church of Jesus Christ of Latter-day Saints, Salt Lake City, Utah, p. 40

23. Rudi Wobbe Oral History, interviewed by Matthew K. Heiss, Salt Lake City, Utah, 1988, typescript, The James Moyle Oral History Program, Archives, Historical Department of the

Church of Jesus Christ of Latter-day Saints, Salt Lake City, Utah, p. 72

24. *Truth & Conviction*, documentary film produced by Brigham Young University, produced by Rick McFarland and Matt Whitaker, written and directed by Matt Whitaker, December 2003, one hour length

25. Rudi Wobbe Oral History, interviewed by Matthew K. Heiss, Salt Lake City, Utah, 1988, typescript, The James Moyle Oral History Program, Archives, Historical Department of the Church of Jesus Christ of Latter-day Saints, Salt Lake City, Utah, p. 72

A P P E N D I C E S

1. Rudi Wobbe Oral History, interviewed by Matthew K. Heiss, Salt Lake City, Utah, 1988, typescript, The James Moyle Oral History Program, Archives, Historical Department of the Church of Jesus Christ of Latter-day Saints, Salt Lake City, Utah, p. 19, reported by Matthew Heiss in the interview

2. Werner Schmidt interview with author, 20 October 2003

3. Rudi Wobbe Oral History, interviewed by Matthew K. Heiss, Salt Lake City, Utah, 1988, typescript, The James Moyle Oral History Program, Archives, Historical Department of the Church of Jesus Christ of Latter-day Saints, Salt Lake City, Utah, p. 19

4. *Ibid.*

5. Karl Schnibbe interview with author, Salt Lake City, Utah, 16 September 1996, transcribed by Don Ricks, p. 43; and Arthur and Marie Sommerfeld interview with author, Salt Lake City, Utah, 18 October 1996, pp. 13-14

6. Rudolf G. Wobbe Oral History, Doublas F. Tobler and Alan F. Keele, 1974, typescript, The James Moyle Oral History

Program, Archives, Historical Department of the Church of Jesus Christ of Latter-day Saints, Salt Lake City, Utah, p. 17; Otto Berndt Oral History, interviewed by Douglas F. Tobler, Salt Lake City, Utah, 1974, typescript, The James Moyle Oral History Program, Archives, Historical Department of the Church of Jesus Christ of Latter-day Saints, Salt Lake City, Utah

7. Otto Berndt Oral History, interviewed by Douglas F. Tobler, Salt Lake City, Utah, 1974, typescript, The James Moyle Oral History Program, Archives, Historical Department of the Church of Jesus Christ of Latter-day Saints, Salt Lake City, Utah, p. 35

8. Rudolf G. Wobbe Oral History, Doublas F. Tobler and Alan F. Keele, 1974, typescript, The James Moyle Oral History Program, Archives, Historical Department of the Church of Jesus Christ of Latter-day Saints, Salt Lake City, Utah, p. 15

9. Rudolf G. Wobbe Oral History, Doublas F. Tobler and Alan F. Keele, 1974, typescript, The James Moyle Oral History Program, Archives, Historical Department of the Church of Jesus Christ of Latter-day Saints, Salt Lake City, Utah, p. 17

10. Otto Berndt Oral History, interviewed by Douglas F. Tobler, Salt Lake City, Utah, 1974, typescript, The James Moyle Oral History Program, Archives, Historical Department of the Church of Jesus Christ of Latter-day Saints, Salt Lake City, Utah, p. 42

11. Otto Berndt Oral History, interviewed by Douglas F. Tobler, Salt Lake City, Utah, 1974, typescript, The James Moyle Oral History Program, Archives, Historical Department of the Church of Jesus Christ of Latter-day Saints, Salt Lake City, Utah, p. 42

12. Otto Berndt Oral History, interviewed by Douglas F. Tobler, Salt Lake City, Utah, 1974, typescript, The James Moyle Oral History Program, Archives, Historical Department of the Church of Jesus Christ of Latter-day Saints, Salt Lake City, Utah, p. 35; Otto Berndt Oral History, interviewed by Douglas F. Tobler, Salt Lake City, Utah, 1974, typescript, The James Moyle Oral History Program, Archives, Historical Department of the Church of Jesus Christ of Latter-day Saints, Salt Lake City, Utah, p. 34

13. Otto Berndt Oral History, interviewed by Douglas F. Tobler, Salt Lake City, Utah, 1974, typescript, The James Moyle Oral History Program, Archives, Historical Department of the Church of Jesus Christ of Latter-day Saints, Salt Lake City, Utah, p. 31

14. Otto Berndt Oral History, interviewed by Douglas F. Tobler, Salt Lake City, Utah, 1974, typescript, The James Moyle Oral History Program, Archives, Historical Department of the Church of Jesus Christ of Latter-day Saints, Salt Lake City, Utah, p. 29

15. Rudi Wobbe Oral History, interviewed by Matthew K. Heiss, Salt Lake City, Utah, 1988, typescript, The James Moyle Oral History Program, Archives, Historical Department of the Church of Jesus Christ of Latter-day Saints, Salt Lake City, Utah, p. 21

16. Rudi Wobbe Oral History, interviewed by Matthew K. Heiss, Salt Lake City, Utah, 1988, typescript, The James Moyle Oral History Program, Archives, Historical Department of the Church of Jesus Christ of Latter-day Saints, Salt Lake City, Utah, p. 21

17. Karl Schnibbe interview with author, Salt Lake City, Utah, 16 September 1996, transcribed by Don Ricks, p. 43

18. Rudolf G. Wobbe Oral History, Doublas F. Tobler and Alan F. Keele, 1974, typescript, The James Moyle Oral History Program, Archives, Historical Department of the Church of Jesus Christ of Latter-day Saints, Salt Lake City, Utah, p. 33

19. Rudi Wobbe Oral History, interviewed by Matthew K. Heiss, Salt Lake City, Utah, 1988, typescript, The James Moyle Oral History Program, Archives, Historical Department of the Church of Jesus Christ of Latter-day Saints, Salt Lake City, Utah, p. 25

20. Rudolf G. Wobbe Oral History, Doublas F. Tobler and Alan F. Keele, 1974, typescript, The James Moyle Oral History Program, Archives, Historical Department of the Church of Jesus Christ of Latter-day Saints, Salt Lake City, Utah, p. 33

21. Rudi Wobbe Oral History, interviewed by Matthew K. Heiss, Salt Lake City, Utah, 1988, typescript, The James Moyle Oral History Program, Archives, Historical Department of the Church of Jesus Christ of Latter-day Saints, Salt Lake City, Utah, p. 68

22. Rudi Wobbe Oral History, interviewed by Matthew K. Heiss, Salt Lake City, Utah, 1988, typescript, The James Moyle Oral History Program, Archives, Historical Department of the Church of Jesus Christ of Latter-day Saints, Salt Lake City, Utah, p. 91

23. Rudolf G. Wobbe Oral History, Doublas F. Tobler and Alan F. Keele, 1974, typescript, The James Moyle Oral History Program, Archives, Historical Department of the Church of Jesus Christ of Latter-day Saints, Salt Lake City, Utah, p. 33

24. Otto Berndt Oral History, interviewed by Douglas F. Tobler, Salt Lake City, Utah, 1974, typescript, The James Moyle Oral History Program, Archives, Historical Department of the Church of Jesus Christ of Latter-day Saints, Salt Lake City, Utah, p. 43

25. Otto Berndt Oral History, interviewed by Douglas F. Tobler, Salt Lake City, Utah, 1974, typescript, The James Moyle Oral History Program, Archives, Historical Department of the Church of Jesus Christ of Latter-day Saints, Salt Lake City, Utah, p. 32

26. Otto Berndt Oral History, interviewed by Douglas F. Tobler, Salt Lake City, Utah, 1974, typescript, The James Moyle Oral History Program, Archives, Historical Department of the Church of Jesus Christ of Latter-day Saints, Salt Lake City, Utah, p. 32

27. Otto Berndt, Jr. interview #1 with author, 20 October 2003

28. Otto Berndt Oral History, interviewed by Douglas F. Tobler, Salt Lake City, Utah, 1974, typescript, The James Moyle Oral History Program, Archives, Historical Department of the Church of Jesus Christ of Latter-day Saints, Salt Lake City, Utah

29. Otto Berndt, Jr. interview #1 with author, 20 October 2003

30. Otto Berndt, Jr. interview #1 with author, 20 October 2003. His son says the injury came from sleeping on wet cement floors in newly built bunkers, but Otto, Sr. says his back was actually broken in two places from an accident. Otto Berndt Oral History, interviewed by Douglas F. Tobler, Salt Lake City, Utah, 1974, typescript, The James Moyle Oral History Program, Archives, Historical Department of the Church of Jesus Christ of Latter-day Saints, Salt Lake City, Utah, p. 46

31. Otto Berndt, Jr. interview #1 with author, 20 October 2003

32. Albert Speer, *Inside the Third Reich* [New York, Macmillan, 1970], p. 103, 194 *Sunstone*, November- December 1980, Vol. 5, No. 6, pp. 20-29, article copyrighted 1975

33. Heinrich Hermelink [ed.] *Kirche im Kampf: Dokumente des Widerstands und des Aufbaus in der evangelischen Kirche Deutschland von 1933 bis 1945.* [Tubingen, 1950], 502

34. Erich Goldhagen, *Weltanschauung und Endlosung, Vierteljahreshefte fur Zeitgeschichte*, Vol. 24 [October 1976], 399

35. Blair Holmes, Alan Keele, and Karl-Heinz Schnibbe, *When Truth Was Treason*, Urbana and Chicago, Illinois: University of Illinois Press, 1995

36. Record of Members, Hamburg District #23403, #994

37. Document of Nazi government, "Helmuth Hübener: Secret," 1942

38. Document of The Superior Attorney General of the Reich, Berlin 28 May 1942 at the People's Court, 8J 127/42g, In Custody!: III-3

39. Karl Schnibbe interview with author, Salt Lake City, Utah, 16 September 1996, transcribed by Don Ricks, p. 25

40. Karl Schnibbe interview with author, Salt Lake City, Utah, 16 September 1996, transcribed by Don Ricks, p. 28

41. Rudolf G. Wobbe Oral History, Doublas F. Tobler and Alan F. Keele, 1974, typescript, The James Moyle Oral History Program, Archives, Historical Department of the Church of Jesus Christ of Latter-day Saints, Salt Lake City, Utah, p. 11

42. Rudolf G. Wobbe Oral History, Doublas F. Tobler and Alan F. Keele, 1974, typescript, The James Moyle Oral History Program, Archives, Historical Department of the Church of Jesus Christ of Latter-day Saints, Salt Lake City, Utah, p. 10

43. Rudolf G. Wobbe Oral History, Doublas F. Tobler and Alan F. Keele, 1974, typescript, The James Moyle Oral History Program, Archives, Historical Department of the Church of Jesus Christ of Latter-day Saints, Salt Lake City, Utah, pp. 10-11

44. Rudolf G. Wobbe Oral History, Doublas F. Tobler and Alan F. Keele, 1974, typescript, The James Moyle Oral History Program, Archives, Historical Department of the Church of Jesus Christ of Latter-day Saints, Salt Lake City, Utah, p. 10

45. Rudolf G. Wobbe Oral History, Doublas F. Tobler and Alan F. Keele, 1974, typescript, The James Moyle Oral History Program, Archives, Historical Department of the Church of Jesus Christ of Latter-day Saints, Salt Lake City, Utah, p. 12

46. Karl Schnibbe interview with author, Salt Lake City, Utah, 16 September 1996, transcribed by Don Ricks interview, pp. 2-3

47. Arthur and Marie Sommerfeld interview with author, Salt Lake City, Utah, 18 October 1996

48. Rudolf G. Wobbe Oral History, Doublas F. Tobler and Alan F. Keele, 1974, typescript, The James Moyle Oral History Program, Archives, Historical Department of the Church of Jesus Christ of Latter-day Saints, Salt Lake City, Utah

49. Rudi Wobbe Oral History, interviewed by Matthew K. Heiss, Salt Lake City, Utah, 1988, typescript, The James Moyle Oral History Program, Archives, Historical Department of the

Church of Jesus Christ of Latter-day Saints, Salt Lake City, Utah, p. 37

50. Blair Holmes, Alan Keele, and Karl-Heinz Schnibbe, *When Truth Was Treason*, Urbana and Chicago, Illinois: University of Illinois Press, 1995

51. Liesollette Prüss Schmidt interview with author 17 Oct 2003

52. Otto Berndt Oral History, interviewed by Douglas F. Tobler, Salt Lake City, Utah, 1974, typescript, The James Moyle Oral History Program, Archives, Historical Department of the Church of Jesus Christ of Latter-day Saints, Salt Lake City, Utah, p. 41

53. Otto Berndt Oral History, interviewed by Douglas F. Tobler, Salt Lake City, Utah, 1974, typescript, The James Moyle Oral History Program, Archives, Historical Department of the Church of Jesus Christ of Latter-day Saints, Salt Lake City, Utah, p. 41

54. Otto Berndt Oral History, interviewed by Douglas F. Tobler, Salt Lake City, Utah, 1974, typescript, The James Moyle Oral History Program, Archives, Historical Department of the Church of Jesus Christ of Latter-day Saints, Salt Lake City, Utah, p. 41

55. Otto Berndt Oral History, interviewed by Douglas F. Tobler, Salt Lake City, Utah, 1974, typescript, The James Moyle Oral History Program, Archives, Historical Department of the Church of Jesus Christ of Latter-day Saints, Salt Lake City, Utah, p. 67

56. Otto Berndt Oral History, interviewed by Douglas F. Tobler, Salt Lake City, Utah, 1974, typescript, The James Moyle Oral History Program, Archives, Historical Department of the Church of Jesus Christ of Latter-day Saints, Salt Lake City, Utah, p. 41

57. Otto Berndt Oral History, interviewed by Douglas F. Tobler, Salt Lake City, Utah, 1974, typescript, The James Moyle Oral History Program, Archives, Historical Department of the Church of Jesus Christ of Latter-day Saints, Salt Lake City, Utah, p. 68

58. Arthur and Marie Sommerfeld interview with author, 18 October 1996 located in MS 5217, Access #23912 Arch-88.

This is the Manuscript History of West German Mission, 1938-1944

59. Document of Chief State Counsel of the Hanseatic Higher Regional Court, Hamburg 36, 25 March 1942, Criminal Case! Juveniles!

60. Document of Chief State Counsel of the Hanseatic Higher Regional Court, Hamburg 36, 25 March 1942, Criminal Case! Juveniles!

61. Document of The Superior Attorney General of the Reich, Berlin 28 May 1942 at the People's Court, 8J 127/42g, In Custody!: sec IIb

62. Document of Chief State Counsel of the Hanseatic Higher Regional Court, Hamburg 36, 25 March 1942, Criminal Case! Juveniles!

63. Statement of Rudolf Wobbe, Rudolf Wobbe, Salt Lake City, Utah, 17 April 1961, Source: Historical Department, Church of Jesus Christ of Latter-day Saints, Salt Lake City, Utah Statement of Rudolf Wobbe, Rudolf Wobbe, Salt Lake City, Utah, 17 April 1961, Source: Historical Department, Church of Jesus Christ of Latter-day Saints, Salt Lake City, Utah: and Ulrich Sander, Helmuth-Hübener Gruppe, in Hochmuth and Meyer, Streiflichter, p. 330

64. Verdict of the People's Court in the criminal case against Helmut Hübener, et al, on 11 August 1942; part II, sec 1

65. Document of The Superior Attorney General of the Reich, Berlin 28 May 1942 at the People's Court, 8J 127/42g, In Custody! II-C

66. Document of State Police Agency Hamburg — Hamburg, 5, 9, 17, 20 February 1942

67. Document of The Superior Attorney General of the Reich, Berlin 28 May 1942 at the People's Court, 8J 127/42g, In Custody!: IIc

68. Document of State Police Agency Hamburg — Hamburg, 5, 9, 17, 20 February 1942

69. Document of State Police Agency Hamburg — Hamburg, 5, 9, 17, 20 February 1942

70. Document of Chief State Counsel of the Hanseatic Higher Regional Court, Hamburg 36, 25 March 1942, Criminal Case! Juveniles!

71. Document of Chief State Counsel of the Hanseatic Higher Regional Court, Hamburg 36, 25 March 1942, Criminal Case! Juveniles!

72. Document of The Superior Attorney General of the Reich, Berlin 28 May 1942 at the People's Court, 8J 127/42g, In Custody!: IIc

73. Document of The Superior Attorney General of the Reich, Berlin 28 May 1942 at the People's Court, 8J 127/42g, In Custody!: sec IIc

74. Document of State Police Agency — Hamburg, 18 February 1942, About the Person: Wobbe, Rudolf Gustav; Document of The Superior Attorney General of the Reich, Berlin 28 May 1942 at the People's Court, 8J 127/42g, In Custody!: III-1

75. Document of State Police Agency — Hamburg, 18 February 1942, About the Person: Wobbe, Rudolf Gustav

76. Document of State Police Agency — Hamburg, 18 February 1942, About the Person: Wobbe, Rudolf Gustav; Document of The Superior Attorney General of the Reich, Berlin 28 May 1942 at the People's Court, 8J 127/42g, In Custody!: III-1, Verdict of the People's Court in the criminal case against Helmut Hübener, et al, on 11 August 1942: part II, sec 3

77. Document of The Superior Attorney General of the Reich, Berlin 28 May 1942 at the People's Court, 8J 127/42g, In Custody!: Indictment section

78. Document of The Superior Attorney General of the Reich, Berlin 28 May 1942 at the People's Court, 8J 127/42g, In Custody!: IIc

79. Blair Holmes, Alan Keele, and Karl-Heinz Schnibbe, *When Truth Was Treason*, Urbana and Chicago, Illinois: University of Illinois Press, 1995

80. Document of The Superior Attorney General of the Reich, Berlin 28 May 1942 at the People's Court, 8J 127/42g, In Custody!, sec IIB

81. Letter from Otto Berndt, Church of Jesus Christ of Latter-day Saints, West German Mission, District: Hamburg 6 April 1942, To the Secret State Police in Hamburg, Stadthausbrucke; Document of The Superior Attorney General of the Reich, Berlin 28 May 1942 at the People's Court, 8J 127/42g, In Custody!: sect. Iic

82. Document of The Superior Attorney General of the Reich, Berlin 28 May 1942 at the People's Court, 8J 127/42g, In Custody! IIC

83. Document of The Superior Attorney General of the Reich, Berlin 28 May 1942 at the People's Court, 8J 127/42g, In Custody! IIC

84. Document of Chief State Counsel of the Hanseatic Higher Regional Court, Hamburg 36, 25 March 1942, Criminal Case! Juveniles!

85. Document of Chief State Counsel of the Hanseatic Higher Regional Court, Hamburg 36, 25 March 1942, Criminal Case! Juveniles!

86. Document of The Superior Attorney General of the Reich, Berlin 28 May 1942 at the People's Court, 8J 127/42g, In Custody! sec III part 2

87. Document of The Superior Attorney General of the Reich, Berlin 28 May 1942 at the People's Court, 8J 127/42g, In Custody!: sec III - pt 2

88. Document of Chief State Counsel of the Hanseatic Higher Regional Court, Hamburg 36, 25 March 1942, Criminal Case! Juveniles!; and Document of The Superior Attorney General of the Reich, Berlin 28 May 1942 at the People's Court, 8J 127/42g, In Custody!: sec III, pt 2

89. Verdict of the People's Court in the criminal case against Helmut Hübener, et al, on 11 August 1942: pt I sec 2

90. Document of The Superior Attorney General of the Reich, Berlin 28 May 1942 at the People's Court, 8J 127/42g, In Custody!: III-2, Document of Chief State Counsel of the Hanseatic Higher Regional Court, Hamburg 36, 25 March 1942, Criminal Case! Juveniles!

91. Document of The Superior Attorney General of the Reich, Berlin 28 May 1942 at the People's Court, 8J 127/42g, In Custody!: III-3

92. Document of The Superior Attorney General of the Reich, Berlin 28 May 1942 at the People's Court, 8J 127/42g, In Custody!: III-3

93. Document of The Superior Attorney General of the Reich, Berlin 28 May 1942 at the People's Court, 8J 127/42g, In Custody! III-3

94. Document of State Police Agency Hamburg — Hamburg, 5, 9, 17, 20 February 1942

95. Document of State Police Agency Hamburg — Hamburg, 5, 9, 17, 20 February 1942

96. Rudi Wobbe Oral History, interviewed by Matthew K. Heiss, Salt Lake City, Utah, 1988, typescript, The James Moyle Oral History Program, Archives, Historical Department of the

Church of Jesus Christ of Latter-day Saints, Salt Lake City, Utah, p. 44

97. Blair Holmes, Alan Keele, and Karl-Heinz Schnibbe, *When Truth Was Treason*, Urbana and Chicago, Illinois: University of Illinois Press, 1995

98. Rudolf G. Wobbe Oral History, Doublas F. Tobler and Alan F. Keele, 1974, typescript, The James Moyle Oral History Program, Archives, Historical Department of the Church of Jesus Christ of Latter-day Saints, Salt Lake City, Utah, p. 2

99. Rudolf G. Wobbe Oral History, Doublas F. Tobler and Alan F. Keele, 1974, typescript, The James Moyle Oral History Program, Archives, Historical Department of the Church of Jesus Christ of Latter-day Saints, Salt Lake City, Utah, p. 8 and Statement of Rudolf Wobbe, Rudolf Wobbe, Salt Lake City, Utah, 17 April 1961, Source: Historical Department, Church of Jesus Christ of Latter-day Saints, Salt Lake City, Utah Statement of Rudolf Wobbe, Rudolf Wobbe, Salt Lake City, Utah, 17 April 1961, Source: Historical Department, Church of Jesus Christ of Latter-day Saints, Salt Lake City, Utah

100. Rudi Wobbe Fireside [youth church lecture], 1987, transcribed by Richard Dewey and Heather Dewey, 1-4 February 2003, used by permission from Herta Wobbe, p. 14

101. Rudi Wobbe Oral History, interviewed by Matthew K. Heiss, Salt Lake City, Utah, 1988, typescript, The James Moyle Oral History Program, Archives, Historical Department of the Church of Jesus Christ of Latter-day Saints, Salt Lake City, Utah, p. 51

102. Rudi Wobbe Oral History, interviewed by Matthew K. Heiss, Salt Lake City, Utah, 1988, typescript, The James Moyle Oral History Program, Archives, Historical Department of the Church of Jesus Christ of Latter-day Saints, Salt Lake City, Utah, p. 51

103. Rudi Wobbe Oral History, interviewed by Matthew K. Heiss, Salt Lake City, Utah, 1988, typescript, The James Moyle Oral

History Program, Archives, Historical Department of the Church of Jesus Christ of Latter-day Saints, Salt Lake City, Utah, p. 51

104. Rudolf G. Wobbe Oral History, Doublas F. Tobler and Alan F. Keele, 1974, typescript, The James Moyle Oral History Program, Archives, Historical Department of the Church of Jesus Christ of Latter-day Saints, Salt Lake City, Utah, p. 8

105. Rudolf G. Wobbe Oral History, Doublas F. Tobler and Alan F. Keele, 1974, typescript, The James Moyle Oral History Program, Archives, Historical Department of the Church of Jesus Christ of Latter-day Saints, Salt Lake City, Utah, p. 8

106. Rudi Wobbe Fireside [youth church lecture], 1987, transcribed by Richard Dewey and Heather Dewey, 1-4 February 2003, used by permission from Herta Wobbe, p. 18

107. Gerhard Kunkel interview #2 with author, 25 February 2003, p. 14

108. Gerhard Kunkel interview #1 with author, 10 October 1996, pp. 3-4

109. Gerhard Kunkel interview #1 with author, 10 October 1996, p. 4

110. Arthur and Marie Sommerfeld interview with author, 18 October 1996, pp. 3-4

111. Arthur and Marie Sommerfeld interview with author, 18 October 1996, p. 4

112. Otto Berndt Oral History, interviewed by Douglas F. Tobler, Salt Lake City, Utah, 1974, typescript, The James Moyle Oral History Program, Archives, Historical Department of the Church of Jesus Christ of Latter-day Saints, Salt Lake City, Utah, p. 65

113. Otto Berndt Oral History, interviewed by Douglas F. Tobler, Salt Lake City, Utah, 1974, typescript, The James Moyle Oral History

Program, Archives, Historical Department of the Church of Jesus Christ of Latter-day Saints, Salt Lake City, Utah, p. 65

114. Otto Berndt Oral History, interviewed by Douglas F. Tobler, Salt Lake City, Utah, 1974, typescript, The James Moyle Oral History Program, Archives, Historical Department of the Church of Jesus Christ of Latter-day Saints, Salt Lake City, Utah, p. 67

115. Otto Berndt Oral History, interviewed by Douglas F. Tobler, Salt Lake City, Utah, 1974, typescript, The James Moyle Oral History Program, Archives, Historical Department of the Church of Jesus Christ of Latter-day Saints, Salt Lake City, Utah, p. 53

116. Otto Berndt Oral History, interviewed by Douglas F. Tobler, Salt Lake City, Utah, 1974, typescript, The James Moyle Oral History Program, Archives, Historical Department of the Church of Jesus Christ of Latter-day Saints, Salt Lake City, Utah, p. 53

117. "The Führer's New Clothes: Helmuth Hübener and the Dilemma of German Mormons in the Third Reich," unpublished essay by Alan F. Keele, Used by permission from Alan F. Keele. A shorter version of this essay was later published as an article in *Sunstone*, p. 27

118. Otto Berndt Oral History, interviewed by Douglas F. Tobler, Salt Lake City, Utah, 1974, typescript, The James Moyle Oral History Program, Archives, Historical Department of the Church of Jesus Christ of Latter-day Saints, Salt Lake City, Utah, p. 73

119. Report of First Area General Conference held in Munich, Germany, August 24 - 26, 1973 [Salt Lake City, 1974], p. 111

120. Alder, German-Speaking Immigration, p. 76; "The Führer's New Clothes: Helmuth Hübener and the Dilemma of German Mormons in the Third Reich," unpublished essay by Alan F. Keele, Used by permission from Alan F. Keele. A shorter version of this essay was later published as an article in *Sunstone*, p. 43

121. Rudi Wobbe Oral History, interviewed by Matthew K. Heiss, Salt Lake City, Utah, 1988, typescript, The James Moyle Oral

History Program, Archives, Historical Department of the
Church of Jesus Christ of Latter-day Saints, Salt Lake City,
Utah, p. 24

122. Rudi Wobbe Oral History, interviewed by Matthew K. Heiss,
     Salt Lake City, Utah, 1988, typescript, The James Moyle Oral
     History Program, Archives, Historical Department of the
     Church of Jesus Christ of Latter-day Saints, Salt Lake City,
     Utah, pp. 106-107

123. Rudi Wobbe Oral History, interviewed by Matthew K. Heiss,
     Salt Lake City, Utah, 1988, typescript, The James Moyle Oral
     History Program, Archives, Historical Department of the
     Church of Jesus Christ of Latter-day Saints, Salt Lake City,
     Utah, p. 99

124. Rudi Wobbe Oral History, interviewed by Matthew K. Heiss,
     Salt Lake City, Utah, 1988, typescript, The James Moyle Oral
     History Program, Archives, Historical Department of the
     Church of Jesus Christ of Latter-day Saints, Salt Lake City,
     Utah, pp. 102-103

125. Rudi Wobbe Oral History, interviewed by Matthew K. Heiss,
     Salt Lake City, Utah, 1988, typescript, The James Moyle Oral
     History Program, Archives, Historical Department of the
     Church of Jesus Christ of Latter-day Saints, Salt Lake City,
     Utah, 0. 108

126. Rudi Wobbe Oral History, interviewed by Matthew K. Heiss,
     Salt Lake City, Utah, 1988, typescript, The James Moyle Oral
     History Program, Archives, Historical Department of the
     Church of Jesus Christ of Latter-day Saints, Salt Lake City,
     Utah, 108

127. Rudi Wobbe Oral History, interviewed by Matthew K. Heiss,
     Salt Lake City, Utah, 1988, typescript, The James Moyle Oral
     History Program, Archives, Historical Department of the
     Church of Jesus Christ of Latter-day Saints, Salt Lake City,
     Utah, p. 109

128. Rudi Wobbe Oral History, interviewed by Matthew K. Heiss, Salt Lake City, Utah, 1988, typescript, The James Moyle Oral History Program, Archives, Historical Department of the Church of Jesus Christ of Latter-day Saints, Salt Lake City, Utah, p. 110

129. Rudi Wobbe Oral History, interviewed by Matthew K. Heiss, Salt Lake City, Utah, 1988, typescript, The James Moyle Oral History Program, Archives, Historical Department of the Church of Jesus Christ of Latter-day Saints, Salt Lake City, Utah, p. 105

130. Rudi Wobbe Oral History, interviewed by Matthew K. Heiss, Salt Lake City, Utah, 1988, typescript, The James Moyle Oral History Program, Archives, Historical Department of the Church of Jesus Christ of Latter-day Saints, Salt Lake City, Utah, pp. 107-108

131. The Diary of Gerhard Düwer

132. Statement of Rudolf Wobbe, Rudolf Wobbe, Salt Lake City, Utah, 17 April 1961, Source: Historical Department, Church of Jesus Christ of Latter-day Saints, Salt Lake City, Utah Statement of Rudolf Wobbe, Rudolf Wobbe, Salt Lake City, Utah, 17 April 1961, Source: Historical Department, Church of Jesus Christ of Latter-day Saints, Salt Lake City, Utah

133. The Diary of Gerhard Düwer

134. Statement of Rudolf Wobbe, Rudolf Wobbe, Salt Lake City, Utah, 17 April 1961, Source: Historical Department, Church of Jesus Christ of Latter-day Saints, Salt Lake City, Utah Statement of Rudolf Wobbe, Rudolf Wobbe, Salt Lake City, Utah, 17 April 1961, Source: Historical Department, Church of Jesus Christ of Latter-day Saints, Salt Lake City, Utah

135. Rudolf G. Wobbe Oral History, Doublas F. Tobler and Alan F. Keele, 1974, typescript, The James Moyle Oral History Program, Archives, Historical Department of the Church of Jesus Christ of Latter-day Saints, Salt Lake City, Utah, p. 12

136. Rudi Wobbe and Jerry Borrowman, *Three Against Hitler,* (American Fork, Utah: Covenant Communications, 1992), p. 39

137. Otto Berndt Oral History, interviewed by Douglas F. Tobler, Salt Lake City, Utah, 1974, typescript, The James Moyle Oral History Program, Archives, Historical Department of the Church of Jesus Christ of Latter-day Saints, Salt Lake City, Utah, p. 51

138. Rudi Wobbe Oral History, interviewed by Matthew K. Heiss, Salt Lake City, Utah, 1988, typescript, The James Moyle Oral History Program, Archives, Historical Department of the Church of Jesus Christ of Latter-day Saints, Salt Lake City, Utah, p. 104

When Truth Was Treason

by Karl-Heinz Schnibbe, Blair R. Holmes, and Alan F. Keele

This riveting, autobiographical account of Karl-Heinz Schnibbe is documented with hundreds of notes and dozens of original documents by professors Holmes and Keele, including all pertinent Nazi government documents and a fine collection of photographs and illustrations.

It is highly recommended as a companion volume to *Hübener vs. Hitler.*

Published originally by the University of Illinois Press, this volume was acquired in November 2003 by Academic Research Foundation, with the last remaining copies available for sale through Stratford Books, Inc.

Academic Research Foundation plans to republish the book under the title of *Schnibbe vs. Hitler* in late 2004 or 2005, as Volume 2 in the Faith in Conflict Series.

Hardback, 467 pages.
$29.95

New ISBN number
for remaining copies:
0-929753-14-3

Note to LDS readers: This book has several passages of harsh language
that will be removed when the book is republished.

To order, see order form on last page.

Porter Rockwell: A Biography

by Richard Lloyd Dewey

The epic biography that traces Porter Rockwell from turbulent Eastern beginnings to battles with Midwestern mobs to extraordinary gunfights on the American frontier. Quotes hundreds of journals, letters, and court records. Illustrated by western artist, Clark Kelley Price.

Hardcover, $24.95   ISBN: 0-9616024-0-6

Look for it in your favorite bookstore,
or to obtain autographed copies, see last page.

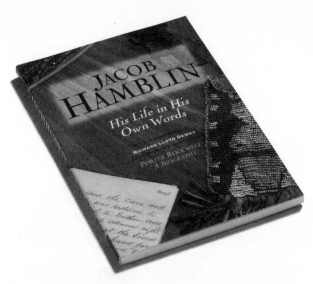

Jacob Hamblin:
His Life in His Own Words

Foreword by Richard Lloyd Dewey

Far from the gun-toting reputation of super-lawman Porter Rockwell, Jacob Hamblin was known in early Western history as the supreme peacemaker.

No less exciting than Porter's account, Jacob's adventures encountered apparent Divine intervention at every turn, a reward seemingly bestowed to certain souls given to absolute faith. And in his faith, like Porter, Jacob Hamblin was one of those incredibly rare warriors who are *absolutely fearless.*

His migrations from Ohio to Utah with life-and-death adventures at every turn keep the reader spellbound in this unabridged, autobiographical account of the Old West's most unusual adventurer among Native Americans.

In his own words, Jacob Hamblin bares his soul with no pretense, unveiling an eye-witness journal of pioneer attempts to co-exist peacefully with Native brothers, among whom he traveled unarmed, showing his faith in God that he would not be harmed.

Easily considered the most successful — and bravest — diplomat to venture into hostile territory single-handedly, Hamblin takes the reader into hearts of darkness and hearts of light.

Softcover, $10.95   ISBN: 0-9616024-5-7

Look for it in your favorite bookstore,
or to obtain autographed copies, see last page.

New Evidences of Christ in Ancient America

by Blaine M. Yorgason, Bruce W. Warren, and Harold Brown

In 1947 California lawyer Tom Ferguson threw a shovel over his shoulder and marched into the jungles of southern Mexico. Teamed with world-class scholar Bruce Warren, they found a mountain of evidence supporting *Book of Mormon* claims. Now the reader can follow their adventure as they unearth amazing archaeological discoveries and ancient writings, all of which shut the mouths of critics who say such evidences do not exist. In this volume, the newest archaeological evidences are also presented.

Endorsed by Hugh Nibley.

Hardcover, $24.95   ISBN: 0-929753-01-1

*Look for it in your favorite bookstore,
or to obtain autographed copies, see last page.*

The Porter Rockwell Chronicles
by Richard Lloyd Dewey

This best-selling, historically accurate biographical novel series renders Porter's life in riveting story form, bringing it alive for adults and teens alike.

Volume 1 begins with his childhood years in New York where he becomes best friends with the future Mormon prophet Joseph Smith. The story continues through Porter's settlement with the Mormons in Missouri, where he fights against mobs and falls in love with and marries Luana Beebe.

Volume 2 covers the turbulent first four years in Nauvoo, where he continues to fight mobs and becomes Joseph Smith's bodyguard.

The Nauvoo period of his life draws to a close in Volume 3 as his best friend Joseph is murdered and his wife Luana leaves him and remarries, taking his beloved daughter Emily with her. Porter must bid a heartbroken farewell as he and the Mormons are driven from Nauvoo and flee west.

Volume 4 continues with his first ten years in Utah, where he is joyously reunited with his daughter Emily, takes on the U.S. Army in a guerilla war, and enters a new phase of adventures as U.S. Deputy Marshal.

Volume 1 (ISBN: 0-9616024-6-5)	Hardcover, $23.88
Volume 2 (ISBN: 0-9616024-7-3)	Hardcover, $23.88
Volume 3 (ISBN: 0-9616024-8-1)	Hardcover, $23.88
Volume 4 (ISBN: 0-9616024-9-X)	Hardcover, $24.88

*Look for them in your favorite bookstore,
or to obtain autographed copies, see last page.*

The Kade Family Saga, Volume 1: In Quest of Zion

by Laurel Mouritsen

Hardcover, $19.95   ISBN: 0-929753-07-0

Sure to delight *The Work and the Glory* fans, the *Kade Family Saga* series of historical novels is steeped in likeable, life-like characters in the fictional story of the Kade family and their adventures spanning from Missouri to the Great Salt Lake basin.

In Volume 1, *In Quest of Zion*, we are introduced to the much-travailed Lydia Dawson, who meets the intriguing Mr. Kade, who writes for *The Evening and the Morning Star*—controversial newspaper for the Mormons, who have recently arrived in Missouri. The reader is pulled into their lives as they endure persecution, physical confrontations with enemies, and eventually deadly battles. The external threats are only half the story, though, as they struggle simultaneously with the emotional conflicts in their relationships.

Told with the skill of a masterful storyteller against a historically accurate backdrop, this story is at once exciting, heart-wrenching, and very satisfying.

ORDERING INFORMATION

Hübener vs Hitler $23.95
A biography of Helmuth Hübener, Mormon teenage resistance leader,
by Richard Lloyd Dewey. Hardcover.
ISBN: 0-929753-08-9

When Truth Was Treason $29.95
by Blair R. Holmes, Alan F. Keele, and Karl-Heinz Schnibbe.
Hardcover, 454 pp.
ISBN:

Porter Rockwell: A Biography $22.95
by Richard Lloyd Dewey. Hardcover, 612 pp.
ISBN: 0-9616024-0-6

Jacob Hamblin: His Life in His Own Words $10.95
Foreword by Richard Lloyd Dewey. Softcover, 128 pp.
ISBN: 0-9616024-5-7

New Evidences of Christ in Ancient America $24.95
by Blaine M. Yorgason, Bruce W. Warren, and Harold Brown.
Hardcover, 430 pp.
ISBN: 0-929753-01-1

The Porter Rockwell Chronicles, Vol. 1   (Reg. $27.50) $23.88
by Richard Lloyd Dewey. Hardcover, 490 pp.
ISBN: 0-9616024-6-5

The Porter Rockwell Chronicles, Vol. 2   (Reg. $27.50) $23.88
by Richard Lloyd Dewey. Hardcover, 452 pp.
ISBN: 0-9616024-7-3

The Porter Rockwell Chronicles, Vol. 3   (Reg. $27.95) $23.88
by Richard Lloyd Dewey. Hardcover, 527 pp.
ISBN: 0-9616024-8-1

The Porter Rockwell Chronicles, Vol. 4   (Reg. $27.95) $24.88
by Richard Lloyd Dewey. Hardcover, 568 pp.
ISBN: 0-9616024-9-X

Utah residents, add 6.25% sales tax (before shipping & handling).

SHIPPING & HANDLING:
Add $1.00 for each book.

Send check or money order to:
Stratford Books
P.O. Box 1371, Provo, Utah 84603-1371

Prices subject to change.